Dr David is Head escent Hospital of the NSW Centre for the Advancement of Adolescent Health. David was appointed Clinical Associate Professor in Adolescent Medicine at the University of Sydney in 1994 and was honoured with an AO in 1995 for 'service to medicine, particularly in the field of adolescent health and medical care'. David is a past President of the International Association for Adolescent Health, and is a consultant with the World Health Organisation. He is married to Anne with four 'adult' children, Lilly, Adam, Sari and Nathan, and is the author of the bestselling book *Growing Pains*. His children are still working on a sequel entitled *My Father the Hypocrite*.

Dr Leanne Rowe (MB BS Dip RACOG FRACGP) is a general practitioner who specialises in adolescent health and parenting and has cared for thousands of different families over the past 20 years. She is Chair of the Royal Australian College of General Practitioners (Vic), Senior Lecturer at the Department of General Practice, University of Melbourne, a medical officer with the Royal Flying Doctor Service, and has just undertaken a Doctor of Medicine degree at Monash University on the topic of adolescent depression. In 1997, she was awarded Best Individual Contribution to Health Care in Australia by the Australian Medical Association for her work with disadvantaged young people at Clockwork Young People's Health Service in Geelong. She has published two other books, *girl_X Recreated* and *Urgent*. Leanne is married to Peter Jasek and has two teenage sons, Chris and Louis.

What to do when
your children turn into
TEENAGERS

Dr David Bennett & Dr Leanne Rowe

DOUBLEDAY
SYDNEY・AUCKLAND・TORONTO・NEW YORK・LONDON

The information contained in this book is based on the research and the personal and professional experiences of the authors. It is not intended as a substitute for consulting with your physical or other health care provider. The names of some of the people described in this book have been changed to protect their privacy.

WHAT TO DO WHEN YOUR CHILDREN TURN INTO TEENAGERS
A DOUBLEDAY BOOK

First published in Australia and New Zealand in 2003
by Doubleday

Copyright © David Bennett, Acacia Arch Pty Ltd & Anne Bennett, 2003

All rights reserved. No part of this publication may be reproduced, stored in a retrieval system, transmitted in any form or by any means, electronic, mechanical, photocopying, recording or otherwise, without the prior written permission of the publisher.

National Library of Australia
Cataloguing-in-Publication Entry

Bennett, David L.
What to do when your children turn into teenagers

Bibliography.
Includes index.
ISBN 1 86471 077 2.

1. Adolescence. 2. Adolescent psychology.
3. Parent and teenager. 4. Parenting. I. Rowe, Leanne. II. Title.

649.125

Transworld Publishers,
a division of Random House Australia Pty Ltd
20 Alfred Street, Milsons Point, NSW 2061
http://www.randomhouse.com.au

Random House New Zealand Limited
18 Poland Road, Glenfield, Auckland

Transworld Publishers,
a division of The Random House Group Ltd
61–63 Uxbridge Road, Ealing, London W5 5SA

Random House Inc
1540 Broadway, New York, New York 10036

Cover and text design by Darian Causby/Highway 51
Cover image courtesy of photolibrary.com
Typeset in 11/14pt Sabon by Midland Typesetters, Maryborough, Victoria
Printed and bound by Griffin Press, Netley, South Australia

10 9 8 7 6 5 4 3

Contents

Foreword • ix
Introduction • xi

SECTION 1: Growing up

Chapter 1 • The perils of puberty • 3

Chapter 2 • Infuriatingly normal behaviour • 23

Chapter 3 • Authoritative parenting • 41

Chapter 4 • Teenagers and the media • 57

Chapter 5 • Corn chips and chocolate • 71

Chapter 6 • It's my body • 87

Chapter 7 • Sexuality: a sensitive issue • 97

SECTION 2: Home and away

Chapter 8 • Middlescence • 129

Chapter 9 • The importance of parents • 145

Chapter 10 • Families getting on together • 159

Chapter 11 • Belonging to school and connected to community • 185

Chapter 12 • Teaching by example • 227

Chapter 13 • Letting go when you want to hold on • 245

SECTION 3: It won't happen in our family

Chapter 14 • Reducing the risk and minimising the harm • 265

Chapter 15 • It's in the mind • 299

Chapter 16 • When, how and where to ask for help • 337

Chapter 17 • What about the future? • 363

Appendix • 369

Index • 377

To my wife Anne, lifelong soulmate and teacher of priorities, and to our children – Lilly, Adam, Sari and Nathan – from whom I gain inspiration and the wisdom born of experience.
David Bennett

To my husband Peter Jasek and sons Chris and Louis with love, always love.
Leanne Rowe

Foreword

Australians live in a land of unique and incomparable beauty which is also abundantly rich in resources. Most valuable of all these resources are our young people.

However, reliable studies of recent times have revealed that around one in five young Australians in their teen years experience significant stress as they strive to cope with the considerable demands of meeting the expectations of parents and peers – and particularly the demands they may place upon themselves – in an ever changing and competitive world. These demands may relate to physical issues or to emotional issues, or both.

Parents often contemplate, with love and concern, the complex challenges that inevitably arise, but they often feel mystified and even helpless in determining how best to respond.

Two eminent doctors, Dr David Bennett and Dr Leanne Rowe, have spent many years working with vulnerable and troubled young people and have shared their extensive knowledge with colleagues in medicine, in teaching and in allied professions.

In this comprehensive book *What to do when your children turn into teenagers*, the authors in frank and clear language, reach out to parents and to all those who are involved with young people, providing valuable insights in negotiating those critical years with greater skill, sensitivity and optimism.

Professor Marie R. Bashir AC
Governor of New South Wales
Patron of NSW Centre for the
Advancement of Adolescent Health

We wish to thank the following individuals for their helpful suggestions: Dr Sue Bagshaw, Margaret Beaton, Ken Buttrum AM, Dr Peter Carman, Dr Justin Coleman, Georgie Ferrari, Alan Gold, Dr Sue Gould, Jenny Houseman, John Howard, Lou Howard, Dr Melissa Kang, Robyn Lamb, Ian McIntosh, Eve and Dr Michael Reed, Narelle Richardson, Jo Sherwell, Anne Slattery, Associate Professor Kate Steinbeck, Professor Bruce Tonge, Kate Toohey, Professor Greg Whelan, Dr Bill Williams, Professor Doris Young, and other colleagues and friends for their encouragement and support.

We'd also like to thank the following photographers from The Geelong College who provided photographs: Sarah Anderson (pages 22, 70 & 96), Joe Ashton (page 226), Jessica Collins (page 244), Stefani Driscoll (page 264), Hanh Le (pages 184 & 362). All other photographs courtesy of photolibrary.com.

Finally, our heartfelt thanks to our wonderful team at Random House: Jane Southward, our publisher, for suggesting and supporting our collaboration on the book; and Sophie Ambrose and Kim Swivel for their fantastic editorial input and attention to detail.

Introduction

Despite all the difficulties teenagers face in this time of rapid social change, world turmoil and worrying trends in family breakdown, we have a shared optimism about their resilience. In our professional lives we have seen creative solutions work to prevent and deal with common and difficult problems such as adolescent depression, drug abuse and family conflict. In our experience, it is never too early or too late to seek parenting information or add to our knowledge about what is happening in the lives of young people. The information and ideas conveyed in our book cover a wide range of health and parenting issues and focus on what teenagers between 12 and 20 most need, individually and collectively, from us. And they need it now.

The voices of young people in the book ring out in a chorus of pain and suffering, frustration, wisdom and hope. Their pertinent and often poignant views inform us about the challenges that they face. Drawing also upon contemporary adolescent health research and our combined experience across several decades (both as clinicians and parents), this book provides sound practical advice and guidance on topics ranging from lifestyle to limit-setting, acne to anxiety, sexuality, mental health and drugs. It also includes an appendix that directs the reader to many helpful books, telephone numbers and websites. The focus of *What to do when your children turn into teenagers* is on what we can do to influence our teenagers' lives and how we can better understand and cope with the things we can't influence.

About 20 per cent of our young people are at risk or in crisis, and this has implications for our whole society. Where adolescent problems are concerned, there is no quick fix. By persevering, enduring difficulties and uncomfortable times and being there for the long haul, we teach teenagers not to give up. We model resilience. The priority is to get the right help early and to keep at it. The abiding message of our book, however, is that we have the power to bring about change, not only with our own or other people's teenagers, but with governments, the media and society at large to improve community involvement and services.

This is more than a self-help book for parents. We see it as a clarion call to action. It is our hope that every parent, grandparent, teacher and health care provider will read it and get active on behalf of young people everywhere.

David Bennett
Leanne Rowe

Section 1

Growing up

Chapter 1

The perils of puberty

I really need my parents to keep reassuring me they love me, but I want to be independent too.
Chris, aged 16

Puberty can be an exciting time for young people, but one that usually includes a few troubling moments for everyone involved. Adolescents are normally preoccupied with their changing bodies, but their anxieties and concerns are often unstated and therefore difficult for others to understand, even for those who care about them the most.

Perhaps one reason for this is that parents' personal recollections of those often embarrassing experiences and noteworthy events have been mercifully dulled by time (possibly some sort of protective device bestowed upon us by Nature). Would we actually want to remember it, in all its agonising detail, even if we could? No wonder our children's puberty often takes us by surprise, particularly with our first born. For one thing, it forces us to acknowledge the passing of a quick decade, more or less, and to recall and relive the experience ourselves.

In the midst of all their hormonal and bodily turmoil, the all-encompassing question that adolescents ask is: 'Am I normal?' Someone must answer. Parents can help enormously by having some idea about what is normal, by knowing what to expect, by tolerating embarrassment and distress (even when it seems unwarranted), and by providing perspective and reassurance.

Is this really me?

The normal changes that take place during puberty are confusing at the very least. At the very worst, kids may wonder if their body really belongs to them – it certainly may not feel like it! They are undergoing the most impressive and rapid alterations in size and shape that they will ever experience, not to mention adding totally new bits and pieces. Puberty is a special and exciting time, unique and different from any other experience in life. In developing sexually, they are also moving inexorably towards reproductive maturity, which adds a significant new dimension to their lives, as well as to yours (we discuss sexuality in Chapter 7).

How does it start?

No one knows precisely what triggers the sequence of events that starts puberty off. The initial message comes from the brain, with increasing secretion into the bloodstream (mostly at night) of a chemical called gonadotrophin-releasing hormone. Most of the responsibility for what follows rests with the pituitary – the 'master gland' – that conducts an orchestra of hormones. Once all this is underway, there's no turning back. Oestrogen and testosterone, present but quiescent during childhood, now flood the brain, causing physical, sexual and behavioural changes that are dramatically different for boys and girls.

The signs of puberty:

As a general rule, the earliest visible changes of puberty are evident around the age of 10 or 11 for girls (usually by the appearance of breast buds) and 11 or 12 for boys (usually by a slight darkening and roughening of the skin of the scrotum). However, it's not unusual for girls as young as eight or nine years of age, under the influence of hormones from the adrenal glands, to develop some pubic hair. This does not necessarily represent the beginning of puberty, although parents may want to seek some medical reassurance about this.

On the other hand, there is considerable international evidence suggesting that girls are maturing earlier. This includes Marcia Herman-Giddens' 1997 study of 17,000 American girls and a British study at Bristol University that tracked 14,000 girls and found one in six with signs of puberty by eight years of age, compared to one in 100 a generation ago. Comprehensive Australian data on the onset of puberty isn't yet available, but it is likely that a similar trend has occurred here. All sorts of explanations have been given for this phenomenon, including: hereditary factors, dietary factors (but definitely not the feeding of hormones to chickens), increases in obesity and body weight, chemicals affecting the endocrine system, and (more recently) the increasing numbers of girls growing up in step-families (almost twice as likely to reach puberty early as girls from non-divorce homes), possibly because they're being exposed to the pheromones of a 'strange male'. Childhood stress or trauma have also been implicated. In the absence of scientific data, we don't know if earlier onset of puberty is happening to boys.

Total transformation

Prior to puberty, differences in the shapes of boys' and girls' bodies are hardly noticeable. The sex hormones, oestrogen and testosterone, soon change that. As girls broaden in the hips, boys broaden in the shoulders, and everybody's supposed to like the shape they've become, which, of course, seldom happens.

Boys experience a major increase in muscle. The chest thickens, biceps flex, and we have a manly hunk in the making. Even thin young men, who are often very conscious of their stature, double their muscle mass during puberty (under the influence of muscle-making testosterone), whereas it only increases by about half in girls. There are few boys who would not wish this process to occur earlier or more satisfactorily. Although less common than with girls, and less publicised, boys can also experience body image concerns during puberty.

These days, with thinness being all the rage (and eating disorders taking such a toll), a good thing for parents to tell their daughters is how normal, appropriate and attractive these changes are. Somehow we have to amend the notion that Nature has got it all wrong.

In girls, important things are happening to their fat stores (adipose tissue), as is listed on the next page.

- There's an increase in the total amount of fat (often referred to as 'puppy fat', although it actually stays around); and, eventually, fat constitutes around 25 per cent of girls' body weight (compared to less than 15 per cent or so of guys').
- There's an obvious increase in fat on hips, thighs and breasts, producing the female shape that women develop naturally.
- As well as providing contours, fat protects muscles, bones and organs, cushions the body, helps regulate female hormones and provides an energy store for future pregnancy and breast-feeding.

What happens to girls?

Some girls don't think twice about the development of their breasts, but others take the whole issue very seriously. They are, after all, inevitably in the public eye. While vulgar barbs from fascinated pubescent boys (often a brother) are a common enough hazard, even a supposedly complimentary remark from a well-meaning adult (often a parent) can bring forth a flood of tearful indignation and embarrassment.

Many girls worry about the size of their breasts. It seems they are too small, too large, or not growing at the same rate. Yet, in most people, the two sides of the body are never precisely the same. Fortunately, the difference in size generally becomes less obvious the more they grow. Teenage girls need to know that the size and shape of breasts have no relationship whatever to the ability to respond to sexual stimulation, produce milk or feed babies.

Sometimes girls also worry about lumps in their breasts. Apart from a 'breast bud', there are two main types of lumps in this age group: single, firm, usually painless lumps that persist (benign fibroadenomas); and multiple, tender areas that vary with the menstrual cycle (fibrocystic lesions). While teenagers should be reassured that these are relatively common and practically never a threat to health, they should be encouraged to practise breast self-examination, a habit that is worth acquiring during adolescence.

My friends all suddenly have breasts but I don't and they tease me about not even owning a bra.
Lisa, aged 13

Changes in the genital area can also be a source of bewilderment. Pubic hair usually appears around the time that breasts start to develop, although initially it may be difficult to see. In due course, there will be little doubt that it's there, but it can be a bit puzzling when it turns out to be a totally different colour to head hair. Underarm hair usually follows, bringing with it the question of what to do about it, if anything. For girls who find it embarrassing and are prepared to work on it regularly, shaving, depilatory creams or waxing is the answer. Otherwise, it can simply be left alone.

Occasionally, dark hair forms on the upper lip, on the arms and around the nipples in some girls, and, although not always welcome, is entirely normal and usually inherited. It is only of medical concern if the appearance of increased or darkened body hair is accompanied by other changes, such as irregular periods or more severe acne, which may suggest the possibility of some hormonal problem.

Then there's the vagina: simple in design but complex in function. Given the general degree of ignorance about this extraordinary female body part, the vagina might be considered 'one of the world's best kept secrets'. Not only do many girls, and women, have little idea of exactly what's there, it may even be regarded with considerable distaste. If girls have not been forewarned about normal vaginal secretions that occur around the onset of puberty, this can be a cause of unnecessary concern as well. Girls often take a lead from their mothers whose attitudes conveyed during childhood can influence a daughter's regard for her genitalia. A negative view might also be subtly endorsed by tampon advertisers, who emphasise the clean and hygienic applicator that makes insertion 'less messy'. The best way for girls to clarify their understanding of this part of their anatomy is to check it out in pictures or diagrams or more directly with a mirror (no obligation to do this, of course).

Sometimes girls worry about their hymen. They may have heard stories about it, particularly its importance as an indication of virginity. Yet often it is difficult even for doctors to know whether or not it is intact. The hymen consists of a tissue membrane of variable thickness with an opening of variable size. It is usually situated where the vagina begins. Girls may wonder what's likely to happen when intercourse takes place. As a general guide, the more complete the hymen is (sometimes it is merely a remnant) and the smaller the opening, the more pressure is required to break it. If this is the case, the girl might feel some pain and may bleed a little after first intercourse.

A sweet secret

Surveys show that many young women view menstruation as a hassle, do not know what the menstrual discharge contains or, more importantly, how it comes about. Parents can help their daughters avoid unwarranted misgivings by discussing menstruation with them, or by providing a book containing simple and explicit information. Here are some useful facts about adolescent periods:

- Most girls experience their first period (menarche) at around 12 or 13, although it may occur any time between 10 and 16.
- A delay in getting started may be due to an inherited tendency, poor nutrition and weight loss (as in anorexia), excessive physical exercise, or a chronic childhood illness.
- The first period usually occurs about two years after breasts have started to develop, and at this time there is a marked slowing of overall growth. A girl will have achieved close to 95 per cent of her adult height when she experiences her first period.
- In a normal period lasting three to five days, the total discharge is only about 100 mls (about half a cupful) and consists of broken-down tissue, blood and a considerable amount of mucus. This material is released from the lining of the uterus when ovulation occurs and builds up again in the next cycle.
- Early menstrual cycles are frequently irregular because the system is still immature and an ovum is not always shed each month; this can last for a year or two before settling down, and rarely requires medical intervention. This irregularity does not, however, give contraceptive security, as some young people might think.
- Early periods are generally painless, but as the cycle becomes more normalised, premenstrual tension and physical discomforts become more common. Painful periods are the most common cause of absences from school and, later, work for young women.
- A healthy girl can exercise, swim, ride a horse, dance at parties or do anything she likes while she menstruates. A parent who can communicate a positive attitude about periods provides a daughter with a gift for life.

During the early stages, having periods takes some getting used to. There are other normal concerns as well. The odour that occurs, for example, when menstrual blood comes in contact with air and airborne bacteria, is something that may worry girls and older women, but this is rarely discussed. It may help to talk about it or at least to reassure your daughter that the odour is perfectly normal and nothing to worry about, even if she feels slightly uncomfortable about it. Washing hands before, as well as after, handling a sanitary napkin or tampon is an important rule of hygiene. Teenagers may have heard of 'toxic shock syndrome' and sometimes fear using tampons for this reason. However, if they are changed regularly (ideally every three to four hours), handled as little as possible before insertion and not left in overnight (use a pad instead), the chances of catching this infection are extremely small. The choice of sanitary pad or tampon is an individual decision and is best worked out by letting your daughter use what she feels most comfortable with, but if she opts for tampons she might find it easier to use those with an applicator at first.

Premenstrual syndrome may include mood changes, tearfulness, tender breasts and headaches. Simple remedies such as vitamin B6 (though note that excessive doses may have serious effects) and herbal diuretics may be helpful. However, medical advice should be sought if symptoms are severe. Painful heavy periods may also be treated with prescription medication.

What happens to boys?

Unlike the caterpillar whose bizarre bodily changes take place in total privacy within a cosy cocoon, there is little escape from close and critical scrutiny for the adolescent boy. For some reason, he is often an object of fun, while the adolescent girl is more likely to be regarded with tenderness. Perhaps this is because boys (of any age) are expected to be always in control (no tears, no tantrums, etc.), so such outward signs of lack of control draw derision.

It's not funny

As the larynx grows and vocal cords lengthen, boys acquire a husky voice that 'breaks' a year or so later. (Voice changes occur in girls too, but are less marked.) Not surprisingly, boys seem to see less humour in the situation than others do. With increasing maturity, the male voice drops an octave or more in pitch, increases in volume and takes on a more even tonal quality.

Another embarrassing development can be breast enlargement in young teenage boys. This is normal and affects many kids; possibly

> My parents show they love me by understanding that some times are good to talk and others are not.
> Michael, aged 17

around as many as 80 per cent, and is mostly quite mild. Changing hormones (possibly a relative increase in oestrogen level) are responsible. It is called gynaecomastia and can be quite alarming, particularly if the boy is not expecting it, or if it progresses beyond the usual small swelling of either or both breasts.

For some boys, fears might even run to, 'maybe this means I'm gay' or 'perhaps I'm turning into a girl'. In most cases it disappears within a year, but if it lasts longer, or is very obvious, it might be worth seeking a professional opinion. Surgery is sometimes considered, especially when psychological stress is great.

Puberty is associated with the development of special body hair, and boys are sensitive about this as well. Pubic hair is okay, more or less, because it turns up early and is usually welcome. Underarm hair, on the other hand, is associated with, and actually preceded by, an increase in the size and productivity of sweat glands. Ask any parents about perspiration odour in their adolescent sons, and the pained grimace which follows will tell all.

In comparison, upper lip fuzz and wispy chin hairs are innocuous and entertaining – that is, to everyone in the family except the owner of the fuzz. Although a boy might be very tempted to shave this off, the need to shave regularly is unusual before 16 or 17. And last, but not least, chest hair might make an appearance, always late and, despite fervent wishes to the contrary, totally unrelated to strength or virility.

A continuing concern

A boy's anxieties about virility are very much related to the size and development of his penis. And let's face it, boys aren't the only ones to worry about the size of their penises. Not only is it a continuing concern of fully grown men, but also of mothers who take their sons along to the local doctor for reassurance.

Penises simply differ in size and, although kids sometimes worry about it, size has no bearing on adequate functioning, which is generally the underlying concern. Differences are most obvious when penises are at rest. Unfortunately, 'do I shape up compared to the others?' is a question that boys and men tend to ask themselves while standing at a urinal or undressing in a changing room. At some point, males have to reconcile themselves to the fact that there is more to life than being well hung.

More importantly, teenage boys should be encouraged to examine their own testicles. A normal testicle is egg-shaped and somewhat firm to the touch. It should be smooth and free of lumps and should have no unusually sensitive areas. Testicular self-examination hasn't really caught on yet, but it is just as necessary as breast self-examination is for women.

A noteworthy event

A boy's first ejaculation is a remarkable experience. It can be as startling as the first period for a girl and has exactly the same biological significance, reproductively speaking, yet we tend to discuss it less.

For two out of three males, the first ejaculation results from masturbation. Some boys will have been practising already for some time and can report the orgasmic sensation known euphemistically as a 'dry run'. Others experience spontaneous emissions of semen.

'Wet dream' is the term used to describe ejaculation of semen that occurs during sleep, but this is not unheard of during the waking hours. This release of semen is involuntary. While not all boys have this experience, those who do may find it embarrassing. The important thing to remember is that it is normal. Men produce sperm cells constantly and this is one way the body has of releasing stored semen to make way for new supplies.

A few facts about boys:

- The nature of adolescent semen is highly variable and often 'lumpy', that is, globulated rather than having a smooth consistency.
- Sperm are actually present in staggering numbers from the very first ejaculation, even though they make up only a tiny fraction of the volume of semen ejaculated. There have been many reported cases of pregnancy occurring where the male partner was a very young adolescent.
- Boys who don't know what semen is invariably imagine the worst, especially if it has appeared in response to their very own (and perfectly normal) efforts.

Confusion and misunderstandings about sexual development, for both boys and girls, can produce a lot of unnecessary anxiety. Open and candid communication between parents and children will go some of the way to avoiding this, if this openness has already been established. But it's difficult if parents are as anxious and embarrassed as their kids and don't know how to raise the subject. Sometimes there is an understanding between parents and children not to talk about sexual development. Everyone has their own level of privacy and it's often easier to seek out information from books and magazines rather than to talk directly about it. If this describes you, then leaving a judicious trail of books, magazines and pamphlets that your kids can pick up at their leisure might be one way of making sure they learn about what's going on. Gentle humour can sometimes help too, and can open up topics for discussion that you and your children might otherwise find embarrassing to talk about.

On the grow

Apart from the first six months of life, puberty sees the fastest rate of growth ever, especially in warm weather. Just before puberty begins, growth actually slows down, as if gearing up for the amazing effort to follow. Then it's on and, before long, that little boy or girl you used to pat affectionately on the head is nonchalantly leaning on your shoulder.

Mainly upwards

Physical growth during puberty is dramatic. It accounts for nearly a quarter of an adult's final height and around half of his or her final weight. This whole process is called the 'growth spurt' and, somewhere along the way, there will be a 12-month period of fastest growth. During this year, a girl can gain up to eight centimetres in height, and nearly five kilos in weight. A boy can gain an amazing 10 centimetres in height, and six kilos in weight. No wonder the bottoms of their jeans constantly creep up their shins to reveal naked ankles!

Girls get started earlier (that's just the way it is), with the onset of the growth spurt generally coinciding with the appearance of breasts. Although boys start later, they have the dubious consolation of growing for longer and usually ending up taller. Initially, however, particularly around Year 6, the size difference between the sexes is considerable. Following the peak, growth slows down in both boys and girls and, except for perhaps a centimetre or so, should be complete by about 18. Then you can look back nostalgically at old photographs and wonder what happened to the cute little kid you once knew.

Some teenagers take their time getting there, while others go through it like a rocket, sometimes in as little as two years. Of course, adolescents yearn to be average, so being even slightly out of step with one's friends is an uncomfortable experience. Parents need to remember that being the first one to shoot up in height can be as difficult for their daughter or son as being the last to experience their growth spurt. In both situations, kindly reassurance is warranted.

> *My mother assumes that now I am older I should be able to deal with everything and that to become 'a man' I should not be dependent on her. But I sometimes need her to interfere.*
> Nick, aged 17

The personal experience of early or late sexual development, which determines when growth will accelerate, has been found to be different for boys and girls. Boys seem to benefit from maturing early, in that they might appear more physically attractive, independent, self-confident and relaxed. Early maturing girls, on the other hand, seem to be disadvantaged – they may be less popular, lack confidence, appear withdrawn and have a less positive body image. The situation for late maturing teenagers is the other way around: boys seem to be disadvantaged, in that they might be less well liked and viewed as anxious, overly talkative and attention-seeking; while girls seem to benefit, often being regarded by peers and adults alike as physically attractive, lively, sociable and leaders at school.

Too short

When it comes to physical size, teenagers will have their own ideas about what's okay and what's not. If you were the shortest in the class, you'd be in no doubt at all. Even if you were not quite the shortest, chances are you'd feel too short. Parents sometimes don't realise the extent to which being short affects their children.

The teenage years are generally the worst for very short people. Short teenagers can be extremely sensitive to stares, curiosity and rude comments. They may have low self-esteem and feel inadequate or, according to research in the 1980s, be shy, anxious or depressed, particularly boys. Boys say they find it more difficult to hold their own socially, especially in regard to the opposite sex. While this is true for both boys and girls, perhaps it is harder for boys because of social stereotyping that says boys are supposed to be taller than girls. But it can be hard for girls too. It's no fun being treated as younger than you are, which can be not only incredibly aggravating, but cause you to be left out of things.

However, a more recent study of 180 boys and 78 girls (quoted by Steve Biddulph in *Raising Boys*) found that short boys, while describing themselves as less socially active, had no more behaviour problems than boys of average height. Short girls in the study often had better mental health than girls of normal height. Interestingly, where the parents were also short, the children seemed to have fewer problems, possibly because everyone was less worried about it. Biddulph comments that perhaps our society is becoming more tolerant of diversity and suggests that 'if a child is praised and valued, and has good communication within the family, then being different will cause much less stress'.

Adult men less than 162 centimetres and women less than 150 centimetres are generally considered short, but when it comes to teenagers it's important to consider whether their height is permanent or temporary.

- Permanently short: The vast majority of kids who are short by nature usually have parents who are also short, although a chronic illness or genetic disorder is sometimes responsible.
- Temporarily short: This is almost always due to delayed puberty; late starters have their growth spurt postponed and, for what can seem like an eternity, are smaller than everyone else. Eventually these children come into puberty and end up approximately as tall as their parents, one or both of whom may have had an identical pattern of development.

If there is any concern about a child's growth, it is important to get it checked out by a GP, as something treatable may be responsible. Most healthy kids are simply heading for the final height they are meant to be, but sometimes it may be reassuring to have a joint X-rayed to check if growth plates are still active.

In a small number of cases, the use of growth hormone is approved for children or teenagers who are not lacking in the hormone but whose growth potential has been seriously impaired by a chronic childhood illness or some other cause. There have been detailed government guidelines for the restricted use of this therapy since 1988, and the daily injections require a strong commitment over several years on the part of the adolescent and the family. It is also very expensive.

Whatever the cause, it is an enormous advantage for short teenagers to have well-informed and sympathetic parents, friends and teachers. To be permanently short, of course, means learning to accept it and dealing with sometimes unsympathetic community attitudes. Often the onus falls on you, the parent, to provide reassurance and realistic support; to encourage pursuits in which physical size and strength are not prerequisites for success and fulfilment; and to point out that there are some very talented and successful short people around (as any die-hard Tom Cruise or Kylie Minogue fan would know).

Too tall

While short stature creates greater problems for boys, excessive tallness can pose particular difficulties for girls. Being head and shoulders above your girlfriends is bad enough, but towering over the boys is even worse (again, because of social stereotyping). Tall girls can't hide; although some stoop, poor posture does not solve the problem. They still stick out in a crowd. The same is true for tall boys.

The most common reason by far for being tall is having tall parents and tall grandparents. Very rarely an endocrine condition (usually involving excess growth hormone) or a genetic abnormality can be the cause of tall stature, in which case, other tell-tale signs would be present. Some parents wonder if there's 'danger' involved in shooting to great height very quickly during an impressive adolescent growth spurt. There isn't to our knowledge. For example, despite what one might think, this is not a cause of later back problems.

A man of 190 centimetres, whose wife is 170 centimetres, described his extremely tall children. The 13-year-old girl was already 180 centimetres and still growing (at school she's called 'giraffe'); his son, at 10 years of age, was also tall and thin (with the nickname 'spaghetti legs'). 'People don't realise the logistical problems involved,' he explained. 'At primary school, long legs don't fit under the desk, certainly not comfortably, and suitably sized clothes and shoes are extremely hard to find.' This dad was empathetic to his kids' plight, but he encouraged them to accept it. He knew from experience that eventually the difficulties would seem less serious. This is true. As with many other agonising bodily concerns of adolescence, the passage of time does wonders.

There was a time when oestrogen pills might have been prescribed for tall girls to stop them growing (high-dose testosterone would do the same for boys), but when you think about it, it is an unsettling idea to interfere in this way with a normal, immature hormonal system. The practice has fallen out of favour and efforts to raise self-esteem and encourage pride and acceptance are now considered preferable and more appropriate. Supermodels and some spectacular female sporting stars have also helped tall women feel less self-conscious, and most end up feeling pretty good about their height.

For parents it's important to be sensitive to a teenager's feelings about their height and to encourage self-acceptance, no matter what size they are.

A temporary mess

The physical changes that occur in adolescence can make kids look like a house on moving day – a temporary mess! Unfortunately, children in the throes of puberty do look, and often feel, rather ridiculous, mostly because the growth of visible body parts is staggered. This is what happens:

- The head, hands and feet grow fastest, and reach adult size soonest (which means that dad might still be able to look down at a kid who's just moved into larger shoes than his).
- The neck, arms and legs follow, and grow significantly faster than the trunk.
- The trunk (which includes the spine, obviously) is completed last, eventually making up the major part of total height gained.

There is no physical pain or discomfort involved in all this, but it explains why young adolescents have such an awkward, ungainly and disproportionate appearance. During this time, kids can feel helpless, out of control, and extremely sensitive about it. At some point, it may be impossible to find clothes or shoes to fit because your teenager is just out of children's sizes and not quite into adult gear, and even when they do fit, either you or your child will feel they don't look quite right. You may come to abhor clothes shopping and feel like killing unhelpful shop assistants and your kid, but it's nobody's fault.

Then there's the face. With an overly prominent nose, a temporarily less prominent chin, and probably a few blackheads for good measure, the overall effect is not going to win first prize in a beauty competition. A pubescent young person is generally not too thrilled about what's happening to the face, and keeps track of it with an almost morbid fascination. After all, practically every time he or she peers into a mirror (which is often), someone new looks back and every little blot or blemish is duly noted. In an Australian study of body image (which is, essentially, the way we think we look), the only people who were able to recognise a photograph of their face upside down were young adolescents.

Acne: the unkindest physical change

Acne is often an unavoidable part of growing up, and one of the least pleasant. At some stage, almost three-quarters of all adolescents will experience it to some degree, most mildly. In its more severe forms, acne is both disfiguring and depressing. There are other problems with it as well: much of the advertising about treatments is misleading (which is disillusioning); and most adults (including doctors, unfortunately) don't take it seriously enough.

At the same time, everybody's an expert on this subject, so it's not difficult to get a bit confused by all the conflicting advice you might receive. Indisputably, acne occurs because testosterone, the male sex hormone, which is also secreted in small amounts by girls, affects sebaceous glands, causing the ducts that lead to the surface of the skin to get blocked. At least, that's how the trouble starts. There are some notorious and common misconceptions about acne and it might help to set the record straight:

- Acne is not an infection as such, although bacteria do become involved in the process. The pus in pimples is sterile and you cannot catch acne from someone, which also means that expensive medicated lotions and creams are unnecessary and may even irritate the skin further.
- Acne has nothing to do with dirt or pollution and can actually be made worse by too much washing and scrubbing (gentle washing with ordinary, bland soap twice a day is quite sufficient). It sometimes helps to use oil-free (rather than oily) sunscreens.
- Bad thoughts and 'dirty habits' have nothing to do with why acne occurs, although many teenagers are not too sure about this.

- ▶ Diet is less crucial than once thought: fat eaten in the diet is not excreted through the skin (which has its own separate supply). Even the dreaded effects of chocolate are overrated. In one study of teenagers, in which one group was given double-dose chocolate bars and the other artificial chocolate bars over a two-month period (the kids didn't know which was which), there was no difference in the number of pimples produced.
- ▶ Some genetic factors may be responsible for the severity of acne, which usually peaks in the mid to late teens and settles over subsequent years. Some individuals, especially young women, have persistent acne throughout adult life.
- ▶ Despite one's most fervent wish (especially when you have a special date next Saturday night), there's no way to get clear skin fast! Acne lesions take their time to develop and, even with the best treatments available, healing takes a minimum of four to six weeks. Changing medications, often through frustration and impatience, only makes matters worse.
- ▶ Acne is a common non-threatening condition and is easily treated in consultation with a GP.

Effective acne treatments include:

- ▶ Application of benzoyl peroxide (a drying agent) to affected areas; 2.5, 5, and 10 per cent gels (use weaker gels for face, stronger gels for back and other areas).
- ▶ Other applications, including Isotrex gel and Differin gel or cream.
- ▶ Topical antibiotic creams such as Clindamycin and Erythromycin.
- ▶ Oral antibiotics, which need to be taken for several weeks before a benefit is seen.
- ▶ For girls with acne the contraceptive Pill can cause marked improvement (through the protective action of oestrogen).
- ▶ A drug called Roaccutane has revolutionised the treatment of severe, disfiguring acne. This drug is highly effective but has side effects (such as dry lips, eyes and nasal linings), poses extreme dangers to an unborn baby (which is why it is used with extreme caution in girls and only in the presence of birth control measures), and has been recently linked to clinical depression.

For health professionals as well as parents, acne is often too readily dismissed as a trivial affliction. But its emotional impact (especially the more severe varieties) can be profound, so empathy and support are called for.

The developing skeleton

It will come as no surprise that active teenagers are susceptible to injury. Bones are developing faster than muscles, which leads to a loss of flexibility at the same time as strength and endurance are increasing. It's a recipe for spills, tears and sprains. There are, however, some important orthopaedic conditions that occur almost exclusively in adolescents that parents should also be aware of:

Adolescent scoliosis: Curvature of the spine of sufficient severity to require treatment occurs in about two to three per 1000 adolescent girls (it is much less common in boys). School screening for scoliosis is much less frequently done nowadays but, if suspected, it should be properly assessed by an orthopaedic surgeon. Scoliosis can be detected by the 'forward bending test' which causes any rib humps to become more prominent (because the ribs are connected to the spine and will twist around as the curved spine bends). This is simply done by having the teenager bend forward at the waist with the trunk parallel to the floor, legs straight and arms dangling, with fingers and palms together. The sooner scoliosis is diagnosed the better as treatment may be needed to prevent worsening of the condition during the adolescent growth spurt.

Adolescent kyphosis: This fairly benign condition is also known as 'adolescent round back' (or vertebral epiphysitis or Scheuermann's disease). The condition is confirmed by X-ray. In about half of the cases, the young person experiences persistent pain in the round back deformity and will need medical attention.

Osgood-Schlatter disease: In this condition, which occurs predominantly in active and sporty teenage boys, there is a painful, firm lump just beneath the knee, where the tendon from the kneecap (patella) inserts into the shinbone (tibia). The disease can be diagnosed simply by eliciting tenderness with a tap on the lump. Treatment is usually at the hands of a physiotherapist and consists of a period of rest from sport, stretching of the hamstrings (the muscles at the back of the thigh) and strengthening of the quadriceps (the muscles at the front of the thigh). Occasionally, surgery is required but only after the bones have fully matured.

Slipped capital femoral epiphysis: An overweight boy with some delay in his development is the most likely contender for this condition, in which the head of the thigh bone (femur) slips on the growth plate (which is made of cartilage), causing pain in the hip or knee and a limp. The condition commonly comes on slowly and can sometimes occur on both sides. Once clinically suspected, the findings can be confirmed by ultrasound, X-ray or bone scan, and the only reliable treatment is surgery.

Some final thoughts

David: Both teenagers and parents can survive the perils of puberty if they know what's going on. After all, these normal biological changes have been around for a long time. In many ways, the most difficult part of the whole business is the related feelings and behaviour. What is most important is that parents are able to encourage their children to greet the changes that occur during puberty with understanding, acceptance and pride. As parents, you may be frequently asked for your opinion about your teenager's appearance, yet when you answer with encouragement you get responses such as: 'Yes, but you're my mum, it looks all right to you.' Your opinions *are* valued, though, even if it doesn't seem so at the time, so don't be discouraged.

Leanne: Despite their sometimes over-confident exteriors, I have found that many teenagers need constant reassurance about what is normal. But then they can be very touchy and easily embarrassed by parents who overdo the advice.

David: No one should be in any doubt that kids are sensitive about puberty. When one of my daughters, then in primary school, heard that I had been invited to speak on this subject to her Year 6 class, she earnestly suggested, 'Please don't go over the top, Dad. We're only children, you know!' At other times, even the most detailed explanation doesn't get through. I know of a 12-year-old girl whose mother gave her the whole story about 'getting her period' and was delighted at how well she handled it when it arrived. When her mum proceeded to say: 'Well, now we can count off approximately 28 days till the next one,' the daughter exclaimed: 'What? You mean I have to go through all this again?'

Parents are sometimes just as anxious as their teenagers. The mother of one boy I was consulted about was most sceptical of my opinion that all was well with her 12-year-old's penis (which she was convinced was too small), and that I could see no reason why it should not continue to grow normally. She actually phoned me after she got home (out of earshot of her son, of course) and insisted that I repeat the reassurance.

I like the joke about a mother who received the following piece of advice from her local doctor in relation to her 14-year-old son's small penis: 'Give the boy plenty of hot, buttered toast,' he told her. 'This will assist his general growth and development and all will be well.' Next morning, the boy was confronted with an enormous plate of hot buttered toast. As he reached out to take a piece, his mother pushed his hand aside and said, 'Leave your father's breakfast alone.'

Leanne: Very funny. It's easy to joke about these things, but really what we are saying is that because teenagers often worry unnecessarily about widespread myths, simple reassurance and acknowledgement of the teenager's concerns can make a big difference.

David: I agree. Teenagers often harbour personal problems. They need to be listened to and taken seriously. A golden-haired 16-year-old boy I saw had only slightly enlarged breasts but was most distressed about it. In his view, they were 'too full'. He felt they were noticed when he was swimming (a common reason for boys avoiding the water altogether) and was 'wondering if something could be done about it'. Another worried teenager was referred to me once, having ejaculated while sitting quietly at a computer. While this problem isn't common, simple reassurance made a great deal of difference to this boy's anxiety.

Leanne: I have also seen highly fraught virginal youngsters convinced they had miraculously contracted some sort of sexually transmitted infection after discovering a normal vaginal discharge. It made a great deal of difference for these young people to hear that they were normal.

Chapter 2

Infuriatingly normal behaviour

My parents show me respect by listening to me even if I'm wrong.
Alexa, aged 14

There is nothing quite like adolescent behaviour. Suddenly the sweet, compliant child of recent memory turns into a moody and truculent adolescent, and parents certainly don't like it. This transition into adolescence, like no other period in a child's life, can make them feel alarmed, angry or indignant, often over what are, in essence, trivial and harmless issues. Or are they? And who suffers the most anyway?

Perhaps an even more important question is, 'Why are parents programmed to expect the worst?' The popular media has never given up on the idea that teenagers are supposed to be puzzling, troublesome, angry and ungrateful. They are almost always depicted as some sort of alien, to be faced with fear and trepidation. This caricature of young people also manifests in the titles of many self-help books (not this one!). If you pay a visit to your local bookstore, chances are you will find a multitude of books on how to love your cuddly infant alongside their companion guides on how to *survive* your spiteful teenager.

It's time to sort this out, because to some extent at least, we are being misled. Not that coping with adolescent ups and downs is ever easy, or that it helps to be told that the behaviour driving you up the wall is 'perfectly normal'. But it might help to know that teenagers are generally as puzzled about it all as we are, that young people are the ones who may be suffering more, and that our relationships with our teenagers do not have to be awful at all. In Chapter 10 we'll discuss relationships in depth. In this chapter, however, we focus on the *infuriatingly normal behaviour*.

Maybe it's the hormones

Even before the earliest signs of puberty appear, children experience vague bodily sensations and emotional stirrings related to their changing internal chemistries. Without knowing how or why, they start to feel different and unsettled, which is exactly how they seem to others. Something has to account for the moody behaviour and emotional outbursts, and hormones are often to blame.

For males, rapidly rising levels of testosterone are responsible for the marked increase in sex drive and desire for risk-taking and excitement that are such features of male adolescence. For girls, oestrogen makes them become almost desperate to communicate (which may explain the verbal diarrhoea you're witnessing). Regardless of the differences in the sexes, however, the teenage years are a time of extreme sensitivity and, particularly during the early stages, literally anything (or nothing) can spark off a mood swing.

Ups and downs

Living with a teenager has been likened to riding a roller coaster of emotional ups and downs. An apparently happy and confident kid can suddenly lash out angrily, become painfully self-conscious or despairingly pessimistic. Sometimes there is an undercurrent of irritability, while at other times, life is just great and nothing is too much trouble.

As ghastly as the miseries can be, bursts of unbridled euphoria are also hard to take (not that one would be so unkind as to complain). It's puzzling when a recently miserable teenager suddenly radiates light and love or prances around loudly extolling the virtues of life. Noisy, continuous giggling at something that seems patently unfunny to the adult mind, or loud yahoos when the football team has won can also really get on your nerves.

During these years, teenagers also need time to be alone. They need 'time out' to quietly ponder momentous questions, such as, 'Who am I?', 'Who will I become?' or 'What should I believe in?' This may mean a physical retreat to the bedroom or other private place, or merely an unwillingness to talk. The latter provides a sort of psychological privacy, as in 'absolutely nothing happened at school today'.

Psychologists call this process 'introspective withdrawal' and consider it extremely important. Some interesting research used long-range beepers to discover what teenagers were doing and how they were feeling at different points in the day. The study revealed that young people are often melancholy while they're alone but, after a while, their mood lightens, as if they've been emotionally refurbished by the experience.

What is one supposed to do in response to these emotional carryings on? Giving in to frustration and tearing out your hair may be one way to go but possibly isn't the most effective option. Nor does seeking an instant explanation work – you are liable to get the 'leave me alone, stop bugging me' response.

Perhaps the best that parents can do is to not get too uptight. If we can stand by without intruding, sympathetically under-react and go easy on the heavy advice, the whole situation can remain manageable. Well, that's the theory. Relationships between parents and teenagers cannot always remain calm, regardless of how much you might want them to be. A lot depends on the nature and extent of the aggravation and how it impacts upon you at a given moment in time.

Living up to expectations

Teenagers feel a lot of pressure to live up to the expectations of their families, friends, school, society and themselves. It may be worth discussing your teenager's expectations. Who is inflicting them and where do they come from? It's clear from the examples given on the next page that teenagers are influenced by information (or mis-information) shared among peers, the misinformation (for example stereotyping) peddled in the media, and the many things that parents, both overtly and inadvertently, convey. These pressures are often unspoken, cause unnecessary stress and tend to be different in males and females.

Leanne: When I visit schools around Australia I routinely ask students about what they expect of themselves during their teenage years and what their parents expect of them. One class of Year 10 boys wrote this list of conflicting expectations:

- to be role models to siblings
- to be interested in cars and sports
- to succeed at school and have career aspirations
- to be tough and brave
- to have big muscles and abs
- to have body odour
- to be interested in the opposite sex
- to get a car, house, wife, kids, job, etc.
- to rebel and live on the wild side.

Another class of Year 10 girls raised these expectations:
- to be feminine and be pretty, skinny, have boobs and good teeth but no pimples, cellulite or body hair
- to like guys not girls and not be a lesbian
- to be smart not dumb but not too smart
- to finish school, get a good job and have kids when you grow up
- to be rich
- to have sex when a guy wants you to and to provide protection such as condoms, the Pill and sex things
- to not have sex
- to smoke if everyone else is so they will be friends with you
- to be perfect
- to never burp or fart or have any problems.

Often the pressure to conform and achieve comes from within the teenager's mind rather than from parents and teachers, but the complexities of trying to sort it all out can be stressful (as we discuss further in Chapter 15). Meanwhile, it may help to explore these sometimes unrealistic expectations with your teenager.

Fidgets and fiddles

Why can't teenagers keep still? They are so much on the go, that early adolescence has been dubbed 'the age of movement'. This is most obvious when they're together. A collection of 12- and 13-year-olds, for example, is a twitching, twittering mass of arms and legs (which, as you'll recall, are the body parts that lengthen relatively early in puberty). Constant movement is usually accompanied by animated talking, giggling and raucous laughter. Catch a morning train or bus on any school day and you'll recognise the scene. Or watch how often teenagers walk in and out of the house, opening doors, closing doors, slamming doors. They just have to be on the go and the house has to move in time with them.

The most plausible explanation for this behaviour is that it is a buildup of energy and tension that has to go somewhere. Rising testosterone levels are at the root of this, making it a nightmare for boys in particular to stay quiet and still (as required of them at school). This is one reason why physical activity such as vigorous dancing and sweaty sports are such healthy and necessary outlets for teenagers.

Of course, outdoor cavorting is one thing. For mums and dads, problems occur mainly when exuberant kids are stuck indoors. That's when not only the fidgets, but also the fiddles (the need to constantly touch things) really take their toll. Boys appear to be somewhat worse than girls in this regard and also clumsier. Practically nothing within reach is safe from detailed scrutiny and handling. When this scourge of so-called 'manipulative restlessness' is upon them, breakages and spills become a routine part of life.

Stay cool, the experts say. Expressing your true feelings about the oil-based paint that has just been 'accidentally' slopped all over the kitchen floor will only damage their fragile young egos. Oh well. What about when kids do incredibly irritating things, over and over again? Bizarre facial grimaces or frenzied hyena impersonations at dinner, for example, can really get you down, especially after a bad day. You can end up wondering if your previously docile child has gone completely mad. Or is this behaviour intended to do that to you?

Realistically, with fidgets and fiddles, yelling and nagging don't seem to help very much. Even a quiet and friendly request to 'please stop it' will rarely work instantly (a bit more fidgeting and fiddling is always necessary, you see, to save face). Some parents get so stirred up by all this that they seek professional advice, usually with disappointing results. Someone is certain to say, 'Don't worry about it, it's only infuriatingly normal behaviour;

it'll pass.' Meanwhile, the idea of setting up a tent in the backyard, and sending the kid out to live in it, may become increasingly attractive.

Don't bug me – I'm rebelling

You know that it's supposed to happen: you've heard about it, read about it, been personally warned about it and, in bygone days, probably done it yourself – teenage rebellion. Even though modern academic research tells us that it's greatly overrated, when you're actually faced with it as parents, it's not much fun. The word itself – rebellion – is perhaps a bit too strong, because this aspect of adolescence can take many forms, from ordinary ungratefulness and disdain, to more outrageous and sometimes frankly dangerous behaviour (the latter applies to only a small minority of young people, fortunately).

Conformity has been described as 'what you do to keep your folks off your back while you are making up your mind what you really want to do'. Doing things differently is, to some extent, what becoming a self-confident, self-reliant, mature person is about. It's what we actually want to see happening. Who'd want an adolescent to be constantly amenable and passive? It might be nice, but it wouldn't be normal.

Messy bedrooms

Benjamin Franklin coined the phrase, 'a place for everything and everything in its place'. This is a deceptively simple idea and the source of endless conflict in millions of homes around the world.

If there's one thing that infuriates parents, it's a messy bedroom. Not just a moderately untidy one, perhaps, but the sort you'd have to see to believe. In terms of gnawing aggravation, a proper messy bedroom can win hands down over many other 'rebellious' adolescent behaviours, such as: the pouty, resentful expression (recognised in most households as 'that face'); the viciously wilful procrastinations; or the ever-so-careless (but really quite studied) disregard for lounge room furniture and general decorum.

Why clean up when it'll just get messy again?
Theo, aged 14

How negotiable should a messy bedroom be?

A teenage photography freak suggested this to his parents: 'If you make my bedroom into a darkroom, I promise to keep it tidy.' Not a bad try. There are two main schools of thought on the approach you might take:

- Parents have a right to enjoy their own homes (which becomes difficult if one of the bedrooms appears to have been converted, without a building permit, into an indoor piggery). Teenagers may argue that their room has nothing to do with you. According to the 'unofficial parents' charter', however, a glance at the signature on the cheques that pay the bills will prove otherwise.
- Alternatively, teenagers have a right to wallow in their own mess ('it's my mess and I love it'), so why not let it be their problem? The door can always be kept closed.

You probably need to work out a level of messiness (or tidiness) that you can tolerate, such as allowing books and sporting equipment on the floor but not dirty plates or clothes left in the room for longer than a day (or however long you can bear it). One smart mother insists that only the small part of the bedroom she can see as she passes by the doorway needs to be kept spotless – the rest of it is the kid's problem! Another negotiated a proper cleanup, took a photo which she enlarged and attached to the bedroom door (which was then kept closed).

Negotiation: turn down the stereo or I'll kill you

Adults rarely like their children's tastes in music and entertainment or how they like to dress and wear their hair. But most parents understand that they need to have at least some freedom of expression and room to discover their individuality. Teenagers also need symbols that show their world is different from that of their parents, and if shocking mum and dad is part of it, so much the better. Styles may change, but the basic idea flows from generation to generation.

There's nothing new about loud music. Of course, in their new-found wisdom, parents are aware that prolonged exposure to ear-splitting cacophony can wreck their teenagers' hearing. What's so concerning about this is that hearing damage is cumulative and irreversible. The results for teenagers and young adults of 'otacoustic emission tests', which measure how quickly the ear can respond to a stream of sounds such as a sentence, in both males and females, reveal a much more rapid decline in hearing than in older people. This is principally a consequence of the advent and widespread use of personal stereos since the late 1970s.

Do teenagers care about any of this? Not at all – their music has to be loud. It's a way to prove you're alive, to tune out the world. What poses the greatest threat to parental sanity, however, is the bone-shattering beat bursting from the bedroom. The explanation that this is an essential aid to study doesn't quite wash.

For a teenager, clothing and hairstyle are intensely personal and important ways of identifying yourself as an individual and as part of a group. Most young people spend a lot of time on their appearance, not only feeling anxious about being normal, but also on doing their hair and makeup, dressing and shopping. When you're stuck in a school uniform all week, dressing up allows you to be creative and to feel more confident. Sometimes, it's simply that you like the way something looks.

Parents were disturbed by the hippie styles of the 1960s and the punk look of the late 1970s and early 1980s, just as we are concerned by the trappings of youth today such as excessive piercings and the return of flares! While 'surfies' have survived for decades, other teenage subcultures appear and change with bewildering rapidity.

Today's parents may be familiar with the following:

- Rappers: rap music-loving teenagers who wear baseball caps back-to-front and baggy pants.
- Skaters: often hugely talented travellers on skateboards and roller blades (which are expensive, as you no doubt know).
- Technokids: computer literate youngsters who spend all their time playing computer games and keeping up-to-date with the latest technology (or accessing adult websites – a subject we address in Chapter 4).
- Goths: young people who dress in black, loose-fitting romantic-style clothes and wear big crucifixes and other religious symbols.
- Ferals: dirty, dreadlocked kids in ripped clothes, affecting 'the poor look'.

Once again, the secret is to under-react. The teenagers whose parents are able to view their 'interesting get-ups', or desire to try them out, with bemused understanding and even refuse to see it as a problem, are doing well. But the whole thing falls apart when 'oldies' go too far and try to emulate these youthful styles themselves. How are you supposed to 'do your own thing' if mum or dad is desperately trying to look the same as you? It's indecent. Generally, the two generations know their place. Perhaps it should occur to us, when we're complaining about our odd-looking kids, that they might not be too impressed with how we look either. If we're lucky, they'll be too polite to say so!

Creeps are other people's children

Human beings are gregarious by nature, but of all age groups, adolescents have the most powerful urge to belong, to be one of the gang. Few parents do not recognise, and at times fear, the powerful influence of the peer group.

For adolescents, friends and acquaintances provide safety in numbers. They provide an antidote to uncertainty, and reassurance in the face of the common foe (you know who that is). Going along with the crowd, even if only in innocuous matters such as dress and musical tastes, signals a distancing from parental influence, although knowing that this is normal doesn't necessarily make it less scary for you at the time. Yet it is often the kid without friends, the social isolate, who is likely to cause far deeper concern.

At the very least, you may view your teenager's friends as 'the blind leading the blind', although it is best not to openly denigrate them – that only makes things worse. At the very worst, you may wonder, 'Are those creeps really leading my nice kid astray?' In which case, it's somewhat harder to know what to do.

There are a number of teenage groups that get parents very worried, namely those that are less mindful of accepted values and social norms, such as religious cults, street gangs and risk-taking groups.

Religious cults: These are characterised by their insistence on mental bondage, absolute obedience to a charismatic (and invariably male) leader and extreme separation from parents. Teenage girls with low self-esteem are particularly vulnerable to being caught up in them.

Street gangs: Gangs are usually made up of young people who, for one reason or another, have to go it alone in the world and find support and companionship by banding together. This is more likely to happen when family and school connections have broken down and the peer group becomes their primary source of identity and affirmation. While these 'tough kids' can teach us a great deal about survival, it's when they deface public property, steal cars and terrorise innocent passers-by that we don't like them; this is 'destructive rebellion' in anybody's language.

Risk-taking groups: Not necessarily 'bad' or delinquent kids (although they may be included) get caught up in dares to do dangerous things as part of these groups; drug-taking can start out this way. As all teenagers can be risk-takers to some degree, taking things to extremes can be influenced by the company they keep.

The fears parents have about such groups and the possibility of their kids becoming involved with them are not unreasonable. But you can't keep teenagers locked up. What you can do is try to keep track of things and say what you think if you have reason to be alarmed. Of course, while young people exercise a choice in the company they keep, sometimes they are pushed into the arms of 'unsavoury customers' by what's happening at home or at school. Families (and schools) that are working well provide insulation that protects young people from a lot of social pressures. But an inhospitable, stressful or dangerous household, for example, is something they will react against. Seeking 'bad company' may be the way they choose to do it.

Even under normal circumstances, dealing with adolescent behaviour can be a supreme test for parents. This is where you need to have a credible track record in regard to establishing clear guidelines, providing a good example, and being willing to allow your own values and opinions to be challenged while standing firm (one of the three principles of 'authoritative parenting' we'll explore in the next chapter and again in Chapter 13). Some of the groundwork will have been established during the pre-adolescent years (hopefully from the earliest years with honest communication and mutual respect). Becoming loudly angry or sullenly silent will not eradicate testing behaviour, while quiet discussion, even when opinions differ strongly, still remains the best way to keep lines of communication open. If things get too much, the sensible thing to do is get outside help (see Chapter 16).

'Wasting time'

Adults have their ideas about what represents good use of time and teenagers have theirs. Not surprisingly, they're rather different. Those activities which seem designed specifically to aggravate parents include: daydreaming, spending hours on the telephone, and just hanging around.

Daydreaming

Young adolescents have an uncanny way of blocking out anything that interferes with their pursuit of happiness. They lose things, are generally forgetful and infuriatingly absentminded. Losing track of time is understandable (and forgivable), particularly when they're having fun, but vacant expressions and vacuous behaviour take a bit more explaining. As an anonymous young graffitist wrote, 'I live in a world of my own, but visitors are welcome.'

During puberty, children start to gain new intellectual abilities. This enables them to generate and explore hypotheses, make deductions, and achieve higher order abstractions or, more simply, they become able to ponder such things as the miracle of thought and the meaning of life. An important manifestation of this is daydreaming, which can make kids look completely spaced out. Sometimes parents think their kid is on drugs and seek professional advice, when what the child actually needs is a T-shirt which states: 'Not stoned – just thinking'.

Many parents and most teachers know a lot about this cognitive phenomenon and it still drives them crazy. As one teacher commented in a school report, 'Jonathon spends a lot of time contemplating matters other than those immediately to hand.' Of course, teenagers do not find this strange in any way. One rather mature young person explained, 'Let's face it, most kids' lives are not what they could be, especially at school.' In any case, all that is happening, generally, is the normal development of thinking processes.

Adolescent daydreams have no simple story. They're often disjointed and vague, sometimes romantic or heroic, sometimes sinister or vicious. They are important, however, for a number of reasons:

- Adolescents try out different behaviours in their imaginations without having to face the hazards of the real world (erotic fantasies would come into this category).
- They can mentally plan ahead and thus gain motivation and confidence.
- Daydreaming also provides a temporary escape from the stresses of everyday life (and who'd blame them for that?).

Vague and inattentive behaviour can, however, indicate a hearing problem. There is much focus lately on this as an educational problem of boys, particularly in the form of auditory processing difficulties, which is more common in boys (we'll look at this in Chapter 11). It's also possible that something else is in play (for example stress, worry or sadness) that may be draining girls' or boys' emotional energy and distracting them from normal routines. The easiest thing to do is to ask 'Is anything troubling you at the moment?' You can usually tell if the matter needs to be taken further (as we discuss in Chapter 15).

Get off the bloody telephone

From a parent's point of view, teenagers and telephones are bad news. Young people can happily chat, giggle or whisper together for hours on end, unless you're determined to take a firm hand. Late night calls, early morning calls, escalating phone bills and mounting frustration are all part of the picture. In the olden days (i.e. before the advent of 'call waiting' and the plethora of juvenile-owned mobile phones), there was also the humiliation of friends dropping in to check on your health because they'd been trying to get through for days.

Why do young people need to spend so much time on the phone? There are several reasons. Connecting with the outside world, when one is temporarily confined to the house, is one – clearly a matter of life and death. Sometimes it is simply a matter of getting help with homework that's too difficult for parents. But mostly it's a way to check out what friends and acquaintances are thinking and doing. If you've accidentally overheard a teenager calling a friend from the phone at home, you'll know that this is usually done with a tone of contrived triviality so that no one knows what they're really doing. The telephone keeps teenagers in touch with what the group is up to and provides endorsement for what they are thinking and doing individually (what psychologists call 'consensual validation'). Talking on the phone is also a way to have a private conversation with a special friend – certainly at school there may not be a lot of privacy. And when the time comes, the telephone is a valuable aid to romance, because it allows intimacy at a safe distance and give-away body language remains private.

Like everything else, a teenager's use or abuse of the telephone may be normal, but that doesn't mean it's not infuriating at times. One knowing teenager wondered if some parents 'get really stupid about telephone socialising because they feel shut out'. This is an interesting thought and there's probably some truth in it. It is now more or less the norm for young people to have their own mobile phone, making it even easier to be private and secretive. Owning a mobile seems to be totally unrelated to socio-economic status. Some kids won't even answer the normal phone – they know it can't be for them! Of course, for parents, it can be reassuring to know that, wherever they are, your teenager can get in touch with you, and vice versa. For example, suddenly a mobile phone rings in the rear of the classroom: 'Yes Mum,' the boy mumbles in embarrassment, 'I'm paying attention.'

The major communications development for young people is the phenomenon of 'texting' messages. A whole new lifestyle has emerged based on instant electronic dialogue about 'what's going on now?' SMS (which stands for 'short message service') provides immediate communication via the tiny display screens on mobile phones in the language of abbreviation: 'The plans have changed . . .'; 'What did you think about what Joe said this morning . . . ?'; 'I'll be there in five . . .' This is great at one level, although one wonders if the 'click-and-go' generation (as psychologist Andrew Fuller, author of *Raising Real People*, has dubbed them) is so imbued with instant gratification that kids are rarely required to think much about or before communicating. It's doubtful that expert phone-using teenagers are too worried about this.

With mobiles, the question of cost can be addressed by using pre-paid cards (or other techniques for limiting use). Otherwise, expenses can really blow out for whoever's picking up the tab. In regard to strategies for controlling phone use at home (after all, somebody important may be trying to get in touch with you), a reasonable limit on the number or length of calls within a given time frame may need to be negotiated.

Mooching around

Just hanging around with friends and 'doing nothing much' is typical teenage behaviour, but, again, not exactly what most adults would consider a constructive use of time. The importance young people give to it is obvious. After all, simply being together in groups is what teenage social life is all about. Aimless and usually harmless 'mooching around', whether at a shopping centre or in a coffee shop, is a pastime they enjoy immensely. In fact, what kids do is often totally lacking in direction and purpose.

Does it matter? Well, probably not, except that parents may want to know what their kids are up to. Parents can't help asking, 'Where are you going? Who with? How will you get there and back? What time will you be home?' But sometimes, the best that honest teenagers can offer is, 'Well, we haven't quite decided what we're doing yet – I'll let you know and keep in touch.' Young people find it hard to justify their pressing need for privacy and intimacy with friends, and it troubles them at times that parents might be thinking, 'What are they hiding?'

The sympathetic and perhaps realistic way to view this mooching around is that young people have only a few short years to have some fun (money, transport and opportunity permitting) before the responsibilities of work, families and households descend on them. Naturally, young people want to enjoy themselves and they know how to do that – their way.

Some final thoughts

Leanne: After reading your earlier book, *Growing Pains*, I made a mental note to avoid making my teenagers' untidy rooms into a moral issue. To a teenager, the bedroom is about privacy and having one's own space. My 14-year-old son once left a note on his door: 'There is no need to clean my room today.' Assuming he had cleaned the room himself, I was more than surprised when I opened the door and found the room had been hit by a bomb (or so it seemed). Sometimes it's best just to shut the door. Parents' and teenagers' perceptions of what constitutes a tidy room vary enormously. I have decided not to waste time worrying about that. However, public space in the house has to be respected.

David: When I look back on my children's teenage years, I remember with a smile the state of my daughter's bedroom – knotted, unwashed clothing; twisted wet towels; assorted paper, pens and other implements of study; apple cores, lolly wrappers, cups, dishes and other evidence of midnight snacks; sporting equipment, magazines, cosmetics and loads of other essential teenage paraphernalia. (What was stuck on the walls was another story – mostly gorgeous and ghostly pop icons as I recall.)

Seeking the middle ground will probably get you a decent cleanup once a week. Surely that's not too much to ask? Meanwhile, some specific limits can be set. In our house, for example, we were more troubled by collections of mouldy old food and knotted wet towels than by general untidiness. I also found it particularly irksome when a desk provided for study purposes was piled high with junk while the student sat cross-legged on the floor, in poor light, trying to work. But in the interests of international peace, I let that one pass.

In retrospect, the tidiness of a bedroom diminishes into insignificance. The issue is more about privacy and space. Important lessons about personal responsibility and mutual cooperation are learnt through a range of experiences and are not determined by the tidiness of a bedroom alone.

Leanne: There's no way to avoid being amused, irritated or even outraged by the way normal teenagers carry on. We may be tempted to think that there are more important things worth worrying about, such as pregnancy, drug and alcohol use or dangerous driving, and we'd be quite right.

Sometimes, however, the very constancy of coping with the daily grind can wear you down. Sometimes, your only salvation is to have a sense of humour, compare notes with friends (so you'll know you're not suffering alone), or take a break in a place where teenagers are off limits. It doesn't hurt to remember also that underneath much infuriatingly normal behaviour, there may be a thoroughly confused kid. He or she may be silently saying, 'Please understand, folks, I'm trying to express my individuality. I'm really a nice person inside.' Perhaps we need to question our priorities. What is really behind our concerns? Will it really matter in the long term?

David: Expressing individuality is another big issue, isn't it? A 14-year-old girl who came to see me had a bizarre, multi-coloured hairstyle, quite different, as it happened, from any of her friends. It made her look as if she'd just been electrocuted. I asked her why she did it, and she explained, 'I know it looks crazy, but at least there's something special about me.' I remember another teenager, a 16-year-old boy with stringy, shoulder-length hair, who burst into tears while telling me that his mother wouldn't even walk with him on the same side of the street. (And some poor kids have parents who insist on walking with them on the same side of the street!)

Speaking in defence of youth, a teenage girl indignantly told me, 'You know, adults have peer group pressure too, but that's all right because it's colleagues, not just useless hooligans.' She went on to explain that 'sometimes groups are brought together because they are all the ones the "nice" kids call weirdos'. Clearly there are lots of non-sinister reasons for being part of a group. As well as learning to be an individual, teenagers need to get together – it's as simple as that.

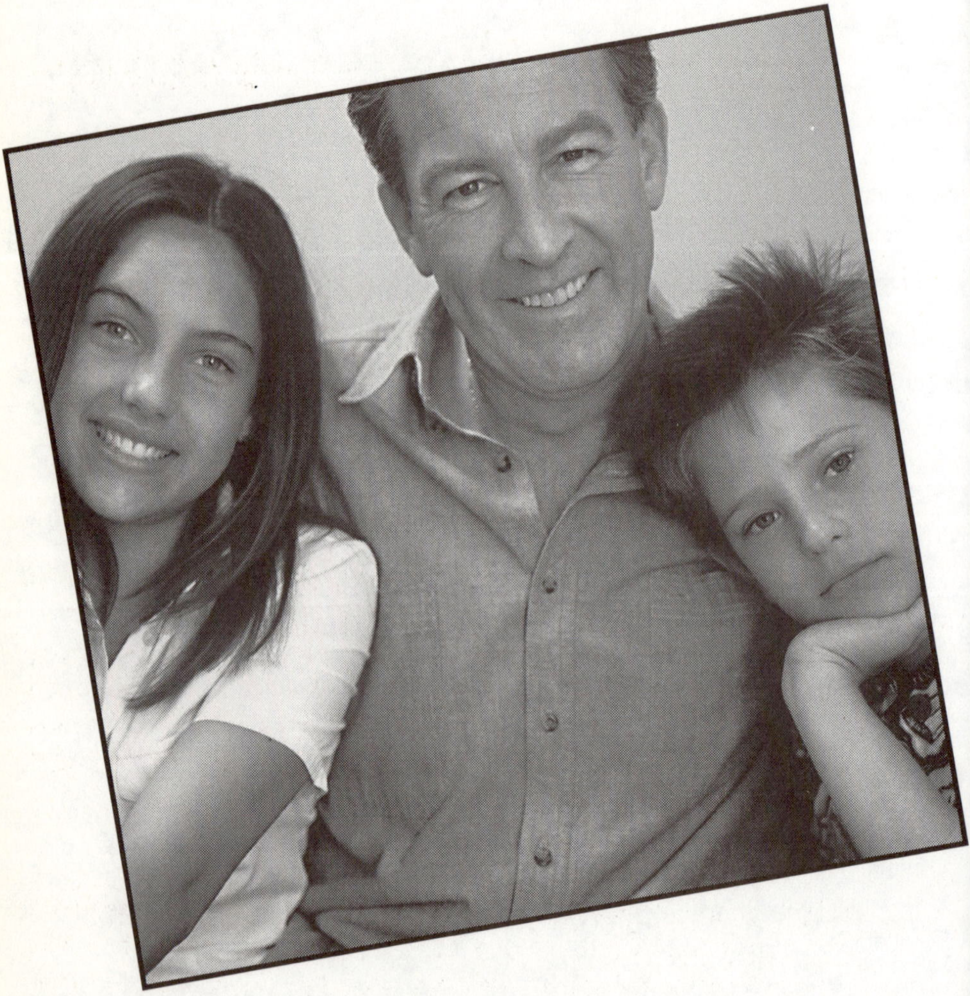

Chapter 3
Authoritative parenting

> *My dad gets upset when I call him an arsehole, but he is.*
> *Jessica, aged 15*

Chapters 1 and 2 have covered what parents may expect during normal adolescent development. As discussed, there is an enormous variation in what is normal and what different families experience in our richly diverse, multicultural society. But we're no longer working in the dark – what we need to do as parents has become increasingly clear and compelling. In this chapter, we highlight the importance of being 'authoritative parents' through showing love and showing respect.

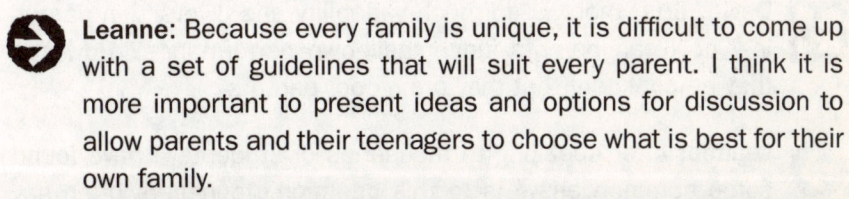

Leanne: Because every family is unique, it is difficult to come up with a set of guidelines that will suit every parent. I think it is more important to present ideas and options for discussion to allow parents and their teenagers to choose what is best for their own family.

This was brought home to me when my 13-year-old son found a flyer of parenting suggestions I received at a Year 7 parent–teacher evening, and I later discovered it torn up in the bin, with his corrections and additional comments in brackets.

42 • What to do when your children turn into teenagers

Memo to my parent

~~Don't spoil me. I know quite well that I ought not to have all that I ask for.~~ I am (not) testing you.

~~Don't be afraid to be firm with me. I prefer it. You make me more secure.~~

~~Don't let me form bad habits. I have to rely on you to detect them in the early stages.~~

Don't correct me in front of other people if you can help it. I'll take much more notice if you talk quietly with me in private.

Don't make me feel that my mistakes are sins. ~~It upsets my sense of values.~~

Don't be upset when I say 'I hate you'. ~~It isn't you I hate but your power to thwart me.~~ (Because I will only hate you for a while).

~~Don't protect me from consequences. I need to learn the painful way sometimes.~~

~~Don't nag. If you do I will have to protect myself by appearing deaf.~~

Don't make rash promises. Remember I feel badly let down when promises are broken.

~~Don't ever suggest that you are perfect or infallible. It gives me too great a shock when I discover you are neither.~~

Don't forget that I cannot thrive without lots of understanding and love. ~~And I don't need to tell you that do I?~~

And to think that I had been quite impressed with the original list! It was interesting to discuss his corrections. Through this discussion, we agreed on our own important list. My son helped me to understand that good parenting is not determined by an outside expert with a set of fixed rules, but about having continual discussion about our important priorities and principles.

David: So if there is so much variability and diversity in parenting, how can parents judge their own performance? How can they be confident that they are 'good' parents?

Leanne: After speaking to thousands of students, I have found some common answers to this question. Teenagers often say 'good parents':

- love and respect you
- give you space when you need it

- support your decisions
- offer advice
- understand your feelings, needs and problems
- respond to you when you ask for help.

This confirms what research tells us about the need for parents to be authoritative parents. According to family researcher Professor Lawrence Steinberg, who recently summarised the results of family research spanning a quarter of a century, authoritative parenting works for three reasons:

Because it's warm: Nurturing and parental involvement make a child more responsive to parental influence, enabling them to socialise more effectively and efficiently.

Because it's firm: The combination of support and structure facilitates the development of self-regulatory skills, which allow the child to function as a responsible, competent individual.

Because it's autonomy-granting: The verbal give-and-take characteristic of parent–child exchanges in authoritative families engages the child in a process that fosters cognitive and social competence, thereby enhancing their functioning outside the family. Teenagers whose parents encourage psychological autonomy are relatively more competent in their interactions with peers than other young people.

Other parenting approaches are not only less successful, in terms of outcomes for children, but can have detrimental effects. (This is discussed further in Chapter 10.) A longitudinal study undertaken by the Australian Institute for Family Studies reported that:

> ... *parenting styles of low warmth, high use of punishment and low monitoring of the child's behaviour, were associated with externalising behaviours (aggression, oppositional behaviour, hyperactivity and attention problems) and with substance abuse.*

If authoritative parenting provides a young person with the best possible trajectory to maturity, as seems to be the case, the challenge is to find ways to educate adults about how to be authoritative, and help those who are authoritarian to change.

This chapter discusses how we can become more nurturing, warmer and firmer parents, and throughout it the voices of young people provide very powerful reminders that the simple things often matter most.

Showing love

Love and respect are threads that weave a family together. Studies have confirmed what we intuitively know: teenagers' most important needs are to *feel* loved and respected by their families.

What helps teenagers feel loved?
Here are some of the things that teenagers say about it:

When I look back on my school years, the most important thing that helped was that my mum really listened to me. I just wanted her to understand but not to worry or over-react, or do anything or give me advice. She would sometimes stop the car and give me her full attention or stay up late with me just talking on my bed. Most of all she would listen with her kind eyes. She didn't even have to tell me. I knew when she did this she really loved me.

My parents show me that they love me by sharing the disappointments and the successes. Small comforts mean a lot. Holding someone rather than talking.

Whatever happens during the day, our family has dinner together and we enjoy talking about the day and make plans for the week. Just asking how my day was is enough proof that they care. Sometimes I know that my parents have a lot of worries, but they try to make this dinnertime together a time that we enjoy together. If there are problems, we talk about that too but they usually spend time with one of us later. Sometimes Mum gives me a back massage or brings up a hot water bottle at nighttime. I talk better at night and this helps me to relax.

My parents sometimes go overboard but they always notice when I do something well or I get an award at school or something good happens. My mum has been there through the ups and downs. She gave me a card and it said: 'We are so proud of you and we love you.'

My dad has a great sense of humour and we have fun together. My parents celebrate everything – from the dog's birthday to Anzac Day. We do family activities and this shows that family matters most. Laughter always helps. They aren't religious but they appreciate the wonder of life – they are very spiritual in the way they find meaning in things and take time to talk about the miracle of normal life. It is a very loving family.

My parents have split up. My mum is sometimes hard on me and tells me off. My dad lets me do anything. I want to stay with my mum. She cares about me. Sometimes I go away with Dad on my own. I wish my mum would come but I know she thinks it's best for me to spend some time on my own with Dad. This way I feel closer to him. I know my mum loves me to let me do this because I know it hurts her to let me go.

My parents look after each other and spend time just together. I know my parents will not disagree with each other about the rules – they stand together even when I think one of them is disagreeing. Sometimes they drive me crazy but they are really like a solid rock that I can depend on. They love me.

My family could sometimes pay more attention to me but it's hard for them when there are four other sisters. I still feel loved.

When I am studying, my dad sometimes comes in and puts a hot chocolate on the desk and then leaves without saying anything. It's when he doesn't say anything that he is actually saying he loves me, respects my work and doesn't even ask for anything in return. I love him.

These quotes come from interviews given by 17- and 18-year-olds and describe some of the small things that parents can do to make a difference. It is worth thinking about your small, reassuring gestures and remembering to show love often. What makes *your* teenager feel loved?

What are some of the common, unhelpful things parents say and do?

The interviews with the teenagers also revealed a number of negative responses about the unhelpful things parents do.

> *My dad gets home late and works every weekend. My mum hates work and takes it out on us and then says: 'I'm doing all this for you.' I feel like saying: 'What exactly are you doing for us?' My parents get up, go to work, get dinner, clean up, get ready for the next day. I feel I should be grateful but this doesn't feel like it's enough.*

> *My dad yells at me and sometimes slaps me. Then he tells me he loves me when he cools down. He says he loves me, but he doesn't.*

We say our families are our priorities. What did we do in the last week to *show* them? It does not seem to be enough to only say we love and respect our children, or to only fulfil their basic needs with material things. Teenagers are sensitive and intuitive. They are mind-readers. But they often get it wrong. Here is another common example:

> *I am not as academic as my brother. My parents don't say anything, but I know they love him more than me.*

Our teenagers know when we have worries or we are not really listening, by our body language, not our words. They often misinterpret our preoccupation with our busy lives and incorrectly assume we do not care. All young people have secret worlds where they experience intense emotions, confusion and concerns about their friends, the world and their future, and they look for constant reassurance that they are loved and understood.

Showing respect

Teenage years are a time of experimentation, self-awareness, curiosity, exploration and search for identity. The challenge is to understand our teenager's individual physical and mental growth and to develop a respect for their changing needs. Teenagers respect us if we show them respect in meaningful ways. Our ways need to be open to change to keep up with adolescent development and to encourage independence, initiative and responsibility.

Here are some comments from teenagers about respect:

My parents' values don't change. When they set rules, we talk about them. I know when no means no. I have learnt to respect that.

My parents respect me and this has taught me to be willing to think of others' feelings.

My parents allow me to totally choose my own path, in terms of subjects, relationships or anything. They have learnt to accept that my talents aren't always academic and they have supported me in my crazy ideas and dreams.

My parents let me have my say, then they offer their views without pushing them onto me.

Teenagers respect their parents when they feel respected. What makes *your* teenager feel respected?

Language

It hurts and humiliates parents to be put down by foul language. As authoritative parents we can set an example and firm limits regarding tone of language. This tends to work better, however, if both parties take time out to cool down before you raise the issue.

Statements like these may help:

- I feel hurt when you use that language or tone.
- What is behind your anger?
- Why are you being disrespectful?
- How can we prevent this happening next time we are angry?

Young people are often disrespectful because they do not feel respected by their parents. It is also helpful to think about the way the language of parents can be disrespectful.

Here is what teenagers say about their parents:

I hate being compared to other people. My parents say they don't have time for me but they give time to my brother. They said: 'You got 90 per cent for that exam, what happened to the other 10 per cent?'

> *My mum says I am just like my older sister. She says: 'I hope you're not becoming like your sister.' It puts me down and my sister down. I hate it.*
>
> *When my mum picks me up from my friends' houses, the first thing she usually says in front of everyone is, 'I hope you behaved yourself. Excuse me, say thank you to Mrs Smith . . .' I feel like hitting her.*
>
> *It is better if my parents say: 'I don't agree with that.' But they usually start with: 'Are you stupid? Can't you do anything right?'*

Young people are sensitive to criticism and embarrassed easily. It is also common for adolescents to become over-critical in return if they are being put down by others.

> *If someone close to you hurts you emotionally, you retaliate, your trust dissolves. You feel alienated. It makes you feel as though you're not normal and you take out your aggression on your family.*

Many teenagers have a strong sense of justice and will admit that unleashing frustration on innocent bystanders is wrong. Parents need a lot of patience to remain calm when they receive the misplaced anger of their teenager. Rather than retaliating, it may be better to ask what is behind the anger. What have they said or done? Does it deserve this outburst? Is there something else going on?

Concern

Teenagers often misinterpret parental concern for disrespect, interference and failure to trust:

> *My parents need to accept there are times when I don't wish to talk and they shouldn't ask questions. I need my own space, especially when I'm in a bad mood. I get really pissed off when they assume I am in a bad mood.*
>
> *Once I told my mum I was not coping and then she told all my friends' mothers. Then my friends asked me if I was coping. It was embarrassing. Mum does not respect me and I don't trust her.*

I have learnt that I am a person of worth and respect and that my opinions count. But when I criticise myself and magnify my faults, I usually begin to doubt myself as a person.

I made a lot of mistakes and my parents keep bringing them up. I feel like I can't make any mistakes without someone jumping at me.

Parents need to understand that things are different from when they were teenagers. They need to loosen up. For example, my parents often ask if I am coping. This is really negative. If I say I am not coping, it sounds like I am inadequate. It would be more positive if they asked me: 'Are you getting enough sleep? Are you okay?' It is just small things like this that make a difference.

A balance is required. Young people need space and to be allowed to develop independence. However, it is normal for parents to show concern. Do not leave a teenager to their own devices if they are depressed, unsafe or uncommunicative. Sometimes it helps to say: 'I respect your need for independence, space, etc., but I love you so much, I need to know you are okay.'

Control

Overcontrol is 'care and concern' expressed as mollycoddling or 'military might'. Some parents feel they have the right to plan and direct every aspect of a child's life. Not surprisingly, undue parental influence rarely works out well.

For the young person with little room to move (an extremely stressful situation to be in), there are several options: to react against it in a normal sort of way (a healthy rebellion); to escape the feeling of being boxed in by getting involved in drugs or some other sort of risk-taking behaviour (an unhealthy rebellion); by abdicating and fitting into the mould set by parents (at the expense, unfortunately, of individual creativity).

It is normal for older adolescents to want more control over their lives and to be respected

I hear my dad say his family is his first priority, but I wish he'd look at when he last put his family over his work and fixing up the house.
Dean, aged 17

and treated like an adult. Our parenting 'style' needs to be respectful. As previously mentioned, a number of studies have identified the benefits of authoritative parenting that is nurturing (warm) and assertive (firm). There are three common types of control exhibited by parents and each deters normal development in different ways.

- Overprotective parents hinder their teenagers' independence by shielding them from potentially challenging or unsafe situations. This style of parenting breeds anxiety and stifles independent development in young people.
- Overexpectation is parental pressure to achieve or perform, which leads to a submerging of a child's personal interests or initiatives. When a 12-year-old kid rushes up to her mother and says, 'Mum, I've just figured out how you can be a lot happier with me – lower your expectations,' she's not joking.

    Some parents program their children to behave in certain ways, and often live vicariously through them. No one would question the desirability of giving young people high ideals, but it is preferable not to push them beyond their abilities or personal interests. The idea, in fact, is to match one's expectations with the likelihood of success – another of those balancing acts for which you have received no training.
- Authoritarian parenting is about punishment, control and domination, by physical and psychological means and is very negative. Teenagers respond with resentment and anger. There is a great difference between authoritative and authoritarian approaches. Authoritative parents have a powerful influence by their gentle but firm confidence. An authoritarian approach is one-sided ('you will do it because I said so') and counterproductive. It paradoxically undermines the power of parents.

As parents, we need to continually ask ourselves:

- Is my behaviour as a parent helping to encourage my child to grow up to be an independent, responsible adult?
- What is the long-term outcome I want for my teenager?

David: I recall an overweight 13-year-old girl whose mother had desperately wanted her to be a ballet dancer. Her efforts to urge this highly valued personal goal onto her daughter led to the girl's opting out by overeating.

What do teenagers say about control?

A cool person stands up for things, is individual and thinks for themselves. This is what I am trying to be. My parents want me to conform to their image. We want completely different things and I need my parents to understand this and to respect me.

My mum yells orders at me. Dinner's ready, do the dishes, put your washing away. I don't mind doing these things but does she have to speak to me like I am a child?

My dad gives me one-sided lectures about things and has to be right. He demands that I listen to him and respect him, but when does he plan to start respecting my ideas?

Limits

Limit-setting is another way of showing and encouraging respect. Teenagers prefer parents to set consistent limits, as this quote suggests:

My dad lets me do anything I like. He doesn't check up if I don't go to school or if I don't come home. But he doesn't care either. My mum's rules drive me crazy and we fight, but she cares.

At other times, limit-setting simply means pointing out a habit that a rapidly developing teenager may not be aware of. For boys a common example is the change in tone of voice, as this quote illustrates:

When I was about 13 or 14, my dad kept saying: 'Watch your tone with your mother.' I didn't even know what he was talking about. Then when my brother turned 13 and his voice changed, I started to notice his tone. I started to say: 'Watch your tone with our mother.' He would give me one of those looks, but I couldn't stand the way he would grunt at her.

> When I get upset, just having a hug from my mum shows me that I am loved.
> Jenny, aged 13

Permissive parenting gives in to the demands of teenagers and takes the short-term, easy-way-out option rather than the best decision for the long term. It does not provide guidance or limits and encourages self-centredness in teenagers. Overindulgence allows kids to get away with murder. According to one definition, 'permissiveness is the principle of treating children as if they were adults; and the tactic of making sure they never reach that stage'. Ironically, overindulgence is also a form of holding on. A parental attitude that lacks firmness fails to provide a model for an adolescent to either identify with or rebel against, and confusion prevails. While they rarely admit it openly, most children are looking for firmness.

Parenting motivated by guilt is very destructive. Young people take full advantage of poor limits associated with overt and unspoken parental guilt.

Coercive parenting also creates common behavioural problems because of poor limit-setting. This scenario illustrates how easy it is to resort to coercion: Mum comes home from work very tired and she has dinner ready at 7.20 pm. The teenagers are watching TV. She says: 'Please switch the TV off.' The teenagers don't move. She comes back a minute later and raises her voice. The teenagers say: 'This is our favourite TV program. Can't we watch TV during dinner?' Mum says: 'No.' The teenagers' anger escalates and she yells at them.

The parent requests, the teenager escalates, the parent is frustrated, the teenager ignores, the parent responds harshly or gives in and the teenager then learns coercion and escalation as normal behaviours. Who can blame the adolescent if they then use this behaviour at school and with peers?

A better alternative is to sit down at a time when the family is functioning well to discuss family limits and rules, agree on limited TV watching times and dinnertimes. When the rules are negotiated and the consequences are drawn up, teenagers learn consistent limits, and common sources of irritation can be avoided. This is better done before the event, rather than during the escalation of anger. It is also important to try to be consistent with negotiated limits and rules once they have been set.

David: Curfews are a good example of limit-setting and a common source of conflict in families. I know of one father who gave his daughter a key to the front door on her 15th birthday, and simply asked her to be quiet when she came in. Most parents feel more comfortable with an agreed upon time. As one young adolescent said: 'In my house we have mandatory retirement, I have to be in bed by 10 pm.'

On the homefront, in a personal, hand-crafted birthday card to me, my elder daughter, then aged 16, included this saying: 'As teenagers grow older, adulthood is no longer pretended; and thanks to understanding parents, their curfews are extended.'

Leanne: This is what one teenager said to me about appreciating limits:

When everyone knows what they are meant to do with the simple things – bedtimes, waking times, chores, party rules, manners, language, cleanliness – the house runs smoothly. We don't fight over stupid things.

Some final thoughts

David: Our message is one of respect for the uniqueness of every family, and the need for parents to discuss with their kids the principles they live by. There is good evidence about what makes a good parent – an authoritative parent. Good parents encourage their teenagers to feel secure. Not surprisingly, the characteristics of good parenting include:

- direct and honest communication
- achieving a balance between warm intimacy and self-confident independence
- showing clear parental authority and responsibility with decision-making, while ensuring teenagers are listened to and given choices
- negotiated family rules and codes of behaviour with firm limits.

Leanne: We will talk later in the book about some worrying trends in statistics regarding teenage suicide, depression, drug use and sexuality. These Australian trends indicate that we need to take a new look at how we are parenting our children. Is our parenting protecting or predisposing our children to problems? Research and experience would indicate that we need to be more nurturing, warmer and firmer.

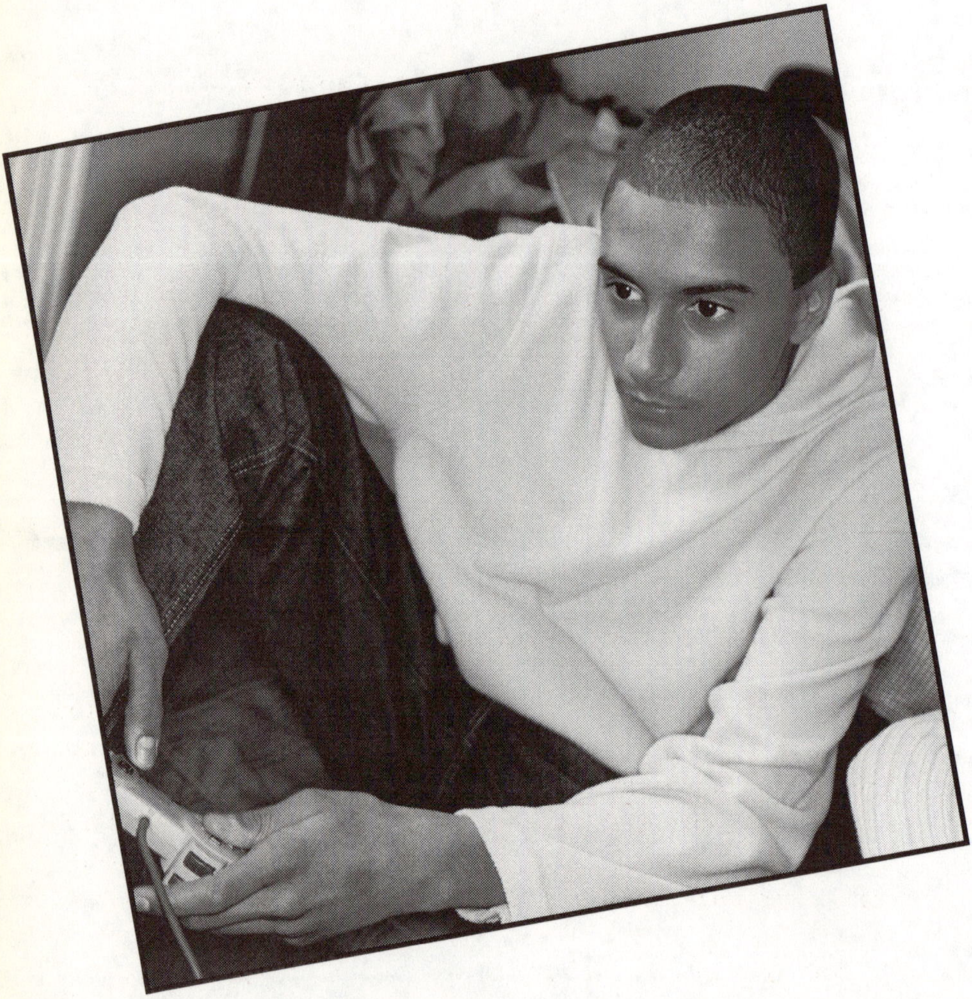

Chapter 4

Teenagers and the media

Everyone seems so happy and looks so beautiful on TV shows. It makes me feel like I'm not normal.
Clare, aged 13

Many of the youngest generation can click a mouse before they can even tie their shoelaces, and are just as comfortable with e-mail and with PCs as with pen and paper, probably more so.

Parents have no problem remembering a time before there was the Internet (after all, it only happened in the 1990s and went from infancy to ubiquity in only seven years), just as grandparents can remember a time before television, a time when radio was king. Between then and now, an entirely new and bewildering world has opened up and, for many parents, there may be a lot of catching up to do.

Are those of us raised during the TV era taking too much for granted where our children are concerned? What do we actually know about the effects of TV and other media on children and adolescents? And are we much too unprepared for the impact of the latest Internet technology and the World Wide Web, let alone for what digital technology has in store for us? This chapter explores these issues and provides a perspective on modern-day media and its importance to young people.

Media violence

According to a 1998 study of over 5000 12-year-olds in 23 different countries, Arnold Schwarzenegger's *Terminator* character was recognised by 88 per cent of the world's children. It seems that American action heroes are the people most likely to be perceived by children as role models. This information should worry us, because research that has been conducted over the past four decades shows that there is a direct relationship between media violence and real-life violence.

Dr Victor C. Strasburger, an adolescent medicine colleague from Albuquerque, New Mexico, and a world authority on this subject, has collated all the relevant studies, and presents some alarming information for our consideration. He pointedly asks, for example, 'Which parents in their right minds would allow a stranger into their home to teach their children and adolescents for three to five hours a day?' Yet television (and its extensions via cable and pay-TV) does exactly that, exposing young minds to a staggering number of violent acts.

The fact is, the majority of shows that children and young people watch contain violence, much of it potentially harmful. Frequently, the perpetrator is a role model, the violence is depicted as being justified or goes unpunished, or the consequences of violence are not shown. Guns are featured in about one quarter of all depictions. And children's shows involving cartoon heroes contain even more violence than programs designed for adults! Researchers involved in an American longitudinal study into the effects of TV violence on children, that has been going on for the past 30 years (with similar work in other countries leading to exactly the same findings), concluded that:

> *Aggressive habits seem to be learned early in life and, once established, are resistant to change and predictive of serious adult antisocial behaviour. If a child's observation of media violence promotes the learning of aggressive habits, it can have harmful lifelong consequences.*

In the Australian context, there is anecdotal evidence that the 'video age' made a difference, in a negative way, to adolescent behaviour. By the early 1990s, violent videos had arrived with a vengeance. Former Children's Court magistrate and author of *Those Tracks on My Face*, Barbara Holborow OAM expressed her concerns, based upon her observations of young people coming through her court, in no uncertain terms. She believed that young people (those in troubled circumstances in particular) were increasingly acting out what they saw their heroes doing in the movies, on TV and on videos. She also noted that the hero in violent videos is often an extremely violent man who, in the end, is successful in violently outsmarting an equally violent bad guy – 'cutting, gouging, blasting, blowing, twisting, crashing, burning and crushing' – but that the videos universally ignored the consequences of violence. If they showed perpetrators going through the whole court system, being refused bail, being sentenced to lengthy stretches in jail and probably being raped, then perhaps they would convey a different message.

> *I see ads all the time about losing weight. It makes me feel I'm not thin enough.*
> *Fatima, aged 18*

Sex in the media

Less is known about the effects on children and teenagers of sex in the media. But while it might not yet be possible to draw cause-and-effect conclusions, as less research has been done, if media violence can lead to real-life violence, surely media sex could lead to real-life sex. Impressionable young teenagers will notice the incredible amount of sexually suggestive material on TV in comparison with the relatively minute amount that depicts birth control, self-control or abstinence. This is also true of movies, which are even more sexually explicit than TV. The impact on teenagers is yet to be properly studied. Dr Strasburger wonders if 'the media could be functioning as a sort of "super-peer", making early sexual activity seem like normal behaviour for some impressionable young adolescents'.

However, the media has become an important access point for teenagers for information about contraception, sexual responsibility and safety. Perhaps the most telling evidence of social change between the early 1960s and now is the difference in popular magazines. In a women's magazine from 1960, the following letters caught our eye:

When I was 13, my best friends were allowed to wear lipstick and high heels. I was annoyed at my parents for not letting me do the same. I felt out of place when I went on outings with my girlfriends and they persuaded me to put on a little lipstick and rub it off before I arrived home. Now I am 15 I have just started to wear lipstick and high heels with my parents' consent. I am very grateful to my parents for making me wait until now and I realise I was too young at 13 to do these things. You aren't missing anything and you can get just as many whistles without these things.

Grateful teenager

And:

I am often invited to parties where they will persist in playing kissing games such as Postman's Knock. I am considered abnormal because I don't like these games and think they are germ-giving. I always have some excuse, if possible, such as a cold but the boys don't seem to mind. I don't mind a little smooching but too much makes me feel sick, especially as I don't like all the boys. Do you think I am old-fashioned or a freak? I am 17.

Germy

The answer to the second letter started like this: 'I don't think you are old-fashioned or a freak: fastidious would describe you with an overdeveloped thing about germs . . .' Another answer to a question about boy–girl relationships in the 1960s received this answer:

You are far too young to be thinking about having a steady boyfriend. No girl of 15 knows her mind romantically; she simply has not had the time to have the experience of love. You are a lucky girl to have parents who have firm ideas about this and in years to come you will thank them.

In contrast, magazines for teenagers today explore topics like 'We've pashed, so now what?', 'We solve your trickiest body dilemmas', 'What guys really look for', 'Sex and your body', 'Party hard', 'Date rape', 'Boobs, bums and everything in between'. The letters in the health pages now tend to read like this: 'While I was giving my boyfriend head, he came in my mouth and I swallowed his sperm. Can I catch AIDS? Also, will it stain my teeth?'

Encouragingly, magazines like *Dolly*, for example, through its 'Dolly Doctor' column and feature articles, provide candid, accurate and helpful answers to teenagers' questions (mostly for girls, of course, although some boys do surreptitiously read this stuff).

The following frank question and answer appeared in a recent edition:

My boyfriend and I went to the movies and he fingered me two times. The first time he used one finger, and half an hour later he used two fingers. When I got home I saw blood in my undies. Am I still a virgin? Also, I got my period two weeks early. What does this mean?

Worried, NSW

Don't worry, I hope you'll be reassured now that you've asked for some advice. Being a virgin means different things to different people, but if you're saying that the sexual experiences you've had involve some fingering and no other genital contact, then you can be reassured that you are still a virgin, even though you noticed some bleeding. The bleeding might have come from some tearing of your hymen when your boyfriend put his fingers into your vagina – this is okay, and provided you didn't feel it was unwanted or painful then there's not much to worry about. If you did find it too rough or you weren't happy about it, make sure you tell your boyfriend and let him know what you do and don't like. If you have never had intercourse (where his penis goes into your vagina) and are therefore at no risk of pregnancy or STIs then it's likely that your early period was a complete coincidence. Depending on what your normal menstrual cycle is like, and how long you've had periods for, your cycle could still be adjusting, and you might find that some periods come early while others are late. Of course, if there is any chance of pregnancy, STIs, or if you have been on the Pill you should talk to your doctor about it.

While the impact on teenagers of viewing sexual violence in the media has not been studied, research has certainly shown that older adolescents and young people are adversely affected by it. For example, it was shown in American studies in the 1980s that the portrayal of sexual violence in X-rated and R-rated material fosters callous attitudes towards the victims of rape and sexual abuse. Violent images in pornography and elsewhere, which portray the myth that women enjoy or in some way benefit from rape, torture, or other forms of sexual violence are particularly detrimental. This is not the sort of stuff we want children to engage with as part of their eager, normal searching for information about sex and relationships (which we will discuss further in Chapter 7). Sexual violence in popular films, as well as material they may access on the Internet, undoubtedly influences their initial attitudes towards sexuality.

A parent reported on her technique of checking the programs that her young adolescent son had been accessing. She noticed that he'd been surfing for information about 'pawn' and was also looking for 'striper' (which turned out to be a fish found off the coast of Queensland). After talking with her son about what he was looking for, she decided to get him some help with spelling.

Drugs in the media

Alcohol and tobacco manufacturers spend billions of dollars on high-impact commercials, many targeting young people. As well as an enormous amount of drug use in popular mainstream TV programs (ever noticed how much the characters drink in 'The Secret Life of Us'?), cigarette smoking has made a big comeback in Hollywood films, with many lead characters lighting up.

The promotional messages are clever and effective. Drinking is normalised for young people and portrayed in terms of its supposed advantages – popularity, prestige, fun, sex appeal. Research shows that brand recognition and positive attitudes towards drinking result from exposure to commercials, making children more vulnerable to experimenting with alcohol. Children who enjoy alcohol advertisements are more likely to drink earlier and engage in binge drinking. Longer term studies leave no doubt about the cause-and-effect nature of the media's influence on both cigarette and alcohol use.

The issues of teenage drug and alcohol use are explored more fully in Chapter 14.

Rock music and music videos

Rock music has represented an important identity badge for adolescents since the 1950s. According to one study of 2700 young people, they listen to music for an average of 40 hours per week (including background). Parents may or may not be aware that, in recent years, song lyrics have become more violent, more sexually explicit and more drug-oriented. How much should we worry about these trends? Based on what little research exists, there is little evidence that sexual or violent lyrics lead to behavioural difficulties. The facts are as follows:

Parents worry too much, so I don't talk about my problems to them.
Gina, aged 13

- Only 30 per cent of teenagers know the lyrics to their favourite songs (or 40 per cent if they are heavy metal fans).
- Even if they know the lyrics, children and young teenagers are unlikely to comprehend their meaning, often missing sexual themes, for example; they come to understand better as they get older (and mature cognitively).
- The themes of sex, drugs, violence and Satanism in some contemporary rock music, while shockingly obvious to adults, often go completely over the heads of young people. Teenagers are more likely to interpret their favourite songs as being about love, friendship, growing up, having fun, life's struggles and other ordinary topics relating to adolescent life.
- A preference for heavy metal music may be a strong marker for substance abuse and other risk-taking behaviour. Although the research is not clear on this point, it's probably more likely that this issue relates more to troubled or alienated young people identifying with the performer and with a negative view of life, rather than the words and music.

Music videos are an interesting phenomenon in the lives of young people. The popularity of Music Television (MTV) is extraordinary, with many teenagers watching for up to an hour or so each day. In so doing, they are also being exposed to an enormous amount of advertising (highly lucrative for MTV!). It's a clever marketing ploy: every time a teenager hears a particular song after seeing the video version, they immediately 'flashback' to the visual imagery in the video, including the advertising. It's hard to know whether or not music videos are actually contributing to attitudinal or behavioural problems in young people, although here's some relevant information:

- A comprehensive content analysis of music videos showed that nearly one in four MTV videos portrays overt violence and involves weaponry, and 20 per cent of all rap videos have violence.

- Around one in four music videos contains either tobacco or alcohol use (which is less than in prime-time TV programs – 70 per cent of which show substance use – and the vast majority of top-grossing movies).
- A legitimate concern is that violence in music videos might desensitise young viewers to violence, and that sexual images in music videos might encourage sexual activity at a younger than ready age.

The Internet

Let's face it, children and teenagers are far more knowledgeable and sophisticated about the Internet and its many facets than their parents are. Of course, if you're among those adults who have enthusiastically embraced its wonders and surf cyberspace with confidence, good for you. This section is designed in particular to inform and reassure the more computer-phobic and technology-resistant types among us, as well as those who have literally no idea what their kids are actually getting into.

The vast majority of young people in Australia have gone online, mostly from home (many from their bedroom – not a good idea!). The Australian Broadcasting Authority's report, *The Internet at Home*, surveyed 310 Internet-using households with children under 18. Almost 50 per cent of the children and young people had seen something on the Internet they thought was offensive or disgusting, such as pornography, tasteless jokes or violent imagery. The good news is that most children said they had ways of managing and dealing with it (for example, deleting a file if it was in an attachment to an e-mail, exiting from a website and so on). It also seems that lots of Australian parents supervise their children's Internet sessions, although it's anybody's guess how many more would have absolutely no idea which websites their children are visiting.

The Internet, or the Net, is simply a vast group of computer networks linked around the world. It was put together originally for academic and military communication and was never really intended for the public. Writing about it in the *Sydney Morning Herald* (in August 2002), journalist Jon Casimir said:

The miracle of the Net is that even though it's slow, unwieldy, prone to crashing computers and full of junk, dumb ideas, misinformation and juvenilia, we love it enough to put up with the grief it brings us . . .

Some of its components are: e-mail for electronic communication (the greatest community revolution of the past decade); bulletin board systems for the posting of information; and chat groups that can be used for real-time conversations. On the World Wide Web, which combines visuals, sound and text together in a manner that allows linkages across many sites related to a particular topic, there are more than eight billion pages – less than five per cent of what will eventually appear.

Things that we used to do by other technologies (such as mail, phones or fax), we can now do on the web – literally everything. Computer literate people are banking, trading on the stock market, buying airline or theatre tickets, booking hotel rooms, accessing the latest news and sports (and listening to games live), finding educational information, looking up addresses (and location maps), sending and receiving photo images and so on. Apparently the two major Internet success stories outside of pornography are banking and travel.

From many points of view, the web and other Internet components are fantastic developments, offering untold advantages and innumerable ways to improve and streamline daily living. Writing in *The Economist* in November 2001, management guru Paul Drucker stated the obvious: 'The next society will be a knowledge society.' This is unavoidable and our children are part of it already. Dr Strasburger, an expert in the impact of the media on young people, along with other specialists in adolescent health, stresses the positive aspects of the expanding educational technology, and the importance for children of accessing and benefiting from it. It's reassuring to know that more young people have used the Internet to look up health information than to download music, play games, buy something, or check sports scores.

What we don't want, however, is for our teenagers to be exposed to 'hard core' sexual content in adult websites, or exploitation targeting children. It's not hard to find and not infrequently it finds you. Many sexually explicit adult sites will state that the site: contains sexually explicit pictures; may be offensive to viewers; and that the viewer must be 18 years of age and, if not, must exit the site immediately. Imagine how often a sexually curious underage person would think, 'Oh, okay, I'd better exit then.' All it takes is a click of the mouse and a small fib about one's age and they can enter the adult site – no problem. From there it's an easy matter to link to others offering further samples of pictures, text and videos of a hard core sexual nature. Unsolicited material comes via e-mail too, and is a common means by which cyber paedophiles distribute child pornography.

Apart from sex, the Net also carries accessible information on how to make bombs or other weapons, material provided by racist and hate groups (which a disappointingly large percentage of people have visited), and websites dedicated to smoking and drinking, with promotional material attractive to young people.

How much is too much?

Complete absorption in something, whether it's TV, Playstation or the Net, is not healthy for young people. These activities do not have a finite end point (like the whistle at the end of a football game), which means they give a sense of 'undiluted time', and create a virtual reality – in other words, a place that doesn't really exist. In his book *Raising Real People*, psychologist Andrew Fuller empathises with the concerns of parents, encouraging them to take note of what their children are up to, by asking the following questions:

- Is my teenager having less face-to-face contact because of their computer use?
- Is my teenager more guarded or secretive than they used to be?
- Is my teenager losing sleep, missing school or declining social opportunities to be on the Net?

Some of the adverse health consequences of being a computer addict include: withdrawal symptoms (moodiness, irritability or aggression) if computer use is restricted; deteriorating eyesight; repetitive strain injury (especially with excessive use of Playstation, which can cause a condition called 'vibration white finger', usually seen in workers with powerful vibrating tools); sleep deprivation (from staying up late or getting up early to use the computer); poor posture; eating irregularities including missing meals.

Even though we're focusing here on potential problems associated with the Net, remember that these are tiny in comparison with the exciting benefits that this technology can bring. Again, we want our young people to take advantage of the incredible world of information and ideas that is now so readily accessible to us. As with anything to do with our kids, as in life generally, the questions are about what's reasonable and what's safe.

In responding to a question about how to restrict computer use in the home when things are getting out of hand, one mother noted: 'I have been known to steal the mouse, disconnect things, or just stand in the doorway and stare!' Here are some other tips for parents about the Net:

- Keep the computer in an open area, not in your teenager's bedroom (although if they're home alone, where the computer is doesn't matter).
- Become more involved and discuss guidelines about Internet use – when it is and isn't okay to be online, how much time is acceptable (for example, not more than one–two hours a day), what sites are off limits, etc.
- Remind your teenager never to give out personal information or arrange to meet someone they've met online.
- If your teenager has set up their own personal webpage, be sure to visit it.
- If your teenager is preoccupied with the Internet to the extent that it is the most important activity in their lives (and they're showing the signs of adverse health consequences listed), seek professional help.
- Help your teenager evaluate the credibility of information they see on a website (for example check if it's an official website).
- Determine if you need to use blocking software to protect your child's safety (by restricting access to pornography, dangerous chat rooms, hate sites and other explicit material). Unfortunately, however, these programs do not work particularly well and need to be improved. And of course, such programs are no substitute for supervision and a lot of nasty stuff comes via e-mail anyway.

Albert Einstein stated: 'It has become appallingly obvious that our technology has exceeded our humanity.' The term 'option shock' was coined to describe the almost overwhelming amount of information and choice to which people are being exposed. At no other time in history has this been more the case than it is now, and it's particularly an issue for children and young people. In our modern society, we need to wonder why the sound of children laughing and playing is being replaced by keyboard tapping. Do they prefer the virtual playground to the real thing? Or are we simply forgetting simpler times amid an ocean of media technology? Sadly, for some young people, their computer world seems more real to them than reality itself.

On the other hand, as parents, we are also part of this brave new world and are not obliged to simply stand dumbly by. The challenge is to grow together with our children, to enter into a different sort of dialogue perhaps, one that recognises and respects the myriad of words, colours and sounds that surround their lives and impact on their hearts and minds.

Some final thoughts

David: Haven't things changed dramatically over the past generation or so? For example, things that might still be embarrassing to someone of my vintage, because of my upbringing and mores of the day, teenagers simply take in their stride. I love the story that the Reverend Bill Crews AM (Chairman of the Exodus Foundation in Sydney) relates. He had taken his two daughters to a movie when 'Suddenly there's bonking all over the screen and my 14-year-old touches my arm gently and says: "Would you rather wait outside, Dad?"' These days children are exposed to many sexual images if they are allowed to watch advertising, music videos and even TV soapies. How do you deal with this with your teenage sons?

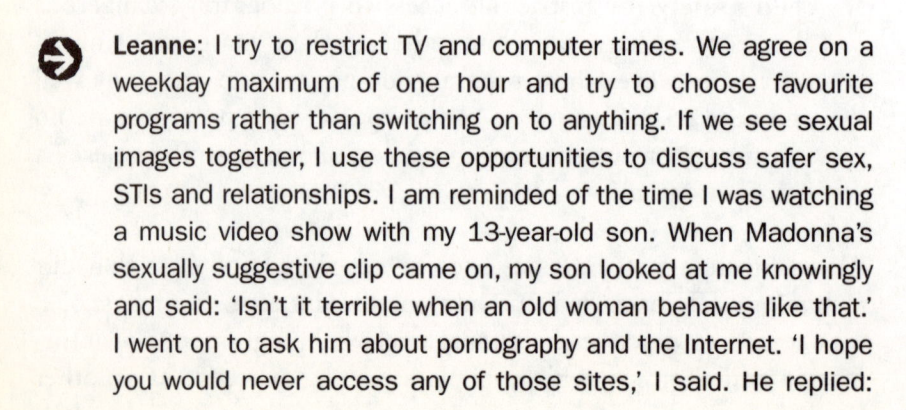

Leanne: I try to restrict TV and computer times. We agree on a weekday maximum of one hour and try to choose favourite programs rather than switching on to anything. If we see sexual images together, I use these opportunities to discuss safer sex, STIs and relationships. I am reminded of the time I was watching a music video show with my 13-year-old son. When Madonna's sexually suggestive clip came on, my son looked at me knowingly and said: 'Isn't it terrible when an old woman behaves like that.' I went on to ask him about pornography and the Internet. 'I hope you would never access any of those sites,' I said. He replied:

'Usually if you don't put X or fantasy after a website name you are all right.' It was difficult to feel reassured!

David: Clare's comment at the beginning of this chapter reminds me of something that Richard Eckersley wrote about the impact of the media 'eroding our sense of personal worth and significance by parading before us the lives of people who are more powerful, more beautiful, more successful, more exciting'. We need to encourage young people to be discerning and not too impressed by this.

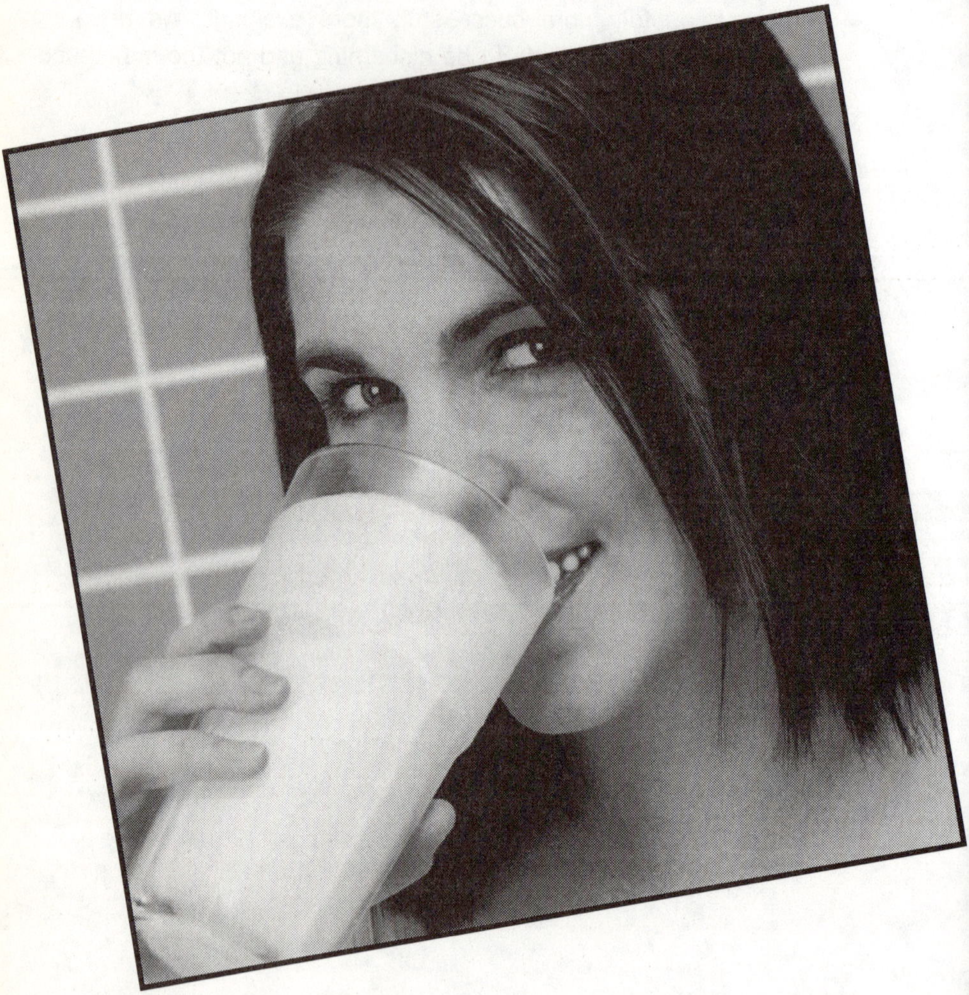

Chapter 5

Corn chips and chocolate

*I eat whatever is at home.
Emily, aged 17*

We are blessed in Australia with a relative abundance of food. What's more, the subject of nutrition is constantly being written about in magazines and books, the health food industry is booming and the importance of weight control and healthy eating is virtually on everybody's minds. Almost everyone knows something about anorexia nervosa and that there are good reasons for concern about chronic constipation, obesity and high blood cholesterol.

While parents may worry about these things, most teenagers seem blissfully unconcerned. Their entire approach to eating is generally one of breathtaking disregard for proper nutrition. They love junk food, snacking and skipping meals. If kids had their way, they'd probably try to live on soft drink, chips and chocolate. What's more, to the chagrin of the nutritional purists among us, they'd probably survive.

How worried should we be about all this? There's clearly more to it than potential threats to health and life. For parents and kids alike, there are also aggravations and conflicts to contend with, a clash of values even. Not all families get knotted up over food and nutrition, but hassles over vegetable avoidance, pigging out on peanut butter or sulking at mealtimes are probably more common than we realise.

What is healthy eating?

Health authorities have been hammering away at us about the basics of good nutrition for some time now, so the message should be getting through. In a nutshell, we need to be eating more carbohydrate foods and limiting saturated fats. As 10 to 20 per cent of us are genetically predisposed to developing high blood pressure on a high-salt diet, we should be cutting down there too.

Teenagers tend to eat a lot of fatty foods such as chips, crisps, fast foods, sausages and chocolate, and sugary things such as fizzy drinks, cordials, biscuits and lollies. Snacking between meals ('grazing') is often a bad habit that encourages teenagers to eat whether they are hungry or not and metabolically encourages fat deposition. To add to this, inactivity itself contributes to obesity in this age group – many teenagers are driven everywhere, watch TV or play computer games for long hours and only play sport if they are good at it.

Fat, salt and sugar can be cut down, simply by not having junk foods and soft drinks at home. Water and low-fat milk can replace sugary drinks. We need to eat more fresh food daily from each food group to obtain all the nutrients our bodies need:

- bread, cereals, rice, pasta, noodles
- vegetables and legumes
- fruit
- milk, yoghurt, cheese
- meat, fish, poultry, eggs, nuts.

It is important to have at least three meals a day, including a nutritious breakfast. Cereals like Weetbix or muesli, wholemeal toast, eggs and fruit provide a good start to the day. Calcium is important for growing bones and this can be provided by milk, yoghurt, and cheese. Vegetarians need to eat foods rich in protein and iron such as nuts, chickpeas, lentils and baked beans.

The basis of a healthy diet for all ages is simply moderation, variety and balance.

What are the major worries?

Let's get right to the most worrisome issues associated with adolescent nutrition. Young people are susceptible to a range of diet-related health problems, most (but not all) of which are well known, some of which are potentially dangerous, and practically all of which are preventable. Parents certainly worry, and for good reason, particularly when kids are too fat or too thin or when an eating problem is starting to seem like an eating disorder.

Too fat

There are scientific ways to tell whether someone is genuinely obese or merely overweight. But in general, if you look too fat, you probably are. The proportion of overweight and obese children in Australia has doubled since 1985. Around one in four school children is now carrying too much fat. This problem is definitely on the rise around the world, leading some researchers to speak of an international epidemic of childhood obesity.

Very obese teenagers have almost an 80 per cent chance of becoming obese adults, which puts them at risk of a wide variety of medical disorders. In fact, obese adults who were overweight as adolescents have a higher chance of experiencing weight-related ill-health and a higher risk of early death than those obese adults who became very fat in adulthood. Not all the health problems occur later in life. Type 2 diabetes (or 'late-onset' diabetes) has now begun to appear among Australian adolescents and is being diagnosed in increasing numbers. Childhood obesity can also lead to joint problems due to postural imbalance and excessive weight bearing (a kilogram of extra body weight places between two and four kilos of extra stress on the knees and hips during all movement).

We still don't know exactly why obesity occurs in some people and not in others, but while other factors are also involved, there is definitely a genetic component. One must be predisposed to it, otherwise it would make no sense at all that food affects different people in different ways, and that some individuals seem immune to every culinary self-indulgence, while others gain weight on the smell of a pizza. Because each individual has a unique genetic makeup, it is not all that unusual for only one of several children in the same family to be overweight.

If there was food in the pantry, I would have eaten it.

Jane, 13, overweight

In addition to this, the matter of eating beyond our needs remains our undoing in terms of gaining excess weight. The current trends are not encouraging. We know that the intake of energy from food and drink increased by over 10 per cent among Australian children aged 10 to 15 years between 1985 and 1995. At the same time, physical activity levels have declined, especially in girls, with particularly low rates in girls from Middle Eastern and Asian cultural backgrounds.

During puberty, there is an increase in the number and size of fat cells. Hormonal changes cause an increase in body fat for both boys and girls. What we used to call puppy fat, however, is just fat, and excess fat gained is unlikely to spontaneously disappear. Overweight teenagers generally fall into one (or more) of the following three categories:

- Some are susceptible to gaining excess weight during puberty simply by eating more food than their bodies need. The problem is predominantly one of inappropriate eating habits, usually in association with too little exercise. The more fat gained in this way, the more difficult it is to shift as time goes by. Normally, an increase in height or a change of habits should see this sorted out. These teenagers have a chance to grow into their weight, as it were.
- Some fat teenagers have inherited their body shape and obesity. The risk of obesity for the offspring of two obese parents is approximately 80 per cent. It's a problem that shows up early in life and responds little (if at all) to weight reduction diets. For such kids, maintaining weight and learning to live with it is the name of the game.
- While the scientific evidence is not yet available, weight gain occurs in some children or adolescents who are under stress, unhappy or bored. The root cause here is psychological, with high-energy food being used as solace. The best way to overcome this is to look at the overall situation rather than merely at the scales. This requires a broad-based and caring approach that, fortunately, doctors seem increasingly willing to take up.

If a child or teenager is growing normally, it is usually a waste of time to go around looking for a medical cause for obesity. Despite the community myth, obesity is hardly ever due to 'the glands'. It is also unreasonable to believe that all fat young people are unhappy or in emotional strife – they may not be. However, other kids can be pretty rotten to 'fatties', and feeling miserable about being ridiculed or shunned may lead to eating even more comfort food, thus setting up a typical vicious circle.

The very best treatment for teenage obesity is prevention before adolescence. If your teenager is currently overweight, all is not lost, but don't expect miracles. A fat boy turned up to see his doctor once with a request for help to become thin by December so that he could feel more comfortable about joining the other kids at the beach. Unfortunately, that was only three weeks away! Fat accumulates slowly and steadily, and that's the way it will be lost too. It cannot be rubbed, vibrated or melted off and there is no known way to lose it naturally from specific parts of the body (as many girls might wish).

For overweight or obese young people, weight loss should not be the only goal. Sometimes maintaining weight while growth is occurring is the more appropriate way to go. Either way, health professionals (including nutritionists who are at the front line of the epidemic) more or less agree on the following:

- Without motivation to change, forget it! The whole family needs to adopt a healthy lifestyle.
- The combination of a sensible balanced diet (smaller portions, less fat, more vegetables and fruit) and increased physical activity is likely to be more effective than either alone. Less time spent in front of the TV and more time pursuing something energetic and enjoyable like skateboarding or cycling is a good idea, even walking the dog. The approach to lifestyle change needs to be realistic, that is, taken in small steps rather than a major upheaval.
- Fad diets and meal replacement diets are not recommended – most cause a loss of body water and muscle but do little to decrease the body's fat stores.
- Appetite suppressant drugs are also out for this age group – they are habit forming and (as with adults) any weight loss achieved will not be sustained after the user stops taking the drugs.
- Behaviour modification techniques (diaries, rewards and the like) may work for a while, although older adolescents find them a bit demeaning.
- Young teenagers enjoy and benefit from a group approach. They stand to gain useful knowledge and a better mental

attitude from well-run programs (even if, in the short term, they stay fat).

Too thin

No one can say exactly what normal eating behaviour is, but severely restricting food intake, hiding food behind the sofa, purposely throwing up, taking lots of laxatives and exercising frantically in every spare moment are definitely not normal. These behaviours to lose or control body weight are common enough in young people to be of concern. According to Australian studies, one in every 200 girls between 15 and 19 years has anorexia nervosa, and about one in 20 young women has the binge eating disorder, bulimia nervosa. Both can occur in boys as well but are much less common. (Eating disorders are covered in more detail in Chapter 15, including information on how parents and friends can help.)

While the causes are complex, social pressures are thought to play a part in eating disorders. Dieting is ever and always in vogue. In women's magazines over the past 20 years, articles about dieting have increased threefold. An American study noted that *Playboy* centrefolds had become progressively thinner over time, reflecting the body form increasingly desired by men. Emaciated mannequins continue to litter our fashionable department stores. Wherever girls look, the message is that being thin is in.

A US study in the late 1990s found that 69 per cent of girls aged 10 to 18 reported that fashion magazine pictures influenced their idea of the perfect body shape, and nearly half reported wanting to lose weight because of such pictures. In the process of compiling her illuminating book, *Ophelia Speaks*, author Sara Shandler read over 800 contributions from adolescent girls, revealing the key concerns in their lives. She reports that the single most written about subject was eating disorders:

In the world of adolescent girls, thinness – sometimes at whatever cost – evokes profound jealousy. We lust for the perfect body. Even when we publicly condemn those who 'control' their food intake, many of us privately admire their 'willpower'.

How unfortunate that many girls (more than half of all 12-year-olds, in fact) actually enter puberty wanting to be thinner, victims of media pressure that makes them feel inadequate, even at the very threshold of womanhood. As discussed in Chapter 1, Nature decrees for pubescent girls a normal increase in the amount of fat on thighs and buttocks – how sad that so many girls resent the feminine shape they are supposed to acquire. In Australia, research suggests that at least 50 per cent of girls in high school (and 25 per cent of the boys) are on some form of diet, while 10 per cent of Australian females have some sort of eating disorder, and an even greater number have an obsession with their body image. Of concern here are the difficulties that young people can sometimes get into in association with unusual or frankly abnormal eating behaviours. These range from depression and other mental health conditions to the sorts of physical health problems mentioned below. For more information on eating disorders see Chapter 15.

From tooth decay to anaemia

Unhealthy eating puts teenagers at risk in other ways:

- Dental cavities are a potent source of personal and financial anguish, and the main dietary causes are: constant sipping on sports and soft drinks, snacking and sticky, sugary foods. And in an ideal world, teens would simply compensate for this by brushing their teeth more often (fat chance). Fluoridated toothpaste and water help prevent tooth decay.
- Approximately one in four Australian children and teenagers eats no fruit or vegetables at all, so it should come as no surprise that about 30 per cent of them are constipated. For reasons that are not yet understood, eating more dietary fibre decreases the overall risk of cancer of the large bowel, and eating more fruit decreases the risk of cancer of the stomach.
- Teenagers, especially vegetarians, run the risk of becoming anaemic if their iron intake is inadequate. Low iron is a common cause of fatigue, particularly in girls, who should eat iron-rich foods such as red meats, liver, poultry, fish, oysters, clams, beans, spinach, tofu, iron-fortified cereals, prune juice, enriched pasta, molasses, brewer's yeast and wheat germ. Sometimes an iron supplement is needed under the supervision of a doctor.
- Girls are also at risk of developing brittle bones if their diets are deficient in calcium, and those who lose too much weight,

to the point of menstrual irregularities, will also be losing bone density. Research suggests that adequate dietary calcium intake and non-excessive exercise can prevent osteoporosis and debilitating hip fractures in older age.

▶ Increased blood fats and high blood pressure do occur in genetically susceptible adolescents, putting them at risk of coronary artery disease in later life.

▶ There seems to be a very small group of children, including teenagers, in whom the ingestion of food colourings and other additives is associated with irritability, restlessness and sleep disturbance. This can usually be ascertained and sorted out by doctors or nutritionists with the appropriate expertise.

Eat your greens or go to bed

As the adolescent years roll on, whether the kids like your chicken soup or not, more and more of the food they consume will be away from your nurturing impulses and prying eyes. Is this inexorably waning influence cause for worry?

During puberty, adolescents have absolutely voracious appetites. They eat constantly and practically anything in sight. If you stock up on food for the week, say on Saturday, chances are you'll be 'cleaned out' by Sunday evening. And it's not just your kids — if their friends stay over on Saturday night, you may have to eat out for breakfast.

Most parents, family budget permitting, handle this pretty well. After all, short of putting padlocks on the fridge and pantry, what can you do? Rapidly growing teenagers have enormous nutritional requirements. If they play sport, an incredible 16,000 kilojoules of energy a day might actually be needed. Of course, less active adolescents need less, but might be inclined to consume that much anyway.

Household conflicts over food are more likely to be about what kids don't, or won't, eat. Teenagers may take up fads like declaring a moratorium on bananas, or refusing to eat anything but bananas. From the age of eight or nine, children also start to understand the concept of death and may become extremely concerned about eating meat. Vegetarian teenagers can give you that look — you know the one that says, 'How could you possibly eat that?'

> *My parents talk about allowing me to make my own decisions, but they only allow me to make the decisions they want me to make.*
> *Mahmond, aged 16*

Actually, vegetarianism is pretty common in adolescent girls, who are also more susceptible to the many diet promotions that target them through magazines and other media. Some young women become vegetarians as an alternative to dieting – enjoying heaps of lettuce and steamed vegetables means 'you don't get flak, because you're eating'. Oh yes. And there are varying levels of commitment. For example, a 14-year-old girl was overheard telling her friends that the only meat she ever ate was a certain famous sort of cheeseburger 'because it doesn't taste like meat'! The important point here is to ensure that dietary restrictions do not compromise intake of needed nutrients. If concerned, parents should consult a dietician.

All of this can drive parents crazy. If you've slaved for hours over a hot stove (or complicated microwave key pad) knock-backs can be disappointing. Perhaps you grew up under strict instructions to eat everything on the plate ('or you can just sit there all night'), an approach that is definitely out of vogue now. People, including adolescents, are entitled to have different tastes, wants and needs and, to some extent, these ought to be accommodated. For example, if the kid doesn't want pumpkin, don't cook it. Making choices is, after all, a normal and important part of growing up. Anyway, according to scientific reports, screaming rows at the dinner table achieve little more than the diminished absorption of food. So it's better to find ways to compromise and keep things calm.

The most important meal of the day

Most children under 11 eat breakfast, but by adolescence about 40 per cent of girls and 30 per cent of boys skip breakfast regularly. Many teenagers say it's a matter of simply not feeling hungry in the morning or running out of time. Girls in particular may be avoiding breakfast in the misguided belief that it will help them control their weight. It doesn't, mostly because they get hungry and eat more (often junk food) at other meals. Furthermore, fasting has been shown to impair intellectual performance, which means that it really is harder to concentrate on school work with nothing in your stomach (an argument that may or may not have the desired effect). More importantly, kids who miss breakfast are more likely to be lacking calcium and iron, just when they need it the most. This is where the good old banana smoothie can come to the rescue or some sort of grab-it-and-go nutritious snack.

Grabbing a bite on the run

As we all know, fast food is a way of life for young people. They rarely have time to do more than momentarily masticate, let alone gently digest the food they have on the run. It's go, go, go – grabbing a bite is just part of the teenage scene. This wouldn't matter if most takeaway foods were not so rich in fat, salt and energy. Salt, for example, makes processed food more palatable, promoting 'eat more', as well as making people thirsty so that they'll buy a soft drink. Of course, if adults demanded a higher standard, things might change, but for now, we're stuck with what the fast food industry chooses to call 'meeting the community demand'.

> **Most fast foods lack complex carbohydrates, dietary fibre and important nutrients like vitamins A and C. For example:**
>
> - A typical cheeseburger contains virtually no fibre at all (although the salty fries that often go with it contain a bit).
> - The local takeaway pizza has about 4200 kilojoules and two grams of salt, approximately four times as much salt and a third of the kilojoules that a teenager would need in a day.
> - Fried chicken and any meal of fish and chips are absolutely loaded with fat.

Teenagers love it all and, in reality, few will be adversely affected in any way from eating it from time to time, particularly those who stay active and make sure that their other meals are more nutritious. However, kids should be encouraged to add salad and fruit whenever they can, and not to eat out every day.

Chocolate, interestingly, may be in a special category, with secret benefits wrapped up with the pleasures and guilt. While not exactly a health food, chocolate apparently can trigger the same chemical reactions as some antidepressants. Of course, if you overdo it and gain 10 kilos, that can be depressing, but there's no doubt that melt-in-the-mouth chocolate has comforting and calming effects. And while it contains a lot of saturated fat, much of this is stearic acid, which does not increase cholesterol or blood clotting. On the heart front, chocolate is also a plant-based food rich in substances called flavinoids, which can act as anti-oxidants, helping the body's cells resist damage from free radicals.

Then there's the matter of what they wash all the junk food down with. Ever noticed how much fluid boys drink? It's amazing, and parents sometimes worry about this too. Gone are the days, of course, when a beverage meant milk or water. Now it's more likely to be soft drinks or beer. In 2001, Australians bought 2.25 billion litres of carbonated soft drink with a retail value of $1.4 billion. While the general population averages around 70 litres of soft drink a year, 14- to 15-year-olds do much better. In one study, Australian girls averaged 148 litres and boys a phenomenal 189 litres. Work it out – a 375 ml can of soft drink contains the equivalent of nine teaspoons of sugar. Today's soft drinks are actually made from high-fructose corn syrup (which arrives intact in the liver and is bad for metabolism) and carbonated water, with a few flavouring agents thrown in for brand recognition.

Another aspect to this soft drink obsession is the fact that young people (anyone actually) can get hooked on caffeine-containing colas (highly acidic drinks that can damage tooth enamel if consumed to excess) or other high-energy caffeine-based drinks. For those consuming large amounts of low-calorie cola drinks, the relatively large amounts of phosphorus in these drinks, together with a low calcium intake, has been shown to contribute to teenage girls breaking bones more easily. It's astounding that there is not more public debate on addiction to these popular liquids. They are certainly marketed seductively and well. We're talking here about the ultimate synthetic food or, 'that wonderful junction where science meets food: calorie-free, nutrient-free, and vaguely immoral'. Despite warnings by doctors, dentists and naturopaths, it seems highly improbable that young people will ever see it as a problem.

On the other hand, some teenagers are heavily into vitamins (though probably only about 5 per cent or so), in the hope that it might do them some good. The likelihood of getting any real benefit, however, is not strong. In fact, evidence is accumulating about the unfavourable effects of mega vitamin therapy. For example, large doses of vitamin B6 can cause peripheral neuropathy (nerve damage) and, for people with the iron-storage disease haemochromatosis, mega vitamin C increases iron absorption and can affect the heart. There is also no evidence that large doses of vitamin C prevent or cure colds.

Even more kids are taken in with so-called health foods, especially of the sticky (and therefore sugary) kind. As noted by Sydney-based nutritionist Eve Reed (co-author of *Kids, Food and Health 3*), 'What's marketed as health foods is not necessarily healthy.' Not only are 'health bars', for example, high in energy, but many of them also contain a lot of saturated fat. Also, much of the stock consists of vitamins and supplements that most people would be getting already from their food. Perhaps the popularity of these types of outlets partly reflects our busy lifestyles – if we think it's 'healthy' we feel less bad about grabbing a bite on the run.

Who's to blame and what to do?

Whether or not you are worried and aggravated, or simply bemused and accepting of the way teenagers eat, it is worth wondering why it's the way it is and what you can do, if anything, to improve matters. First of all, it is clear that teenage eating patterns are influenced by five main factors:

Community trends

Young people are acutely aware of what is happening around them. They notice what adults are eating and adult eating habits have changed significantly (and not for the better) over time. Virtually every meal has undergone changes and the 'special foods' (biscuits and chocolates, pizza, whatever) once reserved for special occasions only, have become everyday fare. An increase in TV viewing and an increase in sedentary behaviour are associated with the increase in obesity in children and young people. TV and noshing (almost always of high-energy snacks and drinks) certainly go hand in hand, so parents can at least try to provide healthy snacks and, even more importantly, limit viewing time and computer games, and encourage physical activity.

Another unfortunate development is towards eating more at each sitting, a community trend aided and abetted particularly by the fast food industry. For example, larger portions are on offer (McDonald's fries have grown by stages from 200 calories in 1960 to 610 calories now) and give-away extras in many drinks and foodstuffs (for example, '20 per cent more for the same price') are commonplace.

School canteens

School canteens can play an important role by limiting the availability of soft drinks and junk food packed with fat and sugar. It makes no sense for good nutrition to be taught in the classroom if high-fat and poor food choices are available in the canteen. Some healthy choices should be on offer, such as fruit, fruit salad, low-fat flavoured milk, yoghurt and nutritious sandwiches. Similar concerns relate to vending machines and the sorts of food available at sporting and recreational venues. One of the resolutions at the NSW Childhood Obesity Summit held in Sydney in September 2002 was for the Government to develop mandatory rules for implementation in school canteens from kindergarten to Year 12 and the recommendation that young people be involved in the development of these rules. In some schools there's now a system of 'smart cards' that are scanned at the canteen to monitor and regulate what students can buy. In this way parents can exert some control over a child's access to food and drink, as well as determine how much money can be spent per day. Kids won't be fazed by an electronic innovation such as this, but whether or not it helps in the fight against obesity remains to be seen. At a simpler level, parents should make their views known to the school's parent committee.

Advertisements

The food choices teenagers make are strongly influenced by the way foods are marketed. Advertising aimed at children and teenagers works, otherwise manufacturers of processed foods would go broke. And if advertising is not such a major influence, why does the food industry get so upset at suggestions that it be banned? Three interesting points to consider are:

- Food advertisements disproportionately promote foods high in fats, sugar or salt and of low nutritional value. Seen many ads for fruit and vegetables lately?
- Many food advertisements are specifically targeted at children and teenagers (those hitting the TV screen during prime viewing time, for example).
- The thin young models and actors with clear complexions and gorgeous white teeth seem miraculously immune to the usual effects of the products they are promoting.

What can be done about this? A World Health Organisation report urges governments to clamp down on TV ads pushing sugar-rich items, and to consider heavy taxes on drinks. While patiently waiting for things to change, however, parents can at least talk about it with their kids and share ideas on these things.

Pressure from friends

If teenagers' friends are filling up on foods with little nutritional value, why shouldn't they go along with the fashion? Kids see no problem with this. For one thing, they are living in the here and now. Since many of the ill-effects of poor diet take so long to develop (months or years, as a rule), most young people wrongly assume, and convey to each other, that it doesn't matter what they eat. And who'd want to look like an idiot? As one young man wryly questioned, how would it sound if you said 'No thanks, I don't want a Maccas today. I'd rather go and get a salad sandwich'? Unfortunately, peer pressure is something that parents can't influence.

Parents

When children turn into teenagers their basic attitudes to eating and drinking are pretty well in place. After all, they've been watching and listening to mum or dad for a long time, and these attitudes are not likely to suddenly change. Parents certainly have a major say about what's eaten at home. In fact, the person who does the shopping is the gatekeeper of the family's nutrition (at least the home-based part of it). It's difficult to pig out on large quantities of nutritionally empty food at home if there's none in the house. But even if your teenager binges on junk every time they walk out the door, your views about and approach to eating can make a big difference.

While it's important to be realistic and reasonable in our expectations, there are a number of things parents can do to help get kids on the right track: teach them a few nutritional facts and try to make nutrition more interesting; encourage a varied diet and a reasonably active life; invite kids to participate in the shopping and teach them how to cook; discuss food labels and the sorts of ingredients you seek to do without; and set an example with your own diet. Finally, if and when possible, encourage the sharing of a relaxed evening meal together – that, at least, will be enjoyable for you as well.

It goes without saying that parents need to look after themselves too. Sadly, too many adults in their 40s and 50s experience problems with serious chronic conditions or die prematurely from preventable causes such as heart attacks, strokes, lung disease, diabetes and mental illness. Smoking is directly responsible for about eight per cent of all disease in our community and alcohol abuse causes far more illness in adults than illicit drug use causes in young people. Good nutrition, regular exercise and relaxation help maintain our health and wellbeing. If we want to stay around for our teenagers (not always within our control), we need to revisit the priorities in our lives and do our best to avoid lifestyle-related illnesses and premature death. We know what to do – we just have to do it. As in all things, young people are quick to pick up on our hypocrisy in relation to health. An outspoken teenager put it like this:

My parents talk to me about drugs, but they smoke, are fat and don't exercise – they are not in a position to lecture me.

Some final thoughts

David: One thousand years ago, what people ate was based largely on intuition and what limited foods could be grown, gathered or hunted. Children had to distinguish between edible and poisonous berries in the bush. Today the average supermarket contains more than 10,000 items, a dizzying array of mostly processed foods, with highly variable nutritional value and lots of clever, man-made chemicals. The challenge facing kids, all of us really, is to be able to distinguish between nourishing foods (the low fat, low sugar, no added salt varieties) and the all too available alternatives.

Leanne: Adolescents need a balanced, nutritious diet in order to grow, develop and remain healthy. This is an area of their lives that cannot be neglected, and not only because of the shorter term problems. The habits and attitudes they acquire now are likely to endure – and there's the next generation to think of as well.

David: Haven't styles of eating changed over the years? I think many families have moved away from high-meat diets, for example. It's pretty unusual to find a restaurant that doesn't cater for vegetarian tastes, at least to some extent.

Leanne: The evening meal is an important time of the day, isn't it? Often exhausted, the family comes together to discuss their day and plans for the next. It's a time to disconnect the telephone, relax and recuperate with nutritious food and real conversations. It needs to be a time to look forward to, a part of the sanctuary of home.

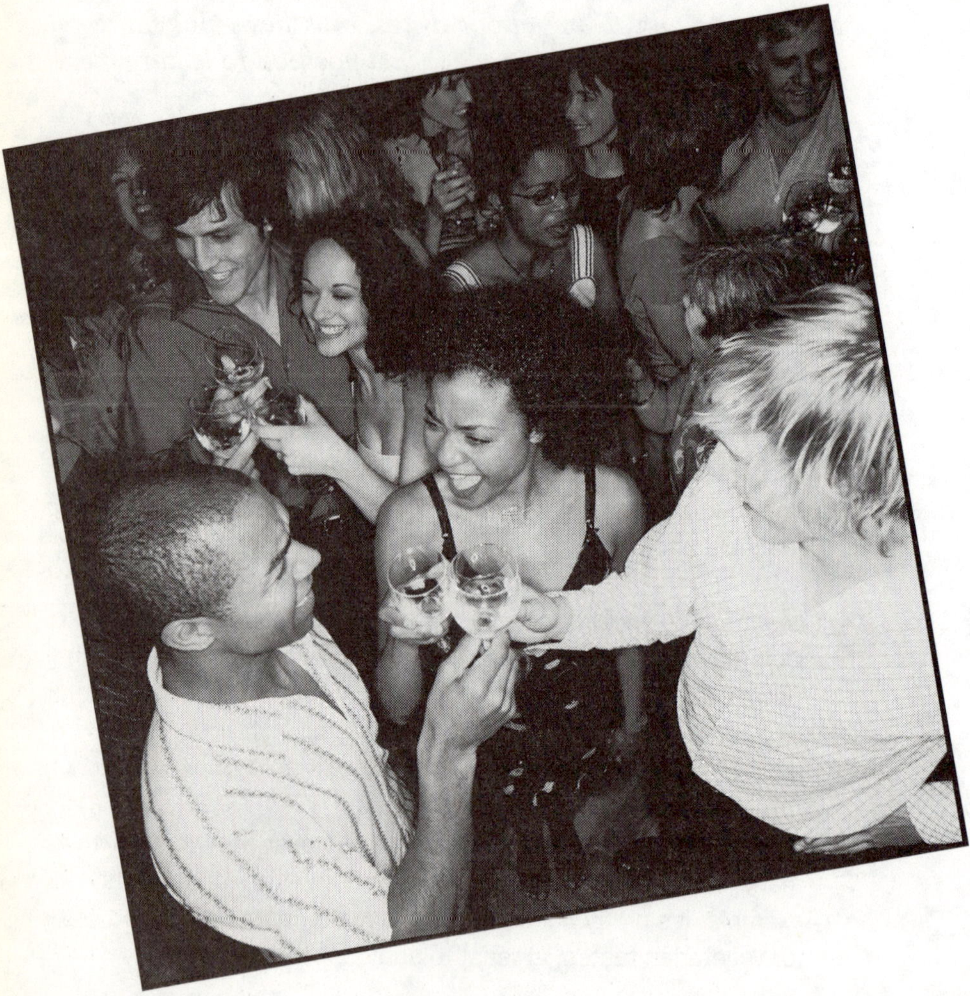

Chapter 6

It's my body

My dad says I spend more time in the bathroom than the whole family combined. He's always asking me what I do in there.
Laura, aged 17

Ideally, kids should already know a fair bit about their bodies well before adolescence. Parents should see to it. In some schools, the subject of 'how the body works' is presented to Year 6 students, and they love it; it's pertinent, it's timely. Soon enough, if not already, they will have to cope with the myriad changes we spoke of earlier: a new body shape, newly developed parts and functions, and all the mixed-up feelings that go along with puberty.

As well as understanding what the human body is about, a child should be encouraged to value his or her own body as a unique and precious gift, and to look after it as best they can. After all, it's the only body they'll get, and it has to last them a lifetime. Of course, how one's body looks and how well it functions may not always be within personal control, but how well one cares for it usually is.

Why a chapter on hygiene and fitness? Is there something special about these mundane-sounding subjects where young people are concerned? Yes indeed. For adolescents, they are sensitive and important issues; for parents, some inspiration is called for, and their brief is to be knowledgeable, supportive and influential.

On being clean

Parents often find the whole question of a teenager's cleanliness somewhat uncomfortable. It is a bit personal really, but it's one of those things that you can't keep to yourself, at least not indefinitely. For better or worse, if you (or your clothing) are not clean, word gets out.

From a parent's point of view, there's more to this than merely wanting a neat, clean and presentable delegate to the outside world (although that's probably a big part of it). A parent has to live with a teenager too. But there are other and possibly more important considerations as well. How we look and how we feel go hand in hand.

Hygiene and health are intimately interrelated, and the way we care for and protect our bodies can influence not only the quality, but also the very length of our lives.

A five-year-old child who doesn't know about the importance of handwashing before eating (notwithstanding the need for incessant reminders) would be an absolute rarity; a teenager who chooses not to wash would not. The point is, during adolescence, the need to attend to personal hygiene simply becomes more pressing. On the teenager's side there are the new bodily interests and sensitivities, while parents have to get their message across without driving the poor kid to rebel and become even more lazy and offensive. The following four factors require our understanding:

An upsurge of modesty

All sorts of interesting and wonderful things are happening to the bodies of young adolescents and, as is right and proper, they become increasingly disinclined to share these with their parents. An excruciating shyness may descend upon them.

What needs to be clean?

What needs to be clean depends on your sex. A group of 14-year-old high school boys were asked to do a drawing of a male body and mark the parts requiring attention. Apart from a few desultory references to earwax and belly button fluff, their giggling preoccupation with the genital area clearly indicated where their principal interests lay. Meanwhile, in the adjoining room, a group of girls were sedately discussing the finer points of menstrual hygiene.

In this entertaining socio-drama, these young teenagers were at least tuning in to the priority areas for cleanliness. Increased biological activity in the sweat glands is an unavoidable feature, albeit a pungent one, of normal pubescent development, so a daily wash or shower (with particular attention to the underarm and genital areas) becomes highly desirable. Deodorants are also essential accoutrements during the teenage years that follow. There are chafing and olfactory discomforts, for both the sufferer and others who may happen to be close by, related to 'jock itch' (Tinea cruris) or 'athlete's foot' (Tinea pedis). Fortunately, these common fungal infections can be prevented by keeping groins and feet as dry as possible by regularly using baby powder or one of the antifungal agents available.

> *Girls should be pretty, skinny, have big boobs and be hairless. I am fat, ugly and have small boobs.*
>
> *Tina, aged 15*

What's the main message?

Where values and attitudes are concerned, teenagers will, in due course, take a lead from their parents. But right now, much of their information and beliefs come from the media. Aids to hygiene and grooming for young people are part of a growth industry, and kids are virtually bombarded with messages about it, from medicated soaps for facial pimples to sweet-smelling aftershave or peppermint mouthwash. Actually, with romance in the air, this 'confident smile and fresh breath' idea probably does hit home. However, they'll do better with toothpaste and floss than with anything they swill.

How gently can you give bad news?

How do you tell someone you love that they have smelly feet, bad breath or body odour? Adolescents often go through a 'disgusting stage', believing people think the worst of them anyway, so why not live up to expectations? A blatant disregard for personal cleanliness can also be a form of rebellion (like messy bedrooms) or an indication of depression. For this reason, poor hygiene is not something to be ignored, because it could reflect something more serious. In terms of intervening, though, an anonymous gift of toiletries with typed instructions is unlikely to succeed. Under normal circumstances there is no good alternative to a direct, firm and kindly approach – you care, and it offends you. Just that.

At some stage, in all probability, the game will change. A teenager may see the light, and suddenly become 'newborn clean'. When that happens, you may as well say goodbye to your bathroom – you may never get in there again!

On being fit

The subject of physical fitness is also one that concerns parents, and rightly so. While some parents are going berserk at the side of a football field (quite clearly a form of child abuse), others may be pondering the fate of the mooching slouch they live with. However, there are things that all parents need to know.

Why be fit?

The evidence that regular physical exercise is good for you is pretty impressive.

> **Fitness would seem to have everything going for it:**
> - With effective muscle control comes better posture; with increased physical endurance comes less fatigue.
> - Physical activity decreases tension and is therefore an effective way of coping with stress and anxiety.
> - It is claimed that exercise, particularly when it involves a lot of jumping up and down, can actually result in increased height (too late for you parents).
> - Exercise contributes to the enjoyment of leisure time.
> - Regular physical exercise helps with weight control and can ward off heart attacks and strokes in later life!

The amount of exercise that is good for you has recently come into question. It seems that the public health benefits of 'exercise in moderation' that some of us have believed in so fervently (only thirty minutes, three times a week; 'a gentle stroll is as good as going to the gym') are exaggerated. It appears that substantial health benefits occur at exercise levels that exceed current minimum guidelines. The Canadian Government has advised that people should get 60 minutes of proper physical activity (you know, the sort that makes you really sweat) every day. This is probably not realistic, and is twice the minimum amount recommended by Australian and American health authorities.

In this context, it comes as no surprise that studies of Australian primary and secondary school children show that their general level of fitness is less than optimal. While some teenagers are getting stuck into it, many others are doing their darnedest to get out of it. For a variety of reasons, a loss of interest in exercise at puberty is not unusual, especially in girls. Possible reasons include: other interests, being overweight, lack of motivation, not doing well in games at school or a response to an overemphasis on competitive sports.

Sporty teenagers

Having sporty teenagers is fun. There's enjoyment and pride in seeing your offspring, bursting with energy and radiant good health, giving it his or her best. Without doubt, many parents go out of their way to do the right thing, ferrying kids here, there and everywhere, barracking and supporting at all times of day and in all kinds of weather. One marvellous couple travelled back and forth, transporting almost a whole soccer team to the match (apparently they had the biggest station wagon) week after week, even though their own kid was the worst player and rarely got a game. Despite their protests at times, teenagers do appreciate the effort and attention, and a parent's interest and involvement are a powerful form of encouragement.

Parents know that team sports build self-esteem and self-confidence, comradeship and cooperation. Teenagers who participate in organised sports have also been shown to do better in school, have better interpersonal skills, and are generally healthier. Female athletes appear to derive some specific additional benefits:

- They have a healthier body image, are less likely to begin smoking and less likely to become pregnant as teenagers.
- They take greater pride in their physical and social selves than their sedentary peers.
- They remain more physically active as they age, suffer less depression and (according to some evidence) are less likely to develop breast cancer and osteoporosis.

As Dr Jordan Metzl points out in his book, *The Young Athlete: A Sports Doctor's Complete Guide for Parents*, sports offer a unique arena in which children can explore and exert their talents. Not only are all facets of life (physical, social, cognitive, psychological) engaged harmoniously in striving towards personal fulfilment, but participation in athletic activities also involves young people meaningfully in an ongoing community composed of their peers and their peers' families.

However, whether your teenager is an aspiring Olympic athlete or simply someone who enjoys an active lifestyle, parents need to make sure that they're getting the right fuel. Good nutrition is vital. For one thing, to perform well, physically active young people need to eat more. Muscles prefer carbohydrates as fuel, so fruit and fruit juice, cereals, bread, potatoes, rice and pasta are the foods to recommend. It's sensible to allow 'enough time' (more than five minutes certainly) after eating before exercising, so that digestion is properly underway. Extra fluid is also extremely important for athletes, especially in hot weather. They need to drink before, during and after exercise to replace the fluid lost through sweating.

Another nutrient that can affect performance is iron, which carries oxygen to muscle cells. Lean red meat is the best source of iron, followed by chicken and fish, because a larger percentage of iron from animal sources is absorbed in the gut (which is why it's called 'well-absorbed iron'). Other sources of iron (not as well absorbed but still good) include enriched breakfast cereal, beans, tofu and deep green vegetables. It's useful to know that vitamin C, for example in fruit and vegetables, increases iron absorption from these plant-based sources, while the tannins in tea and coffee can inhibit it. Better to have herbal tea and get maximum benefit from the food.

What about vitamins and other supplements? Someone once said: 'What do you get when you add a vitamin supplement to a poor diet?' Answer: 'A poor diet plus a vitamin supplement.' In other words, a pill is not the answer. Likewise, expensive protein powders do not seem to be beneficial. The most recent studies indicate that athletes do need more protein than their couch-potato counterparts, but because they eat more, they almost always obtain enough protein just by eating normal food.

So the message to active kids: eat enough to meet your fuel needs, especially carbohydrates; drink more water than you think you need to; and enjoy both being active and eating well!

In the pursuit of added muscle bulk or enhanced performance, unfortunately, some young people take steroids. Apart from being illegal, steroids can have disastrous side effects: acne, aggressive (even homicidal) behaviour, stunted growth and, in the longer term, liver cancer. An American study showed that 6.6 per cent of 16-year-old boys had used steroids for body-building purposes. Australian trends are estimated to be similar. Boys also sometimes go for high-protein diets, but these are unnecessary for building muscle, and foods like powdered milk formulas only make you fatter.

Success in sports is not just about winning (that is, beating the opposition). Success includes concepts such as improving your skills, fulfilling your potential, doing something you love, and building character and perseverance. Remember that undue pressure can actually tarnish a promising young talent, and that really is a shame.

Non-sporty teenagers

Some people have little or no interest in physical pursuits, and little or no aptitude for them. If this describes your teenager, chances are it describes you too – athletic propensities (or lack thereof) are often inherited. For example, not everybody is well coordinated. If you have difficulty hitting a ball with a bat, or you're endowed with a talent for tripping over your feet, certain sports are simply not for you. Some groups of young people, such as the disabled, have special needs, while those who are obese need appropriate alternatives to athletics and team sports. The important thing, though, is that no one needs to miss out on exercise.

We all know teenagers who would much rather be playing computer games or chasing notes up and down a piano than outside chasing a ball up and down a field. What do you do then? You can only lead a horse to water, you say? All is not lost. There are many possibilities for getting that blood pumping. For younger teenagers, careering around the neighbourhood on a skateboard or a bicycle, playing table tennis or even indoor bowling are all better than doing nothing. Getting out in the surf isn't bad either.

Perhaps the clue to success here is tapping into a kid's interests and trying to find some physical activity that's somehow connected to them. For example, an aesthetic type might be prompted into yoga or creative, non-competitive dance; an overweight young person with an interest in animals might be encouraged to join a dog-exercising/training group; a shy kid might get into a bushcraft group. Who knows what sorts of ideas might start to flow during an enthusiastic open discussion about the options. Sometimes more encouragement may be needed, like in the family where mum just confiscated the cable TV card or 'mislaid' the Playstation cord and pointed towards the park ('Get on your bicycle and go there').

My mum yells orders at me. She wouldn't speak to her friends like that so why does she speak to me in that tone?
John, aged 16

This is also a situation when 'doing with' may serve a better purpose than 'sending away', as in 'Let's go for a walk together' rather than 'Off you go and get fit'. This approach kills two birds with one stone: exercise and spending time with your kid – you never know, it might even lead to talking! By the way, going for a jog not only enables you to see the glorious outdoors but is considered just about the best way to achieve endurance fitness which, unlike mere muscle tone, is a key factor in longer life.

The aim in promoting at least some energetic pursuits in young people is not necessarily to get the non-sporty into sportiness as such, but to encourage physical activity that is also nourishing for the person in terms of it becoming a source of pleasure. Apart from certain obsessive middle-aged adults driven largely by mortality fears (narcissism is another matter), people usually don't exercise because they have to, but because there's an element of fun in it. Physical activities that exercise the heart, lungs, metabolism and muscles (aerobic exercise) need not consist of an organised exercise program. Simple pleasures in a context of sociability and enjoyment, such as bushwalking, mowing the lawn and a host of other homely physical activities, also do you good. Creating such opportunities means thinking outside the square.

Sometimes 'non-sporty' teenagers can surprise us. A 14-year-old boy at a school sports carnival, suddenly decided to compete in the 100 metre sprint, the 400 metre and the 800 metre, after which he could barely move for days. On other days, according to his puzzled dad, he didn't lift a finger by choice.

Some final thoughts

David: Encouraging a child to have a positive regard for his or her body is an important task of parenting, and one that must be administered with tact, sensitivity and love. For all of us, how we look and how we feel go hand in hand. Perhaps this is especially true for teenagers in whom appearance (body, clothing, demeanour), gaining a sense of control and having a sense of belonging constitute the main ingredients of self-esteem. Much of this plays out in company, whether in the family, socialising with friends or taking part in competitive sport.

Leanne: Simply knowing that hygiene and fitness are integral to a teenager's good health and wellbeing is not enough. Sometimes it's necessary to walk that fine line gingerly between interest and intrusion, as a too heavy hand can have the opposite of the desired effect. But it is important to start early (preferably well before adolescence arrives) because, when the teenage years are in full bloom, you are likely to be told in no uncertain terms that it's no longer your business.

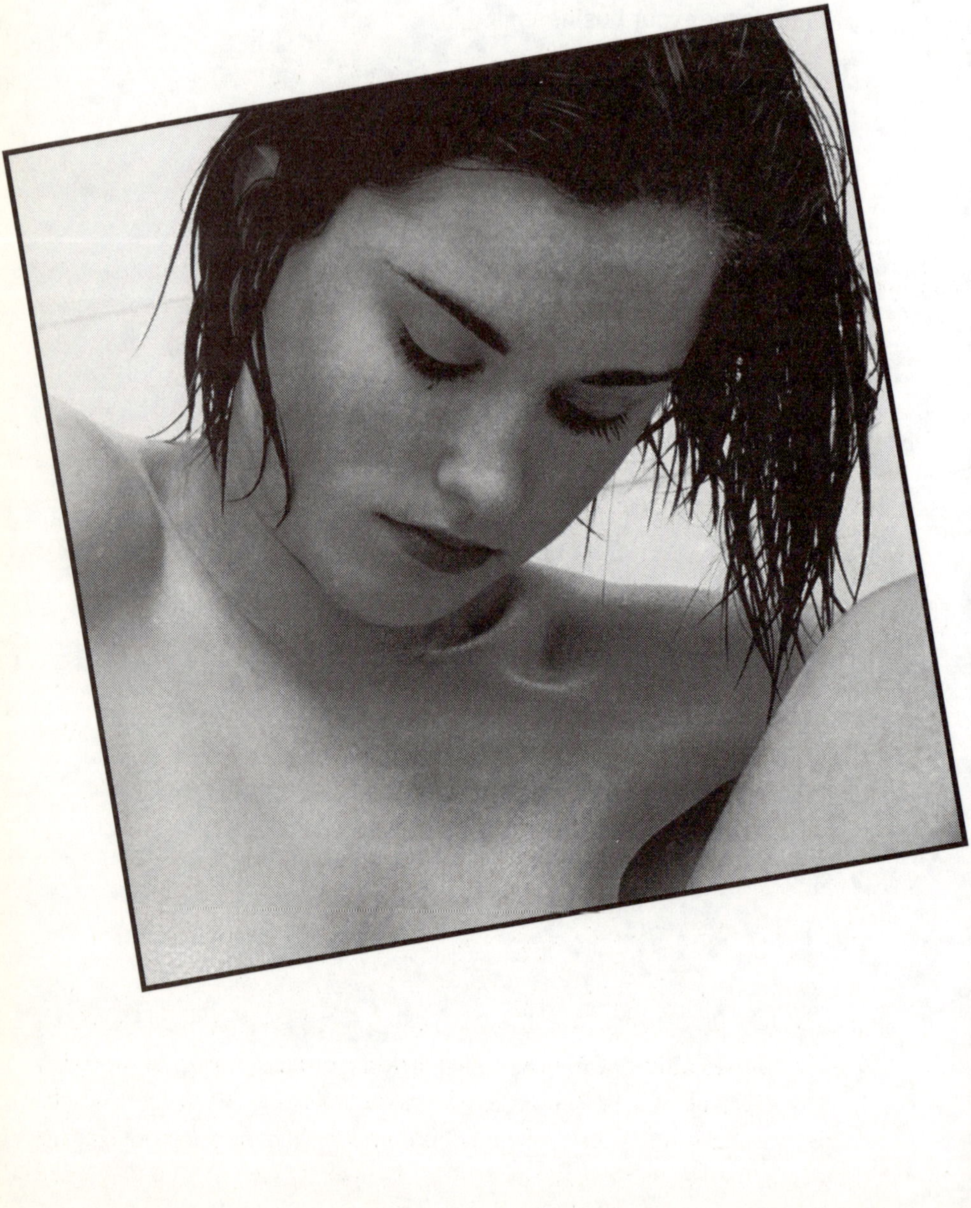

Chapter 7

Sexuality: a sensitive issue

Sex is better when it's with someone you love.
Claudia, aged 18

Where teenagers and sex are concerned, parents worry a lot. They worry that they'll have sex too soon, with the wrong people, of the wrong kind, or not at all. All this would be of little concern if parents were in possession of the sexual 'on-off' switch to their children's lives. No such luck!

Whether or not adults are comfortable with the idea (mostly they're not), teenagers are sexual beings. Sexuality is an integral and inescapable part of living, from birth until death. It is a vital and important, if somewhat confusing, part of growing up. It should concern us, and not just because there are risks involved.

Why are young people confused?

Why not? Everybody else is. In no other area of human need and activity are there so many mixed messages and double binds as there are about sexuality. Previous generations more or less accepted a 'birds and bees' approach (otherwise known as an 'ostrich' approach) to sex. Today, while the subject is less of a taboo, young people are frequently confronted with both their own uncertainty and the uncertainty of their adult mentors.

Three obvious sources of confusion are: prevailing stereotypes, double standards and moral hypocrisy.

Stereotypes

As early as three or four years of age, children have not only decided which sex they belong to but have also learned something of the behaviour expected of that sex. We are born either male or female (most of us – in some babies it's less clear cut) as a result of purely genetic and biological factors. How masculine or feminine we feel and behave (which is what 'gender' means), however, depends on how we are treated by our parents and by what we see and hear going on around us. For example, boys are generally encouraged to find out how things work, while girls are generally encouraged to find out how people work. This process of identification as a boy or a girl is pretty powerful. Even subtle messages and clues taken in as a young child have a major influence on our self-perceptions and behaviour.

Things hot up during adolescence. Consider the different sorts of publications targeted at teenagers. Girls' magazines and novels are loaded with romantic pap, usually with just a hint of sex at the end. The overriding message is that happiness is a thing called boys and there is a lot of advice on how to attract them. Boys' magazines, on the other hand, are also about boys or men, all doing something tough. The emphasis is on action, achievement and hardware. And while, in reality, happiness is also a thing called girls, they're not encouraged to admit it so, of course, they don't – a pattern which sets them up for life.

Despite much change and discussion in the past 20 years, sex role stereotypes are alive and well, limiting personality options for both males and females. At the same time, new role models are appearing too. At home, for example, an increasing number of men are starting to pull their weight with domestic and parenting chores, while women are continuing to take on and maintain professional careers.

Double standards

Comedian Billy Crystal put it succinctly: 'Women need a reason to have sex. Men, they just need a place.' One of the most unfortunate aspects of gender inequities is this double standard related to sexuality. It is so entrenched and so well known, yet so unfair, and, in the game of love, girls get the worst deal by far. Parents (often fathers) are more suspicious and more controlling of their daughters for a start, and probably always will be, simply because the daughters have more to lose if things go wrong (namely, an unwanted pregnancy). But more insidious is the ruthless double standard that operates among young people themselves. It works like this:

- Teenage girls come under a lot of sexual pressure from teenage boys, who are also under pressure from other boys, because it's masculine to 'score' (preferably as often as possible). But the girls are damned if they do, and damned if they don't: sexually active girls are regarded as 'sluts' by both boys and girls, and those who don't come across are 'frigid' or 'teasers'.
- Despite all the efforts to encourage masculine involvement in birth control and the prevention of sexually transmitted infections (STIs), the burden of responsibility still rests unfairly on girls.
- An unfortunate outcome of all this is that boys are almost always less experienced than they say, while girls are at risk of becoming more experienced than they might want to be.
- The double standard works in the opposite direction with same sex contact, in that it's okay for girls to muck around sexually (hold hands, kiss) but not for boys (for further discussion of the issue of homosexuality see pages 109–112).

Moral hypocrisy

In the past half century our sexual knowledge, attitudes and behaviour have changed dramatically. The advent of the Pill, and the women's movement and gay liberation, have given us greater freedoms. On the other hand, the rise of casual sex has brought with it new moral conundrums and fears.

No doubt, the gradual move towards greater openness and honesty has been for the better, but we are still grappling with the dilemmas change has provoked. Not least among them is the issue of premarital chastity. Although this remains important in some religious and ethnic communities, in general, the ideal of the 'virgin bride' has been abandoned, and young people are being increasingly pressured to be sexually active. They are bombarded with sexual images and innuendoes in virtually every form of media at our disposal.

> I've never heard of anyone getting pregnant under 16. It's just something adults make up to put young people off having sex.
> Ling, aged 16

Alongside these more permissive social attitudes, however, there is an enduring moral hypocrisy that takes the opposite line. Most adults have misgivings about the whole issue of adolescent sexuality and openly (more or less) disapprove of it. The message kids are getting from the adult world is 'be sexy but also be good' and for many the net result is uncertainty, guilt and stress. Having the opportunity to talk with parents or other caring adults about these 'mixed messages' is often reassuring and helpful for young people.

Pornography

Pornography is not something that's on everybody's mind – some people may even pretend it doesn't exist. But we live in an era of unavoidable visual turn-ons; they're literally everywhere – in advertisements and magazines, on TV, videos and the Internet. Seeing all that exposed skin and the setting off of a normal, enquiring interest in sex are not the problems. Even the fact that boys tend to access a good deal of their 'sex ed' through porn is not as alarming as it sounds.

Pornography encourages neither tenderness nor caring (and typically quite the opposite as we mentioned in Chapter 4). And the scary thing about it is that it can become addictive and, like any other addiction, can mess up your life. What we're talking about here is a diet of humourless, mechanical, degrading or violent sex that can adversely affect young and impressionable minds. Pornography is fantasy, and if a teenager is constantly thinking about it, it's time to get some help. It's less addictive if it can be seen for what it is and some boundaries are set regarding what is and what is not acceptable.

In some situations, it's the extreme parental reactions to discovering pornographic material in the house that is the more damaging. What if you find sexy magazines under your 14-year-old son's bed, for example, or learn that your 16-year-old is perusing porn websites on the Internet? Conflict in the family can get out of hand and further confuse the issue. For example, dad might be the outraged and furious one, while mum's saying, 'Hey, let's stay calm about this' (or vice versa). Meanwhile, there's a younger sister who's completely revolted by it all and the 'techno-kid' brother is loudly protesting that 'It just comes over the e-mail, I don't ask for it'.

As Steve Biddulph suggests in *Raising Boys*, 'the problem is where, when and with whom'. Images in magazines and on the Net should be kept private and the girls and women in the house shouldn't have to see such pictures glaring out at them. Fathers also have concerns about the explicitness of magazines and sites nowadays (in their day more was left to the imagination) but know that prohibition will not work. Parents need to find the balance between close enough monitoring to prevent really objectionable material circulating among boys, while at the same time not shaming them for being interested and curious.

Young people need to know, however, that pornography affects their thinking. It devalues people – usually women – into objects and reduces them to one-dimensional *things* that are reacted to only on a sexual level, rather than seen as being real multi-dimensional humans. Pornography can negatively influence a young person's understanding of his own sexuality and the sexuality of those around him. It can also adversely affect how people treat others, especially their ability to form close and caring relationships. What parents want is for boys to see women as people with attractive bodies, not just objects to lust after.

From giggles to romance

Boys become more wary of girls as they progress through childhood. In an interesting experiment, four-year-old boys were asked to walk up to a girl and get as close as they felt comfortable – they made it in real close, almost nose to nose. Nine-year-old boys, on the other hand, invariably stopped within several metres of the girl. Over the next few years, it doesn't get any easier, and the reasons are largely biological. Boys feel increasingly attracted to girls, under the influence of testosterone, but have no skills to find out how they feel. So, while pubescent girls, under the influence of oestrogen, are sympathetic, socially active and ready to communicate, boys often find it difficult to talk to girls in an ordinary way.

As puberty approaches, however, children become intensely curious about sex. With eager delight and giggling apprehension they share their fantasies with each other and actively seek out information wherever they can find it; in magazines and novels, medical books, dictionaries and encyclopaedias. 'What must a sexual experience be like?' they wonder. 'Where on earth do people put their legs?'

Later on, some of the distortions, rumours and wild tales that filter down from above get sorted out. But with puberty in full swing, there are other things to cope with. Put together an anxious preoccupation with bodily changes and the hypersensitivity associated with this, and sexuality becomes an emotional minefield in early adolescence.

First infatuations occur at this time (say, around 11 or 12) and involve strong, new feelings. This is the stuff of romantic daydreams which may be directed at either sex. Often nobody else knows about them and kids get over them quickly. Of greater concern to some parents are the close relationships that form between young adolescents of the same sex, and the experimental sex play that often goes along with this. Stories about groups of boys seeing who can ejaculate the furthest are true! but this is really just a way for them to learn about physical sensations at a time when the opposite sex is pretty threatening.

In most instances it's preferable for parents to keep their distance and not be too alarmed about this sort of thing. It will generally become obvious through a child's behaviour if there's emotional distress involved or if relationships are becoming too intense.

Then there's the matter of masturbation. The Scottish comedian Billy Connolly remembers his first sexual experience as a very frightening one: 'It was dark and I was alone'. And there's the immortal line from the play, *The Boys in the Band*: 'The best thing about masturbation is that you don't have to look your best.'

It goes without saying that adolescence and masturbation are related, but for many parents and kids, this remains an area of discomfort. Myths and fantasies abound and, although many young people take it in their stride, others experience guilt, anxiety and shame. Boys who masturbate early in puberty (as most do) before they're sexually mature enough to ejaculate, can experience a 'dry run' – an orgasmic sensation without semen. Some boys think that they are only given a certain number of ejaculations and if they use them all up in this way, bad luck! Girls may feel guilty about touching 'down there' or may not even know that masturbation provides a multitude of ways in which they can gain sexual pleasure for themselves, simply because they have more erogenous zones than boys. Boys discover masturbation at around 12 or 13 (or whenever puberty starts). Interestingly, sex researcher and author Shere Hite reports that girls masturbate more and begin earlier than has been generally known, with more than 60 per cent masturbating by the age of 11 or 12.

Steve Biddulph (in *Raising Boys*) has it right: 'Masturbation isn't just harmless, it's good for you.' Advantages include: the release of tension and having a good time; the lack of any ill-effects (it is not possible to masturbate to excess); safety, in terms of not being able to catch anything; and it also helps kids to know and understand their bodies and their strong sexual feelings. For boys, it's also a simple mechanism for keeping sperm renewed (in the privacy of their rooms after lights out, with tissues!). Perhaps we should be encouraging kids to stick to masturbation until about their mid-thirties! At the very least, if parents (and doctors and other health professionals) communicate that it's okay, it will take an enormous burden off a teenager's mind. It's simply a matter of saying so.

Parents usually become more anxious about what their teenagers are up to sexually during the middle years of around 14 to 16. This is the time when they start to act so grown up but, to you, they still seem so young and immature. There is increasing contact with the opposite sex during these years, which initially takes place within the relative safety of mixed groups – 'relative safety', because in no way does this preclude a good deal of affectionate, sexual interaction. Sensible kids won't say a lot about this, but as a guess, innocuous-sounding activities like 'video parties' are often merely comfortable, home-based 'tickle and grope' sessions. The settings may have changed somewhat, but parents can remember what they got up to in their teens. What better reason to worry?

When one mother returned home to find her 15-year-old daughter sitting, red-eyed and stunned, in the middle of her bedroom floor, the first guess was correct: the shattered girl had just broken up with her boyfriend. Where there's love there's trauma for all concerned. Boys in their mid-teens might not so readily show their feelings but still feel the same emotional wrench when things go wrong. As part of a general sexual awakening, romantic emotional attachments are likely to occur at this time. They are characteristically short lived. But being head over heels in love involves feelings of desperate ecstasy, or ecstatic desperation, that may never be experienced in as intense a way again. Those who have survived such relationships are not sorry about this at all, because the experience is exhausting, bewildering and frequently bruising, for both kids and parents.

For adolescents, getting older generally means becoming more sensible and level-headed. In the later teens, having a 'good sort' at your side is less important than sharing interests and establishing some give-and-take, although for some young men, this will always be a factor. Relationships are likely to be longer term and to involve mutual caring and loyalty, a reasonable setting for the more serious expression of sexual needs. The reasons for being in a relationship also broaden with maturity. Older teenagers whose identities are becoming more secure are also in better shape to cope with the emotions and responsibilities involved, but breakups can be shattering on both sides.

Going 'all the way'

A study of nearly 4000 teenagers in Victoria in 1996 showed that the average age of first sexual experience is 16 years. About 40 per cent of boys and one-third of girls had experienced sexual intercourse by Year 12. More recent research confirms that more teenagers are having sex and at an earlier age. They are also having oral sex much earlier than their parents did. According to the first national sex survey of Australians' attitudes and practices (based on phone interviews with 19,300 people aged 16 to 59), 60 per cent of young people between 16 and 19 in 2001/2 have had vaginal or anal intercourse or oral sex.

On the other hand, half of all young people in this age group are still virgins, that is have not had intercourse. Contrary to common belief, adolescents are not promiscuous. Most sexual experiences appear to occur in the context of a steady and 'loving' relationship. For example, it was reported in one Australian study that around 60 per cent of 17-year-old girls and boys who had had 'full sex' considered it as part of a 'meaningful relationship'. How long such a relationship lasts before another takes its place is, of course, another question. Casual sex still represents an important part of young adult sex, and is all too often unsafe, despite better understanding about sexually transmitted infections and AIDS (see pages 116–119 for more about this).

Other studies give us a more detailed profile. Young people from well-to-do families who attend private schools (and particularly if they are religious) are less sexually active than other teenagers, especially those who have left school, are unemployed or homeless. Co-educational school students have higher rates of sexual experience than those who attend single-sex schools.

I'm tired of watching everyone else falling in and out of relationships – intoxicated sex and empty promises.
Nicola, aged 18

Country teenagers are less sexually active than their city peers. More adolescent virgins than non-virgins feel closer to, better understood by and have easier communication with their parents, who are also more likely to have discussed sexual matters with them.

The first time

Woody Allen said: 'Love is the answer. But while you're waiting for the answer, sex brings up some pretty good questions.' Before looking at the whys and wherefores, though, here are some facts about first intercourse:

- The average age of first intercourse has become younger over the past few decades. It has declined from 18 (the average age 30–40 years ago) to 16. For women, the median age of first intercourse has fallen from 19 to 16. (It's possible that many teenagers think you're *supposed* to start having sex at 16, because that's the 'age of consent' for heterosexual intercourse.)
- First intercourse has a seasonal tendency, with a peak in the summer, for obvious reasons!
- For teenage girls, male partners tend to be older boys or young men (common wisdom suggests that if a 15-year-old girl has a 19-year-old boyfriend, at some point intercourse is inevitable).
- First intercourse may occur literally anywhere, but often at home, her place or his (yes, parents go out, leaving the house reliably vacant at an opportune time).
- First intercourse rarely comes up to expectations, particularly for girls; in fact, it may happen so quickly (usually in silence, in darkness and without preliminaries) that it is difficult for some girls to know if they've had it at all. It's highly unlikely for girls to have an orgasm either.
- Not surprisingly, girls are more likely to experience feelings of anxiety, worry, guilt and embarrassment afterwards, while boys are more likely to report being excited, satisfied and happy (at least, that's what they say).
- Over 90 per cent of young people use contraception the first time they have sex (Australia's approach to sex education appears to be working, but of course we cannot be complacent about this and *consistent* condom use is not the norm).

For far too many girls it may occur under duress, before they're fully ready. According to the Victorian study quoted on page 104, while 84 per cent felt they could say 'no' to sex, a worrying percentage could not. The consequences of forced sex, whether 'date rape' or occurring outside a relationship, is a particularly awful way to start out. And when first intercourse is the result of incest or rape, the emotional consequences are disastrous (as discussed further in Chapter 10).

A question of readiness

You cannot forbid sexual behaviour in teenagers. This part of growing up is private and you are not going to be around when it happens. This is definitely an emotive subject and parents tend to have definite ideas and feelings about it. Some may think that adolescence is the golden age of sexual growth and that such opportunities to learn by experience will never come again. Other parents think that kids are too immature and irresponsible to have sexual intercourse and that the potential consequences are too devastating. Some parents may accept that adolescents have to learn to cope with personal relationships and negotiate the sexual component within them, which may eventually include intercourse.

There is much food for thought here, but no clear answer on the question of readiness. Individual teenagers and their situations vary greatly. Some handle sexual involvement without undue stress, while others find themselves totally out of their depth. One thing is clear, though: the earlier they start, the greater the likelihood of bad experiences, and the impact of these can be enduring.

One's fervent hope is that a young person will have thought it through beforehand and had the opportunity to talk about it with somebody sensible (a parent or trusted adult friend), preferably before it happens. A young woman reflecting on her sexual initiation shared the idea that it can be helpful to seek a variety of opinions, but highlighted the value of an honest and open discussion, including the topics of birth control, condoms and unwanted pregnancy.

Why do they do it?

So, why do girls go along with it? Part of the answer lies in the submissive role that females are conditioned to accept. But there's always at least one other factor involved. She might simply have not wanted to hurt his feelings. Feeling as if you're 'in love' is a pretty common reason why girls agree to sex, or why they might feel ready to take that step. At least the presence of feelings of love makes it a potentially more pleasant and pleasurable experience. But unfortunately, for a lot of young people sex and drugs are related. Both are trendy and involve pressure from friends. Having sex when drunk or under the influence of drugs is not uncommon. As well as leading to behaviours that place adolescents at higher risk of contracting sexually transmitted infections, this is the situation in which females are more likely to be victims of male sexual aggression.

> *One mistake shouldn't mean that people don't trust or respect you any more.*
> *Lara, aged 16*

Other reasons for having intercourse can involve psychological needs and, again, put young women in particular at great risk. Intercourse can be an effort to gain affection denied by parents, a form of rebellion, or a cry for help. Promiscuous sexual behaviour in girls can also be a manifestation of depression – a way to get close to someone, however briefly, when they're feeling low. This is true of boys too. In fact, the relationship between 'risky sex' and a whole range of mental health conditions is an important one to know about (as discussed further in Chapter 15).

'It can't happen to me'

When it comes to using birth control, sexually active young people are dismal failures, apart from the first time they have intercourse. On many occasions they will take the risk of unprotected intercourse. Whether or not they are showing increased responsibility in other areas of their lives, there is some sort of block about 'protected sex'. They generally know about the risks of unwanted pregnancy, sexually transmitted infections such as HIV/AIDS, and at least something about what's available to prevent these problems, but do not seem to believe the advice applies to them.

The 'reasons' young people give for not using contraceptives include the following:

- Sexual relations should be held under natural and spontaneous conditions; you don't *plan* to have sex ('I shouldn't look as if I'm expecting it').
- 'It can't happen to me' or 'I'm too young to get pregnant'.
- Contraceptives are too troublesome and inconvenient; they interfere with sexual pleasure (a common complaint boys make about condoms).

- Contraceptives are unnatural or potentially harmful to the body.
- Contraceptives are too expensive.
- Parents might discover such incriminating evidence at home.
- It's embarrassing to ask for contraception and thus declare that you are, or are intending to become, sexually active.
- Contraception is a female responsibility.

Contraception

Teenagers usually become sexually active long before their parents suspect they are. This leads us to advocate for earlier education by parents and schools about safer sex. Getting this information as high school seniors (year 10 plus) is leaving things a bit late.

Here is a quick revision of the steps to effective use of condoms:

- Check the use-by date and standards mark (the indication of quality) on the packet.
- Store condoms in a cool place, not in your wallet or in the car.
- Open the packet carefully, making sure fingernails and jewellery don't tear the latex. Put the condom on before having any contact with your partner's genitals. Use some water-based lubricant on the outside of the condom to help prevent tearing.
- Wait until the penis is erect, then squeeze the teat at the end of the condom to expel air so it will not burst upon ejaculation. Hold onto the teat and roll the condom down over the penis. Make sure the condom is down as far as it will go.
- After ejaculation, hold the condom rim firmly onto the penis, roll the condom away from your partner and gently withdraw, before losing the erection. Be careful not to spill any semen. Wipe the penis with a tissue. Condoms should never be reused, even if you don't ejaculate.
- If a condom breaks or leaks, contraception may be prescribed by a doctor.

Oral contraceptives are the best way to prevent pregnancy. The combined oral contraceptive contains oestrogen and progesterone, the two hormones naturally produced by the ovaries. The Pill stops eggs maturing in the ovaries; therefore ovaries do not release eggs. When taken every day, at the same time and according to the directions, oral contraceptives are about 99 per cent effective, but of course teenagers using oral contraceptives should also be told to use a condom to prevent sexually transmitted infections. Emergency, injectable and implant contraceptives may also be prescribed by a doctor.

All this is good advice, but as psychiatrist Dr Jeffrey Cubis points out:

> *At a practical level it is expecting a lot from the average adolescent to know when they are likely to have sex, obtain condoms in advance, maintain secrecy from peers and parents, and use condoms appropriately in a situation of great unfamiliarity, emotional arousal, and with the risk of social and personal embarrassment. The difficulties of obtaining them from chemist shops are real.*

Similarly, use of the Pill requires foresight, consultation with a GP, and the commitment to take it every day. And even if we were able to remove all the impediments to taking proper precautions, the use of contraceptives by the young might not increase substantially simply because risk-taking, so much a part of adolescence, enhances the thrill of guilty pleasures. It's a difficult issue and quite a challenge for parents and other sex educators to tackle. However, contraception is something that parents should talk to their teenagers about because it's so vital. We want our sons and daughters to be protected from grief and to remain safe. Of course, not everybody would be as blunt as the mother who announced to her kids: 'Your father keeps his condoms in the drawer next to the bed. Nobody's counting.' We might also make them aware that family planning clinics exist.

Not everybody's heterosexual

In our culture, being homosexual is not a particularly easy path to follow. Fears of homosexuality can cause fathers and mothers to behave in certain ways towards their children in the hope of preventing it. For example, fathers might discourage dressing up and dolls for little boys, or mothers limit their affection for fear of 'making him queer'. These fears are totally unfounded. Throughout the school years and beyond, any male who doesn't quite fit the stereotyped image of masculinity is at risk of being labelled a 'poofter', a term of utmost derision. Because our society is more accepting of physical affection between females, there is somewhat less consternation about girls not conforming to accepted stereotypes.

This is a complex subject. Most teenagers worry about their sexual identity and about their ability to attract and perform sexually with the opposite sex. At some time or other, most will wonder whether or not they are homosexual. Having crushes on the same sex, whether it's a best friend or a class teacher, is very much a normal part of growing up. But feeling uncomfortable about it would also be the norm. In *Ophelia Speaks*, in which adolescent girls write about their search for self, Sara Shandler writes: 'Newly felt physical attractions and sexual arousal throw nearly all of us into confusion. When these feelings don't fit heterosexual expectations, fear often transforms into upheaval.'

Here are some facts about homosexuality:

- Homosexuality is defined as a predominant and persistent attraction to individuals of the same sex, plus absent or weak attraction to the opposite sex.
- It is now believed that one's sexual orientation is determined early in life – before or shortly after birth – and is not amenable to 'cure'. The discovery in 1993 of a gene for male homosexuality provides some scientific support for the view that sexual orientation has a genetic or biological component.
- The notion of 'gay' or 'straight' is often too black or white; there is a spectrum of sexual orientation with most people falling somewhere between the two extremes. Sexual orientation involves a number of aspects, including sexual fantasy, emotional attraction, sexual behaviour and cultural affiliation, all important to the individual to varying degrees.
- Between 20 and 50 per cent of adolescents are said to have had a homosexual experience. This is not necessarily a harbinger of homosexuality (although it could be), but can subsequently cause anxiety about future sexual adjustment.
- The occasional attraction to a person of the same sex is also not homosexuality, but for some can be extremely troubling and very difficult to discuss and seek reassurance about.
- Adolescent and older homosexual men and lesbians can often trace their earliest suspicions about being gay back to primary school. In high school, clues might include a predilection for erotic fantasy about friends of the same sex (particularly while

masturbating) and not being attracted to the opposite sex when peers are becoming besotted.
- Homosexuality does not equal or lead to paedophilia or result from it. The most likely person to sexually abuse a child is a heterosexual male. Statistically paedophiles who molest children of the same sex are unlikely to be homosexual in their adult sexual relations.
- According to a survey of 3500 students in Years 10 and 12 in 118 schools throughout Australia, 6.3 per cent of students were attracted to people of their own sex or people of both sexes, while another 2.3 per cent were not sure. In other words, almost one in 10 senior high school students are saying that they're either homosexual or bisexual in their orientation or not entirely sure they're heterosexual.
- Gay adolescents feel different, that is, 'not straight', but for a long time struggle alone with uncertainty, confusion and fear ('If anyone were to find out, I'd die'). They often have low self-esteem and feel like second-class citizens, experience loss of friendships and verbal and physical abuse from peers. Gay adolescents may be two to three times more likely than their peers to attempt suicide.
- Young homosexuals are reticent to 'come out' and fear confronting their parents (concerns about parental disapproval are not always unfounded), so it comes as an enormous relief to meet other gay people and share experiences and concerns.
- Young gay and bisexual males who engage in unprotected rectal intercourse (not all gay men have anal sex) are at extreme risk of contracting sexually transmitted infections, including HIV/AIDS and hepatitis B.

When the subject of a young person's homosexuality is ultimately broached with parents, it usually comes as a shock. As this is often not what they wanted for their child, there is a grieving process to go through, involving denial, guilt, self-doubt and anger. 'What will family and friends think when they find out? Am I to blame in some way? Could it have been prevented?' Or more selfishly, 'Why are you doing this to us?' Getting used to the idea can take time, and it is often helpful in this situation to talk with other parents of gay youths (see the Outreach website listed in the Appendix for more information). The support and advice that can be provided by a group is usually worth enlisting.

On the other hand, many parents take great pride in their gay and lesbian children and express outrage at the unfair societal victimisation they often suffer. Posters declaring such sentiments as 'My mum blamed herself when she found out I was gay – now she wants to take all the credit' are being used in campaigns around university campuses and elsewhere to promote a more positive attitude. Without doubt, gay and lesbian young people fare better in terms of their health and wellbeing when they have family acceptance and support! They also draw inspiration and encouragement from gay or lesbian role models like Justice Michael Kirby and Dr Kerryn Phelps.

Sexual intercourse – a health hazard

Can you get AIDS the first time you have sex?

I feel really embarrassed. I've been really stressed lately and I went to a party last night and we all got really drunk. I don't usually do this but I went up to a guy and something went 'in and out and in and out' so I think I had sex, but I don't know. I'm sure the guy wouldn't have an STI. Can you do a pregnancy test?

These sorts of statements from teenagers raise the need for better sex education and more availability of reliable contraception and protection from infections. Sadly, many young people have already experienced unprotected intercourse before they come to a GP for help. Education must be provided about access to general practice, use of Medicare cards and information about young people's rights to confidentiality (these issues are taken up in Chapter 16). Learning about sexual health needs to include information about everything: hormones, physical changes, periods, wet dreams, reproduction, body image, emotions, sexual feelings and same sex attraction.

There is no evidence at all that sex education of any kind leads to earlier or increased sexual activity. In fact, there is a body of research which tells us that such education means that young people are more likely to delay sexual intercourse and to be better prepared for it when the time comes.

What needs to be discussed includes: use of condoms, information to increase the reliability of the Pill, the advantages of injectable progesterone, and the option of emergency contraception. Failed contraception is a major factor in unplanned pregnancy. It needs to be emphasised that the side effects of any form of contraception are considerably less than the long-term consequences of an unwanted pregnancy.

> My mum gave me condoms. I wasn't even having sex and I thought it was weird.
> Alec, aged 17

Teenagers must understand that failing to use a condom effectively – just once – can also lead to long-term consequences. Sexually transmitted infections, such as HIV, hepatitis, chlamydia and herpes are real and very serious.

There is an ancient saying: 'For a little love, you can pay your whole life.' This section looks at why unprotected sexual intercourse is so risky.

Teenage pregnancy

Despite the population growth in the past 20 years, fewer teenage girls are having babies in Australia. The decline has been highlighted by the national sex survey of 2001/2 which revealed that almost a quarter of the surveyed women in their fifties had been pregnant in their teens compared to 17 per cent of women in their twenties. The marked decrease in very young mothers can be attributed to greater access to sex education, contraception and abortion (certainly not to any decrease in sexual activity).

Nevertheless, there are about 16,000 births per year to Australian teenagers and an equal number of terminations of pregnancy, the second-highest rate in the Western world. So, adolescent pregnancy is no small matter. In terms of the emotional and financial costs, it's still a major health issue.

Some teenagers choose to be parents and, although this represents an enormous challenge, with support, many do a great job. However, an unwanted pregnancy is a tragedy for all concerned, whatever the outcome. Usually it is unplanned, in about 90 per cent of cases, although some girls seek a pregnancy (not necessarily at a conscious level) as a way to meet psychological needs. Such girls generally have low self-esteem, are underachievers, have experienced losses or are in some sort of strife. For them, motherhood is a means of achieving a sense of self-worth or independence.

In some traditional societies, adolescent pregnancy is an integral part of the culture and, even for unmarried girls, occurs under the protection of the family community. Western society is very different. A frightened teenager with an unexpected pregnancy anticipates parental and social disapproval and will often try to keep it a secret for as long as possible.

The main issues and problems regarding teenage pregnancy are:

- As a result of fear and uncertainty, pregnant teenagers often present late for antenatal care, and in delaying they put themselves at medical risk; and, the younger and less mature they are, the greater the risks. In terms of risk for the baby, this appears to be related to the number of antenatal visits that the young mother attends: the fewer the visits, the greater the risks.
- Approximately one in two teenage pregnancies in Australia ends in termination, the physical, psychological and social consequences of which are not always evident in the short term. However, young women seeking an abortion appear to have a more sophisticated ability to project themselves into the future, in comparison to those who go on to have a baby. They are better able to imagine the impact that a completed pregnancy might have on themselves and their potential offspring.
- When teenage girls choose to continue with their pregnancy, as about half of them do, their lives are permanently affected, usually adversely. These are also the girls who feel their lives are more controlled by external events and influences, and subscribe to far more traditional sexual stereotypes than those who have abortions.
- Just over one in 10 pregnant girls in Australia marry, but teenage marriages are notoriously unstable, with many ending in divorce.
- About four in 10 who have their babies raise them as single mothers, a situation fraught with difficulty. If 'having a baby' was romanticised as a 'solution' to a host of personal problems, disappointment at the reality of parenting a child can be extreme. The children of adolescent mothers are more likely to be exposed to illness, injury and deprivation and go on to become teenage mothers themselves.
- Some people openly resent the government allowance that single mothers get, the Sole Parents Benefit, viewing it as an unnecessary burden for the taxpayer. Contrary to popular belief, girls rarely seek a pregnancy and then keep their baby for financial gain; once there, however, the financial support they receive is minimal, and to suggest they should receive less is unthinkable.

This is not a happy litany of facts and figures. Pregnant teenage girls face an agonising dilemma and somehow must choose for themselves the 'least worst option'. While we now know that there are personality factors involved in the choice they make, it is a decision that is not easily made alone. Understandably, a girl in this situation is going to feel pretty scared about how her mum and dad are going to react when they find out. They're not likely to feel pleased! But, as a rule, it works out better than teenagers expect.

Of course, a teenager may have an abortion without her parents finding out (a particularly heavy secret to carry). Sometimes there is conflict over what should be done, and pressure may be brought to bear upon her to pursue a course of action contrary to her wishes. Fortunately, most parents tend to rally in a crisis and give all-important moral support and guidance. However things turn out and whatever the difficulties along the way, this can make an enormous difference.

The young father, long neglected by researchers and counsellors, is coming under increasing scrutiny. Teenage boys generally do not handle their girlfriend's pregnancy at all well, and the relationship often falls apart. Statistically they are likely to be unemployed and have relatively poor prospects for the future, as well as ongoing emotional problems. Somehow or other, they need to be included in the difficult process of sorting things out.

When a girl decides to keep her baby and raise it as a single mother, her parents (unless they have thrown her out and severed ties – fortunately not a common scenario) often become very involved in its care, even if with some ambivalence at the outset. After all, just when they thought that nappies and broken nights were well behind them, here they are starting anew. However, having to raise a grandchild, more as parents than grandparents, while a frequent bone of contention for the child's young mother, is not without its pleasures and satisfaction for the 'oldies'. Many in this situation tackle it philosophically and with goodwill.

Sometimes 'premature grandparents' have unrealistic expectations and consider that the adolescent mother, now with a child of her own, should become an instant adult. She can't. She still needs to be a teenager, and this means going out and mixing with unfettered friends from time to time. Having to turn her back on all the normal things that young people like and do is hardly conducive to her growing up.

Sexually transmitted infections

Sexually transmitted infections (STIs) are acquired during unprotected sex with an infected partner. There may be symptoms such as discharge from the penis or vagina, bleeding, pain, odour or redness and a rash on the genital areas. However, some sexually transmitted infections are invisible and painless and can only be detected by having tests.

STIs include genital warts, genital herpes, chlamydia, gonorrhoea, candida (thrush), trichomonas, hepatitis B and HIV/AIDS. (Hepatitis C is transmitted via blood to blood contact such as sharing needles and tattooing, but there is a small risk that it may be transmitted during intercourse if bleeding occurs or menstruation.) All these infections need to be confirmed by pathology testing, which can be arranged very simply by a doctor. Many infections can be treated, others have life-long or life-shortening consequences.

The incidence of STIs continues to rise worldwide, with young people being largely responsible for this trend. In developed countries, more than two-thirds of all reported cases of gonorrhoea involve people under 25. Chlamydia and trichomonas are thought to be even more common than gonorrhoea. More than 20 infectious agents are now known to be transmitted sexually.

For various reasons, including inadequate sex education and poor communication between parents and kids, teenagers remain dangerously ill-informed about these diseases. Although, as already noted, knowing about risks does not always change adolescent behaviour, we must keep trying to get the message across. The frightening reality of AIDS makes it even more critical to encourage adolescents to adopt safe sex practices. In particular, the risks involving anal intercourse (which is probably more common among adolescents and young adults than is generally recognised) need to be conveyed to all adolescents, not just homosexual and bisexual young people.

Many adolescents believe that having a stable partner (which could really mean 'three weeks: so far, so good!') is all they require to protect themselves against HIV/AIDS or other STIs. We all know, however, that adolescent partnerships can change often and quickly, increasing the risk of meeting and having sex with someone infected.

Other strange ideas many young people have include: nice people don't catch things; you have to sleep around; you can tell if a particular person poses a health risk; and the best way to get rid of it is to 'give it away'. All this means that they don't take proper precautions, don't recognise symptoms for what they are and don't readily seek help when they do have symptoms. Teenagers also need to know that disappearance of symptoms does not mean that the disease has gone.

Having, or fearing the possibility of having an STI, is not something that a teenager would readily discuss with parents, unless they are very 'askable' people. Unfortunately, parents themselves are often ill-informed and scared about these diseases, a situation that can be remedied by getting hold of the clear and explicit pamphlets available from the Health Department.

Here are a few pertinent facts:

- 'Thrush' (monilia or candidiasis) causes an itchy white vaginal discharge. It can be sexually transmitted but is more commonly associated with antibiotics, the Pill, and the warm, humid environment created by tight jeans and nylon underpants. It can be treated with tablets or vaginal creams. Men can carry it too, and unless both partners are treated, a couple can pass it back and forth.
- Trichomonal infection ('Trich') is caused by a protozoan – a microscopic, one-cell animal – and produces an itchy, smelly vaginal discharge. It is treatable with tablets (needed for both partners). Condoms offer good protection against Trich.
- Gonorrhoea presents itself in many symptomatic guises, such as a very sore throat; usually causes discharge and discomfort in men but may be symptomless in women; homosexual transmission is very common. In women, gonorrhoea can cause pelvic inflammatory disease (PID), an infection in the fallopian tubes, which can result in ectopic pregnancy or sterility.
- Chlamydia is a kind of bacteria that is sexually transmitted. Most people are not aware that they have the infection, which is why it is being referred to as the 'silent epidemic'. Up to 85 per cent of women and 40 per cent of men have no symptoms. For females, chlamydia, like gonorrhoea, represents a serious risk of PID and the complications mentioned above. Chlamydia is easy to treat with antibiotics.
- Genital herpes, rare before 15 years of age, is found in 28 per cent of sexually active females by age 20. It causes blisters that are distressing when active and are likely to recur. Acyclovir is used to reduce the severity of a primary attack and the frequency of recurrence. Recurrences are sometimes related to emotional, physical or health stresses.

- Genital human papillomavirus (HPV) infection is the most commonly diagnosed STI in the Western world. It may present as anogenital warts, which can be removed, but there is no cure for HPV. HPV has been linked to the development of cancer of the cervix in young women, with girls who start having sex early and have multiple partners being at particular risk.
- Hepatitis B, about 300 times more contagious than HIV/AIDS, is transmitted sexually as well as through contact with infected blood (in particular, shared needles and syringes or by tattooing or acupuncture performed with unsterile needles). As well as the dangers of liver disease and death, a proportion of infected people become asymptomatic carriers, and represent an unwitting hazard to their sexual partners. The World Health Organisation recommends that all young adolescents be vaccinated against hepatitis B at about age 12.

It's almost enough to put you off sex, especially with anyone you don't know extremely well. With medical concerns about STIs now including the longer term risk of infertility, cancer, chronic liver disease and AIDS, no one can afford to have a laissez-faire attitude. While 'crabs' or pubic lice (also sexually transmitted) and thrush can be cured, blocked fallopian tubes and AIDS can't. Teenagers need to know, from an early age, what the dangers are and that it pays to be careful.

Some facts about HIV and AIDS

AIDS is caused by a virus called HIV (human immunodeficiency virus) which can damage the body's defence system so that it cannot fight certain infections.

HIV is transmitted in three main ways:

- Through unprotected sexual intercourse, both anal (which represents a particularly high risk) and vaginal intercourse.
- By injecting: drug users sharing equipment especially syringes and needles.
- From an infected mother to her unborn child.

Other possibilities exist. Transmission could occur through oral sex if there are cuts or sores in the person's mouth, or by sharing sex toys (like vibrators). Any device that punctures the skin, including tattooing and acupuncture needles, equipment for ear- or other body-piercing, and removing hair by electrolysis may be contaminated with infected blood and could, in theory, pass on the virus.

Body-piercing is becoming almost mainstream for young people (much more so than tattoos), for many a rite of passage, so the risks of being exposed to HIV or other nasty germs in this way are very real. Getting pierced is costly too (around $60 for the belly button job, $100 for genitals), forcing some kids to do it themselves at home. Add cheap jewellery to the mix and you have a recipe for skin infections and irritations at the very least.

Now for the good news: everyday contact with someone who has HIV or AIDS is perfectly safe – the virus cannot be transmitted through touching, shaking hands or hugging. We also know that you cannot be infected with HIV by touching or sharing objects used by an infected person such as cups, cutlery, glasses, food, clothes, towels, toilet seats or door knobs. HIV cannot be passed on by sneezing or coughing, through tears or sweat or by mosquitoes and other insects. Scientists have also confirmed that the odds are virtually zero of catching HIV from a trip to the dentist, sharing a toothbrush infected with the AIDS virus or even kissing someone with the virus (apparently the saliva in the mouth reduces HIV's ability to infect). Swimming pools are safe too.

In Australia, HIV continues to be transmitted overwhelmingly through sexual contact between men. The number of new HIV infections continues to fall (in men, from 11,061 in 1992 to 602 in 2001; in women, 633 in 1992 to 94 in 2001), which is very encouraging. The decline in new AIDS cases is attributed to improvements in therapy, which are also enabling longer survival with the disease. The bottom line, however, is that AIDS causes premature death.

Dr Jonathan Mann of the World Health Organisation said in 1987, at which time the epidemic was getting into full swing: 'The only means of containing the disease is health education – frank, explicit and repeated.' In the past two decades, media campaigns and HIV/AIDS education programs have targeted young people in schools. As parents, health professionals and caring adults in general, we must do our bit too.

Adolescent mental health and risky sexual behaviour

Researchers in New Zealand have demonstrated the increased probability of risky sexual behaviour occurring in young people across a wide range of mental health diagnoses. This is important because around one in four adolescents has a 'mental health' problem (this issue is discussed in Chapter 15). Even the most prevalent mental health disorder in young people, clinical depression, is associated with increased rates of risky sex, sexually transmitted infections and early sexual experience. For teenagers with serious psychiatric impairment, as with those under the influence of alcohol and other drugs, the ability to assess risk and behave in a self-protective way may be severely impaired. Risk-taking in these circumstances (including risky sex) may also represent an indirect expression of anger, or a means, albeit dangerous, of exerting some control over one's life. For a seriously disturbed young person, sexual activity might also be used for diversion, to relieve tension, and as a salve of affection-seeking – a sort of self-medication with sex. One must also wonder here (especially in regard to early sexual initiation) about the role that may have been played by sexual abuse, a major precursor to mental health disorder as well.

A famous child psychiatrist, Professor Barry Nurcomb, once told a group of wide-eyed medical students that if a way could be found to prevent child sexual abuse, the need for a major portion of adult psychiatry would vanish. He made this observation because people who have been sexually abused in childhood have a higher incidence of mental health problems such as major depression, conduct disorder, panic disorder, alcoholism and other substance abuse disorders, post-traumatic stress disorder, eating disorders, psychosomatic disorders, and borderline personality disorder.

Fortunately, not all children who are sexually abused develop a significant mental illness. Protective factors can lessen the likelihood of such bad outcomes, for example disclosing the abuse to someone who is not only supportive but active in ending the abusive relationship, and when the abuse is of shorter duration and less severity. On the other hand, there are risk factors for developing mental illness: severe abuse involving attempted or completed intercourse (which applies in about 5.5 per cent of women who were sexually abused as children and 2.5 per cent of men); longer duration of abuse; physical restraint or violence; an incestuous relationship with the abuser; not being believed or being punished for disclosing the abuse. Sexually abused children may also develop an unusual interest in or avoidance of all things of a sexual nature and experience relationship difficulties (for more information on abuse, see Chapter 10).

An important message for both parents and health care providers is the need to carefully consider what might be happening sexually in the lives of young people suffering with depression, anxiety and other mental health disorders, and the need to coordinate health care.

What do teenagers say about sexuality?

I made a stupid mistake at a party. I want sex to mean something, unlike many of my friends who already feel spoiled and let other people use their bodies. You watch sex on TV, hear it on the phone, read it in all the mags, get sent it by e-mail. It's not special any more and people seem to have sex without being prepared for what can happen.

Virginity is not valued. It is expected everyone should lose their virginity as soon as possible. I got to a point where I had to have sex to keep my relationship going and in the end it broke us up. I didn't enjoy it at all. When Dad found out I had sex, I felt degraded.

My mum said to come to her before I did anything – I did when I was ready.

Most people in high school have already had sex – you have to be cool. I really wish I had waited with sex because the guy I am with now should have been the first one. I felt pressure from older friends. Sex is not private or clean – a lot of my friends have had sex in the toilets. It's too embarrassing to buy condoms.

Boys feel threatened by homosexuals. Girls are punished severely at school for girl-to-girl contact – this wouldn't happen if it were girl-to-boy contact.

When I was 14, I was scared of girls and felt sexually attracted to other boys. It made me very depressed and I decided to come out. For the rest of my schooling, I was bullied. I joined the armed forces and, at 19, I realised I was not gay. I still don't know why I had to tell everyone.

I am gay and inside I always knew this. But when I talk to other gay friends, they usually feel confused. Probably you don't really know until you are about 18. There are two helpful books that talk about these confused feelings – My Child is Gay *by Bryce McDougall and* Inside Out *by Erin Shale.*

Dealing with sexuality

Let's bring the subject of teenage sexuality back into the home. Nothing terrible has happened, but there are sexual vibes everywhere. You are hassling about the usual things – dress, hairstyle, friends and curfews. Most parents don't realise that these are often thinly disguised attempts to control sexual behaviour. Another approach is to say or do nothing that could lead to discussion, conflict or personal revelation about sex. Kids play this game too, knowing their folks need protection from their emerging sexuality.

This is not the way to go. We get ourselves so tied up in knots about it that we create more stress and anxiety than is necessary. Admittedly, by the time your child becomes a teenager, there is a lot of water under the bridge: attitudes arising out of our own upbringing have already been conveyed; our marital (or equivalent) behaviour has already been modelled. But it is still possible to change the state of play. To do so requires a rethink of some enduring misconceptions:

That teenagers are knowledgeable about sex: They may appear so at times, but this is deceiving. Research studies have demonstrated that many teenagers believe such rubbish as: females have to have an orgasm to conceive; the 'safe period' (good grief!) is in the middle of the menstrual cycle; and you don't get pregnant if you have sex standing up. Even if young people get the basic facts straight, what they learn from soap operas, films and videos is that being sexy is good; that you have to have sex in different positions; that orgasm is the main goal. No doubt this falls far short of the attitudes and understanding that most parents would wish them to have.

That if you tell them, they'll want to do it: The fact is, they already want to do it. Far more important questions are: how soon and with what degree of forethought, consideration, and safety? As already mentioned, the evidence suggests that teenagers 'in the know' are actually more likely to postpone sexual intercourse and be more responsible generally in their sexual behaviour.

That you have to be all-knowing: The information explosion and technological advancement in the areas of sexuality and conception are dizzying. Not knowing the answers to complex or even simple questions is no crime. In fact, sometimes it might even be an advantage not to know, in that it gives you the opportunity to bridge the gap between yourself and your child. In saying things like 'I don't know' or 'my views are not firm on that subject' or 'I'll find out and we can discuss it again', you show your honesty and your care. Young people really appreciate a candid or humble response on these matters. And for the parent, doing a little research is a good way to learn.

That you have to be liberal in your attitudes: Who says you have to take a carte blanche attitude to your children's developing sexuality? Is it so terrible to be labelled old-fashioned, traditional or boring? A pseudo-liberal posture with undertones of disapproval is worse, and kids can pick it easily. An open and responsible approach is preferable, which includes being as well informed as possible. The important thing is being able to listen, even if you're aghast at what you hear.

That you always have to be comfortable about sex: For one thing, it's impossible. Talking about it won't always go smoothly, even if you subscribe to the view that questions must be answered frankly and at the adolescent's level. Anyone can be taken off guard. It's okay to say 'I feel a bit embarrassed talking about this'. In fact, sometimes just verbalising your embarrassment can alleviate it.

Some final thoughts

David: The subject of sexuality for young people is broad. At the very least, it covers identity issues, relationships, communication, moral values, experimentation, societal pressures and, increasingly, the risk of disease and mortality. Young people need information (there's no such thing as too much information), opinions and ideas about human sexuality from the adults in their lives. They need opportunities to discuss their sexual feelings and get them into perspective. They need to be encouraged to take things gradually and to enjoy a relationship for the other things it has to offer as well.

When the time comes to experience a sexual relationship, young people need access to counselling and contraceptive advice. Hopefully, by that stage they will have achieved enough maturity and self-regard to be discriminating, careful and caring. They will be aware of the implications of sexuality for physical and emotional health and take all necessary precautions. Their decisions about who they share their bodies with, however, are their own.

Leanne: So that's the theory. Then there is the question of what you do when you are confronted by your teenager's sex life.

David: At the age of 17, one of my daughters suddenly announced while we were washing up together: 'I think I'm just about ready to do it, Dad.' Apart from smashing a few dishes, I blustered: 'Don't do it, darling. It will drain all your energy away from your brain. You'll fail your exams.' She simply replied: 'Okay, Dad,' no doubt, thoroughly pulling my leg.

Leanne: Suppose your son or daughter wants to bring their girlfriend/boyfriend home for the night or the weekend or on holidays? What do you say then? There's the indignant 'not in my house/separate rooms or nothing' approach (even though you know that they might be sneaking around in the wee hours); or there's the 'turn a blind eye/open acceptance' approach. A lot depends too on their ages and the nature of the relationship. You need to have the debate about what is right in your own family.

David: Some time ago, I recall finding our old copy of Alex Comfort's *The Joy of Sex* lying open on our bedroom floor. 'Somebody in our family's getting educated,' I thought as I returned it to the shelf. It's not easy to broach the subject of sexual intercourse with your kids and sometimes you can feel very uncomfortable about it. In many families, it's often easier to leave such things unstated and, ironically, this is often what teenagers would prefer. Have you ever tried to bring it up and heard, 'Good grief, Mum, I know all that'? There are, of course, more subtle ways to deal with it (by the high quality literature we leave around the house, for instance).

Leanne: I see many teenagers in my practice who have too little information and suffer the consequences. Here are some of the common statements I hear from my young patients over and over again:

It wasn't proper sex.
It wasn't actually unprotected sex – it's just that the condom came off.
He said he hasn't got anything. I think I've got something. I've got an itchy virginia.
Does Mum have to know?
I don't know if I had one last month or not.
I'm not planning on doing it again.
I'd say it's a stable relationship – two weeks next Saturday.
I can't take the Pill – it makes me put on weight, it makes me moody. I won't be doing it regularly anyway.
I think the condom broke.

Section 2

Home and away

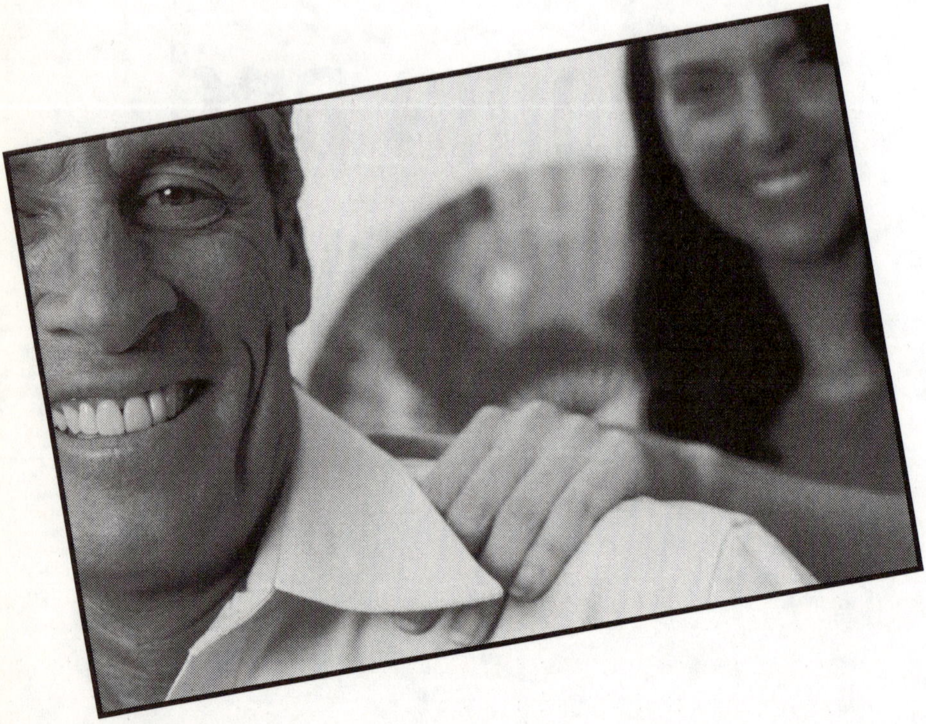

Chapter 8
Middlescence

> *Sometimes parents show too much concern. They want to solve everything instead of listening.*
> *Will, aged 14*

Middle age has an impact on teenagers. Sooner or later, mum and dad will go through it, nothing surer, because Nature has arranged things rather strangely: while kids are going through adolescence, parents are going through 'middlescence'. Have you ever thought that you, too, are in transition and that a number of interesting life changes are happening in parallel?

Adults have their own special needs and problems that young people are often unable to recognise and unlikely to understand (to them, anyone over about 26 seems ancient anyway!). Inevitable differences in circumstances and attitudes give rise to all sorts of conflicts and misunderstandings. There exists what we might call an 'empathy gap', often related to differing perceptions and expectations.

What does it mean to be grown up?

Some people do seem pretty grown up, in the sense that they say and do the types of things one expects of adults – you know, express opinions on current affairs, hold down a job, go to meetings and help out at the school canteen. But how they feel inside generally remains hidden.

One thing is certain: maturity does not descend upon you like a gown of honour on your 18th birthday. There is a lot more personal sorting out to do, and it literally might take forever. At some point, however (probably during the thirties), you sense a subtle change in self-perception. You gradually become aware of being more confident in your own beliefs and actions and less concerned with the expectations and demands of others (the boss excluded, of course). The world looks real because you are able to see it as it is and better accept the good and bad as part of life.

When is middle age?

Middle age is a touchy business. Can you count on the fingers of more than one hand people who admit to it willingly? A fifty-something man vehemently denies that he is middle-aged. 'Not even close,' he states bravely, 'I will be suddenly old one day, when it suits me!' Some people feel young inside and that's the way they'll stay.

Attitudes to ageing have clearly changed. Nowadays, depending on your vantage point, of course, even 60 or 70 can seem positively young. One reason for this is that there are more very old people around – a tribute to the wonders of modern medicine. It gives middle-aged folk something to be optimistic about.

When are you a middlescent?

There can be much satisfaction in reaching middle age, resting on your laurels a little (unless you're an incurable workaholic) and accepting things as they are. But descriptions of middle age, for some reason, rarely emphasise the positive. The following is a check list of generally accepted symptoms:

- A growing preoccupation with one's body, its changing shape and assorted discomforts.
- A less starry-eyed view of male–female relationships. So this is the way it is, you realise.
- A sometimes painful evaluation of one's personal goals, objectives and achievements. Has it all been worth the effort? If you knew then what you know now, would you have wasted so much time?
- A feeling of being sandwiched between two generations (and not particularly appreciated by either). It's harder to find clothes that are just right, not too young and not too old.

► An acceptance of oneself as an older, rather than a younger person (some people are born to it) and a tendency to think more in terms of how much time is left, rather than of what has gone before. You stop looking forward to birthdays.

The urge for change

Just when society wants stability from its adult members, the urge for change is strongest. Middle age demands a fresh outlook on life, and the struggles involved in this can be complicated and taxing. Some people weather it with relative ease, while others experience a major mid-life crisis that can blow families apart. However, few are immune from the emotional upheavals involved. A comparison of the two sorts of 'menopause' should help clarify what's going on.

The so-called **male menopause** (an unfortunate name for it, because the *men* in menopause comes from *men*struation, which has nothing to do with men at all) is an important concept. There are actually two issues here. One is to do with hormonal changes (that have a bearing on a man's sex life) and the other is the all-too-familiar mid-life crisis. While the causes are different, there can be overlaps in symptoms which can make the whole situation hazy.

For men, a mid-life crisis is essentially a problem of psycho-social adjustment to major shifts in career, marriage and parenting that often occur in mid-life. The crisis occurs when these changes and disappointments are difficult to deal with. So somewhere between the late thirties and mid to late forties, many men become 'ratty'. At the very gateway to middle age they fall apart (relatively speaking); just when everything in life seems to be going well, they experience an illogical and consuming need for change, a vague and constant sense of frustration and failure.

A previously reasonable man may become irritable and short tempered, hypochondriacal and complaining, listless and morose. Or, he may become frenetically busy, drink too much (coffee, tea, alcohol, anything) and turn into a restless, nocturnal prowler. Or more seriously, he may start dressing young and trendy, stay out late 'keeping up with the boys' or going out with young floozies (in search of sexual adventure to bolster his flagging ego). Of course, what he most wants and needs is understanding and care, something he may feel unlikely to find at home.

Male menopause (perhaps better called andropause or male climacteric), on the other hand, is more specifically related to changes in a man's sexuality with advancing age. It is a distinct physiological phenomenon that has some parallels with the female menopause in terms of declining hormone levels. It has been found that even in healthy men, by the age of 55, the amount of testosterone secreted into the bloodstream is significantly less than it was 10 years earlier. Also with ageing (or with illness and stress), a relative increase in circulating oestrogen (which competes with testosterone for cellular receptor sites) can unfavourably tilt the testosterone–oestrogen balance and decrease the availability of testosterone to target cells.

The symptoms of male menopause are similar to the ones women experience and can sometimes be as overwhelming. However, the male menopause does not affect all men, at least not with the same intensity. Approximately 40 per cent of men between 40 and 60 will experience some degree of lethargy, depression, increased irritability, mood swings, hot flushes, insomnia, decreased libido, weakness, loss of both lean body mass and bone mass (making them susceptible to hip fractures) and difficulty in attaining and sustaining erections (impotence). Of course, nothing is ever this simple and there are many other causes for the general decline in libido and potency that occurs in a significant proportion of men in the population. These include excessive alcohol consumption, obesity, smoking, hypertension, prescription and non-prescription medications, poor diet, lack of exercise, poor circulation, and psychological problems, notably mid-life depression.

Apart from getting a thorough medical checkup (possibly including hormonal tests) and reviewing your life circumstances, the self-help approach could include: finding new ways to relieve stress; eating a nutritious, low-fat, high-fibre diet; getting plenty of sleep; exercising regularly; finding a supportive friend or group and talking to them about what you're going through; limiting your consumption of alcohol and caffeine; and drinking lots of water.

The **female menopause**, as everybody knows, is very much a hormonal phenomenon, usually occurring some time between the ages of 42 and 58. Menopause occurs when the ovaries stop releasing eggs and a woman has her last period. Sometimes this happens suddenly. Perimenopause refers to the gradual changes that lead into menopause, often a stop-start process that may take months or years.

Hormone levels fluctuate, causing changes just as they did during adolescence. The most distressing symptoms include hot flushes (waves of upper body heat that can last from 30 seconds to five minutes), sleep deprivation (from insomnia due to drenching night sweats), vaginal dryness (which can make intercourse very uncomfortable) and loss of libido. There are other symptoms that a woman might not even realise are related to menopause, for example fatigue, achy joints, having difficulty concentrating or recalling things, headaches, frequent urination, early wakening and mood changes. As with men, a woman's experiences during menopause may also be influenced by other life changes and all the uncertainties and pressures that come with mid-life. And increasing numbers of perimenopausal women also have young children to care for.

There are many therapies for the symptoms and conditions associated with menopause. However, lifestyle evaluation and advice (including nutrition, stress management, exercise, and giving up smoking and alcohol) remain the most important aspect of managing the menopause. Exercise is important – particularly aerobic, weight bearing, and stretching exercises – as is a diet high in fruits and vegetables and low in saturated fats. Many women try complementary therapies for treating menopausal symptoms. For example, natural remedies such as Remifemin have been shown to be effective for relief of some symptoms. There are vaginal lubricants for intercourse and moisturisers for skin dryness.

Other complementary therapies such as homeopathy and Chinese medicine (acupuncture and herbal treatments to harmonise a person's life energy) have varying results and are often expensive. Soy products such as soybeans, tofu, soymilk, and roasted soy nuts, which contain phytoestrogens (plant chemicals similar to oestrogen) have been shown to give about a 40 per cent improvement in symptoms, which is similar to the effect of a placebo.

Hormone replacement therapy (HRT) works for millions of women. As well as protecting against osteoporosis, hormone replacement therapy (HRT) is also helpful when hot flushes and sleep deprivation are getting out of hand, as well as other benefits. Hormone replacement therapy also:

- reduces dryness of skin and hair and vagina
- improves energy, mood, and sense of wellbeing
- may restore sexual desire
- may improve concentration and memory
- reduces the risk of Alzheimer's disease and the risk of colorectal cancer.

But the hormones used in HRT may pose risks as well as benefits. For example, it may cause vaginal bleeding, bloating, breast tenderness, nausea and headaches. The well-publicised Women's Health Initiative Study in 2002 showed a slight increase in breast cancer for women (average age 63) who were taking combined oestrogen and progesterone therapy. In this study there were 38 cases of breast cancer per 10,000 women taking HRT compared with 30 per 10,000 taking a placebo. This difference peaked at four years after taking the HRT and then declined, suggesting HRT was 'growth promoting' for the tumour rather than the cause. The study also confirmed a very small increase in cases of heart disease, stroke and clots in the veins. However, many of the women in the study were overweight, smoked or had high blood pressure, which may have predisposed them to these complications. The decision about HRT is therefore very individual and will rest on one's health and family history and a careful weighing up of the pros and cons with the help of a knowledgeable doctor.

There are a number of other treatments available for menopause including:

- Tibolone (Livial), which improves menopausal symptoms and maintains bone density but causes less breast tenderness than HRT.
- Venlafaxine, which is an antidepressant (selective serotonin release inhibitor) that also reduces hot flushes sometimes in low doses. (Antidepressants are also very helpful when moodiness and depression are predominant features of menopause.)
- Clonidine, which has been used for many years for hot flushes (but is often discontinued due to side effects, whereas Propranolol has a similar action and fewer side effects).

From a younger age, women can also experience feelings of uselessness and redundancy that are not hormone-related. They can have lots of self-doubts, aided and abetted by society's double standards about ageing, which says it's okay for men but not for women. Research clearly indicates that women who have developed interests outside the home and family (such as paid or volunteer work, study, hobbies, etc.) suffer less 'suburban neurosis' and generally fare better psychologically in middle age than those who don't. Of course, few would not welcome hearing, from time to time, that they still look attractive.

For both men and women, the essence of the mid-life crisis is grieving the loss of the possible. It requires you to graciously give up the idea that you will ever become a sex goddess, achieve fame and fortune as a trapeze artist or single-handedly change the world.

Differences in common

Large or small, people are people and, beyond the basics – food, clothing and shelter – we all crave and need certain things. We want to be understood and appreciated, cared for and loved, and acknowledged for our efforts and achievements. We seek variety, enjoyment and meaning in our lives. In as many ways as parents and teenagers are different, therefore, they are also alike. Having some insights into the various concerns that adolescents and middlescents somehow share, can help a lot if and when the going gets tough.

Changing bodies

They say middle age has arrived when someone tells you to pull in your stomach and you already have. One does tend to notice, by contrast, that teenagers are blessed with young, nubile bodies, all supple and firm. Any mother who's shared a bathroom with a 15-year-old daughter getting ready for a date will recognise the feelings involved – there's a fine line sometimes between admiration and resentment.

A couple of decades of living has to make some difference to a body, and the fact that most of the changes that come with middle age provide little cause for celebration is something we just have to deal with. Of course, adolescents are not necessarily revelling in their bodily changes either. As we've discussed, teenage concerns about these changes are many and varied, but to a 40-year-old parent who's starting to discover 'worn bearings and large patches of rust', this might not rate too highly at all.

Not tonight, I'm too tired

Seen through adult eyes, teenagers appear to have a powerful sexuality. And it's true, those in the throes of puberty do tend to find practically everything erotic. A young character in a popular TV sitcom said 'Even the lino makes me horny'. But while this is not always troubling in itself, grown-ups can feel troubled by it in a number of different ways:

- By feeling uncomfortable and anxious, which can lead to feeling the need to control or reject the adolescent. For example, fathers who feel threatened by their daughters' emerging sexuality (even though they may not be aware of this at a conscious level) may behave distantly or exert heavy authority concerning, say, modest dress and behaviour.
- By feeling aroused by teenagers, which is not all that unusual in itself (although acting on these feelings is wrong and dangerous for both parties).
- By feeling envious, because they seem to be having all the fun (going to parties and having the stamina to stay up late).
- By feeling disappointed and resentful, because you're not having any fun at all (stuck at home watching TV, possibly because they've got the car!).

Middle age can be tough from a sexual point of view. It is often a time of extremes. The stereotype of sexual decline is not entirely wrong. Work pressures, financial worries or any of the myriad concerns of everyday life may render sex simply a low priority. Performance can suffer and hormones also play a role in this. For example, stress and loneliness in males are known to lower testosterone levels and stimulate oestrogen production (the reverse happens when you're winning and on a high). The other side of the coin is a sudden resurgence of erotic fantasies and sexual energy. And it can have a snowballing effect – the more you get, the more you want! It's either feast or famine.

One of the problems many middle-aged couples face is a discrepancy in sexual interest. While it obviously matters, this is not entirely about how much sex they are having (or more likely, not having). Hearing that Australians say they are having sex on average 1.8 times a week is not helpful and can create guilt and resentment, especially in the partner who believes it. But there are other dangers too. The attraction between couples may simply wane and desire can fade. You may even wonder if you want to push on with your partner (who may be wondering the same). Those who successfully weather these troubling changes of mid-life can consider themselves extremely fortunate.

> I get the feeling my dad wishes he was back in 1974 when his life was free and easy – before we came along.
> Joshua, aged 16

Taking stock

For most people, the middle years are not too bad; for some, never better. By dint of hard work or good fortune, they will have achieved as much authority and standing as they are destined to achieve. Certainly, it is an appropriate time to take stock and, if one is spared the more drastic forms of restlessness we've described, you might find middlescence is quite a nice place to be. With the struggles and frenzy of earlier years behind you, you might now find it possible to enter more tranquil waters and enjoy the fruits of accomplishment and security.

Teenagers 'with tomorrow in their eyes' cannot relate easily to their parents' situation. They are caught up in school pressures and vocational anxieties. To them, the relative success and comfort that age apparently brings seem light years away. Parents are generally well imbued with the good old work ethic too, which can make it even more difficult for them to empathise with modern-day dilemmas facing the young, especially unemployment. These particular differences in status and circumstance are not easily bridged.

Did someone say 'independence'?

Independence is a nice idea, but probably a bit of a myth. Teenagers certainly want it, passionately, and in their struggle for it, parents can go quietly crazy. It's a tug of war about freedom, control and responsibility, all the things that kids seem to think grown-ups have. Meanwhile, parents may be discovering that they have a little more responsibility than they need. Middle-aged people largely run the country, manage the businesses and carry the various burdens related to community life. It doesn't always feel great.

If you're lucky, of course, your parents are still alive, self-supporting and supportive of you. Even so, there is often a distinct feeling in the middle years of being squeezed from both sides. (Ever wonder why kids get on so well with their grandparents? They have a common enemy.) So much for independence! Whatever one's age, our parents continue to exert a powerful influence over us. We may not always understand it, but chances are we do take it seriously.

Everybody has unresolved issues related to their parents; these can range from minor irritations about their attitudes and behaviour, to deep-seated emotional pain persisting from childhood. Coming to terms with these feelings is an important task of adulthood. Sometimes, as Harold H. Bloomfield points out in *Making Peace With Your Parents*, what you have to deal with is the 'internal conflict between you and the parents you carry inside your head'. While your children won't understand this now, they will later, when they experience these mid-life confrontations themselves.

Irrespective of our childhood experiences and how we've resolved them (or not), there's invariably everyday stuff to deal with now. Of course, some people have relatively little to do with their folks and are not necessarily troubled by this at all. For others, there are two main possibilities: either we're getting on well and enjoying mostly happy, respectful, relaxed and mutually helpful exchanges that are nice for everyone; or we're struggling to keep our cool with parental behaviour that we find infuriating (no need to spell out why).

What does it all mean?

Young people and their middlescent parents also have in common a search for meaning in their lives. Both are asking: 'What is it all about?' 'Where am I headed?' Middle-aged people are not doing this for the first time, but they are offered a golden opportunity to do it again. This new bout of self-questioning is a way to resolve certain leftover bits of adolescence that didn't get sorted out before. There is time also to reflect, even to get in touch with one's spiritual self. This can be an uncomfortable and unsettling process, however, and your canny kids will know how to prod it along. But chances are you'll come through it a better person (and possibly a little more mature).

In a sense, too, the rapid social and technological changes of the past 20 years or so, as well as general fears and uncertainties about the future of the planet, have brought the two generations closer together. For example, the necessity to become computer literate, and concerns about terrorism and global warming are shared by kids and parents alike. Young people may get churned up about what they view as a 'tarnished legacy', but most adults aren't too happy about it either.

The impossible dream

So, there we have it. Nature, society and the passage of time set us up. For young people, the world is their oyster and they are the future. For middlescent parents, the realisation dawns that certain goals and ambitions will never be achieved. They become aware that there is a limit to the length and quality of their lives, and they're not necessarily going to take it lying down. Teenagers don't have a clear picture of this. How could they? Nobody explains it to them. But they know something's going on and it can be extremely puzzling.

> **Consider some of the stranger things that some parents do in their middle years:**
>
> - To be successful, they spend all their time at work or sitting on committees (usually with people they can't stand).
> - To be healthy, they get heavily into vitamins and health tonics (even if they don't feel better, it's nice to be helping a struggling growth industry).
> - To be fit, they jog and pound inner-city streets (deeply inhaling toxic fumes and risking injury or death in the unfeeling traffic).
> - To be in touch with their inner selves, they embrace special therapies (for the scientifically inclined, biofeedback; for those who want to start all over again, primal therapy).
> - To be calm, and when all else fails, they get into alcohol or tranquillisers, which can get very out of hand.

The stiff upper lip

What about the brave souls who merely grin and bear it? Aren't grown-ups supposed to be rational and responsible at all times? No matter what's happening in their lives, aren't they expected to be strong, to cope, to have no problems, confusions or self-doubts? If this is what you think, read on – fast.

Middle-aged parents are notoriously reluctant to discuss their personal difficulties. They believe that adults should be able to solve their own problems. This stoic attitude not only doubles the burden, but it isn't too good for the kids either. It's really hard to relate to a stiff upper lip!

Teenagers need parents who are comfortable with themselves, who accept the ups and downs of life and who know what to do when life becomes really stressful and demanding. One of the most important goals for middle-aged parents is to reduce the empathy gap, to keep the lines of communication open so that mutual understanding can grow. This requires, first of all, that you give up being a closed book and, secondly, that you are able to put yourself in their shoes (to some extent, at least).

It's not what they say, it's how they say things. I hate clichés. I always hate it when people say one thing and mean another.

Habibi, aged 16

So open up a little

Children and adolescents love parents to talk about themselves. Have you ever noticed that? 'Tell us again, Dad. What other crazy things did you do when you were a child?'

There is nothing quite so humanising as self-revelation. This is different from wearing your heart on your sleeve. We're talking about a judicious sharing of one's thoughts, feelings and experiences – from funny little things that happen at work, to major, embarrassing gaffes. After all, this is who you are. Why keep it to yourself? It's part of keeping the lines of communication open.

An ability to do this makes it more likely that you will avail yourself of support when you need it and possibly also makes you more open to being supportive of the kids too. Given its amazing health promoting qualities, support is one of our most underrated therapies. It consists of anyone or anything that makes a person feel better, function better or be more optimistic. Often it's a matter of gaining a different perspective by talking things through or simply feeling understood and affirmed that give one a sense of being more in control. The most powerful sources of support open to an individual are one's intimate relationships with family or friends, teenage children included.

There are things you can do today to improve your own self-esteem (which also benefits everyone you know and love). Often this involves taking little steps in a variety of ways that immediately make a difference to how we feel and act. The following reflections by Ron Luyet, an international human relations consultant (Managing Director of BCon WSA International), provide a helpful guide to this process:

- **Tell your truth.** Let yourself and others know what your personal truth is.
- **Realise that you choose.** Eagerly accept responsibility for everything that is happening in your life. Know that only you can make yourself whole.
- **Seek deeper self-awareness.** Read, discuss, meditate, involve yourself in activity that aids your awareness of your old programs and deeper levels of meaning.

- **Respond emotionally.** Allow yourself to 'feel' yourself. And *have* your feelings rather than them having you or you numbing them out. Realise that all emotions are acceptable, but not all actions.
- **Give up blame and postpone judgement.** No one is guilty. Rather seek to understand what is happening and your part in it. Attempt to listen and clarify one another's viewpoint before defending, teaching, or making them wrong.
- Seek not to consciously hurt others.
- **Take time to envisage yourself as you want to be.** Create motivation from your future rather than be shoved through life by your past.
- **Consciously change your limiting beliefs.** Don't wait for experience to change it for you.
- **Assert yourself.** Be aware of your boundaries and stand up for yourself. Explore alternatives and give up being 'right' and 'winning'.
- Be as sincere and as vulnerable as possible.
- Be in touch with your body and its wisdom.
- Seek a higher meaning or purpose in your life.
- **Treat your growth, unfolding, and inner life with respect, excitement, and patience rather than judgement and fear.** Realise that darkness has much to teach and you need to reject nothing within your own being.
- **Give to give.** Give yourself away daily to the purpose, people, places, and things you love. Stop waiting for others to love first, to make it safe, accept you, agree with you. Start being who you want to be . . . today.
- **Laugh a little.** Some things are much too important to be taken seriously.

© Ron Luyet, BConWSA, 2000

Sometimes, of course, problems are such that more is required. What you need then is a good 'therapist', someone who's not only competent, but also empathic, warm, and seems genuinely interested in you. You can find a good therapist by asking around – your GP or local community health centre is usually a good place to start.

Take a nostalgic trip

The novelist L. P. Hartley said in *The Go Between*, 'The past is a foreign country, they do things differently there.' But memory is a wonderful thing, for it enables you to go back there. One important way of closing the empathy gap is to picture yourself as a teenager. What did you look like and what caused you embarrassment? Do you remember your first heavy date or your first sexual experience? As if anyone doesn't! What was it like? Who was your best friend and what did you do together? What was going on around you? What was most likely to cause arguments with your parents and what were the things they did that bugged you the most? What didn't you tell them? How did you get along at school and who was the teacher you hated most? What was very important to you at the time and what were your dreams for the future?

This is terrific fun to do in a group, particularly if you all went through it in the same decade. Be prepared for a lot of laughter, but the memories might be bittersweet (or even a touch painful). That is, after all, what adolescence is like too.

Some final thoughts

David: Bad jokes about middle age are pretty common, but for many men and women, being there is no laughing matter. Some people buckle under and seem to devote all their waning energies to accelerating downwards. Others (the majority hopefully) seem to cope well, hold onto their idealism, revel in second chances and face the future with optimism. Meanwhile, of course, your kids are going through their own upheavals and will benefit from you being just a little less confused than they are.

Leanne: There is nothing easy about being a middlescent. The 'differences in common' that we come to share with our teenage offspring – issues related to our changing bodies, changing sexuality, changing self-concept and changing responsibilities – can at times be overwhelming. Fortunately it is possible to choose not to be overwhelmed, to work many things out and, if necessary, seek support from others. Even as mature adults, our self-esteem is fragile and needs to be nurtured and protected. Doing so improves our ability to be in a relationship (the topic we focus on in the next chapter).

David: I've been thinking about my changing body shape. As a young man, even as a newlywed in my mid-twenties, I continued to believe that it was important to build up my muscles. I worked at home with a contraption called a 'bullworker', which was supposed to strengthen one's arms and chest. Well, it didn't work then and it certainly doesn't seem to matter now. Do you have a personal comment on enjoying midlife (or not!)?

Leanne: About five years ago I worked as a doctor at a menopause and women's clinic in Geelong, Victoria. The patients were women in their mid-forties and fifties and most cried about the same problems – distant partners and ungrateful, unruly teenage children. After the session I would change from my suit and heels into jeans and a T-shirt and walk two blocks to the adolescent health clinic where I would work for the afternoon. There I saw 'ungrateful, unruly' teenagers who complained their parents did not listen or understand. It struck me how society sets women up to fail. Some of the expectations teenagers feel are listed on page 26. Many women in their forties and fifties tell me they are expected to:

- Balance family (including extended family), home and work and never say 'no'.
- Do most of the parenting and home duties.
- Always respond to the sexual needs of their partners.
- Live with the hot flushes, heavy periods and fatigue of menopause as it is natural.
- Be an interesting person.

This work has led me to look for more meaning, balance and enjoyment in my own life. One of the aspects I enjoy is my work with the Royal Flying Doctor Service, flying out to remote areas to provide women's health clinics. Years of struggle on the land are character building and I delight in meeting women who regard the next stage of their lives as a challenge rather than a downhill slide. Their resilience is inspiring and I have learnt a great deal about generosity of spirit and enjoying the simple pleasures of life (such as nude rain dances in the desert).

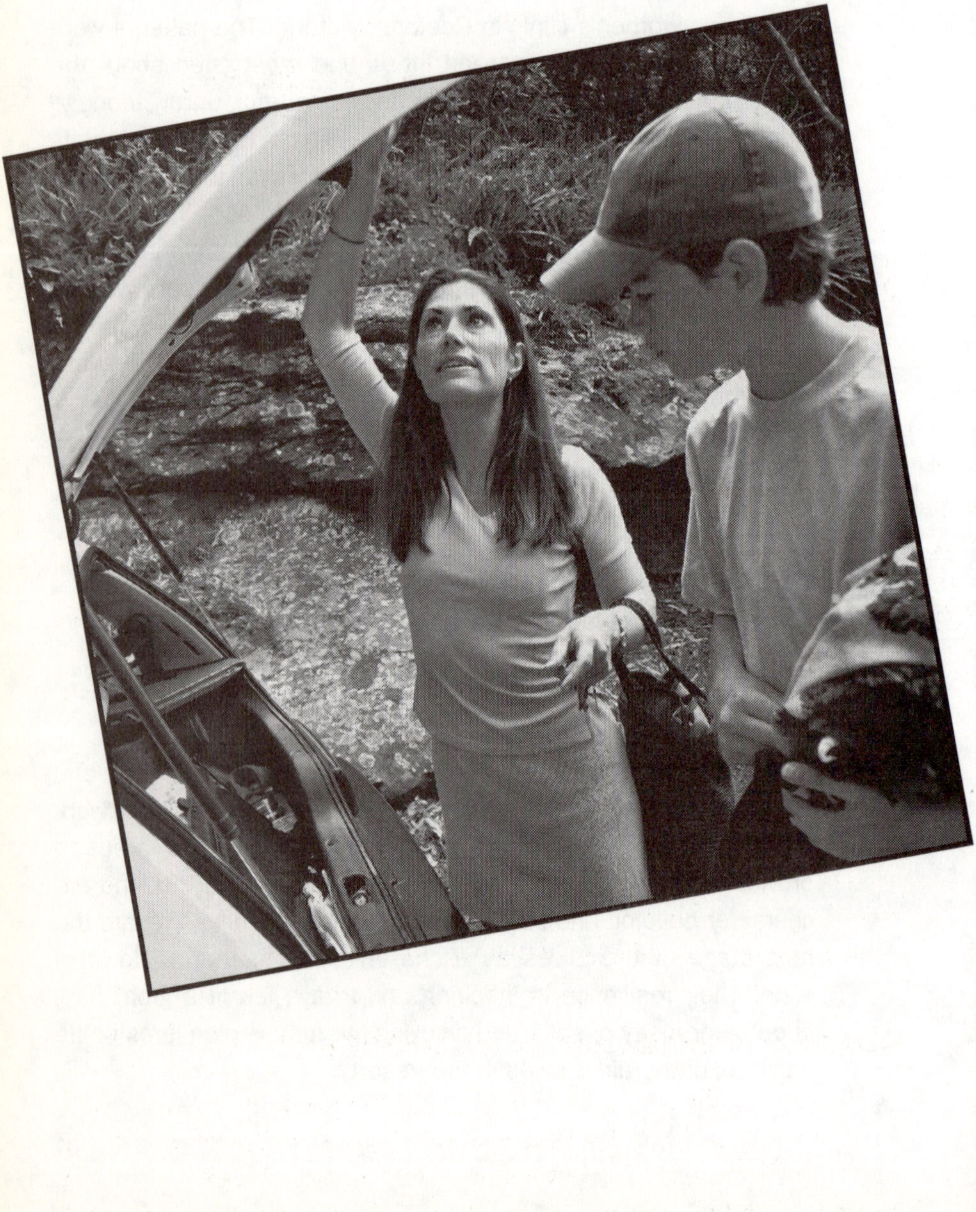

Chapter 9

The importance of parents

How can family, friends and teachers support me? Just by asking: 'What can I do to support you?' rather than assuming or pressuring.
Tom, aged 17

All teenagers have a fundamental yearning for belonging and connectedness with other young people and adults. Not surprisingly, they need to feel valued for who they are, not for what they do. Young people have complex and secret inner worlds. As they develop through adolescence they are quietly asking: 'Am I normal?' 'Who am I?' 'Where am I going?'

Different questions arise in relation to others: 'Do my parents understand me?' 'Why are we not getting along together?' 'Is my family going to be all right?'

These ideas will be explored throughout the rest of Section 2. In this chapter, we focus on achieving connectedness in your immediate family – mum, dad and the individual young person.

Connectedness to parents

Teenagers' resilience is promoted and enhanced by feeling cared for and connected. They develop self-esteem by participating and contributing. Unfortunately, our secular Western culture promotes individualism, materialism, competition and stressful lifestyles which can work against these important developmental goals. Young people with a history of family breakdown, unhappiness at school or dropping-out, unemployment, homelessness and isolation or chronic illness, are at particular risk because their ability to bounce back from adversity is weakened. The challenge is to promote connectedness with family, school and community, to alleviate the risk of losing hope and self-esteem.

Here is what young people say about this risk:

Half the people I know say one thing and mean another. It's important not to judge people purely based on the first impression. Little things can set you off – you feel unworthy, no one cares or pays attention to you.

I think that the media – TV, newspapers and the Internet – play a big part in helping kids grow up thinking the world revolves around the terrorism, explosions, corruption and the evil that they see every day. Kids have their own personal heartache – rejection from parents who are too busy with their careers, yearning for money, or keeping marriages together, too busy to notice the desperation in their children's eyes. Schools are too busy and worried about their reputations to help and counsel troubled students, which leaves them vulnerable to vultures on the street. And abuse. Everyone is angry about the state of the world and this leads to abuse in one form or another.

These deeply felt thoughts and fears are rarely shared with parents. Parents need to take time to have meaningful conversations with their teenagers about personal, local, national and world issues. Home should be a sanctuary.

Early childhood is the foundation. Neuro-scientific research has provided powerful new evidence about the importance of the early years of development, from conception to age six, as a base for learning, competence and coping skills throughout life. For example, it is no longer conjecture (as obvious as it might seem) that children's development and behaviour are greatly influenced by the nurturing that parents provide in those early years. It appears that particular parts of the brain need positive stimulation to develop properly, while lack of appropriate stimulation, loss or neglect prevent this happening, with significant and sustained negative effects. The following poem says it all:

Many things we need can wait, the child cannot.
Now is the time his bones are being formed,
His blood is being made,
His mind is being developed.
To him we cannot say tomorrow,
His name is today.

Gabriela Mistral
(Chilean Nobel Laureate 1889–1957)

Similarly, many studies confirm what we know intuitively about teenagers. They develop resilience and self-esteem by experiencing at least one caring relationship, positive expectations, and opportunities for participation and contribution. And their name is today.

Sadly, in a growing number of cases, life is far from ideal and many young people do not experience even one caring adult relationship or any opportunity to participate in ways that are meaningful to them. Not surprisingly, young people are at risk when their families experience divorce (which occurs in over 40 per cent of first marriages and over 50 per cent of second marriages), loss, poor support from extended families, mental and physical illness or financial and work pressures. Yet even when life for young people seems easy, their inner worlds may be turbulent because the outside world is in turmoil. Here is another example:

I was really happy in primary school. I look at old photographs of me as a baby and family holidays and you could not get a better family. My parents are fantastic. I know they love me and only want what's best for me. But now I am in Year 9, I worry about all these things. My friends' parents are splitting up, a girl in my class has got cancer, genocide, animal testing, the environment and terrorism. On a lot of days, I feel empty and don't even know what I feel. I get really moody.

Some teenagers react to their problems by quietly isolating themselves rather than behaving badly. Whatever the reaction, listening to their thoughts and concerns often helps us understand the cause. Sometimes this takes time and parents need to be patient.

But during difficult times, how do we as parents remain resilient? How do we create sanctuary in our homes and keep our families connected?

Marriage and partnership

Teenagers bring a whole new dimension into your life. Having survived as a couple for so long is no mean feat in itself, and just when you are getting out the champagne glasses, here comes a potentially testing (although not necessarily awful) time. However, it's important to remember that the state of your marriage or partnership (any long-term committed relationship, not only those who are legally married) also has an enormous impact on your children. Good, bad or indifferent, your children know what's going on and react to it. The state of the marriage largely determines the climate in the home, how secure and well loved kids feel, and whether or not it's something they might consider for themselves in the future. And when partnerships don't make it, that takes its toll too. People who are separated or divorced don't stop being parents.

Keeping it afloat

First of all, don't be put off by young people's attitudes today. Things have changed. Although most teenagers still admit to a desire to marry one day, enthusiasm has waned somewhat. Thirty years ago, surveys showed that nearly 80 per cent of students intended to marry. Today that figure would probably be less than 50 per cent. As well, there is no longer a sense of urgency about it. All in good time, they say.

Chances are, too, that young people are simply not inspired by what they see. Even when you think you're doing okay, teenagers may perceive your partnership as humdrum or perfunctory. You've spent many years nurturing a relationship that seems reasonably stable, caring and supportive, and they see it as boring or stultifying. Little do they know how much hard work, persistence and goodwill may have gone into keeping it afloat (and boring).

Of course, we can thank the 'baby boomers' (the huge generation born between 1946 and 1964) for setting the trends with marriage. As well as being part of the 'free love' movement, they made divorce mainstream, mostly married early and had their children young. They pioneered living together before marriage, brought homosexuality out of the closet and spawned women's liberation. However, despite their reputation as marriage-breakers and philanderers, it is anticipated that baby boomers will enjoy the longest marriages in history and there will be more elderly couples around than ever before. Clearly, if you can make it into old age, still together, you're there for love.

Another interesting fact is that Australian researchers now say those who live together first are just as likely to have enduring marriages, and that cohabiters are no less content than married couples.

How does it all work out?
The *Housekeeping Monthly* of 13 May 1955 provides an historic insight into this question. The following marriage tips come from an article entitled 'The Good Wife's Guide' and we might be hunted down and shot for dredging it up:

- Have dinner ready. Plan ahead, even the night before, to have a delicious meal ready, on time for his return. This is a way of letting him know that you have been thinking of him and are concerned about his needs . . .
- Prepare yourself. Take 15 minutes to rest so you'll be refreshed when he arrives. Touch up your makeup, put a ribbon in your hair and be fresh-looking. He has just been with a lot of work-weary people.
- Be a little gay and a little more interesting for him. His boring day may need a lift and one of your duties is to provide it.
- Clear away the clutter. Make one last trip through the main part of the house just before your husband arrives.
- Be happy to see him; greet him with a warm smile and show sincerity in your desire to please him.
- Make him comfortable. Have him lean back in a comfortable chair or have him lie down in the bedroom. Have a cool or warm drink ready for him.
- Arrange his pillow and offer to take off his shoes. Speak in a low, soothing and pleasant voice.

If this were to happen in the average home today, the average husband would call for the mental health team to come and take his wife away. It's fun to think back to bygone times but, thank God, male–female relationships work a lot differently now.

The success or otherwise of a marriage or partnership is influenced by many things, not the least of which is why people got together in the first place. Experience teaches that, as a basis for an enduring partnership, the following do not rate too highly:

- Romantic love – it feels great at the time, but the rosy glow wears off fast.
- A neurotic need – disappointing because it soon becomes obvious that someone else cannot solve your personal problems.
- Extenuating circumstances – the 'shotgun' wedding of yesteryear (much less popular now).

Take two highly complex individuals, each moulded by a unique upbringing and life experience, each with a full set of personal needs and expectations, and ask them to chant with sincerity 'till death us do part'. They are somehow supposed to mesh together and make a go of it. How does it ever work out? Where is the training one needs for such a difficult job? How can it sometimes last for so long?

Of course, two people may have clung together over the years because they were too anxious to do anything else, or too tired, or 'too stuck'. But it is more likely that they had something going for them in the first place. They probably knew each other reasonably well, perceived each other without too much distortion of reality and felt sort of 'right' about it from the start. In an atmosphere of mutual goodwill, they also probably worked at the relationship – success certainly requires that.

At this point, let's clarify the question of whether men or women are happier in or out of marriage. It has long been thought (based on a famous early 1970s American study) that marriage enhanced men's mental health but could drive women crazy. Australian research now disputes this, showing that both sexes are okay inside marriage, with similar (and low) rates of mental health problems (with women being more vulnerable to depression and mood disorders; men to alcohol and drug disorders). The good news (depending on where you're situated) is that both married men and women have better mental health than the divorced, separated and never-married.

Never plain sailing

Making it to the middle years is certainly commendable. Consider some of the rough spots that one has weathered along the way: the initial adjustment to intimate living; the dreadful first year; the maintenance of relationships with each other's families; the birth of the first child; the toddlerhood of the first child and the birth of the second child, the chickenpox and head lice . . .

As you can see, the list is grossly inadequate, but the point is clear.

People soon figure out that life is not about candlelit dinners and romantic strolls at dusk (well, not often anyway). This important relationship is actually conducted against a background of trivia, a kaleidoscope of mundane events and pressures such as bills, repairs, shopping, appointments and household chores. By middle age, in fact, wedding anniversaries are celebrated with either growing wonder or growing dismay. Friends you haven't seen for a while greet you with mock admiration, 'Good heavens, still together!' And they'll want to know the secret of your success.

Is there a secret of success?

Who knows? Maybe you like each other. One thing is certain, it hasn't been easy. There is no such thing as a perfectly harmonious relationship; this is, in fact, a contradiction in terms. Henry Kissinger once remarked that 'No one will ever win the battle of the sexes; there's too much fraternising with the enemy'. And Erica Jong said: 'Men and women, women and men. It will never work.' But according to clever analysts of human behaviour, a successful marriage or partnership is definitely achievable, at least when it incorporates the following basic elements, the so-called 'Four Cs':

- **Conflict:** This is a normal and necessary component of any relationship, but one requiring skill and goodwill to reach constructive solutions. Compromises are required.
- **Communication:** Saying what you feel will not always solve problems, but it's a good place to start (few people have sufficient psychic powers to read minds). Often it's how you say what you feel that's important.
- **Change:** It's unsettling and unavoidable, but a sign of life. Flexibility, tolerance and sensitivity to a partner's changing needs are necessary, and couples need to regularly monitor progress in the relationship and make adjustments along the way.
- **Commitment:** Ah, an old-fashioned concept embodying such chestnuts as mutual care, respect, concern and loyalty, and a belief in 'coupledom'.

Happy couples around the world are the ones who put their relationship first. They have a strong sense of being a couple, while retaining their own individual identities. They look after each other

> *My parents argue all the time. I get really scared that they will split up.*
> *Larissa, aged 15*

and are willing to give more than they receive. They are 'the president of each other's fan club'. There is also a place in a good marriage for mirth and merriment (being able to laugh with one another plays a big part in staying together), for sharing responsibilities, for talking through plans, aspirations and troubles (which means setting aside 'couple-time'), for affection and love and, of course, for sticking it out through the bad times. None of this is easy. But in this situation it's far more likely that the kids will feel more connected to their well-connected parents, and we know that's a good thing.

What about now?

Marriages can get into difficulty during the middle years. Spouses may have matured at different rates, couples may gradually grow apart, or the marriage may become the focus of dissatisfaction as part of a mid-life crisis. Powerful psychosocial forces can also contribute to different connubial behaviour and personal discontent in the relationship. For example, changing sex roles, work roles or the allure of a companionship marriage, in which equality is the key, can upset the balance, particularly in more traditional marriages.

As already noted, this is often the time, too, when children are turning into teenagers. If the normal, inescapable rigours of everyday life leave you emotionally drained and exhausted, bad luck, because living in close quarters with teenagers brings new stresses and strains. These take many forms, but at the very least, there will be:

- More encroachment on your private time – they stay up later at night and need to be taken places at weekends.
- More demands on your energy and resources – physical, emotional and financial.
- More conflicts over behaviour and rules (although 'authoritative parents' will know how best to handle these).

Your marriage is affecting the kids

Who knows what goes on behind closed doors? From the outside, it's impossible to tell what other people's marriages are like, and we should be cautious about making assumptions. A picture of joy and light might be a charade. The couple who bicker in public might actually have a very solid relationship.

Likewise, nobody can rate your marriage either. Only you know whether it's 'dawn to dusk ecstasy' or 'sheer bloody murder'. Chances are, however, that it falls somewhere in between these extremes, probably in one or other of two major categories: not too bad or not too good. The distinction is an important one to make, because, for better or for worse, young lives are being affected.

Not too bad: Many married couples at this stage of life will describe a relationship that's reasonable. There's a discernible amount of affection, understanding, mutual appreciation and companionship. The individuals concerned are able to feel okay about themselves and have enough emotional energy to devote to their parenting tasks. This situation isn't bliss, far from it, but it provides a stable enough base from which family members can get on with their lives.

Not too good: This kind of relationship is characterised by ongoing conflict, lack of communication and withdrawal. But even if things are not quite that bad, if the ingredients that go into making a reasonable marriage are missing, and there is little or no emotional support, feelings of poor self-worth and bitterness are likely to flourish. Most importantly, parental energies are spent on coping with a difficult situation, rather than on nurturing the kids. A poor or deteriorating relationship is also imbued with sadness and there's really no way to hide it.

They know what's going on

No matter what's happening on the surface, children know when something's not quite right. More than we realise, they worry about their parents, about their health, their happiness and, increasingly, the state of their partnership. They sense what family therapists know too well, that the parental relationship is pivotal to the functioning of the family. Inevitably, this affects them in an intense and personal way.

An unhappy home life is an enormous burden for children of any age. It is sadly reflected in their behaviour, their school work, their relationships and their general state of mind. Parents may resent being unreasonably blamed for all sorts of things

I get really moody and sometimes I feel my parents don't understand me any more.
Kylie, aged 16

to do with their kids, but there is no ducking this one. Even though it's probably nobody's fault, the consequences can be serious and far reaching, especially for teenagers, who may become seriously depressed or dramatically display their feelings.

It's no fun living in a home that's tense, uncomfortable and humourless, worse still if it's downright dangerous. Children and young adolescents of violent relationships are particularly at risk. They can become fearful, anxious and withdrawn, develop nightmares, bedwetting or other stress-related symptoms, or become aggressive towards others. Even when things are less dramatic, life's not great. Teenagers soak up vibes like a sponge, and when the vibes are bad, it's like taking poison. It saps your energy and troubles your mind. But a surprising number of such kids suffer in silence, dreaming of happier places and longing for better times. What they most need and want, however, is a sense of connectedness to family. This becomes rather difficult under endlessly trying circumstances.

Sometimes, things can improve. Maybe mum and dad get their act together somehow, and push on a little more hopefully. On the other hand, sometimes it really is better for all concerned if they cut their losses and end it.

Calling it quits

About 50,000 children a year in Australia see the formal end of their parents' marriage. The implications of over 40 per cent of marriages ending in separation or divorce are complex and, for those involved, the outcomes uncertain. People outside the situation cannot always appreciate the traumas of an unworkable and destructive marriage and the relief and freedom that separation can bring.

Alternatively, sometimes people plummet headlong from an unsuccessful marriage into an unsuccessful divorce. Some people remain neurotically tied to each other even after they separate, and the conflict continues indefinitely. Others embark upon divorce politely, in mutual agreement that this is for the best (although occasionally without properly thinking things through), and end up in a vicious circle of bitterness and strife. But even when a marriage has been awful and calling it quits is welcomed, there is still a lot to come to terms with.

In the midst of these distressing games that grown-ups play, whatever the reasons, the major losers are the kids. For them, a disintegrating family causes a special sort of bereavement. Feelings of sadness, anger, fear, guilt and disappointment are to be expected, although teenagers often express these less openly than adults. Adjustment is most difficult, and suffering most prolonged, however, when there is ongoing strife and conflict. Even then, there is a fervent hope that parents will be reunited. Getting caught up in parental battles, being used in 'play-offs', shunted from place to place like unhappy packages and being forced to make impossible choices are incredibly hard to handle.

Parents can lessen the pain of separation and divorce by:

- Not being afraid to ask for counselling or guidance for the family.
- Seeking similar help for themselves when they need it. Self-defeating guilt and other feelings can be pretty intractable.
- Creating an open climate of communication in the home. Being allowed to speak about what's happening and how they feel is possibly the greatest gift a child or adolescent could receive at this time.
- Allowing them to relate lovingly to the 'missing parent' – even if this means biting one's lip and declaring a truce.
- Separating problems with your partner from problems as parents. It is possible (but not necessarily easy) to work on and resolve parenting issues, and avoid dividing the kids' loyalties. Although parents may not be together, and may have ongoing problems in their own relationship, they are still parents and always will be. Perhaps the most caring act you can do for your kids, if you have separated, is to make the decision to share the responsibility of parenting together.

There's no doubt that divorce puts children at risk. Studies in different countries and over different decades consistently highlight the vulnerability of children of divorced parents compared to children whose parents stay together, at least in the short term. They face about double the risk of problems, such as learning difficulties, early sexual experiences, depression, substance abuse and juvenile delinquency. This is not a simple cause-and-effect scenario. How children turn out is related to a host of factors such as the quality of parenting they receive, parental education levels, parental mental health, social isolation and poverty.

Despite the added risks, most children prove to be incredibly resilient and emerge unscathed. In other words, the vast majority of kids from divorced families (four out of five) do fine, with no long-term damage. They grow into adults with no greater problems than anyone else, establish careers, form intimate relationships and build meaningful lives. Ideally though, considering our high divorce rate and the effect this has on children, all parents need to take steps to nurture their relationships with partners. For those who are divorced there is a life beyond and an ongoing need to stay connected to loved ones, old and new.

Some final thoughts

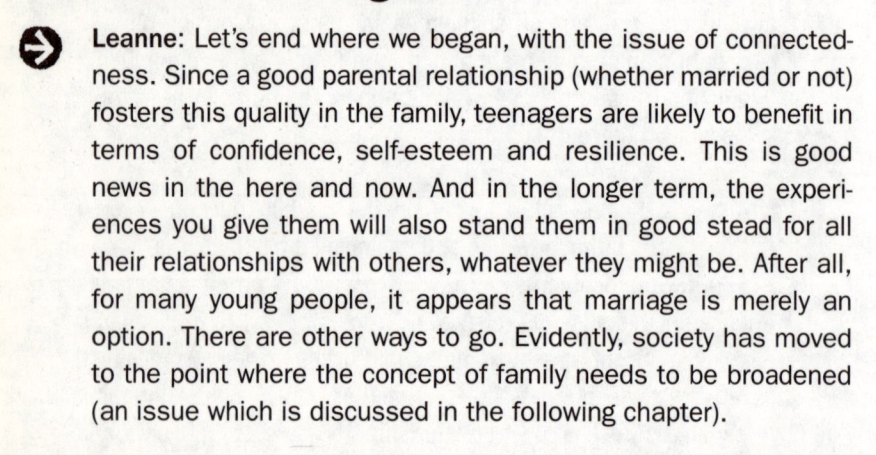

Leanne: Let's end where we began, with the issue of connectedness. Since a good parental relationship (whether married or not) fosters this quality in the family, teenagers are likely to benefit in terms of confidence, self-esteem and resilience. This is good news in the here and now. And in the longer term, the experiences you give them will also stand them in good stead for all their relationships with others, whatever they might be. After all, for many young people, it appears that marriage is merely an option. There are other ways to go. Evidently, society has moved to the point where the concept of family needs to be broadened (an issue which is discussed in the following chapter).

David: I like what Eleanor Berman, author of *The New-Fashioned Parent*, says about marriage:

No one has yet devised a better way to serve our fundamental human needs for emotional security, the preparation of children for responsible adulthood and a framework that gives meaning and happiness to life.

Leanne: I agree, but it doesn't always serve our need. Many teenagers worry about their parents' marriages. Despite their cool exteriors, their underlying fears may interfere with other areas of their lives. One boy who was refusing to go to school said this:

My friend's parents split up suddenly. I stayed at their house one night and everything seemed great. Then in the next few weeks they split up. They must have been pretending. Now I wonder if my parents are pretending and when they are in a bad mood I get really worried that they are going to tell me they are getting a divorce. I can't ask them whether they are going to split up. It would be horrible if they said yes.

David: Tony was 15 when he first came to see me, unhappy about the size of his nose, his lack of friends at school and the difficulty he was having concentrating on his studies. During one of our talks, he described his parents' marriage as loveless and his home life as barren. He said, 'We all just do our own thing. We're not connected to each other at all.' Tony also felt that no one understood him, and he viewed the situation as unfixable. His disappointment and sadness were touching all areas of his life. If a teenager is having problems it is important for parents to be courageous enough to examine what is happening in all areas of family life including the marriage or partnership. And whatever our circumstances, our relationships must be respectful and nurturing.

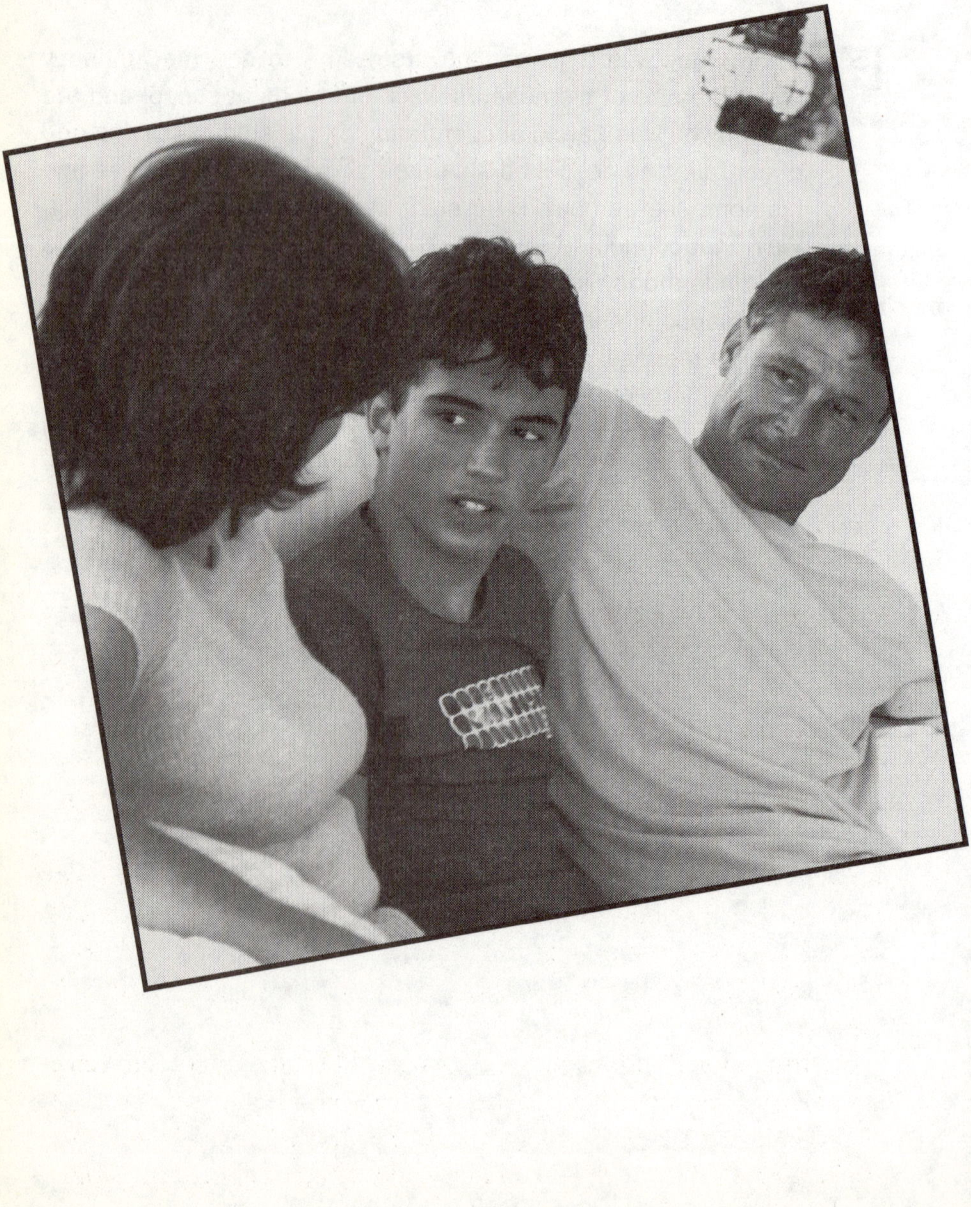

Chapter 10

Families getting on together

> *My dad doesn't even have to say anything for me to feel his pressure and his too-high expectations.*
> *Luke, aged 19*

The family, somewhat under siege but still the cornerstone of society, has a powerful and enduring influence on people's lives. For most children, it is the centre of their operations and it is very, very important. It has been said that what is most needed in the modern home is the family. This sounds good, and raises some important questions. For example, what is a family these days?

Everybody knows that families come in all shapes and sizes; that they are special groups of people who develop unique styles of relating and coping, of showing affection and expressing outrage. How they do this, however, and where teenagers fit into the scheme of things, also bear looking at. Show us a household where the kids don't get on their parents' nerves, and where the opposite doesn't equally apply!

Getting along with each other is what life's mainly about. Since parents and teenagers have their own needs and rights, some sort of workable balance has to be arrived at. For most of us, whatever we do in the outside world, and whatever the setup at home, the people we live with are the ones we need to relate to and cope with.

Different families and relationships

There's no such thing as 'the family'. Only about five in every 100 families would fit the TV image of two parents and two children, one of each sex, with the father in paid employment, and mum looking after the home.

A family has been described as 'a group of people irrationally committed to one another's wellbeing'. Would that this were always the case, but it's certainly the general idea. Depending on the person, the context and the culture, family has many meanings. The sociologist thinks of it as a social group or construct; the psychologist imagines a fount from which the personality flows; the politician talks about the family in an idealised way, using it to represent traditional values. Inspirational author Thomas Moore in his book *Care of the Soul* gives this insight:

> . . . we all know the family in its particulars. This is the nest in which the soul is born, nurtured and released into life. It has an elaborate history and ancestry and a network of unpredictable personalities – grandparents, uncles, aunts, cousins. Its stories tell of happy times and tragedies. It has moments of pride and skeletons in its closets. It has its professed values and its carefully constructed image, as well as its secret transgressions and follies.

As an Aborigine, family means more to me than just having a mum and dad. I've got aunties and cousins who are always there and who I can turn to. Some of them aren't even directly related to me.
Allira, aged 14

A family is much more than a collection of individuals who call themselves a family. Whatever is happening to any member of a family system affects everyone else. Within this group of intimates with a history and a future, the key issue is the quality of relationships between family members and the sense of belonging that these relationships provide. The family is the first emotional and social support we experience, our first teacher, our first health care provider. A family also exists over decades and its effects are powerful and enduring. The World Health Organisation considers the family 'at the very heart of human growth and development'.

And such is the rich tapestry of life that families

range from the usual or the ordinary to the interesting and bizarre. (Let's give up on the idea of 'normal' right here.) One of the important factors in this regard is the amazing cultural diversity that defines our nation and, with it, a kaleidoscope of family types. There are a number of readily indentifiable family groupings that will serve as a basis for discussion.

The traditional family

Families have become smaller. Approximately one in three Australian children is an only child, and just over half have no sibling of the opposite sex. There's room to swing a cat, of course, but fewer people per household to turn to for solace.

The nuclear family has been described as 'society's act of violence against itself'. Isolated, struggling and stressed, and much too mobile for the good of children, it often falls far short of the ideal it has been portrayed to be. When community supports are lacking (or seem hard to get at) and relatives are few and far between, 'nuclear' parents bear the full weight of parenthood on their sagging shoulders. And when teenagers are being difficult, it can feel an especially heavy load to bear. Nevertheless, many parents cope reasonably well with this arrangement, work hard, raise their kids and rarely give a thought to the alternatives. It's probably the only sort of family they've known.

The single-parent family

What about when there's only one set of shoulders at home? Consider this: one in every four parents will at some time be a single parent.

A single-parent household comes about when a parent has never married (about 10 per cent), a spouse dies (around 15 per cent) or a married couple split up (more or less the rest). How well or badly things work out will depend upon the nature and circumstances of the single-parenthood, the emotional stability of the parent, and the quality of family and community supports. If the other parent is still around, that is, not dead or out of town, the relationship of the ex-spouses and how the kids fit into this are the most crucial factors.

Regardless of how it comes about, adolescents are devastated by a loss of this magnitude, and the early stages in particular are likely to be terrible. They can be aggressive and lash out or become sullen and withdrawn. This can be very difficult to handle for the suddenly single person who, one way or another, already has a lot to contend with.

> *My parents just say, 'Grow up, get over it.' They don't trust me and don't respect my feelings.*
> *Ian, aged 14*

For one thing, personal grief can consume virtually all one's resources.

In the case of divorce, the exhausting legal merry-go-round can add immeasurably to the drama and strife. The custodial parent (usually the mother) is often faced with financial difficulties, a lack of practical assistance and little moral support. Things are not necessarily very good for the non-custodial parent either. If it's the father (which it usually is), he is two to three times as likely as his married counterpart to need treatment for mental health problems. From his children's point of view, the most important thing he can do is to keep telling them he loves them. They will want to hear this. After all, even if he's not living with them, he is still their parent.

For teenagers of divorced or separated parents, there are often divided loyalties, and they can become extremely skilled at playing parents off against each other. Sometimes, through difficult behaviour or symptoms of illness, kids are expressing a sad and desperate hope for reconciliation. They think, 'Maybe, if I'm enough of a problem, they'll have to get back together again to sort it out.' Of course, it rarely works out that way.

A teenager in a single-parent home (or a younger child, for that matter) may become 'parentified' and take on the role of the missing parent. Having too much responsibility can speed up adolescence and rob such young people of the opportunity to enjoy these years. They are unable to develop more gradually, as was intended, or sometimes even to take part in normal teenage activities or experimentation. This does not always have serious consequences, although, as noted in the previous chapter, children who are affected this way do appear more prone to depression and other problems.

The evidence suggests that it can take up to five years or more after separation for the dust to settle. Eventually, as the necessary adjustments are made, life can get, more or less, back to normal – whatever that is. Without doubt, a parent raising children or teenagers alone can be extremely effective, cope with the extra demands, and allow the kids to be kids. Especially where there are other adults providing support, the family is able to push on, diminished but undaunted.

The blended family

When people remarry and take children with them, things can get pretty complicated. As one teenager explained with a resigned air, 'I've got one proper brother, two stepsisters and there's a half a something else on the way.' When it comes to figuring out uncles, aunts and cousins in a blended family, most people give up.

If you're thinking of getting into this situation, stop watching television immediately. Those ghastly, sickly sweet family situation comedies will have you feeling inferior in no time. They model love, harmony and joy and the successful resolution of all crises. Real life isn't like that.

Let's take one step back, to before the 'deed' is done. Teenagers get used to the way things are in a single-parent household. When all is going well, they know their place and pull their weight. So one can forgive them for being less than thrilled when a parent's lover comes on the scene and great upheavals are set in train. When there is a succession of part-time lovers things can be even more confusing.

In one troubled family, a woman underwent a complete personality change after divorce. Having been an excessively devoted and self-sacrificing type of mother to her four children, she eventually broke away from what was, for her, an unsatisfactory marriage. Suddenly free and head over heels in love with somebody new, she became a star-struck kid, totally besotted by her gallant lover. A frenzied courtship left the kids, for the first time in their lives, often in the hands of somebody new. The change in their mother's behaviour and attitude, let alone the marriage that soon followed, left the kids completely bewildered.

On the adult side, new step-parents don't have it easy at all. They want to make inroads with the children they haven't fathered (or mothered), but this can be a slow process. There's the possibility that they've gone into a second marriage without having completely worked through the difficulties related to the one that's failed, and often have unrealistic notions about how wonderful things are going to be now. It takes time for children to accept and trust a new parent figure (especially if emotional traumas are fresh), and teenagers can make life very awkward indeed.

It's also normal to feel protective towards one's own children (or guilty about doing things with your new spouse's offspring when yours live elsewhere). Petty jealousies and resentments are pretty usual. Blended families can work out extremely well, but most often some difficulties and compromises simply have to be lived with.

> **Teenage reactions to parents' new relationships:**
>
> ▶ For most teenagers, the new situation is likely to provoke a new bout of grief because it puts an end, once and for all, to any remaining hope of reconciliation for their parents.
> ▶ For a teenage girl, coping with the reality of a mother's re-awakened sexuality can be difficult, and occasionally leads to sexually provocative behaviour (for example, she may compete with her mother for the attention of her new partner). And for a boy it can make him jealous and protective.
> ▶ For older adolescents in particular, there may be a change of role to adjust to. Having been the special male or special female in the family, someone has arrived to take his or her place, and this can lead to competitive behaviour and resentment.
> ▶ Many teenagers voice their resentment of the new partner and desire to oust him or her from the house. Some kids might go to extreme lengths to get rid of a new partner.

The extended family

Families can be extended in all sorts of ways. Grandma or Uncle Fred can come along and stay indefinitely, perhaps because of old age, illness or becoming widowed. Maybe you and your family move in with a relative while you're saving for or refurbishing your own home.

The image that comes most readily to mind, of course, is of three or more generations of people, all living together in glorious peace and supportive harmony. Part of the myth surrounding extended families, and the reason that people in nuclear families think they're missing out on something, is the idea that 'the others' (meaning, not the biological parents) will help discipline and care for the kids. The notion of sharing these roles and responsibilities is attractive, is it not? Perhaps, at times, it really does work out just like that, but often it doesn't.

One does hear of tensions, intrusions and strife. A lot depends on how the family came to be extended and the degree to which roles and expectations have been clearly sorted out. If elderly grandparents (or other relatives) know that they make an important contribution by their willingness to baby-sit, for example, but otherwise are not expected to behave like a parent, well and good. The alternative, where nobody knows who's supposed to be doing what, can get pretty messy.

The grown-ups involved must also be able to relate to one another in a mature way, adult to adult, acknowledging and resolving difficulties as they arise, and accepting compromise. It's when teenagers see their parents not being able to sort out things with their own parents, or when older relatives behave in a divisive way (for example, by joining with children against their parents), that trouble can occur. In all likelihood, the kids will simply up the ante with behaviour that forces their sandwiched folks to take charge. (You can see this happening, in fact, even when grandparents are merely paying a visit.)

The adoptive family

Over the past thirty years, there has been a dramatic drop in the number of adoptions. It is no wonder that adopted children feel different; they often grow up never meeting a peer in a similar situation. From the peak of almost 10,000 in 1971–72, numbers dropped to a mere 514 adoptions in Australia in 2000–2001. The reasons for the decline include the use of contraception, abortion, and social acceptance of single parents. Another contributing factor is that step-parents, who previously tended to adopt their partners' children, are now encouraged to become legal guardians. That principle also applies to other relatives, such as grandparents.

Most children adopted now come from overseas, in marked contrast to the early 1970s when most adoptions were of Australian-born children. There were 289 inter-country adoptions in 2000–2001 (56 per cent of all adoptions), the major countries of origin being South Korea, India, Ethiopia and Thailand. But even adoptions of foreign children are falling.

The secret nature of adoption so prevalent in the 1950s and 1960s has changed dramatically. In Australia, the Adoption Information Act of 1990 enables adoptees of 18 years of age to have access to their original birth certificate and enables birth parents to have access to details of their child's adopted identity when the child they surrendered turns 18. So, young adult children of adoption now have the opportunity to discover their name, religious background, ethnicity, health history and other aspects of their origins. While many embark on this search, few do so without a sense of guilt that they are betraying their adoptive parents.

Adoptive parents, on the other hand, need to be prepared for a greater involvement with birth families than they might have expected. This, too, has its difficulties. Experts now agree, however, that the more open the situation from the start, the better it is for the adjustment of all concerned. In adoptive families there are many issues of loss – all those involved need a chance to grieve, to work through the associated pain and suffering that may exacerbate when children reach adolescence.

While not all adopted teenagers become preoccupied with their adopted status, most will wonder about its meaning for them and struggle with identity issues: 'Why did my parents give me up? What was wrong with me? Why me?' Even looking in the mirror raises questions such as: 'Who do I look like?' Adoptive families in distress, as many are when adopted children start searching for answers, need help to cope with the stresses involved.

Foster families are pretty special too and deserving of recognition. Many children and teenagers are placed with foster parents because of family breakdown, parental neglect – a host of reasons. Many have been before the court and placed in care as wards of the state. Fostering is difficult for teens. Sometimes things work out extremely well, in which case the benefits are enormous, sometimes not. There's no doubt that such troubled childhoods take their toll and many fostered children are damaged and difficult, with special needs. There's also no doubt that foster families need additional support, far more than is usually available to them.

The alternative family

There are many other styles of family living. Sometimes they work out, sometimes they don't. The following are examples.

- Communes are based on principles of cooperation and goodwill, and vary from loosely organised shanty towns to more stable groups of committed families (often with shared political, cultural or religious views, as in the Israeli Kibbutzim).
- The share household family consists generally of youngish people who live together under the same roof either by choice or necessity, sharing ideas, tasks and incomes.

- The homosexual family is a family with two parents of the same sex and one or more kids. Australian research has recently confirmed that children are just as likely to thrive in families with homosexual parents as they are with heterosexual parents. And most lesbian and gay parents enjoy a high level of acceptance and support in the community.
- The 'stretched' family involves arrangements whereby families or single people provide some sort of support for each other, either in the home (as when a family takes in a helpful boarder) or through meeting regularly to share problems, exchange services and perhaps enjoy leisure pursuits together.

'Alternative' families may pose problems for teenagers, who essentially do not like being different. One young woman in her early twenties, who grew up in the country as part of an alternative community where several home-schooling families supported each other, reflected that what she most wanted as a teenager (between, say, the ages of 12 and 16) was a 'normal family, not mung beans on toast'. Her strongly held view is that most kids prefer a family with a mum and a dad, if at all possible, 'a family that's okay, one that does normal things'.

From a psychological point of view, where the boundaries between people are less clear, as is the case in some of these situations, young people may feel vulnerable or experience a degree of general or sexual anxiety. As a result teenagers in alternative families may thus experience a greater struggle in growing up, achieving independence and establishing relationships.

Getting along together

A family is clearly different things to different people. But essentially, it is an organised group held together by the power of its dominant members. When children reach adolescence, there may be questions raised as to who the dominant members actually are, but the point remains valid.

It is beneficial for a family, like any other group, to have a sense of purpose and direction. This comes about when the leadership has goals and aspirations (such as what to do when the kids leave home). But how it feels to belong to a family largely depends on what's happening within those four walls, on the presence or absence of inner cohesion. How are people getting along together? What is their degree of cooperation, mutual understanding and goodwill?

> **Like all groups, a family has certain basic needs. These are:**
>
> - An identity: usually determined by such things as your family name, how neat you keep the garden and other special traits.
> - A place to protect its resources: your dwelling, however humble that may be.
> - A committed membership: you, the kids and whoever else is currently in residence.
> - Effective leadership: hopefully yours.
> - Inner cohesion: related entirely to how members get along together.
> - A value system and rules governing conduct.
> - A sense of history and wider connectedness, gained from the celebration of such things as birthdays, anniversaries, religious and other important occasions.

Communication is the key

Communication is the lubricant that enables people to get along together. Internationally renowned management guru Paul Drucker has said: 'The most important thing about communication is to hear what isn't being said.' It really is impossible to overstate the importance of this. Of course, one's style of relating is pretty well established by the time children turn into teenagers, but when the tone of the interaction changes, as it often does when children turn into teenagers, it can come as a bit of a shock.

Ever wondered why teenagers find parents such a pain in the neck? No matter what they say or do, sometimes, poor old mum or dad just never seem to get it right. For example, a 15-year-old girl came sobbing to her mother, saying that the earrings she wanted to wear to a party were nowhere to be found. Her mother said, 'Never mind, dear. I'll let you borrow some of mine.' The daughter stormed out, slamming the door and saying, 'Thanks a lot. You really don't care, do you!'

Many a parent has looked to heaven and wondered, 'What did I say wrong?' Where parents and teenagers are concerned, the message sent is frequently not the message received. The complexities of human communication have been neatly summed up as follows: 'I know that you believe you understand what you think I said, but I'm not sure you realise that what you heard is not what I meant.' In 1969, in his book *Between Parent and Teenager*, psychologist Haim Ginott explained that, for teenagers: 'Help is perceived as interference, concern as babying, advice as bossing.' Things haven't changed much since then. Or perhaps it's simply that, as Woody Allen put it, 'kids put their parents under a pedestal'. A parent might politely ask a teenage daughter to kindly pass the pepper; her mumbled reply: 'What did your other slaves die of?' When a simple enquiry is an interrogation; a simple observation, an unfeeling intrusion; and a simple request, a monumental imposition, what do you do?

It doesn't appear to pose as much difficulty in the other direction. Teenagers just know what not to tell their parents – they are masters of the smokescreen. This is a skill they cherish, as if their survival depended on it. They develop a sixth sense about the sort of response particular information is likely to bring (especially when it involves behaviour that comes perilously close to the limits set). They think, 'Why buy trouble?' So, when a kid says literally nothing for days on end, you know something's up.

Eventually, of course, it's all going to work out fine. The Reverend Bill Crews AM, Chairman of the Exodus Foundation in Sydney, made the following remark during a public forum on adolescent depression and hopefulness: 'At some point, we all become folks sitting around the table. We can talk to each other. It's nice.'

Setting the record straight

We've come a long way in the past 25 years towards understanding what's happening between teenagers and their parents. In the first place, the situation is nowhere near as bad as it was once thought. Prior to about the mid-1970s, before proper research on this subject was done, parent–teenager conflict was simply assumed to be normal. If adolescent rebellion and oppositional behaviours weren't happening, families felt that something was wrong, that they were somehow missing out. Studies then started to show that approximately 75 per cent of teenagers reported happy and pleasant relationships with their parents! What is more, most of the remaining 25 per cent of families had histories of family difficulty that preceded their children's entry into adolescence, which tended to explain their situation.

Despite these illuminating findings, the notion of an entrenched 'generation gap' seems to have stuck in everyone's mind. Even though the idea that adolescents must detach or separate themselves from their parents (in order to be healthy) has become outdated (with the need for connectedness now in vogue), the portrayal of the adolescent period as a difficult one, and the image of teenagers themselves as troublesome, angry and ungrateful, persist. But this is unhelpful and wrong. High-intensity, angry fighting in families is just not normal!

This is not to say that the course of family relationships is necessarily easy or smooth. To the contrary, as everyone knows, bickering and squabbling occur frequently during the early adolescent years (as one parent commented: 'arguing with your teenagers is like being pecked to death by ducks') and infuriatingly normal behaviours (as we explored in Chapter 2) are very much part of the scene. But the evidence suggests that this is more upsetting to parents, especially mothers, than it is to teenagers themselves. The kid generally walks away from such interchanges feeling far less troubled than mum or dad. As surprising as it may seem, parents are the ones who hold on to the negative feelings, sulk and remain miserable about it.

The reasons for this are related to differing perspectives and expectations of parents and teenagers, which are difficult or impossible to reconcile:

- Parents tend to see mundane conflicts as being about codes of right and wrong (moral debates, rejection of basic values) – in other words, serious stuff.
- Teenagers are simply less hung up about it. They think more in terms of personal choices – 'I just didn't want to do it. What's the big deal?'

About 40 per cent of parents suffer emotional distress as the family moves into adolescence, even when nothing unusual is happening. During this important transition, parents may experience lowered self-esteem, diminished life satisfaction, increased anxiety and depression, and more frequent rumination about middle age (for reasons discussed in Chapter 8). What an interesting twist – the mental health of parents can suffer at the hands of totally normal teenagers doing completely normal (albeit aggravating) things.

The benefits of authoritative parenting

As we've discussed in Chapter 3, adolescents benefit from having parents who are authoritative: warm, firm, and accepting of their evolving need for psychological autonomy. Authoritative parenting is firm, confident but warm and nurturing. Authoritarian parenting is domineering. It says: 'You will do this because I told you to.'

Family researcher Professor Lawrence Steinberg from Temple University in Philadelphia has spent the past 25 years confirming the validity of this finding, and the evidence appears iron-clad. Adolescents from authoritative homes achieve more in school, report less depression and anxiety, score higher on measures of self-reliance and self-esteem, and are less likely to engage in antisocial behaviour, including delinquency and drug use. They also show more positive social behaviour, self-control, cheerfulness and confidence.

What about the effects of differing parenting styles within the same household? How much does this matter? Studies have shown that mothers and fathers are in agreement about 75 per cent of the time anyway, but parental consistency in dealing with teenagers turns out to be less important than the presence at home of at least one authoritative parent. There's more:

- Having two authoritative parents is slightly better than having one.
- Having one authoritative parent is better than having none, even if having one means having parents who do not see eye to eye.
- Either of the above scenarios is better than having parents who agree, but who are permissive, authoritarian or neglectful.

What this amounts to is an ideal context for connectedness within families – as well as doing better in general, teenagers in families where authoritative parenting is the norm get along better with their parents and with others.

Partly a matter of time

This is all good stuff. But when is all this authoritative parenting and positive interaction supposed to happen? There is a saying that the best inheritance parents can give their children is a few minutes of their time each day. It's true. In our busy world, having a little time, some undivided attention, makes a child of any age feel wanted and important. Even the most gorgeous and extravagant material gifts cannot compensate for this. A mother of two young adolescents described her family's home life as follows:

> *The kids come home from school, have a quick bite and do their homework. After dinner, we go to bed. My husband usually comes home much later. On weekends, they want to be with their friends. Of course, sometimes we're all together, watching television like zombies.*

Perhaps she should be pleased that they spend any time together at all. When everybody's rushing around, meaningful discussions are likely to be very rare, unless some special effort is made. Some families take active steps to enable communication as a group and this certainly has its merits. There are a number of possibilities:

- You can organise a regular meeting at which everybody gets to have a say; whether this is tightly chaired or more of a friendly free-for-all is a question of preferred style.
- Families more taken with bureaucratic procedures might prefer a suggestion box, the contents of which serve as the basis for a thorough discussion from time to time.
- Others simply prefer to deal with issues as they arise – frequently, it would seem, over dinner.

This notion of a shared meal, in fact, has much to recommend it. Sitting down together around a table is a ritual that can build the familiarity and tolerance that make a family strong. Reflecting on family meals in an article in the *Sydney Morning Herald* (31 December 1994), Morag Fraser recalled them as:

> *occasions for honing of conversational skills, for airing grievances, learning patience and ritual, for exchanging the experiences of the day. Meal tables were the sites for confession, laughter, revelations of catastrophes, for rites of passage and initiation.*

She's absolutely right, although there's a tendency these days for families to watch TV while eating instead of talking. Based on a review of research over the past 50 years, the evidence is strong that family routines and rituals are highly beneficial. They provide a sense of competence to everyone in the family and offer stability during times of stress and transition. Studies show that the repetitive nature of family mealtime, for example, allows families to get to know each other, which can lead to better parenting, healthier children and improved academic achievement. The key seems to be responsive and respectful communication and the benefits are experienced irrespective of the family setup. Under conditions of single parenting, divorce, and remarried households, family routines may actually protect children from the proposed risks associated with being raised in non-traditional families.

The point is that people's ideas and views need to be taken seriously. Whether you're six or 46 years old is not the issue. The people who communicate well, at any age, are those who know how to listen. There is probably no single skill more valuable in this regard. And, of course, the important thing is to make time so that communication can happen.

Between parents and teenagers

Within families there is always a special dynamic between parents and children. How this works differs greatly between families and depends on such factors as who's there, parenting styles, the atmosphere in the home and the personalities of the players.

For example, families vary enormously in the way they express affection. Some families are extremely cuddlesome, while others might prefer a firm handshake at bedtime. Touching is very powerful. Children who grow up in a physically demonstrative and warm home will probably raise their own kids the same way. Of course, there are also many subtle and non-physical ways to indicate affection. The caring things we say and do clearly convey the message as well.

There are four basic parent–teen relationships, each with its own special characteristics that can either enrich or disrupt the family – or both!

Mothers and daughters: These two have something in common – they're the same sex. This should be good news. However, as her own biological clock ticks on, a mother has to deal with her feelings concerning her daughter's emerging sexuality, and this is not all that easy. According to sex researcher and author Shere Hite, this is probably also the reason why most mothers have such difficulty discussing sexual and anatomical matters with their daughters and tend to hide their own sexual lives.

During the early teenage years, girls will gain the distance and privacy they need, usually through frequent withdrawals to their bedroom. However, if lines of communication are open, they will seek closeness and support from their mothers when they need it. A daughter who has been more or less 'missing' for days can suddenly turn up in desperate need of some item of her mother's clothing. And at any time she might want to gossip about girlfriends or talk about the meaning of life – and boys. They will have their ups and downs, but in due course, there is much comfort and enjoyment to be drawn from this relationship on both sides.

Mothers and sons: A boy going through puberty can be pretty hard for his mother to take, particularly in regard to his personal hygiene, smutty humour and physical awkwardness. But emotional distance and physical closeness are not mutually exclusive in the adolescent boy. Sometimes boys can become sweetly protective of their mum, or angry and intimidating. In the latter situation, if dad's around, he needs to intervene strongly on mum's behalf. If a teenage boy wants to get close to his mum, he may simply pick her up – at which time her best response is simply to be incredibly impressed by his marvellous strength!

On the other hand, sometimes a mother looks to a teenage son for the closeness she is not experiencing with her husband (whether or not he's physically present). This can give rise to a special, stable and not overly healthy twosome within the family.

Fathers and sons: These relationships are usually less intense and personal than those between mothers and daughters, but more competitive. This is thought to be because certain things are important to them both, simply because they're male: having strength and agility, being attractive to women (both within and outside the family) and being successful. As boys flex their newly grown muscles, dads can expect to be tested out in all areas.

Boys are very fortunate when they have a confident and committed father who can handle the situation with tolerance and good humour. This has been called the 'loving fight' and without love, mutual respect cannot develop and a boy's self-esteem is likely to suffer. Fathers who are struggling with their own identity issues may either opt out or over-react in a very heavy-handed way. On occasion, an adolescent boy's emotional and behavioural problems can be traced to this cause.

Fathers and daughters: A dad's approval, affirmation and affection contribute enormously to a teenage girl's self-perception and her developing confidence in dealing with other men. According to research, just having a father around helps to protect her against the risk of future depression and relationship problems. It's important for a father to listen to his teenage daughter, to check out what's happening in her life and how she's feeling, and to enquire into her dreams for the future.

Most fathers handle the flirtatious behaviour of their teenage daughters with knowing reserve, or tactfully withdraw from closeness. Of course, when other males start to take an interest in his 'little princess', paternal hackles can rise rapidly. Fathers are notoriously protective of their daughters and can be overly restrictive at times in an effort to restrain their daughters' developing sexuality. One teenaged girl, who had been lectured about her provocative dress, asked: 'Why does he have to make such a tragedy of things?' Girls from some cultural backgrounds in Australia often experience problems in this regard, which can add immeasurably to the stress of growing up (particularly since they are often egged on by friends whose parents are less strict).

As in life generally, how well or badly two individuals get along together in a family impacts on others. The four basic relationships described here can evolve and change over time but they will remain important forever.

Sibling strife

With two or more kids in the family, the variables of family dynamics go off the scale. Not all kids fight with their siblings – only about 99 per cent of them. Ultimately, there is likely to be a special bond between siblings, something that parents like to see. But during adolescence, this can get extremely stretched. Why do teenagers frequently not get along with their 'partners in crime'? The factors involved include the following:

- An excruciating sensitivity to any comment or glance in reference to their bodies or embarrassed interest in the opposite sex. An 11-year-old girl, for example, who spent what seemed like hours doing her hair, ribbed her older brother about his small crop of juicy pimples. He retaliated with: 'And you love yourself, don't ya?'
- An exceptional degree of physical gratification related to pushing and shoving: so when he squeals, 'she keeps pushing me', he might not actually want to be rescued.
- An exquisite sense of fair play coupled with a climate of constant inequity. Have you noticed how kids measure things? We line up four glasses and pour milk – woe betide if the levels do not turn out exactly equal! We take great care in choosing their birthday presents – they do mental estimates of their relative value.
- An exhausting and ruthless struggle for scarce parental attention (usually when parents are absolutely exhausted and have practically nothing left to give).
- An extraordinary resistance to any adult-inspired measure to prevent or stop their tussles.

Of course, one cannot assume that because kids fight they don't get along. Underneath they may have a strong and supportive relationship. And children who never fight are not necessarily close to one another – they may simply be uninvolved. Nevertheless, you can hurt inside when kids are constantly at each other's throats. Especially when it's occurring in a confined space, murder seems entirely reasonable. On a long car trip, for example, you may feel inclined to put them out on the footpath and let them fight there forever. No one is ever wise enough to know who really starts a sibling fracas, so level-headed parents do their best to butt out. They don't always succeed.

Acceptable levels of conflict and boisterousness need to be worked out, but parents need to remain authoritative – even when they can't be heard above the din.

Some teenagers have problem parents

Tolstoy, in *Anna Karenina*, points out that 'All happy families resemble one another; every unhappy family is unhappy in its own way.' In happy families, people enjoy each other, there's mutual respect, negotiation and expression of feelings (even if loudly at times). The style of parenting is almost invariably authoritative.

Dysfunctional families tend to be characterised by marital discord, manipulative behaviour, poor boundary setting, alcohol and substance abuse and domestic violence. There is wide diversity here, but the style of parenting typical of dysfunctional families is almost always authoritarian, with ineffective and inconsistent punishment and discipline. In this context, too, children are more at risk from abuse – physical, emotional and sexual – and neglect. Sexual abuse (as discussed in the next section), for example, occurs more frequently in children from socially deprived and disorganised family backgrounds.

Sexual abuse

A friend of ours was shocked when his 10-year-old daughter announced: 'Forget about strangers, it's fathers you've got to be careful of.' An important message was getting through, although her own dad was momentarily less than comfortable about the implication. Not every parent is an abuser.

When a father (more commonly a stepfather) exploits his position of power and authority and draws his child into sexual activity with him, relationships have gone badly wrong. There is no doubt that feelings exist between fathers and daughters, but acting on them in this way is illegal, a clear betrayal of trust, and causes humiliation, confusion, fear and rage.

Incest appears to cut across all races, religions, ethnicities, ages and classes, affecting rural, urban and suburban lives. With increasing community awareness of child sexual abuse, ever so slowly, the health, welfare and legal systems are trying to sort out how best to deal with it. There's a long way to go because it's a wretched and apparently growing problem. Consider the facts listed on the next page about child sexual abuse.

- Child sexual abuse is not uncommon in our society but has long been ignored or condoned. Its incidence is grossly underestimated, not only because the majority of children and teenagers, through fear of being disbelieved (or perhaps not believing it themselves), do not report it, but also because it's so terrible, there's a general resistance to 'knowing'. After all, recognising the high incidence of sexual abuse challenges one's perceptions of the world.
- Workers in the field estimate that as many as one in three girls under 18 years has experienced an unwanted sexual incident. Boys are sexually abused too (one in seven, but this may be an underestimate; it comes to light less often because of the enormous shame involved in being a victim).
- In more than 80 per cent of cases it is perpetrated by a family member, or an older person for whom the child has positive feelings; 30–40 per cent involve an alcoholic parent.
- The vast majority of perpetrators of sexual abuse of both girls and boys (over 95 per cent) are heterosexual men.
- It involves the abuse of different children in a family more often than abuse of one only, and is more likely to happen in blended families where incest taboos between children and step-parents are weakened. It has been reported that girls living with step-fathers rather than biological fathers are five times more likely to report having been sexually abused. Girls are also at increased risk from the boyfriends and suitors in situations where their mother may be seeking a new partner.
- It is generally secret and ongoing, isolating the young person from healthy relationships or activities.
- It involves considerable overlap between physical, emotional and sexual abuse – children who are subject to one form of abuse are significantly more likely to suffer other forms of abuse.
- It is linked in adult life with higher rates of depressive symptoms, anxiety symptoms, drug abuse, eating disorders and post-traumatic stress disorders.
- It has relevance to criminal behaviour as a significant number of offenders in youth training centres and prisons (estimated between 40 and 70 per cent) were previously wards of the state due to abuse (including sexual abuse) and neglect.
- It contributes to homelessness, with an estimated 60 to 70 per cent of homeless children leaving home to escape abuse by one or both parents.

When to suspect abuse and how to respond

Sexually abused children may: develop depression, withdraw, run away, use alcohol and other drugs, develop eating disorders, self-injure, attempt suicide, have poor self-image, behave overly seductively or promiscuously, lie, have recurrent physical complaints (including puzzling symptoms such as abdominal pain or strange turns), have delinquency and conduct problems, be unusually aggressive, have a negative attitude towards and fear of sex, have school problems and poor peer relationships. Not surprisingly, the experience of incest is often associated with longstanding emotional, social and sexual problems for the abused girl or boy. After all, if a child or teenager cannot trust those closest to him or her, how can it be safe to trust anyone?

If abuse of a child or teenager under 16 years of age is even suspected, let alone disclosed, there are now strict laws in place that make it obligatory for people from many professional and vocational groups to report it to the welfare authorities. However, it's a matter of such importance that literally anyone with a concern for the well-being of children and young people should see themselves as being in a position to help. We can't always close our eyes and ears to what goes on in other people's homes and lives.

Sexually abused children and their families need immediate professional evaluation and treatment. With proper help, abused children and young people can regain a sense of self-esteem, cope with feelings of guilt about the abuse, and begin the process of overcoming the trauma. Hopefully, too, such treatment can help reduce the risk of developing serious problems as an adult.

Working parents

Let's take a brief look at the mad rat race many of us are caught up in. We scurry back and forth, day after day, building mountains out of molehills, or even larger mountains out of mountains, our energies and resources all but consumed by work of some kind. And this goes equally for fathers and mothers.

Working fathers

Working fathers have the most plausible excuse in the world for neglecting their family: 'But I'm only doing it for you.' No one will deny that there are pressures and responsibilities involved, particularly when you're the only income earner. But the personal losses can mount up and, especially if your spouse is at home full time, empathy might be in short supply. This is not only because there's practically nothing as thankless as full-time housework, but also because the man seems to have the best of both worlds. He has the stimulation of an external setting, people to relate to (both male and female), a generally structured environment, clear expectations and tangible rewards. Then he comes home to hot food and clean clothes (if not other welcoming behaviours as recommended in 'The Good Wife's Guide' of 1955 quoted in Chapter 9).

Working fathers also inspire the ire of their children, partly because they're not around and partly because when they are around they're not really there. Preoccupations of the mind are not conducive to close and comfortable relationships. So, here we have the horns of a dilemma. Dad gives at the office, as he must, and returns to the fold, tired, cranky and off the air. Balancing the needs and pressures of both work and family is never easy.

Here's what young people say about their working dads:

My dad hates work – he comes home and constantly complains about all these problems and the people he works with – I hate him being so unhappy and irritable and it puts me off working that hard or taking a responsible job.

Dad pressures me. He's very clever and expects more of me. Now he wants me to choose a financially rewarding career. He was disappointed with my Year 12 results and he wants me to be like him. His pressure causes me a great deal of stress. He didn't care about my excellent art score. It's not a legitimate subject in his eyes. Life is all about work for him.

We unknowingly say a lot to young people about their future work, based upon our attitudes to our own work. Do we also talk about the good things we achieve at work? Let's give a thought here to the single dad as well – he's often an unsung hero.

Working mothers
Mothers who work in paid employment often are worse off than fathers. Generally they have to effectively do two jobs, and some-

how do justice to both. Fathers are increasingly sharing domestic tasks, some are participating more fully in bringing up children, which is even better. But in most cases, where care of the children is concerned, responsibilities still rest mainly with the mother. The ideal, of course, is where mothers and fathers are both in paid employment and share the housework, rather than mothers carrying the burden of the two.

> My mother always worked and it didn't bother me at all.
> Edward, aged 14

Working mothers, particularly full-timers, can end up chasing their tail. They have less free time (or more likely none) and less vigour and energy. They often feel out of touch with the kids, and guilty when their home runs less than smoothly. A husband's resentment adds insult to injury.

One young person expressed the heart of the matter:

I didn't mind my mother working. It would have worried me if she chose to sit home all day and do housework. Her work helped our family financially and we were more organised and responsible for our own stuff when she was working. But what worried me was the way she was always rushed, irritable, stressed, preoccupied, distant and getting ready for the next day. She also felt guilty and would over-react to things. I learnt that I could get away with murder when she was tired – she didn't have the energy to keep the rules. On weekends she was too tired to be with friends or to do other things. It was not her work that worried me. This gave us financial security and I liked that. It was the way she reacted to it.

What kids often don't seem to understand is that running a home is work. Even mums who don't work, WORK.

Pitching in

There's only one rational solution: everybody has to 'pitch in'. This brings us, finally, to the touchy subject of household chores. Families need to set priorities and decide together what's important and who needs to do what.

In homes with one parent or with two who both work, the family might agree to things being somewhat less than shipshape. Of course, some people really thrive in creative squalor (and have the advantage that burglars think someone else has been there already), but most of us prefer some semblance of order.

For some, rosters work well. Others prefer a more casual approach. For example, when help is needed, whether it's to set the table for dinner or bring in the washing, one simply asks for it. Whatever system is adopted, certain jobs for teenage offspring should probably be obligatory. For example: putting their own dirty clothes in the washing basket (anything that's not there doesn't get washed), putting their own washing away, and tidying up their bedrooms at least once a week (or whatever has been agreed to).

In some families, kids are expected to prepare meals, do the shopping and take on the lion's share of household cleaning. Under certain circumstances, there's probably no alternative. But young people need some leisure time and are quick to complain if, as they see it, they are being treated unfairly. When approaching the topic of chores, yelling won't work, while flexibility and negotiation will (well, mostly). We shouldn't weaken on this point, however, because we're teaching kids important life skills that they need to have. And we're fostering that all-important sense of connectedness. In all families young people are greatly advantaged by their involvement in chores.

Some final thoughts

David: Many people blame the problems of adolescence on working mothers, absent fathers and lack of extended families. Whether parents work or stay at home, are divorced or married, there are no set rules for the right work and family balance. When it comes to balance, it's about what is right for the individual family. How does anyone really know what is right when families, workplaces and society are changing at such a rapid pace? How can we really know what is right for single and step-families in a time of escalating divorce? What is certain is that young people need their parents to be there for them, while encouraging a sense of responsibility and independence.

Leanne: Families are invariably interesting, very diverse and incredibly important. There's always a lot going on, not the least of which is the development and moulding of young lives. Hopefully a place of dignity, respect and trust, a family should provide a safe and reasonably predictable environment. For teenagers, the family home is the security base from which they take off to check out the world. Whatever its shape or size, it should be their sanctuary.

David: You know, we haven't said much yet about families shrinking as kids grow up and leave home (although the issues involved in 'letting go' are mentioned later in the book). My wife Anne and I are a bit further along with this now, with our four 'children' in their twenties and thirties and only the youngest still at home. While we miss them being around, it's been a bit of a surprise to find ourselves feeling okay about it. We're freer to pursue our own interests. What are your thoughts about returning to being a couple when your two boys head off somewhere?

Leanne: On one hand I look forward to having more time for our marriage and ourselves. On the other, I have very painful emotions about the thought of my teenage sons leaving home in the future. I suspect these conflicting feelings will stay with me forever.

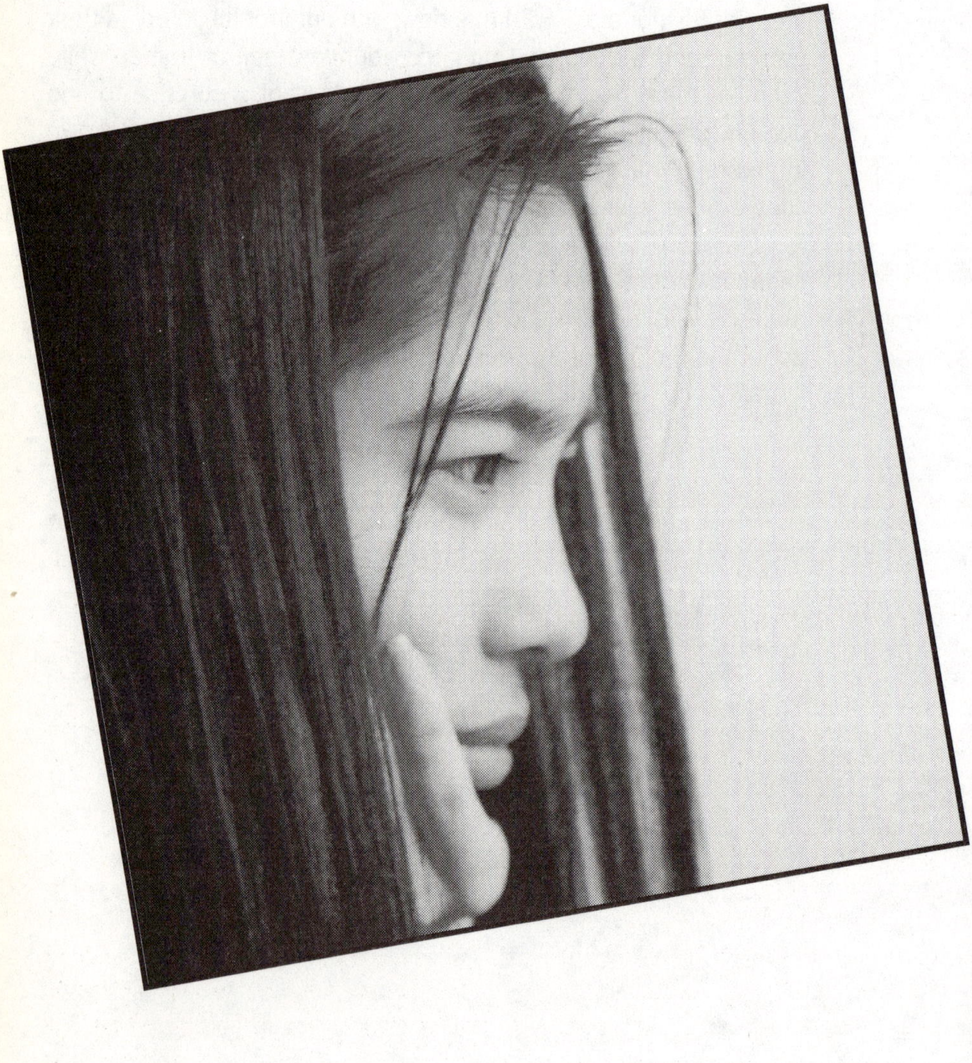

Chapter 11

Belonging to school and connected to community

I like school because the people there like me.
Jamie, aged 13

In Chapters 9 and 10, we discussed the importance of feeling connected to parents and to family. A sense of belonging to school and community also nurtures resilience in teenagers. However, many teenagers need guidance to persevere through the difficulties of school, tertiary education or a job. Chapter 11 covers the good and bad about education and getting a job, including what teenagers say about teachers, peers, bullying and learning difficulties.

Do I have to go to school?

Getting an education used to be something you just did, more or less. It was simply the way one spent those particular waking hours, no questions asked. Then, as now, the demands for achievement were not always matched by our thirst for knowledge. Then, as now, the constraints and authority that epitomise school were not always in keeping with our innate desires for freedom and independence. But there, perhaps, the comparison ends.

Our high school system was developed in the expectation of full employment – an expectation, as we now know, that may never be fulfilled. This simple but shattering fact has put a gigantic question mark over the whole deal. Teenagers today have particular reason to wonder: Education for what? Relevance to whom? This hallowed institution, our education system, surrounded by controversy as never before, appears no match for the rapidity with which society is changing. This section looks at the high school scene, how parents can help and some of the problems that may arise.

What are high schools about?
Like any other system, the education system has its good and bad points, its extremes and its middle ground. Optimists say that things are changing, ever so slowly, for the better; that there really are discernible moves in the right direction. Some of these are emerging from within the education system itself, while others are occurring in response to outside influences.

School children have the benefit of modern teaching techniques: there is less of a focus on the rote learning of factual information (but it still has a very important place – we all use rote-learned facts daily); experiential learning is in vogue, enabling teenagers to gain knowledge and understanding through active involvement in the learning process; and some schools do justice to the teaching of skills for living, including health education. Modern education has the capacity, at least, to engage young emotions as well as young intellects.

Schools are also having to adjust to our increasingly multicultural society; the changing aspirations of girls (more of whom now complete high school than boys); and a more aware public that is exercising a much more effective say in what's happening.

The pressure's really on
Meanwhile, for a lot of kids, school is not all that great a place. It should be a responsive and caring place; more than a centre of learning and stimulation, it should be a place that draws young people to its heart and serves their needs. In reality, many are merely 'stuck' there, victims of pressures beyond their control. One study of school leavers showed that the self-esteem of young women increased as soon as they left school. Educators, too, are recognising that high school can be a bruising experience for young people, especially for those who are not achieving well – a problem that deserves our serious attention.

The outside pressure on kids involves the compulsion to be at school and stay there as long as possible. It is exerted by parents, schools and, increasingly, governments. Anxieties are transmitted to school children down through the years, even to kindergarten. These days, a little kid who fails at blocks is being watched very closely – as a future could be in jeopardy!

Kids are affected by internal pressures too, mostly relating to conforming and achieving. What's wrong with pressure to conform? Isn't this what society demands of us all, with its precise rules and bureaucratic systems? However, if school is about getting on with the job (one that is devised and perpetrated entirely by adults, as it happens) in an atmosphere of mindless obedience, lots of kids are in hot water.

Of course, persistently wearing your tie crooked is a different brand of recalcitrance, perhaps, to always turning up late and, one would imagine, less outrageous than punching up small kids. But even in matters of dress and etiquette, in some schools, transgressions can get you into very serious strife indeed.

How many kids involved in the normal questioning of authority have heard the challenge, 'And what makes you think you're special, Buster?' Sadly, many schools seem unable or unwilling to view emerging individuality as a positive attribute. If education is designed to shape rather than to encourage growth in young people, we may indeed be training them for docility.

What's wrong with pressure to achieve? Surely that's not altogether a bad thing either? Surely everyone wants kids to do as well as possible? It depends. Pressure to achieve academically is often what this is about, but it can also apply to athletic and creative pursuits. High school students cope with these pressures in several ways.

There are those who compete and win:

- Teenagers who do well in the academic arena bring pride to their parents, kudos to the school and seem pointed towards a bright and successful future. But this is not always without cost.
- Some 'brainy' kids are ostracised by their peers or become social isolates by choice, which is not the best way to become a fully functional and well-rounded person.
- Success may be achieved at the expense of emotional or physical health; many high-achieving students are on legal medications such as analgesics or tranquillisers for headaches or other stress-related symptoms.

- Some of the most stressed (and unwell) high achievers attend notoriously high-pressure schools, where kids without supreme potential are not allowed in to start with – mustn't mess up the school average. Knowing that pupils who don't make the grade are likely to be gently 'encouraged to leave', and that their parents know this too, is a heavy burden to carry.

There are those who compete and lose:

- Some kids do less well than they would wish, or others would wish, despite trying hard. Studies have shown that concerns about school, including test results, are rated highly by teenagers. Struggling on without success damages self-esteem and leads to feelings of guilt for not living up to personal, family or teacher expectations.
- As one young struggler put it: 'If I didn't feel that everyone was on my back so much, I think I'd probably do better.' Young people who constantly fall short of expectations are at risk of depression – a chastening thought. There is value in parents talking to the teenager and teachers with a view to agreeing on realistic expectations. It makes a big difference.

Then there are those who refuse to compete at all. The most frustrating of all for parents and teachers alike are those teenagers with demonstrated ability who simply do not put in the effort. Such kids may be naturally non-competitive, fear failure or give up in the face of excessive expectations. For non-academic pupils, for example, the main problem is lack of gratification. The system doesn't meet their needs, they become bored and disruptive and usually opt out early, either by physically leaving or attending in body only. Of those who leave early, a lucky few will find a job, but most will merely join the ranks of the restless unemployed.

Early school leavers

One in three teenagers leaves school each year without completing Year 12. Teenagers from lower socio-economic backgrounds or isolated geographic areas are more likely to drop out of school early. Only 40 per cent of Aboriginal students stay at school until Year 10.

Leaving school early is also associated with poor achievement in the lower levels of schooling, and a strong dislike of school. The disadvantages ahead include lower participation in the labour force, higher unemployment rates (generally more than 20 per cent) and lower incomes in comparison to Year 12 completers. Some school drop-outs, in cahoots with kindred spirits, will get up to no good (which is unfortunate for public telephones and train seats), and research shows that risk-taking behaviours are much higher in teenagers who don't attend school.

Much thought is being given to the problems associated with leaving school early and the potential solutions. When asked for their views, early leavers identify the need for 'adult learning environments'. They are asking to 'not be treated like two-year-olds', to have an adult relationship with teachers, and opportunities to gain knowledge and skills directly related to their work goals and aspirations. They want their education to be meaningful. Most young people want to apply their learning.

What happens in the first year after leaving school is crucial. Getting full-time work reduces the risk of chronic unemployment over the long term, but currently there is little labour market assistance for early school leavers wanting to enter the workforce.

The commitment that needs to be fostered in Australia is twofold:

- All young people should have the opportunity to complete 12 years of schooling or its vocational equivalent; and
- All young people who have left full-time education and want to participate in the workforce should be able to do so.

With 20 per cent of young people in Australia between the ages of five and 18 years (or around 700,000 children) living in disadvantaged households, this is an enormous challenge. However, the costs and cost benefits of achieving these ambitious goals have been carefully worked out. A comprehensive learning and work commitment for young people makes sense – it will reduce risks for individuals, improve the skills base of the workforce, impact positively on productivity (which is good for society), and enhance the capacity of young people as a whole. Whether the political will exists to effect this solution remains to be seen. Meanwhile, non-government organisations like The Smith Family are helping tens of thousands of disadvantaged young people remain in school.

What makes a good school?

A good school is one that fulfils the most important and basic needs of teenagers, which are: having good friends; having good teachers; believing that you fit in at school; feeling that you are respected by your teachers; having an adult other than a parent take an interest in you.

A good school connects with families and the community and looks after its teachers. It has strong programs in the areas of literacy and numeracy, but encourages: a love of learning, creativity (art, theatre, music, creative writing, poetry), leadership, citizenship, participation and contribution, sport, community service, social responsibility, ethics and debating. A good school is not about what it looks like, but what it feels like. It feels positive and safe.

Do the school and class fit the student? This often depends on the focus of the school. Sometimes it helps to change schools when problems arise, but it is generally better in the long run to teach teenagers to persevere and to overcome their problems. School problems are addressed later in this chapter and in Chapters 14 to 16.

If we wish to deal effectively with the time-consuming behavioural problems of students, teachers must be more available to deal with students' emotional problems. Teachers provide very significant support when they do simple things, such as remember names or show an extra interest. Concern and care from a teacher is often more effective than counselling from the school welfare coordinator, doctor or psychiatrist.

Teachers are people too

What is a good teacher? There is no single, universally accepted answer. Is it someone who is knowledgeable in the subject area and can put it across in a stimulating manner? Is it someone who cracks jokes from time to time and shows a human face? Probably all this and more. Adolescents need room to move as individuals, and greatly value a teacher who provides it. They also need positive reinforcement, as everybody does, and someone they can trust.

A good teacher is long remembered, an inspiration for life. For example, one English teacher encourages her high school pupils to communicate

> *Teachers help by asking me if I'm having problems instead of waiting for me to approach them.*
> Tamsin, aged 15

with her through a journal. This is purely voluntary. Kids can write to her about anything they wish, knowing they will receive back a caring comment, a simple word of encouragement or advice. They would probably describe her as a 'good teacher'.

Some parents are intimidated by teachers, whether they're good, bad or indifferent, and avoid them at all costs. Parent and teacher nights come and go and they stay at home. For those who do go, however, it can be an extremely informative and worthwhile experience. There are other gains as well. Knowing who you are, teachers say, makes a difference to their attitude to the pupil, who then becomes more than just a face in the crowd. The triangular relationship between school, child and parent is an extremely important one, and educators are certain that their efforts are more potent when parents are aware, encouraging and involved in what's happening. As a result, you too can get things into better perspective and your teenager, who'll be aware that you've taken the trouble, cannot help but feel good.

What do teenagers say about teachers?
Here are some positive comments:

I need to be given guidance from teachers, with efficient studying and extra privileges when I do well. The teachers are genuinely interested in my work and wellbeing and give me constant help and advice. I was also invited into the staff room for cups of tea. But they made me realise it is up to me to pass Year 12.

The best thing about the final years of school is the improved relationship between teachers and students. My teachers show they respect me by speaking to me and treating me as an adult or friend. I feel like a person not just a student when teachers outwardly praise a well-earned achievement, remember my name or take the effort to make conversation. Teachers can be snappy and sometimes so can students. They need to understand that we all have bad days. Teachers should explain things in detail rather than criticise me.

I put a lot of pressure on myself. When I'm doing something difficult, I always think of the hardest thing I've ever done. Then I think, well if I can do that, I can do this too.

As school goes on I have more independence, more responsibility and more fun. Teachers should make themselves more approachable and need to be more patient, no matter how stupid my problems are. Giving me the benefit of the doubt is really important. There should be an acknowledgement of my own ability to use commonsense and do the right thing.

Everyone at our school backs me up; other students, other parents, the teachers and even the canteen ladies. Sometimes it's tempting to believe I can't rely on relationships. But there is always someone to listen.

Here are some negative comments:

Students need to be dealt with individually. Some adults try to make superficial conversation with me to try to show off that they know how to get on with adolescents.

When a teacher likes me they talk to me. A lot of teachers don't care and they ignore you if you pass them in the corridor. I try not to let teachers bring me down.

I have found that often teachers mainly focus on the louder, most open students. As quieter, shyer students, we are often just left to our own devices. We need the most help and have great ideas we could share with the class if given a chance.

If teachers encourage and have input into what I do, I want to do better and it's very encouraging. I definitely need encouragement. Some teachers put a lot of pressure on me. They say things are harder than they really are. I get really psyched out. It's hard to tell teachers things even if I trust them. They are authority figures.

From these quotes we can see that the difference between a 'good teacher' and a 'bad teacher' seems to be very small and much to do with attitudes and small kindnesses. However, teachers cannot be everything to students. It must be acknowledged that teachers have very challenging careers and need the backup and acknowledgement of other teachers, the school principal, the council and parents.

Peer influence

Peers have a very big influence on the experience of school life and learning. What do teenagers say about their friends?

> *Why aren't my friends here when I need them? I write, I talk to my cat. I talk to my pillow – I abuse it, I yell at it and I tell it everything I wish I could say. I'm scared my friends will backstab me. They gossip if I don't act the way they want me to.*

> *I look at other kids in my class. Some of them are really depressed because their parents have split up or died. One guy is in a wheelchair, a few are getting bullied because they are fat or different or something. Others do some pretty bad things at school and might be expelled. I don't have any real problems like this. I can do my work really well and I have some friends. But deep inside something feels really bad and I just keep quiet about it.*

> *Life can be very complicated – relationships, peers, etc. I don't need unrealistic goals as well. A lot of the reason that kids leave school is related to drugs. They can't be bothered and they would rather do the drugs. A lot can't cope with the school work and some don't bother turning up for exams. We can watch our friends destroying themselves and do nothing or we can offer help. But there is no point helping if we end up getting hurt ourselves. I tried to break away from my smoking friends. My other friendships made me strong enough to do this. Friendships split up because people are self-destructing and I have learnt to accept I can't do anything about it.*

> *After my father died suddenly last year from a stroke, I had to do many things to try to get back on track. Of course, it still upsets me and I still miss him but I have learnt to cope with it. I have found a group of friends that support me and care for me. I have learnt to cry when I need to. I have found activities like netball and singing help me cope. I have found that I enjoy my leadership role at school and being a role model to younger students. I have also learnt to talk to people about my problems.*

> *We constantly worry about friends but usually quietly. It is time to really worry and act if a teenager expresses concern about a friend.*

Peer pressure competes with parental influence and often wins. When asked what would most help him kick his drug habit, one boy replied: 'Get some new friends.' Usually we are given very few opportunities to influence our teenager's choice of friends. It is therefore important to tune in if a teenager asks for help with peers.

Why school is not working for boys

When it comes to schooling, from kindergarten to tertiary level, boys are not doing as well as girls:

- Boys lag well behind girls in literacy levels, with the gap in attainment levels in final-year examinations favouring girls by up to 19 per cent.
- Year 12 retention rates are 12 per cent higher for girls.
- Admission levels into universities are six per cent lower for boys (that is, over 56 per cent of students in higher education are women).
- Boys comprise 80 per cent of the estimated 100,000 suspensions from Australian schools that occur each year.

These findings come from a report called *Boys: Getting it Right*, released in October 2002 by the Commonwealth Government's Standing Committee on Education and Training. Boys are underachieving compared to girls for almost every socio-economic group (the disparity being greatest for those in the most disadvantaged socio-economic groups) and education departments around the country are being asked to do something about it.

The research shows that, on average, boys do not perform as well as girls in each aspect of literacy: reading, writing, listening, viewing and speaking. These differences emerge in primary school and persist into high school. Poor literacy is linked to: early school leaving (because such students are more likely to become alienated and disengaged from learning); lower rates of entry to further education; and higher rates and longer periods of unemployment (which ultimately affects personal and economic wellbeing). There are also strong correlations between poor literacy and social problems such as crime, rates of

When they ask me what I like doing at school, I say, 'Pissing people off.'
Jake, aged 16

imprisonment and substance abuse. Around 65 per cent of people in jail today cannot address an envelope. All these problems affect boys more than girls and their causes are complex. Here are some of the suggested reasons why girls are achieving better in school than boys:

- Girls develop ahead of boys, right from the word go, with boys having more difficulty adjusting to school and seeming less ready than girls for the demands of the classroom in the early years.
- Boys are more likely to get into trouble for their behaviour at school (while girls tend to be praised) and more likely to have difficulties with learning (learning and behaviour problems often go hand in hand).
- A higher proportion of boys than girls have 'auditory processing problems': they may be able to hear well, but process sounds more slowly. With less information getting to the brain to be analysed, they're able to recall less of what they've heard (which impairs their early grasp of literacy skills), a major disadvantage in the verbal environment of the classroom, where the main method of instruction is 'teacher talk'.
- There's a tendency for boys to favour the mathematical and the logical in preference to language-based ways of thinking (although despite the enduring stereotype, girls do just as well at mathematics as boys).
- Some primary schools have no male teachers and only 15 per cent of teacher trainees are men (this has been called the 'feminisation of primary school'); there are concerns that this lack of male role models might be sending a message to boys that education is not important.

The report, *Boys: Getting it Right*, goes to great lengths to make clear that efforts to raise the educational achievement of boys (and engage them in education) can be undertaken without threatening the gains made by girls in recent decades. The wide-ranging recommendations include courses to help teachers cater better for the differing learning styles of boys and girls, assisting boys with auditory processing difficulties, providing more boy-friendly texts in the English curriculum and mounting campaigns to attract more male teachers. The priority, according to the Federal Minister for Education, Science and Training, Dr Brendan Nelson, is 'to get the very best educational outcomes for both boys and girls. The next generation will pay a very high price if we do not get it right and get it right soon.'

High school is a family affair

Parents don't need to be told that high school is important. In the classroom and in the playground, important life dramas are being played out and destinies are being determined. We may be totally confused as to what our kids are supposed to be learning (although it is possible to find out). We may share their uncertainty as to how pertinent it all is to what lies ahead for them. We may even be unaware of whether or not they are receiving the best education available.

It is our duty and responsibility as parents, however, to encourage and support young people in their efforts to learn what there is to learn, to cope with school and to make the best of it. Being interested in what is going on and getting involved when the opportunity is there cannot be underestimated.

First things first

Anticipation of high school really hits home in Year 6. Some kids are starting to develop physically at this time and become more independent. Others seem too little, too immature for what is facing them. But if they're the right age, and they've made the grade, off they go to join the 'big guys'. The question is: 'Which high school?'

Many families are committed to public education as a community asset and social right. Others have few options because of geographic and cost factors. For those who have a choice, there are decisions to make, pros and cons to consider and conflicts to resolve. Some kids will want to go where their friends go, and cannot see much beyond that (and it's a valid case, particularly if they're anxious about the whole deal). Parents, on the other hand, are thinking ahead and wondering what's for the best. Their own aspirations and values come into the picture, making it an emotive subject.

About one in three Australian high school students is receiving a private education and there appears to be a community trend in this direction. In making this choice, parents are motivated by a number of issues:

> *I've learnt things like maths and English at school, but it's my experiences that have taught me life skills.*
> Greg, aged 17

- A desire to find a school that more or less reflects the family's values or religion (and sometimes this can include an element of snobbery).
- A desire to find a school that will suit the particular needs of the child. For example, a sensitive kid will usually be more comfortable in a smaller school.
- A belief that higher educational standards will be available at a private school (although Australian studies show that tertiary success rates are higher for students from government school backgrounds); even people who strongly support public education mostly have or aspire to have their own children in a private school.
- An interest in discipline, usually of the traditional, 'character-building' sort.

As for single-sex versus mixed-sex schools, the debate rages on, although the differences may in fact be small and not matter much. Girls tend to do better academically in single-sex high schools (hence the joke about having to choose between a coeducational school and an educational one). Attitudes favouring single-sex schools focus on the idea that boys and girls learn differently. But when boys' and girls' schools have amalgamated, achievement levels in maths and English have not greatly suffered. Also, there appears to be no guarantee that any academic advantage gained by attending a single-sex school will carry over into tertiary education.

An important transition

Moving on to high school is a major milestone for children, one that often stirs mixed feelings of excitement and apprehension. Primary school has provided a highly structured, predictable and relatively low-pressure environment. Primary school children know that high school is different, that it involves new subjects, assorted teachers (some of whom are sure to be awful) and class to class moves. There are also more people to cope with and, most importantly, a sudden change of status – you become the youngest again!

Anxieties are short-lived, however, decreasing usually within the first few days. After three weeks, it is estimated that nine out of 10 Year 7 pupils feel comfortably settled in. Some schools have 'peer support schemes' in which older pupils take an interest in the newcomers, show them the ropes and lend a helping hand. This seems to work well and everyone involved feels good.

Helping with homework

If an adolescent seems uptight about something, it means a lot when a parent quietly takes note of it. 'I bet you're feeling a bit anxious about school,' you might say. It's a question of empathy. You can also listen to a tirade about dastardly injustice in the classroom or mayhem in the school yard, and feel well within your element. This is a manageable parental role. But when it comes to helping with homework, good intentions may not be enough! How can you possibly help if you've never used a computer? You might well know how to get the right answer to a mathematics problem (your way), but find they do things differently now.

Depending on the year and the school, homework is really piled on. Multiple assignments and self-directed study are hallmarks of modern secondary education and are, no doubt, all for the better. But there's so little time for fun, to just muck around. For high school students, out of school hours (certainly on weekdays) are regimented and serious – there's sometimes no other way to cope with the load.

This is particularly the case for children and teenagers who receive coaching, even worse for those who get coaching to help them cope with homework related to the other coaching they're getting (which really does happen apparently). Extending the school day in this manner might not only exhaust the student (in the same way that occupational stress can afflict workers forced to do overtime), but it might also not be worthwhile in terms of academic outcomes. Too much homework leads to increased stress which in turn interferes with performance. A study of more than 1700 girls at a Sydney girls' school found that the high school students who had no out-of-school coaching actually did better at end-of-year exams than those coached for specific subjects. So, if the quality of the school education that your child is getting is high, consider saving the money.

Fortunately, there are ways for parents to help, without losing face:

- Show an interest from time to time in your teenager's subjects. The options here are to do a little research, by glancing through set texts and novels, or simply make encouraging noises (even if you haven't got a clue what the subject is about).
- Try not to nag about homework. It's more effective, as a rule, to exhibit a quiet acceptance that homework is important. The school will let you know if there are problems, or, if you're concerned that homework is not being done, let the school know

about it – they may have excellent ways of dealing with this issue.
- Encourage good study methods, such as the making of regular summaries in each subject.
- If possible, create a calm and studious atmosphere while homework is underway (family squabbles can be scheduled for another time maybe?).
- Be strong – limit weekday television and non-work-related computer use, which are deadly enemies of home-work.

> **David:** I have a friend who tells me about the regular maths coaching he gives his son. I listen in awe. Personally, it troubles me that my own kids will remember me as an utterly inept homework helper. Their subjects seemed too complicated for mere parental mortals. At 14 years of age, one of my sons wanted ideas for a cover design for Harper Lee's classic novel, *To Kill a Mockingbird*. 'Not a bloody chicken with an arrow through it,' he cautioned. He'd read my mind.

Exams take their toll

Exams serve their purpose, but are not always beneficial to one's mental health. More final year students are turning up with emotional problems than ever before. Near exam time, anxious teenagers may be consulting their doctors with headaches, sore elbows and wrists and all sorts of other stress-related symptoms.

What can parents do to help? The general advice we've given still applies, only more so. Apart from walking on eggshells and discouraging visitors, parents can further oblige with a predictable home routine, meals that are served hot and exactly on time, and a flexible approach to household chores (the harried student's participation in them, that is). This is called 'understanding'. Of course, a decent place to work and a utopian home life are not adequate in themselves. Teenagers also need 'exam preparation skills' – something, hopefully, the school can provide. A school counsellor tells students: 'If you fail to plan, you plan to fail.' With good preparation, confidence will increase and stress levels go down, although some students experience free-floating anxiety anyway. For them, more specific relaxation training or counselling may be called for.

> **David:** I know of one set of parents who had no idea their daughter was doing an important exam until the very morning it was on! Between total nonchalance and gut-churning panic, however, there's a good deal of concern and worry. For the majority, exam tension is unavoidable. Even now, seeing jacaranda blossoms gives me butterflies in the stomach, their association with summertime exams etched forever in my brain.

The school report

The school report, another interesting phenomenon, is designed to indicate, directly to parents, how a pupil is getting along. Much time and effort usually go into its preparation. With its interesting array of marks, symbols, averages, comments and exhortations, it is meant to provide a clear blueprint of the current state of affairs. The comments are particularly important, although sometimes you have to read between the lines.

In his Year 9 first-term report, a teenage boy received the following 'compliments': in maths he was 'polite and cooperative'; in home economics (which he topped) 'a zealous worker with an excellent attitude'; in history, 'thoughtful and positive in discussion'. In geography, however: 'He must learn that the teacher's decision is final. It is not his place to oppose the teacher.' School reports tell you something about the teacher too.

Often parents pay too much attention to the mark and too little to the record of effort, a mistake to be avoided at all costs. Some schools send instructions home on how to deal with the report, and encourage parents to respond sensitively. After all, it is not the intention to create unnecessary tension and unhappiness. The main don'ts are:

- Don't talk to other parents about the results (not too specifically, anyway).
- Don't openly compare the reports of siblings.
- Don't refer back and openly compare with earlier reports – it's now that counts (although a steady decline could certainly be an indication that something stressful is happening in the teenager's life).
- Don't offer bribes for future improvement – there are better incentives than a trip to Surfers Paradise or Disneyland. Your personal modelling of high standards, your respect and your interest in their progress should pay dividends in themselves.

▶ Don't panic, hit the roof and pile on more counterproductive pressure – expectations might be too great already.

School problems

Actually, high school teachers don't have an easy time. They need holidays (which some people seem to resent) to save their sanity. As well as having responsibility for as many as seven separate classes, material to prepare daily, tests to mark and standards to maintain, teachers are also expected to identify and help kids with problems.

School problems are common, with possibly as many as three in 10 students having academic or behavioural difficulties. The major concerns are about poor performance and the many causes of it (such as bullying or learning difficulties), poor attendance and poor behaviour. Here is some information about these problems.

Poor performance

The essence of underachievement is expectation. Someone thinks the student can do better, and is usually right. The reasons may not be deep: bright kids may become bored and stop trying; some are turned off by excessive emphasis on an irrelevant curriculum or feel that future employment prospects are bleak anyway and that 'learning this stuff' won't help; others simply have different priorities and 'march to the beat of a different drum'. Another reason for poor performance may rest with the quality of the teaching – teenagers may do badly in subjects taught by teachers they don't like (usually because they're boring, ill-prepared, sarcastic or punitive). More importantly, poor or deteriorating grades can also indicate emotional problems or specific learning difficulties.

Emotional problems are the most common of all school problems, and should be suspected when a teenager is anxious, sad or angry in relation to events in their life. Worry and stress short-circuit energy away from the task of learning, which makes falling marks a particularly sensitive indicator that something is amiss. It may be problems at home, but teasing and other hassles at school, either by peers or teachers, can really get kids down too. Refer to Chapter 12 for ways to deal with stress and emotional problems.

Bullying

More than half of all students have been bullied at some time and around one in six reports being bullied at 'detrimental levels' each week or more frequently. Even more concerning is the fact that a decade of intensive efforts in Australian schools to stop bullying has failed. According to a survey of 4500 high school students from Western Sydney, bullying is as prevalent as it was 10 years ago. But this does not mean we can afford to be complacent, because the problem is a serious one. Long-term effects may include low self-esteem, sleep problems, headaches, bed-wetting, anxiety and depression. These problems affect school peformance significantly.

Bullying occurs when someone is subjected to behaviour which is hurtful, threatening or frightening.

> **Three main types of bullying:**
> - Physical: pushing, pulling, hitting or physically attacking someone; damaging, removing or hiding another person's possessions without their permission; manhandling someone under the guise of 'horseplay'.
> - Verbal: spreading rumours, 'put-downs', name-calling, teasing, ridiculing others and their achievements; verbally attacking someone about their race or religion; making physical threats; making sexual comments about another person.
> - Social and/or psychological: purposely excluding someone from an activity; glaring or making menacing gestures at another person; totally ignoring someone, as if they don't exist; causing someone to feel afraid through intimidation.

As one might expect, boys are more likely to be physically abusive than girls. Boys aged 14 to 16 have been shown to be the least tolerant of all young people, which might have some bearing on such behaviours in this age group. In terms of bullying, girls are just as guilty as boys but more likely to use verbal or 'silent treatment' tactics.

For the victims, such experiences are distressing, isolating and unfair. There is evidence to show that teenagers who are bullied have lower than average self-esteem and are more inclined than others to stay away from school. Victims of ongoing bullying are likely to feel depressed and troubled and sometimes the consequences are devastating – in some studies, a number of youth suicides are blamed on bullying. Contrary to the old rhyme, 'sticks and stones will break my bones but words will never hurt me', verbal and social bullying are actually more likely to cause alarm and serious depression.

Bullying usually involves an imbalance in size, strength, power and numbers of children – many bullies act in groups. Sensitive, shy, and introverted adolescents who over-react or under-react are the common targets, as are those who are 'different', for example those who wear glasses or are overweight. But any child or teenager can be bullied.

Parents of teenagers who bully others should note that not all bullies were hot-headed, temperamental and impulsive infants who grew to enjoy inflicting pain on others (although this is apparently true of some). The reality is that family background, ethnicity and whether or not there are two parents or one in the home appear to have little bearing on who might become a bully. Even the stereotypical bully as the child substituting aggression for low self-esteem and social shortcomings turns out to be a myth. Some bullies fit this description but others are among their environment's more self-assured members (some even go on to become successful business leaders and politicians!). In other words, it can be cool to be a bully, at least in the bully's perception. Bullies place a high value on the domination of other people and feel more respected because of their behaviour. However, there could be trouble ahead – a Scandinavian study concluded that bullies were three times more likely than other children to graduate to adult crime.

Bullies tend to be angry. Anger puts impulsive adolescents most at risk. From a young age, children need to learn to express their anger in constructive ways. Bottling it up can be just as destructive as letting the volcano burst. It is helpful to identify what the real feeling is and then the real cause. Rather than anger, the feeling may be loneliness, restlessness, fear, irritability, anxiety, boredom, depression, panic or despair. The angry adolescent needs to be asked: Is the anger really justified? Is the issue worth wasting energy on? Would it help to talk to the person concerned? How can one let off steam in an acceptable way?

> Kids at school ask me: 'Why do you look different? What's wrong with your nose?'
>
> Mai, aged 14

All schools should have a whole-school approach and policies to address the issue of bullying. The culture of the school may be more important than any program implemented. Too often, subtle forms of bullying, harassment or racism are overlooked. Most anti-bullying programs fail because of a lack of consistency in implementation. The more successful programs reduce the numbers of students victimised by teaching them skills to protect and defend themselves. Newington College, a private boys' school in Sydney, has done this extremely well, dispelling myths about bullying and widely publicising to students and parents the recommendations and procedures for dealing with the problem. The policy includes the following responses to common misconceptions:

- *I was just mucking around, can't he take a joke?* This is the most common response from the bully. In fact, bullying is not a joke. It is not funny to ridicule and hurt someone, to make them feel uncomfortable or to push them around.
- *I don't want to cause trouble.* This misconception comes from the victim, who thinks he is the cause of the problem. All students have a right to feel safe at school, and during their travel to and from school. You are only standing up for yourself when you report being bullied.
- *It is just a natural part of growing up.* This misconception comes from adults, but the truth is that there is nothing 'natural' about being victimised.
- *No one can do anything about it.* Most cases of bullying are sorted out very simply, especially if the bullying is reported sooner rather than later. The school is committed to solving these sorts of problems, but students must communicate with staff if the school is to have any chance of helping.
- *Dobbing is a bad thing to do.* Bullying is the bad thing, telling the truth is a good thing. By telling the truth you are standing up for your rights as a human being. It takes character and intelligence to stand up for your rights, which is something that bullies are afraid of. Bullies try to intimidate people into maintaining a 'code of silence' because they can then continue to hurt other people for as long as they wish. Bullying continues when people fail to report what is happening.

Not all schools are quite so proactive or well prepared. If parents become aware that their child is being bullied, or if they suspect the bullying is being tolerated, they should contact the school immediately. They should speak to the teachers, principal or school counsellor. It is preferable not to approach the parents of the bully, however, as this tends to escalate the whole affair – let the school handle it.

At home, there are things that parents can do for kids who are or are at risk of being bullied. Teach your child relaxation skills – a less uptight kid is a less attractive target. Build confidence and self-assurance by, for example, encouraging involvement in non-competitive sports and drama (which helps build communication skills and expression). And pass on playwright Harvey Fierstein's excellent advice: 'Never be bullied to silence. Never allow yourself to be made a victim. Accept no one's definition of your life; define yourself.'

> **Leanne:** I remember one 14-year-old girl who was refusing to go to school because other children in the bus were burning her neck with cigarettes. She had been told she just had to stand up for herself as the bus driver could not be responsible for controlling the behaviour of other students. Bullying out-side schools and throughout our workplaces is widespread. Sometimes, it only takes good people, including bus drivers, to speak out to make a difference. Bullying only occurs because we tolerate it.

Racism

Unfortunately racism is also common in and out of schools. These experiences of young people are heart-breaking:

One day I overheard a fight between two boys at my school. It went like this: James yelled out, 'Scott, you are nothing but a stinking Abo.' Scott yelled back, 'No one's worse than an Abo.' And then they started laughing hysterically. I felt a tightness around my chest. I am Aboriginal. I have been called Abo, coon and boong. Words like that should be banned from the English language.

One of my 'friends' thought that us Kooris got too much money from the government and wasted the money on alcohol and cigarettes. Fellow students make racist jokes and remarks just

> within ears' reach. The racism became even worse when a teacher (who thought she was making me feel important) was singling me out to ask if facts or events about Aboriginal history were correct.
>
> I've always felt that I did not fit in anywhere and that people are just pretending. Kids at school say: 'You can't even tell that you are Aboriginal.' I was hurt on Sorry Day when friends said: 'Why do we have to say sorry to you? We didn't do anything wrong.'
>
> Why do people carry negative preconceptions on something that they have not been exposed to? To take a stance on an issue they know nothing about? To judge a person not because of their personality but because of their physical appearance or race? Something happened today after school that really upset me. A man came into work and refused to be served by an 'Asian Gook'. What would possess a man who was probably himself a descendant of an immigrant or maybe even a convict to pass judgement on my racial background? How am I supposed to react to such ignorance and pain? How am I going to cope if or when this sort of agonising encounter happens again?

At one school, the question of the advantages of multiculturalism was raised. Many students were able to talk about the need for respecting other cultures and beliefs. However at the same school here is what a group of Muslim girls said about how they were treated:

> We are expected to be terrorists and to hate Westerners yet we were born in Australia. People say things like 'Where are you from?' We are perceived to be illiterate and uneducated. They think we don't have free rights, freedom of speech or equality with our men. They expect to hear we are forced to cover up and have arranged marriages. When we walk down the street, people call us 'threats to society' and 'extremists'.

The injustice and negative impact of these experiences cannot be overstated. Poor school performance and school drop-out often are the result. Racism must not be tolerated.

Martin Luther King wrote: 'In the end we will remember not the words of our enemies but the silence of our friends.' It is a powerful reminder for good people to be fiercely outspoken against racism.

Learning difficulties

Specific learning difficulties should be suspected when there are particular problems with spelling, reading and mathematics; left/right confusion; and a sort of 'absentminded professor' approach to information. Learning difficulties are more common than we realise. Fifteen per cent of students have learning or behavioural difficulties that are significant enough to impact on their lives. The earlier they are picked up the better. Behaviour problems, related mostly to frustration, are often the clue to the existence of learning difficulties and are extremely common in boys. In fact, the two problems are often linked and one can lead to the other – learning problems can lead to behaviour problems and vice versa. The frustration that girls with learning difficulties experience is generally not quite as obvious since it is not acted out, and for this reason their learning difficulties may be under-identified. Some of these kids are reluctant to go to school or may develop some other form of anxiety.

There is some evidence that children from homes with domestic violence have attention difficulties. They may not actually have attention deficit disorder, but have problems concentrating or problems with hyperactivity. Anxiety and depression are conditions that often exist alongside this sort of hyperactivity as well.

Attention deficit disorder (ADD), first described almost 100 years ago, is now recognised as an important cause of learning and behaviour difficulties. Few conditions and their treatment have created more controversy and confusion than this, although decades of extensive research and experience have led to better understanding in treatment and education. The link between attention deficit disorder and learning difficulties (present in about 50 per cent of cases) has become more widely accepted as professionals, parents and people with the disorder collaborate.

The classic presentation of a frenetic, disorganised and infuriating kid used to be referred to simply as 'hyperactivity'. Nowadays it is called attention deficit hyperactivity disorder or ADHD. Without hyperactivity, the appropriate label is attention deficit disorder, or ADD (a condition which often goes unrecognised, particularly in girls, adolescents and able children). What we know for sure is that ADHD is more common in boys than girls. It is often hereditary. Most affected children will have a close relative, usually male, with some features of the condition and more than half will carry some elements of the disorder into adulthood.

Experts on ADHD find it affects up to five per cent of those under 18, with approximately two per cent considerably disadvantaged by it.

ADHD merges with normal behaviours and abilities, and unfortunately there is no foolproof diagnostic test. The three core behaviours – inattentiveness, impulsiveness and overactivity – are usually intense or frequent from as early as the pre-school years and are highlighted by the demands of school. Although ADHD tends to improve with age, some 60 per cent are affected in adolescence when it is complex to sort out, with the surge of hormones and all the other factors which influence a teenager's functioning and behaviour. By high school, longstanding problems with self-esteem and peer group relationships are the main difficulties, even after diagnosis and counselling. Some teenagers may display oppositional or conduct disorder (which are separate problems often accompanying ADHD), while others may become demoralised and depressed. These compounding issues need to be addressed along with the ADHD.

An intelligent and broad-based approach, focusing on the relative impact and implications of ADHD in a young person's life, is essential. ADHD has many causes and effects and, in the absence of a biological test, the diagnosis requires various perspectives, certainly more than a parent's story alone. Other factors such as emotional difficulties, chronic illness, hearing and vision problems can contribute to the behaviours. Pointers to ADHD include persistent patterns of strengths and weaknesses in school reports and specific psychological questionnaires. Comprehensive assessment also includes a thorough medical/neurological examination and a family interview. This all takes time and patience and needs to be well coordinated by someone you trust – for example, your local GP or community health centre. Remember also that most schools have school counsellors who can play a pivotal role.

There is a bewildering array of suggested interventions from medication to special education, behaviour support and counselling.

Unfortunately, many alternative practitioners promote quick-fix, ineffective and expensive treatments such as spinal manipulation, mega vitamins, diet restrictions, eye exercises, tinted lenses and EEG biofeedback.

Adolescents, like younger children, need more structure in their learning strategies, and patience, praise and encouragement are crucial. While it can be reassuring to have a 'medical label', all of life's difficulties are rarely due to a single organic cause or response to a single solution. This is particularly true where teenagers and their families are concerned. Perhaps the two most practical things you can do are join an ADHD support group (these can be found all over Australia and provide valuable information about services in your local area) and educate yourself about ADHD.

The major controversies with ADHD/ADD have been over stimulant medication which, in Australia, usually must be initiated by consultant paediatricians or psychiatrists. Extensive research and clinical experience certainly demonstrate that medication is an effective form of intervention, particularly as part of a comprehensive package of help. As with the use of any drug, the treating doctor needs to inform you about side effects and closely monitor progress, repeat prescriptions and possible misuse. Some teenagers are not too impressed with this approach, however, like the 15-year-old girl who said: 'I tried Ritalin once. I could concentrate. It was boring.'

We must also carefully nurture self-esteem and confidence in these teenagers. The following quotes bring out the fragility of self-esteem and the pain associated with learning disorders:

From Grade 5 to 11 was the hardest time for me growing up with ADD. At school, none of my friends knew that I had ADD and I didn't want them to know because I thought they might think differently of me and I thought they wouldn't want to be my friends any more. I didn't like taking tablets – they made me feel different – they changed my mood, my personality and I wasn't as talkative to my friends. But I found that everything was more organised. I was given heaps of help from teachers and tutors, but I hated it if my tutor was in the classroom with me. All the other students would know that she was there to help me. That made me feel really stupid.

One of the worst days was when one of my friends was searching my bag for food and he found my tablets. He told my friends and they all went quiet – I didn't like the way they reacted – it still hurts me to think about it. Then I changed schools but left the next school soon after.

Love, hugs, understanding, one-on-one time, a balanced lifestyle and a positive focus are all important in nurturing children and teenagers, particularly those with learning disorders.

Poor attendance

Going to school can sometimes be a real drag, but as already discussed, it's not simply a matter of choice. For better or worse, secondary education has been compulsory in Australia for children under 15 since World War II. There was a time when not showing up would soon see the authorities knocking on your door. The truant officer of old has been replaced (in some states) by a network of officers whose role is to liaise between the home and the school to identify reasons for non-attendance and seek solutions in a friendly, supportive way.

Teenagers fail to attend school for various reasons. They may be seriously ill or disabled, often needing time out to visit doctors or physiotherapists or to be treated in hospital. Parents may actually encourage them to stay at home to help out with the domestic chores or child care; this is not uncommon in families where education is not greatly valued. Then there is truancy, which is an unauthorised absence from school that is usually concealed from parents. This is different from school refusal, which is associated with severe emotional upset and a tendency to stay at home. These two conditions are approached in different ways and both need to be managed early by parents and schools.

School refusal: This is otherwise known as school phobia, and occurs when a child or adolescent fears or is reluctant to attend school, despite a desire to do so. When a young person consistently says 'I've got a headache' on school mornings, and is perfectly well and happy on weekends and holidays, something's going on. Although they say they have physical problems such as headaches and tummy aches, no medical cause is found. They may also complain of just 'feeling sick' or more specific symptoms such as 'butterflies in the stomach', aching muscles, a racing heart, tingling in the limbs, sweating, clammy hands, lump in the throat, choking, or shortness of breath. These are all signs of anxiety.

It may appear that a stressful situation or event at school is responsible, but in most cases the underlying problem is getting out of the front door and leaving home. Teenagers with this condition are often anxious about losing a parent (usually the mother) and staying at home is a way to keep track of things. Many of them (about half) are depressed, timid individuals who are afraid of new experiences. Of course, the involved parent may also be holding onto the child out of their own psychological neediness. Often family therapy or some other sort of counselling can help the young person gain the courage to move towards independence, and help the family relinquish control. Reassurance and encouragement or daily relaxation exercises are also helpful for these teenagers (as described on pages 228–30), who also suffer less in the long run if they are taken back to school gently and as soon as possible.

Truancy: This occurs when young people consciously 'wag' school in order to do something more enjoyable, such as playing in the park, seeing a movie or refining their electronic skills at video arcades. While some kids play truant just for the hell of it (hoping, of course, that no one will find out), sometimes they become involved in other problem behaviours such as stealing, vandalism and drug abuse. Then it is obviously a more serious problem.

Truancy can be dealt with by enlisting the support of teachers, maintaining attendance records and acting on absenteeism promptly. Continued communication, consideration of different subject choices and rewarding school attendance also help, as do opportunities for school participation, contribution and positive feedback. Teenagers will feel and want to be connected if they have someone to talk to and to trust, as this young person pointed out:

I was given a hard time by other kids and teachers. I hated some subjects, had trouble taking tests and was worried about doing things in front of the class. Why wouldn't I want to leave school to do things I want to do? Then I left for a while and felt lost. A youth worker got me into an alternative school – I learnt to set some goals. I learnt that it's really up to me.

> **Here are some helpful questions to ask teenagers who have difficulty attending school:**
> - What sorts of things do you do when you don't go to school?
> - What are the best things about wagging school?
> - What are the worst?
> - What things have made it hard for you to go to school?
> - Did something happen at the time you started avoiding school?
> - What are the sorts of things that you and others have done to make school easier for you to attend?
> - What would it take for you to go back to school regularly?
> - If you could change anything about school what would it be?

Poor behaviour

'Are teachers there to teach you or are they there to get you in trouble?' asked a girl in Year 7. This plaintive question raises an important point: what is 'poor behaviour'? Lack of attentiveness? Some kids explain that it is very difficult for them to be 'bright-eyed and bushy-tailed' at 8.30 in the morning. Some teenagers, it seems, are just not 'morning people'.

A pattern of aggressive or oppositional behaviour, on the other hand, is a worrying sign, especially when accompanied by school failure. Teenagers who resist the usual limit-setting and consistently infringe the rights of others are in a special category. For teachers, such kids are extremely taxing, often intimidating and ultimately soul-destroying. It is worth noting, too, that violence in Australian schools is gaining momentum, a situation which is causing serious concern in education circles.

Corporal punishment is no longer acceptable, but has been part of a spectrum of measures designed to control kids. Teachers and schools vary greatly in their handling of discipline problems. Other techniques include: a sympathetic exploration of the underlying reasons for the behaviour; a symbolic gesture such as 'demerits' or loss of privileges; suspension from classes (the ignominy of working alone); physical detention after school hours with or without the writing out of lines; the use of peer discipline (for example, having to clean a prefect's shoes); or expulsion from school – usually a drastic last resort. Many schools have a list of infractions such as these so that you can at least know where you are on the trajectory to expulsion. But some take a more preventive view based on a 'whole of school' culture, by fostering a sense of community, remembering to catch kids doing something good and perhaps even inviting the student body to actually make the rules.

To what extent the more serious measures are deserved, necessary or helpful is difficult to say. Some kids seem too readily labelled as bad, when there are clearly other factors at play. Some kids who play up are those who cannot see the relevance in what they're doing, lose respect for educational values and become disenchanted with the authority of teachers.

There's another worrying thought. The people who do best in life are those who have self-confidence and feel good about themselves. These attributes are less likely to develop if the measures used to control students' behaviour involve fear, stress, uncertainty, confusion and failure. Enlightened schools know this and act accordingly.

Treatment of school problems

Not all kids with school problems have specific learning difficulties or require disciplinary measures. As teachers well know, a class is made up of individuals with a wide range of abilities and personalities. In a given situation, it will be necessary to look closely at the young person causing concern in order to work out what is best.

Tutoring or a change of school may be needed in order to make a fresh start. If children are unwell, they will need treatment. If this is a stress-related disorder or there are other emotional problems involved, professional counselling may be needed. In most situations, the school will be able to point parents in the right direction.

Connected to community

In the normal quest for independence, many young people choose or are forced to suddenly sever connections with family and school. Emerging from the incubator can be a painful experience and it is here that connectedness with community becomes particularly important. Teenagers need to be encouraged to take the initiative in being involved in community, but parents can lead by example. We can encourage young people from early adolescence to take an interest in their communities. These activities may be very simple, such as involvement with neighbours, work experience, sporting clubs, theatre, clean-up days, charities, fundraising activities for local youth services, youth leadership opportunities with local councils, community vegetable gardens, bushwalking groups, environment groups, land care, and writing letters to local councils and politicians about issues that concern them.

These are the words of a well-connected 17-year-old:

In a world that is civilised, problems are still sorted out by war and terrorism. In our own communities there is so much pain and people resort to drug use. Globalisation is a worry. We think about materialistic stuff too much. Politics, the environment, logging, pollution, youth unemployment, East Timor, racism, suicide, Aboriginal people and poverty. There are so many ignorant and intolerant people who don't care. Well, I care, but I have learnt to put my energy into one cause rather than being paralysed by being worried by everything.

Our community needs to reflect on fundamental questions affecting our lives and shrug off cynicism.

How connected are you to your own community?

Getting a job – the next step in life

Having a job means having an answer when someone asks, 'What do you do for a living?' Getting a job is what's supposed to happen when you leave school or complete your training. It's what kids, and their parents, plan for and look forward to – a ticket to self-reliance, security and self-worth.

Unfortunately, whatever one's expectations or desires, there are no guarantees. While a good job can mean status, fulfilment and the chance for advancement, a bad job can mean stress, danger and boredom. The only thing worse, perhaps, is having no job at all.

For most teenagers, the world of work is school – that's where they are most of the week. Their whole effort is directed towards an imaginary afterwards. A badge on a teenager's lapel said, ever so simply, 'School's out – what's next?' This is the haunting question facing our kids from the moment they step into the high school years.

Early forays

Children tune in to the harsh realities of the commercial world early in life. How long does it take for kids to realise that there are things to buy, from essential consumer items (such as lollies, drinks and ice-cream) to commodities of more enduring value? At some point, what they really need is an income, and that means pocket money.

Pocket money is a financial handout which comes with or without strings attached. Family attitudes and practices vary widely here. Questions of how much, how often and what it's supposed to cover need to be resolved. Sometimes the older the teenager, the larger the investment (a common source of irritation for younger siblings). An only child seems to do best of all. One father we know puts a whole year's worth of pocket money into an account for each of his two teenagers, and lets them manage it as they see fit (his 13-year-old daughter is currently dabbling on the stock market). Then there are those of us who are willing to be 'touched' on a weekly basis.

Many parents are wary of promoting the idea of 'something for nothing' and prefer to connect a regular allowance (or even sporadic payments) to the carrying out of certain household tasks. This is most likely the case with a family's oldest child. Alternatively, and more fairly perhaps, a reasonable basic rate might be agreed to for sundry minor needs, with a bonus for voluntary duties. Whatever the system, pocket money introduces kids to the give-and-take of the commercial world, even though, in this instance, the 'boss' might be a bit of a pushover.

Adolescence can be expensive. A study by researchers at the University of Canberra showed that parents spend over $200 a week on 15- to 17-year-olds, almost four times what they spend on kids under five. A teenager's needs and desires (at least for all but the most indulged) will soon exceed the family coffers. Making a few dollars on the side becomes the only way to go. Enterprising kids look first within their immediate neighbourhood, taking virtually anything that pays – paper runs, baby-sitting, helping out at the local garage. For students, part-time work after school or at weekends might involve a bit of travelling, but it shows a growing sense of responsibility and is generally worth encouraging.

What about a 'proper' job?

When it comes to looking at life, let alone future job prospects, the early teens provide a high-flying vantage point. Idealism is rampant and, for most, anything seems within grasp. With the gaining of a little more maturity, say at 15 or 16, it is more a question of options, of weighing up possibilities, although fantasies about lavish lifestyles remain strong. Only later will kids become aware that high-paying, sophisticated and exciting jobs are mostly figments of one's imagination. By the time it's okay to be practical, say at 18 or 19, aspirations will need to have shrunk to match a somewhat more sober reality.

Teenagers know that work is important. Unfortunately, what we often forget to mention is that a proper job, something a young person would be happy to stick at, is relatively hard to come by. A job that doesn't challenge one's abilities or afford an opportunity to explore and discover, can make arrival at the workplace a terrible disappointment.

The pressure on young people to stay at school, obtain extra training and generally prepare themselves as extensively as possible for a better job later on, will provide definite advantages for some individuals (as well as keeping down the official unemployment figures). But what a let-down, when the time eventually comes, for those who cannot find a job to match their qualifications.

Ever counted the number of pimples at supermarket checkouts or behind the sterile counters in fast food stores? Yes, they are filled with teenagers trying to earn even a little spare cash. There are jobs available for young people, but in terms of vocational satisfaction, many leave a lot to be desired. If the only job a teenager can get is part-time, there are two sides to the argument. On the positive side, one could argue (as employers might) that these jobs enable kids to learn the ropes, cope with people and achieve at least a small measure of self-sufficiency. On the other hand they: don't constitute an adequate income; are frequently menial, repetitive and boring; provide only the most tenuous toe-hold into the workforce; rarely lead to something enduring and worthwhile.

The point is, as most parents will know, underemployment (even in a full-time job) does little for human dignity, and rapidly turns youthful exuberance and enthusiasm to dust.

The world of no work

In June 2001, the Australian Bureau of Statistics reported that the rate of youth unemployment was 16.09 per cent for 15- to 19-year-olds and 10.3 per cent for 20- to 24-year-olds. We are talking about almost three-quarters of a million unemployed young people, around the same number who are employed in either full- or part-time jobs. In 2000, Australia had the eighth-highest rate of youth unemployment in the industrialised world.

Everyone is aware of the enormity of the youth unemployment problem. Many people are touched by it directly. It is an issue that concerns young people, parents and governments. In reality, it's not that vast numbers of kids go for years without a job, it's that many of them are in and out of jobs (long-term unemployment is actually more of a problem for older workers than for teenagers). In any case, the bald statistics give little sense of its impact on the lives of individuals and their families.

Surely there's a job out there

Comfortably employed people take a perfunctory glance at the fat employment sections in our major newspapers and wonder what all the fuss is about. Those who regularly do battle with these pages of promise, however, know differently. Changes in the job market over the past 20 years or so have been profound. With increasing technology, many full-time jobs previously available to young people, such as factory, trade and farmwork have simply disappeared. For those that remain, competition is fierce.

A government survey of the job market showed that 25 per cent of unemployed adolescents had trouble getting work because they were too young. Insufficient work experience ruled out another 10 per cent or so, in what has become the classic double bind for young job seekers: without a job, you can't get experience; without experience you can't get a job. It's not easy!

What about motivation?

One often hears adults talking about the laziness or lack of motivation of young people in regard to work. Employers say they have difficulty filling jobs at times, and accuse unemployed teenagers of being too choosy. Many parents seem to hold this view also, and believe that there are plenty of things kids could do if they really wanted to. Well, yes and no. It clearly depends which side of the problem you're on.

Most young people who have been surveyed are very keen to work and gain experience. They are a very mobile group, often willing to travel long distances to seek employment. What they are always hoping for, of course, is to be able to do something useful, something they can feel good about. But what they do not always realise is that success requires more than motivation.

Others factors are important, such as: your level of schooling and academic achievement (this is where young people with a poor foundation in literacy and numeracy, more commonly boys, are at such a disadvantage); current abilities; personality, attitude and appearance (that is, how you come across in interviews); and past work history. Unemployed young people with recent references from previous work fare better than those without. For unskilled workers, there just aren't a lot of jobs around, however keen you might be to find one.

Teenagers who do have jobs, on the other hand, are notorious for doing a half-hearted job or just opting out if things don't suit them. The boss, of course, perceives this as unreliability (which is the most common reason for young people losing their jobs). The big worry is that employers may ultimately feel disinclined to take on young people, thus adding immeasurably to the difficulties they face.

Motivation takes a beating, too, when young people experience repeated or prolonged periods out of work. They become depressed and demoralised by the vicious circle of unemployment. They become bored and listless, which makes it increasingly difficult to give a good impression at job interviews. So it's not surprising that the long-term unemployed become increasingly unemployable.

What's it like being unemployed?

Being unemployed for two weeks is like a holiday – being unemployed for three months or three years is like a sentence without a reprieve. Constantly looking for a job is an exhausting and disillusioning task in itself. As a young person who knows explained:

> *I go to the Commonwealth Employment Service only to wait in line. I go to the Department of Social Security only to wait in line. 'They' talk about statistics. I know what they mean – I'm just an unemployment statistic waiting in line.*

The many difficulties that face unemployed young people fall into three main categories: practical problems, health problems and family problems.

Practical problems: Living on the dole, a single meagre cheque once a fortnight, provides for little more than a spartan existence. When the basics – rent or board, food and travel – are barely covered, anything you might want to do is limited by financial constraints. New clothes are often well beyond reach. A major problem is not having enough money to get around, which can lead to social isolation and loss of contact with friends. An unemployed 19-year-old girl sums it up: 'When you can't afford to go anywhere, you're just stuck there. You feel confined.'

Health problems: Lifestyles that often accompany prolonged unemployment are not particularly healthy. Unemployed young people admit to staying up late, not eating regularly or well, not exercising, smoking too much and drinking too much, behaviour related in part to simply having too much time on their hands. To be homeless as well greatly compounds the problems.

An unemployed 16-year-old boy was referred to a specialist by his local doctor because he was feeling tired and dazed (sort of dizzy all the time). The symptoms were no more specific than that, although he looked a bit pale and seedy too. On closer examination, his daily timetable seemed relevant to his current state: during the week, he'd routinely sleep till about midday, have a bite to eat, then sit and watch television till midnight; on weekends, he'd go 'raging' with his friends and drink himself into oblivion. This had been his life since leaving school several months previously. He'd not tried to get a job and said he'd lost all confidence.

Unemployed young people are more likely to report health problems, both physical and emotional, than employed youth. Of these, emotional problems are considered the more serious:

- Unhappiness and depression have been widely reported, as well as high suicide rates.
- Feelings of loneliness, frustration, guilt and anxiety are common.
- Many have low self-esteem, an absence of goals and a lack of purpose in life.
- Most feel alienated, powerless and disillusioned (a recipe for major social unrest and violence).

Family problems: Looking to one's family, a traditional source of help and support, doesn't sound unreasonable. But this can be a big disappointment. Unemployed teenagers living at home often feel resentment at not being fully contributing members of the family. When they are nagged and hassled, as they often are, it adds insult to injury. They feel they have lost respect, that their parents see them as failures (which is exactly how they see themselves).

Parents are also frustrated and worried. They find it difficult to accept young people as adults when they don't have a proper job. It's aggravating when teenagers sleep in late, slop around the house like death warmed up, and don't seem to be making a major effort to get a job. Parents may resent having to support kids on the dole, particularly if they embrace an attitude of 'the world owes me a living'. They may be torn between feelings of helplessness and an urge to force them into some sort of employment 'for their own good' (some parents give this as a reason for taking a big chunk of the dole as board – a measure more likely to be experienced as punitive than helpful).

Arguments and tension can reach the point where leaving home may seem preferable to enduring the hassles or shame. Some kids are literally thrown out, often to face worse and deteriorating circumstances (which frequently include joining the sad ranks of the homeless). But it doesn't always end up like this and it doesn't need to. Some families seek more constructive solutions and cope better – they encourage unemployed young people to maintain hope and accept that the overall problem is not of their making (which it most definitely is not).

Parental hopes

Very few parents would not want their kids to find a niche, to end up doing something worthwhile. Many have hopes and aspirations, sometimes in multiple areas of their children's lives – relationships, hobbies and, of course, career. Some parents have it all worked out. To them, children are not just little kids with a future of their own (as uncertain as that may be). At three years of age, they are already doctors, lawyers or business tycoons.

It would be very unusual for fathers and mothers not to want good things for their kids. Whether in relation to appearance, sport, education or future success, parents can be motivated by two powerful desires:

- For their children to do as well as, or better than they did.
- For their children to do what they were unable to do.

This may be called the 'achievement imperative' and is either good or bad for the teenager, depending on degree. There's a fine line sometimes between setting a standard and encouraging effort, on the one hand, and coercing with heavy pressure and unrealistic expectations (usually because of one's own needs) on the other. It's important to know the difference and worthwhile thinking about what your motives are next time you're running up and down the sidelines of a football field or putting pressure on your daughter to stay in all weekend to study.

Such children bear the promise of becoming what their parents could not be, of achieving what their parents could not achieve. Some people merely want their offspring to follow along in their own footsteps, to validate and continue their parents' efforts. Parents who live through their kids put them under enormous pressure, and it can work out badly.

An 18-year-old boy with crippling stomach pains told his doctor that he desperately wanted to choose a different career path to his father's, but couldn't muster the courage to tell him (although eventually he did and his stomach pains mysteriously disappeared). There are other cases in which bright and talented young people have opted out of tertiary education rather than following a prescribed professional career. Teenagers need to develop a separate and special identity of their own, but hopefully not a life path determined by an act of rebellion.

All parents wonder what lies ahead for their kids. In today's world, to not worry about this would be unusual. It's impossible not to be involved, to enjoy their successes and suffer their failures. At the same time, we should allow them to live and create their own reality. We can be supportive, but we cannot do it for them.

Teenagers may need assistance, at first, in writing appropriate letters of application to potential employers and preparing a résumé. But the most important thing they have to realise is how crucial it is to present well in person. In *The Teenager and You*, student counsellor Jan Wilson offers young people some practical hints for the interview:

- Make an effort to create a good first impression.
- Be neat and clean; sneakers, thongs, excess makeup or outrageous gear can prejudice an employer.
- Have available in a folder: your school records, any certificates or special awards, birth certificate and references, any samples of past writing or a hobby that may be relevant.

- Arrive five minutes early; do not become impatient if you are kept waiting (the employer may be delayed).
- When asked to enter, step forward and speak clearly, be prepared to shake hands, do not sit until asked to do so.
- Always look directly at the interviewer.
- Do not smoke.

Parents can encourage good presentation and attitude and provide support and reassurance. We cannot determine our teenagers' futures. In the end, it is up to them.

Keys to the future

According to the experts, the keys to finding a place in today's ultra-competitive job market are training and knowledge. The better your skills the better your chances, so continuing your education in order to become more employable later makes good sense.

In the future, workplace training and upgrading of skills will become an ongoing part of the work environment. This means that as jobs change, workers will be re-educated, with TAFE (Technical and Further Education) playing a more and more important role. No doubt, given its vocational orientation, TAFE will become increasingly viewed by young people (even before Year 12 at high school for some) as an alternative to university.

In recent years, the university population has risen by about 30 per cent, but the jobs are not meeting the demand. Therefore, for those who choose a university education, it is advisable to keep an open mind about what lies beyond graduation. There is still a reasonable chance of getting a job in medicine, dentistry and optometry, but job opportunities directly related to the degree obtained are far less likely in almost all other occupations. This is not doom and gloom. It is simply the way it is. At these times young people can be active in their communities. It's about keeping them connected until their job opportunities arise.

Some unanswered questions

As incredible as it sounds, a growing percentage of bright, able-bodied and eager young people face the prospect of a future without work. At one time, such an idea would have seemed preposterous.

Today, it is a reality, a situation brought about by our new technologies and changing priorities.

What we are seeing is the creation of a new social condition in which an increasing number of young people are frozen in limbo between school and work. What was already a long period of dependence on parents is being extended.

In our society, so much of one's identity is wrapped up in work. Without it, there is no way to avoid feeling like a second-class citizen. Unemployment is clearly a complex social problem with far-reaching consequences. For one thing, it renders the traditional function of schools invalid. Should we, in the light of current reality, be educating kids for unemployment? Or is that a defeatist attitude? There are a number of other pertinent and perplexing questions as well:

- Does long-term unemployment always have negative effects on young people? Not necessarily – the research on this remains inadequate. There are very few studies that follow young people from school into unemployment and note the changes. Surely it is wrong, therefore, to assume that all unemployed young people will regress, deteriorate or self-destruct. Some will maintain social competence, while others will strike out in new, effective directions.
- Is it possible that some young people find temporary advantage in the role of unemployment, as a respite from academic or social pressures? Taking a break from work and living on the dole (particularly when several incomes are pooled) is not all that tough. Needless to say, those few dishonest individuals who live well on several dole cheques bring discredit and dishonour to their struggling peers. The unemployment benefit was first introduced as a stopgap between jobs (it was never intended as a permanent lifestyle).

Some final thoughts

David: Did it ever occur to you that parents get a double dose of schooling? Firstly there's your own, then there's your children's. If your school days were the very best days of your life (well, it's possible) and your kids are doing okay, this is fine, no big deal. If not, it can seem like an endless and exhausting saga.

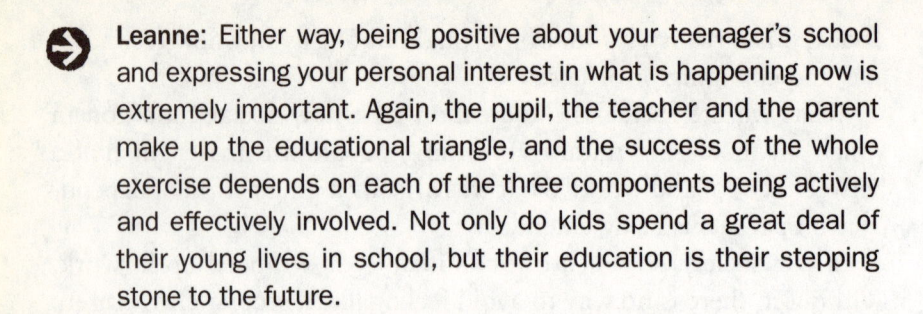

Leanne: Either way, being positive about your teenager's school and expressing your personal interest in what is happening now is extremely important. Again, the pupil, the teacher and the parent make up the educational triangle, and the success of the whole exercise depends on each of the three components being actively and effectively involved. Not only do kids spend a great deal of their young lives in school, but their education is their stepping stone to the future.

David: Throughout the world, studies of young people's worries about the future put unemployment into first place. Society has to find a satisfactory solution to this and not merely accept it as part of the inevitable cost of progress. The ultimate outcome of disrupting, confusing and alienating an entire generation of energetic young people is surely a high price to pay. Despite growth in adult employment in Australia, youth unemployment is still unacceptably high.

Leanne: For young people, a sense of belonging to school, tertiary education and work contributes to their resilience and wellbeing and is a crucial element in one's trajectory to successful adulthood. We must work harder to keep them connected.

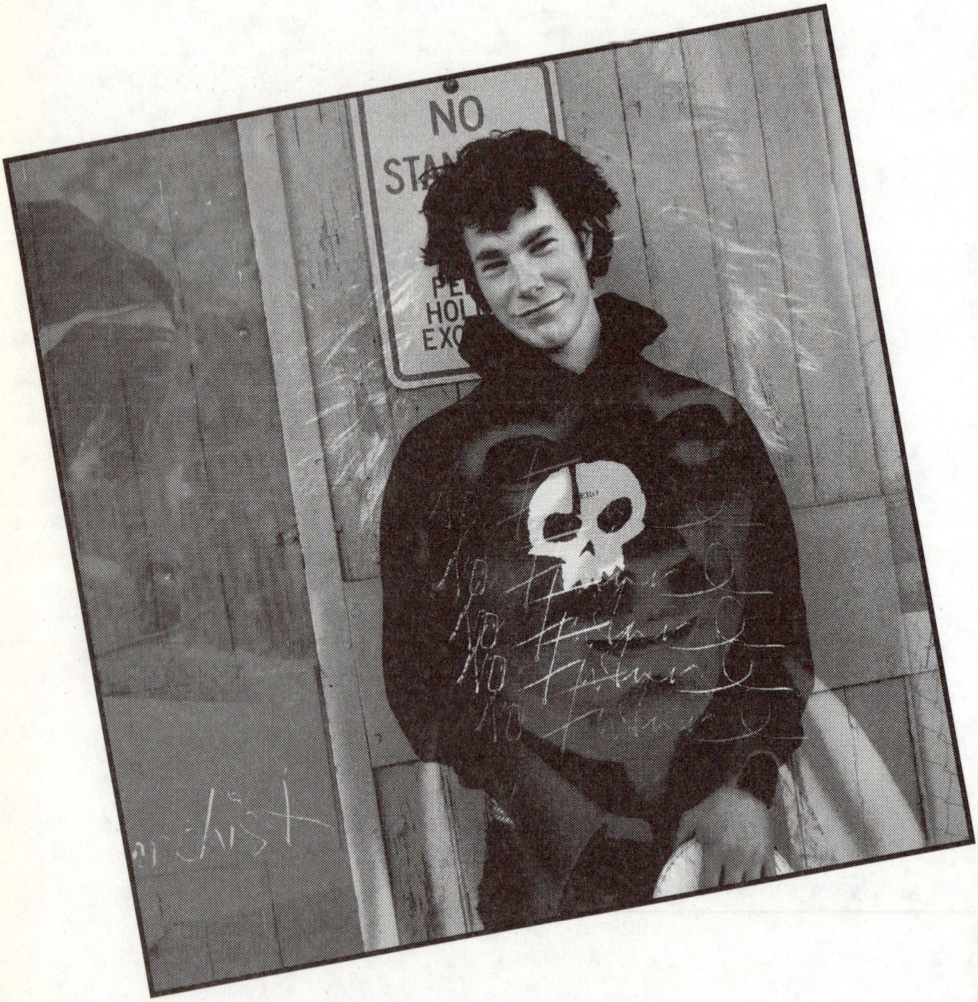
NO

Chapter 12

Teaching by example

> When my parents say 'I feel very hurt when you say that', it makes me stop arguing.
> Andrew, aged 16

Teenagers search for recognition, independence, respect and understanding. They learn who parents really are by questioning their values and taking control. They have very sensitive 'hypocrisy and injustice meters' and tend to learn more from example than words about everything from healthy lifestyle to spirituality.

Thinking depressed

Parents teach their children ways of thinking and communicating. Teenagers who become depressed tend to 'think depressed' and have difficulty identifying and expressing emotions. Usually they respond to the idea that there are other ways of thinking about things. Adults, on the other hand, tend to be more resistant to changing their thinking patterns.

Negative thinkers tend to ask the wrong questions about life situations. We need to consider what our own attitudes are and to think more about the ways our inner thinking makes us feel. Are our thoughts positive? Are we asking helpful questions?

Here are some questions to think about:

- Am I only noticing the negative side of things?
- Am I worrying about things I can't do anything about?
- Am I taking things personally?
- Am I always exaggerating everything?
- What is the real evidence of my thinking?
- Am I blaming myself for things that are not my fault?
- Am I seeking solutions or just complaining?
- Is this thinking helpful or unhelpful?
- Am I assuming things can't change?

One teenager said this about negative thinking:

I have all these negative thoughts. That I have no real future, that I will fail miserably in my future job. That I am a terrible person. The thought of gaining weight. Embarrassment. The thought of someone demanding respect from me when they don't respect me to begin with. The thought of losing the people I love and confronting the people I dislike. I don't know how I got all these fears but they are constantly in my mind.

Parents who try to maintain their mental health teach their teenagers to think more positively. We can unknowingly 'transmit' our positive as well as our negative attitudes.

Helping teenagers deal with stress

Adults have become very interested in the idea of stress management, but obviously the earlier such skills are learned, the better. It is generally accepted that:

- People with strong support systems and a strong sense of connectedness and caring live longer and suffer less stress-related disease than those who feel isolated and lonely.
- Certain lifestyle habits are helpful in strengthening us against the effects of stress: a sensible diet, adequate sleep and regular exercise; an ability to 'slow down', do one thing at a time and achieve a reasonable balance between work, rest and play.

Parents can set the scene throughout childhood. They can encourage kids to view pressure as a challenge, to cope with hard knocks courageously and well, and to develop skills for dealing with the more serious threats to their emotional equilibrium. Much has been written on this subject, but the keys are rehearsal, relaxation, 'self talk' and assertiveness:

> *I constantly worry that I might do something stupid and embarrassing.*
> Angela, aged 13

Rehearsal: It is extremely important that children and teenagers are able to anticipate stressful or dicey situations they might encounter and mentally 'practise' possible solutions. (This is obviously relevant to risk-taking behaviours, which will be discussed in depth in Chapter 14.) For example, a teenager might decide to avoid being exposed to something stressful (such as unprotected sexual intercourse) or be prepared to take some sort of positive action (such as talking things through, soon, with someone he or she trusts). Parents can help simply by talking openly with kids about their concerns and ideas in such matters.

Relaxation: Being able to relax is a potent antidote to stress and a major advantage to a young person facing, say, an exam or a public performance (such as giving a speech or having an interview for a job). Since transcendental meditation was introduced to the West in the early 1960s, millions of devotees throughout the world have taken it up in order to achieve 'a state of conscious restfulness' (usually for about 20 minutes twice a day). Teenagers might not be too taken with this approach, but it will be useful for them to know how to get calm quickly. They can easily learn the following technique:

- Take several slow, deep breaths, relaxing the shoulders while breathing out, then allow breathing to become quieter and more peaceful.
- Relax the muscles of the face and jaw. Once your facial expression becomes tranquil and at ease, the mind and body tend to follow.

'Self talk': When things go wrong, most people put themselves down ('I probably deserved it, anyway'). Positive 'self talk' is the opposite, a magic mental tool for building up self-esteem in the face of adversity ('Well, I tried my best in the ballet exam – next time will be better').

> **Kids need to be actively encouraged to be kind to themselves. They should be reminded that:**
> - Every person is unique and of value, so think often about all your good points.
> - Positive thoughts absorb anxiety, so focus on the good things you are looking forward to in the future.
> - People with a sense of humour handle stress better (smiling reduces tension and makes you more likeable), so reach out and make contact.

Assertiveness: This is probably the most important anti-stress attribute one could possibly acquire, and one we tend to underestimate. Assertiveness simply means saying and doing what is right for you (without being aggressive or threatening) in situations where there is pressure to do otherwise. Assertiveness is about communicating effectively in situations of stress and if that means saying 'NO' (the most important assertiveness tool of all), then that's what you say.

The message for parents is to teach your children and teenagers to think about what's likely to be upsetting to them; to talk about it (both with their parents and with others); and to take positive action in their own interests.

Resolving conflicts

Family conflict is one of the most common and distressing problems. In the adolescent years, minor irritations can escalate. But are teenagers only to blame? Parents teach their children how to solve conflict by their calm, patient example.

Parents may find it helpful to categorise conflicts. Are they minor irritations? Unnecessary? Unwinnable? Not negotiable? We can learn to respond differently to different categories, to avoid over-reacting to minor irritations or under-reacting in situations where safety is paramount. Consider the following:

- Conflicts which are minor irritations can be negotiated and prevented with incentives (who sits in the front of the car, who opens the gate, when they watch TV, when they do chores, when they go to bed).
- Sometimes conflicts occur through unnecessary parental interference in situations that inevitably lead to consequences at school (not doing homework, late for school, forgetting sports equipment, lunch, etc.). In these situations young people learn from their mistakes by their consequences.
- Arguments about control (over clothes, makeup, haircut, pierced ears, tattoos) simply cannot be won by parents unless enforced by the school. You can say: 'I strongly disagree with you getting a tattoo.' 'I totally disagree with you piercing your nipple.' The most important priority is to ensure safe piercing or tattooing, rather than arguing ineffectively on whether it can be done at all. Short of locking your teenager in their room (which we would not recommend), it is impossible to prevent young people conforming to the latest fashion.
- For more important issues, parents must pull rank to ensure the safety of their child (travelling with a drunk driver, riding a bike without a helmet, accessing pornography on the Internet). However, the issue of safety must be discussed before the event in routine conversation from an early age, as well as strategies to resist the pressure of peers.
- If we are in constant conflict with our teenagers, we need to ask ourselves about our priorities. What is the result we want? In the long term, does this conflict matter?

In the Smith household, there were arguments every night over cleaning up after dinner. Sarah and her parents made an agreement that she would clean up the kitchen by 9 pm. The next night, her father yelled at her at about 8.45 pm, because the dishwasher was not packed. To Sarah, this was much more than a minor argument about the dishwasher, but was more to do with her parents having inconsistent rules that they broke, and about control and domination. This pattern was repeated in many conflicts in the household; Sarah and her parents admitted they had all behaved badly and that the conflicts had escalated. The issue is not about the unpacking of the dishwasher, it is about the process and having to learn another way of approaching a conflict. For instance, when families come to us for help with this sort of problem, we try to teach them how to deal with the conflicts in another way, rather than try to solve it for them. We work through the following process:

- Choose a small conflict.
- Define the problem. What is the real problem? Describe it exactly. What is the real argument?
- What are all the solutions? Every family member should nominate even the silly or impossible ones. All ideas are to be respected. Try to use language like 'I feel...', rather than 'You make me feel...'
- Choose the best solution for everyone. List the positives and the negatives for each idea. Is it a helpful or unhelpful solution?
- Is there anything else behind the argument?
- How can this be communicated in the future?

A common example would be arguments at the dinner table. One family sought help because their 13-year-old daughter, Kate, would pick fights with her younger brothers at the table and a family argument would escalate, often with one parent throwing food and ordering Kate to her room...

What is the real problem? Kate described the real problem like this:

> Mum and Dad both get home from work late. We are starving. They expect me to set the table and do everything around the kitchen. The boys don't have to do anything. My younger brother, Damian, always starts it by pulling faces when Mum is not looking. Then I tell him off and it all starts.

Mum described the real problem like this:

> Kate makes me feel guilty for working. I work hard all day without a rest and I come home to a house in chaos. Kate only helps if I nag her and I think I will have to give up work because she is not showing any responsibility.

What are all the solutions? Kate and her Mum nominated these:

> Get a bigger table.
> Eat earlier.

Give up work.
Tell Damian nicely not to pull faces.
Share the chores evenly between the kids.
Offer to do chores before asked.
Spend special time together on weekends to make up for the busy week.

Is there anything else behind the argument? From this discussion, we were able to open up the issue about mum's work. Kate admitted that she did not want her mother to give up work because she realised it provided advantages for the family. This greatly relieved the guilt of her mother, which led to a calmer handling of future conflicts.

In this process, the family solved the problem and learnt a different and more constructive way of solving other conflicts. Kate explained:

> *We used to have arguments and then later I didn't know what they were even about. Then my parents started this thing where they'd say: 'I feel very hurt when you say that.' It makes me stop arguing. I say: 'I feel really angry about . . .' It makes us stop and think what the real argument is about.*

What if the teenager refuses to see the problem and a conflict arises over their selfishness and lack of responsibility? Punishments in the form of denying privileges, grounding, fines and extra household chores can be imposed but it is usually better to inflict these when everyone is calm. If things start to get out of hand, it is important to bring the support of a third party into the situation, such as extended family, a teacher, student welfare coordinator or GP, to allow a different perspective.

Household chores, as we've discussed, are a frequent source of arguments, but you can do things to stop them escalating. Involve the whole family rather than only the offending adolescent; list all the chores in the household, and come to an agreement on a fair distribution of responsibility and a system for completing them. Rather than asking for help with chores, which implies a favour, ask for family members to share and to cooperate.

On the next page is another example of the process of resolving conflict.

What is the problem? Jeremy spends too much time glued to the computer.

What are the possible solutions? Sell the computer; limit the time spent playing on the computer; reduce the use of violent games; let them play games only with friends; play games with your teenager; move the computer out of the bedroom; turn the computer off at 9 o'clock each night.

Advantages and disadvantages of each suggestion: Some homework is done on the computer and so selling it will interfere with school work. Playing games with friends and parents will increase Jeremy's social interaction. Turning the computer off at the end of the day and moving it out of the bedroom will allow other members of the family to have access to it. Both parents work late so it's difficult to monitor computer time. Jeremy's parents always lose games and feel defeated!

The family then decided on the best solution together: Turn off the computer at 8 o'clock every evening and spend time as a family after this. This solution was the easiest for the family to monitor and be consistent about. If the rule was not complied with, the plug was to be pulled out of the wall and the computer lead confiscated for a week.

Review of progress: It worked!

Conflicts need to be seen as opportunities to learn and to teach. Here are some perceptive positive insights young people give on the issue of conflict:

> *It always hurts when we fight with a friend or family member, but it doesn't have to mean the end of the relationship. It helps to try to put yourself in their position, see things from their point of view. To do this, you need to be alone for a while and although it is painful to think about the situation, really analyse it from your side, but from theirs as well. Try to understand where they are coming from and you may see why they are angry or worried. Once you have thought long and hard, if possible make another approach or write a letter explaining your point of view. Let them*

know you understand how they feel and give them a chance to explain it to you without arguing – wait until they have finished, to tell them how that makes you feel. Then remind yourself you have done your bit and now it is up to them, but remember they may need time to think about it in the same way you did. Do not blame yourself, but do not blame them either – there are always two sides to the story.

Sometimes things work out and this new understanding that you have with each other really helps. But sometimes things may not work out and you have to accept this and wait until things have smoothed over a little, to try again. I was having a lot of conflict with my family but I realise now that I need to compromise to make life easier for myself. I need to be less selfish – otherwise it's not fair on my family and it backfires.

Our response to conflict is often emotional. We can learn to stand back and change the way we deal with it. One of the great things about being a parent is that we can grow with our children. Next time a conflict arises, use it as an opportunity to teach by example.

Problem-solving

In the same way, parents can teach their teenagers to solve their own problems and encourage them to take initiative rather than 'rescuing' them every time they have an issue. Many problems do not cause conflicts but they are nevertheless time consuming for parents. It is better to offer a method for solving a problem. The method can then be used to solve other problems and this leads to confident, independent thinking. Here is a simple example:

James recently qualified to play in a top tennis team at school. This was a great achievement but the announcement to his parents led to a prolonged discussion about how they were going to change their arrangements to drive him to before-school training and weekend tournaments as well as to his social engagements.

James was asked to follow this process:

What is the problem?
Transport and time.

List all possible solutions

Walk.
Give up sport.
Ask Mum and Dad to drive me to everything.
Explore the bus timetable.
Ask friends if their parents can share the driving.
Organise to sleep at a friend's house.
Arrange to go to school earlier with neighbour.
Get my learner's permit as soon as possible so I am independent next year.

Write down the main advantages and disadvantages

I am not that fit but walking would help me get fitter.
Giving up sport would solve the problem but then I would have another problem – boredom.
My parents can't do everything but they want me to be safe.
If I stay at a friend's house, I have to be more organised and pack my sports equipment but it would be good to have a change.
I feel embarrassed to ask our neighbour but she drives past the school on her way to work anyway.

Decide on the best solution

A combination of all of the above except giving up sport.

List the steps you need to come up with the solution

Telephone friends and neighbours and speak to the tennis coach.
Ask the school about buses.
Ask my parents if they could share some of the driving.
Get fitter.

Review your progress and what still needs to be done

Need to write up a roster to remind me how I am getting to places. My sport and social life make it hard to fit in my homework. New problem . . . what is the problem?

Learning about life

Leanne: A few years ago my then 11-year-old son announced he had won the school debate. He was a speaker on the negative side for the topic: 'The world is getting better every day'. Here is his speech:

I know that most of you think that the world isn't getting better every day. But for those few who think that it is, I will run over my team's points to remind you how much worse it is getting. More pollution, animals are dying, the ozone layer is getting damaged and eventually the world will be covered in smog. Oils and fuels are running out. Wild animals are getting introduced to make other habitats perish. More modified food is being sold. The population is expanding and there are more homeless and unemployed. Diseases are spreading. People aren't caring about others. There are more wars. You are working for the same amount of money you would get 10 years ago.

The speech prompted me to think about how he had accumulated this pessimistic view of the world and I requested a copy of the positive argument from his 10-year-old opponent. It read:

More and more things are happening. Every day inventions are getting built, food is being made, problems are being solved and scientists are discovering things. All through your life you have had sad days, fun days and exciting things have happened. You might have broken your arm or leg, your spine or neck, but it will get better and if it doesn't, you can still see what happens the next day. Every day gets closer to your birthday, Christmas or Easter and, of course, all those days are special. But they only come once a year and just because you get presents on your birthday and at Christmas and maybe get chocolate at Easter, it doesn't mean that every other day is bad. It's exciting waiting for your birthday to open all your presents and just before Christmas you get to decorate a Christmas tree. We have colour TV, computers, fax machines and Nintendos. Having all these things surely makes every day get better.

> *I have all these negative thoughts. I am miserable and lonely and can't admit it.*
> Eliza, aged 15

The result of the debate troubled me greatly because children learn their views from their parents or from others when their parents are not proactive in communicating their views. My son and his friend had picked up their pessimistic and materialistic views of the world from someone. Who?

Do your teenagers know that you have values, morals, goals, dreams and hopes for the future? Do they see that you are self-confident, compassionate and that you have the ability to persevere through difficulties and to seek long-term fulfilment? Would they have observed how your relationships are enhanced by your social skills, including your good communication skills? Have they observed you seek help in times of need and take time to relax in times of stress? Do they know that you have a commitment to community service, an appreciation of cultural diversity, a spiritual life and a wonder of the world? Do they understand what your definition of success is? How would they know? When did you talk to them about all this? Who is teaching them about life?

Upon being asked about her inner concerns and pressures, one teenaged girl said:

> *Sometimes I worry about all the choices on leaving school. Then about conscription for the war on terror. At other times I worry about what to do when my friends do drugs or cut themselves. It all becomes too much to think about and I start to forget about world peace and think more about getting my P-plates, having a good formal, keeping my family happy and having a boyfriend. Call me shallow but I am only a teenager.*

When asked to imagine what they thought the world would be like in 100 years' time, some of the most common answers teenagers gave were:

- the world will not exist then
- no forests or animals
- war-torn countries
- lots of pollution
- limited water

- people won't care
- people will stop having babies
- more unemployment and homelessness.

Positive responses, on the other hand, were difficult to elicit. Here are some examples:

- computers will fit into your pocket
- a cure will be found for the common cold
- people will be living on other planets
- there will be more hippies.

The feeling of unexpressed hopelessness predisposes many of our young people to depression. While the world is in turmoil there has never been a more important time to talk about hope. Overwhelmingly young people feel it's better to talk about community and world problems, but, unfortunately, many feel excluded from conversations about issues like terrorism and the future because adults often assume that it is just too terrible to talk about. While discussing these sorts of issues raises many uncomfortable visions adolescents have of the future, such discussion also gives young people the opportunity to share their own inspirational stories of resilience, hope and courage in adversity.

Teenagers will readily express their hopes and dreams for the future. Here is what one group said about what they hope the world will be like when they are adults:

No discrimination
Reconciliation
No homelessness
No hunger
Freedom of speech
An older generation who listen
No animal cruelty
No GST
A healthy environment
Totally 100% recyclable products
No capital punishment
Women's rights including being able to breastfeed in public
A complete ban of nuclear weapons

A world free of war and terrorism
World peace.

Teenagers also readily identify the need to turn the energy of their fears and frustration into positive action by focusing on one local cause that will make a difference rather than feeling overwhelmed by all the problems of the world.

Here are some of the things that young people have taught us about life:

Small minds discuss people. Average minds discuss events. Great minds discuss ideas.

Self-esteem is a big issue. Lots of kids have problems with self-confidence. Confidence is knowing yourself, feeling comfortable with yourself, accepting yourself before others accept you, listening honestly and closely to another person. You need barriers and shields to protect yourself – it takes a lot of energy to maintain this.

Morals are like guidelines for life. If you don't follow them then you lose respect for yourself and others' respect. I stick to my morals – they are selected morals handed down by my parents but shaped to suit me. Values are about being yourself, being strong – you don't change yourself just to fit it.

For me, inspiration can arise from anywhere, from people I meet in the street, to people I've known for my entire life. I read once that the Buddhists look at everything as though it is the first time. Instead of seeing a tree as a tree, it is seen as a magnificent structure that provides the world with oxygen and beauty. Looking at everyday objects and obstacles in this way has provided me with an abundance of inspiration. I have learnt that inspiration has to come from within.

Success is self-satisfaction. It is not achievement at school. Year 12 results are not a reflection of how you are as a person. I like this quote from Ralph Waldo Emerson:

What is success? To laugh often and much. To win the respect of intelligent people and the affection of children. To earn the appreciation of honest critics and endure the betrayal of false friends. To appreciate beauty. To find the best in others. To leave the world a bit better, whether by a healthy child, a garden patch or a redeemed social condition. To know one life has breathed easier because you have lived. That is to have succeeded.

Find the right time to talk to your teenagers about life's big issues, about morals, success and spirituality. However, be prepared to listen, rather than advise, as this teenager suggests:

My dad suddenly got the idea that he should talk to me about all sorts of personal things. It was like he had read a book and was very artificial. I hope he got something out of the discussion.

Some final thoughts

David: Emotional pressures are a fact of life while you're growing up and forever more. It's important to learn how to cope with them and not to let them grind you down. But there's more to success and happiness than merely coping with stress. There's hope. As child and adolescent psychiatrist Professor Ken Nunn puts it: 'With hope, you have a belief that you're going to be okay, that you will get some of the things out of life that you want. With this sense of hope, you feel that you have some control over your future.' It's important to create opportunities for kids to not only receive care, but to also give care. This capacity to give to others creates hope.

Leanne: In this chapter we have said a lot about teenagers learning from our example. But we have as much to learn by listening to them as they do from us. One mother said this: 'My father was in hospital with a stroke and then my 10-year-old son developed appendicitis in the same week. I was up all night and got home late the next day. Exhausted, I collapsed on the couch, wondering how I would find the strength for the next day. Then I felt my daughter's hand on my back and she gently ran her fingers through my hair. I felt intensely loved and cared for and her small gesture gave me hope that things would get better. The next day I sat by my father's bed and ran my fingers through his hair. I knew it meant everything.'

David: Dr Sue Bagshaw, an adolescent health colleague in New Zealand reminded me of the three Ps: *perspective* (there are bits of your life that are okay!); don't take it *personally* (of course God doesn't make it happen just to you!); and it won't *persist* (this time next year you'll probably be laughing). I found these three Ps helpful when I was going through a difficult time. Kids need to know about them too.

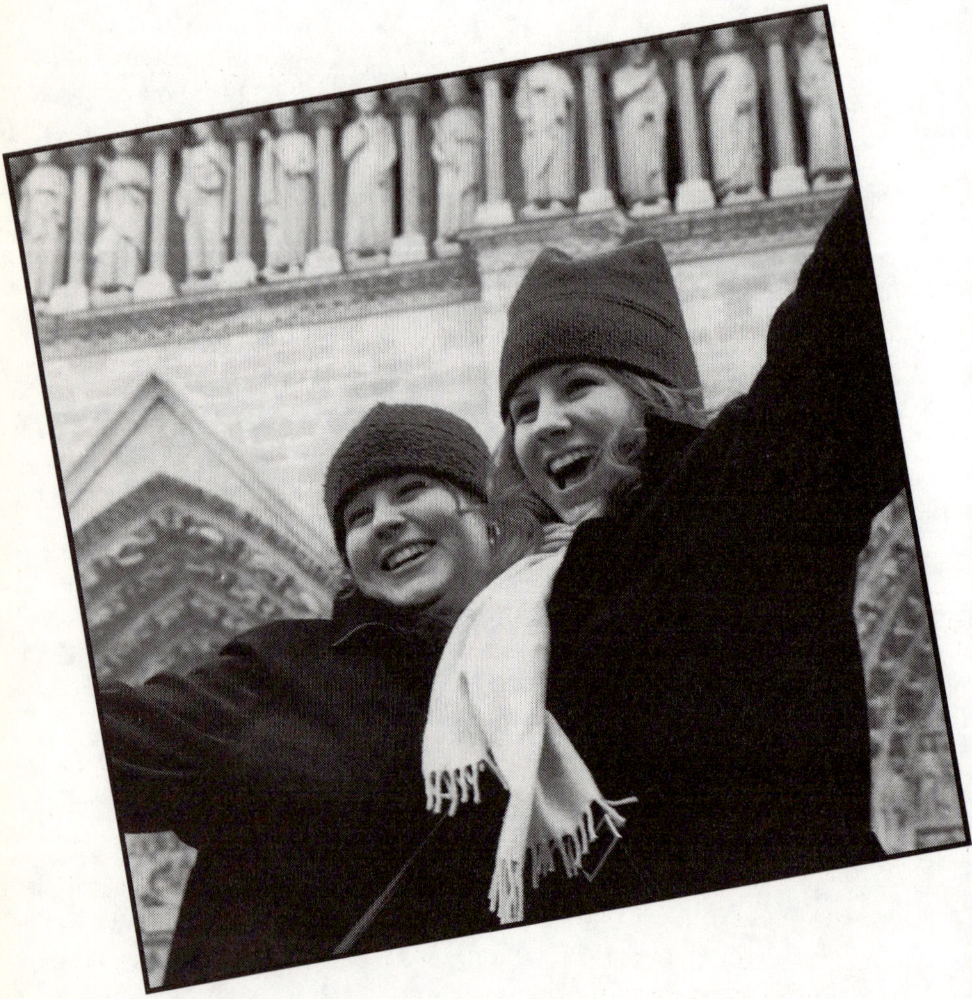

Chapter 13

Letting go when you want to hold on

My parents are so overprotective. They're always asking me where I'm going.
Georgia, aged 17

By the time your children turn into teenagers, you've come a long way as a parent, and there's much to be proud about. Those treasured baby snaps and photos of little puffed out cheeks over smoking birthday candles bear testimony to less complex times. These memories are to be enjoyed, because parenting adolescents is not easy!

For one thing, life is less predictable. At no other time in the family life cycle is there likely to be more uncertainty and confusion. Parents may approach their children's teenage years with elation or with apprehension, but few are prepared for the feelings of bewilderment, sadness and inner conflict that frequently arise. Providing guidance and support, while at the same time progressively loosening the reins of control, is no easy brief.

Letting go is a challenge. As a parent, one has to bear many small losses in order to gain a greater prize – a mature and self-sufficient young person who can relate to you, ultimately, as an adult. But the process of separation is painful, and there is ambivalence about it on both sides. As teenagers move increasingly within their own circles and do more and more, their own way, we are called upon to adjust to a progressive loss of status and a lessening of control. This is unsettling. But holding on to poignant memories of how they were as little kids is to no avail, for we cannot turn back the clock. On the other hand, the future is uncertain and many parental fears are rooted in reality. We will not always be there to smooth the way.

Learning to trust

There is no simple knack to letting go. Some parents who are particularly keen to get on with their own lives may prematurely retreat from parental responsibilities and let go too quickly, pushing their kids out. Others hold on too tightly, perhaps because the alternative is to face new priorities or a new middle-aged identity or unhappiness in their marriage. But for most of us, it is not an all-or-nothing phenomenon, rather a gradual relinquishing of control over time. It has been said that raising children is like baking bread: it has to be a slow process or you end up with an overdone crust and an underdone interior.

So much depends on it and yet, for most of us, letting go almost goes against our every caring fibre. American psychologist and author Haim Ginott in his book, *Between Parent and Teenager*, has said it well: 'This can be our finest hour. To let go when you want to hold on requires utmost generosity and love. Only parents are capable of such painful greatness.'

Absolutely right. And how does one achieve this state of grace? Much of it lies in learning to trust. Teenagers need a parent's trust in order to be themselves and to become responsible for themselves. Giving it, however, is somewhat less straightforward. Consider some of the difficulties involved:

- How do you trust a teenager who you're certain is up to no good? Shifty eyes and convoluted stories don't make it easy.
- How do you trust a kid who constantly hands you the implausible line 'But everybody's doing it/going there/sleeping over?'
- How do you trust a teenager when the people with whom they keep company raise all sorts of suspicions in your mind? (As a mother said to her daughter, 'In you I have all the faith in the world, it's the other people in the world I have trouble with.')
- How do you trust a kid who's got you as a parent? You certainly remember what you did when you were that age!

This is a dilemma. Parents know that their offspring are gullible, that there are all sorts of dangers to their health, safety and peace of mind out there. But whatever the reasons, lack of trust is no secret. Certain behaviours loudly proclaim it: asking too many questions; nagging and lecturing; showing overprotective concern. From time to time, we are all guilty of these things. For teenagers, however, they are high on the list of 'most abhorred parental traits'.

> *Sometimes I worry about all the choices and pressures on leaving school.*
> *Lachlan, aged 16*

What do you do? Occasionally it is necessary to literally bite your lip and quietly sit on your misgivings. It can pay off. A couple once tried this by not 'suggesting' that their eldest daughter miss an outing on Saturday night in order to prepare for an exam on Monday. She made this decision herself without any help at all. Teenagers like to feel trusted and generally live up to the expectation. In a self-perpetuating cycle of happy outcomes they'll make better choices and more mature judgements and you'll be able to worry less and everything should work out fine. (Well, that's the theory, anyway.)

Of course, misplaced trust is disappointing. On occasion, you'll realise that you've been lied to. Kids sometimes start out with a small deception or thoughtful omission and a major fabrication builds from there to cover up. With your firstborn, this always seems worse (you become wiser later). It's generally better not to completely fall apart. You could perhaps say something powerful like 'I'd like to know why you felt you couldn't tell me the truth.' Then proceed to outline the consequences.

I'm sleeping at a friend's house

An adolescent phenomenon requiring a good deal of parental trust is sleeping over at a friend's place. Almost all teenagers (and many younger children too, of course) want to do this, and increasingly as they get older. It's normal. It's wonderful too, sometimes, to have them out of the house. But sleeping out does raise some parental concerns, simply because you're out of the picture. For one thing, you are trusting them to be where they say they'll be, hopefully with people you know or know something about. You won't know what time they get in if they go out. The next day, you'll wonder if they got any sleep – when you see them it won't be hard to tell.

The mother of a 16-year-old boy described her reaction when she received a call from his 14-year-old girlfriend at 9 pm saying that he was 'too tired to come home'. When he eventually got to the phone, he sheepishly announced: 'It has been suggested that I stay the night.' His mother, not amused, 'suggested' that if he didn't appear at their front door in 15 minutes, she'd be down to collect him.

Some parents do not permit their kids to sleep over at all, often for logistical reasons (too complicated with lots of children; too much chauffeuring around, etc.). However, most parents do permit it, viewing it as part of their exploration of the world out there, of seeing how the other half lives. Obviously, it is also part of a normal desire to gain distance from you. All that remains to be resolved is when and how often. School nights would probably be out (including Sunday nights), and exam time too. Other than that, as always, it's a personal decision.

One thing you can do to allay some of your fears and concerns is to telephone the other parent involved. However, even kids with the most suspicious parents in the world (experienced parents can get to be like that) will sometimes find a way to exploit the situation.

David: For example, a distraught mother once called us to say she'd returned home from a weekend away to discover 'subtle clues' of a teenage party. Her trusted daughter had entertained a multitude of 15-year-olds, 15 or 20 of whom (it's never possible to be certain) had spent the night. Our son, ostensibly sleeping at a different friend's house, was one of them. 'Why did you do that?' my wife Anne asked. He explained: 'It happens. I took a chance. If I hadn't been caught, it would have been worth it.' We set to work, yet again, trying to make sure that it wasn't worth it!

The ubiquitous party

What if it's all happening at your place? If ever you want to experience shellshock, allow your teenager to throw a rip-roaring party at home. The noise and mess are the least of it – you expected that anyway. The scary part is that you are there in the responsible role of adult chaperone (a euphemistic expression if ever there was one). Not unreasonably, you might wonder about the following:

- Who's there? Don't ask. Probably more kids than were invited. They're physically bigger than you imagined and generally disinclined to give you the time of day (which is disappointing

if you personally prepared the food and helped with the decorations).
- What are they doing when you can't see them? Don't ask. Even if you wander around 'unobtrusively' all night offering savouries, you'll never keep track of them – there's outside too, you know.
- There isn't any alcohol here, is there? Don't ask. That was the deal, but check around in the morning – you'll discover what sort of 'do' you really had. And it's best not to serve punch as some clown is sure to lace it!

David: Only after having this experience myself (with 16- and 17-year-olds), and talking about it with other parents, did I fully realise what a contentious issue it is. Parents worry about teenage parties, suspecting that having fun might mean more than just hotdogs, innocent games and loud music. Sex, alcohol and goodness knows what else is the combination we fear. Some people simply refuse to have teenage parties, preferring to let it be somebody else's headache. However, if you are willing to play host or hostess (the preferable attitude, I would say), there are three main positions you can take:

- Exercise militant control. Insist on a guest list and tick off kids' names as they enter the house, introduce everybody to the bouncer, give out printed rules about expected behaviour and proposed punishments for transgressors. This approach is only appropriate for a one-off affair as no kid would want to come to a party at your place again.
- Go out for the night. That is, let them get on with it and hope for the best (the furniture needs replacing anyway). It might be a good idea, however, to let the police know where they can contact you, and to expect to hear from them.
- Be there and be fair. Most parents would probably seek the middle ground. This involves negotiating beforehand what's acceptable and what's not, agreeing to maintain a friendly 'arm's length' presence and trusting your offspring and his or her friends to be a bit responsible. Mostly, it works out okay.

If taking the reasonable approach, there are many things to consider: Have you spoken to (warned) the neighbours? How many people are coming? Should entry be by invitation only? Where are people going to leave their valuables? Have you considered fire safety? In which parts of your home is the party going to take place? How will people make their way home? What will you do in the event of drugs, alcohol, smoking? Are you aware of your responsibilities in respect of minors consuming alcohol in your home? Who's supervising? How will you prevent people from gatecrashing? Have you registered your party with the police?

There are such a lot of questions to address, but your kids will really appreciate your effort – even if they consider you a complete dag.

Those outside influences

While we're on this subject of trust, a word of reassurance about the apparently growing influence of 'outsiders'. Teenagers undoubtedly look to their peers in matters concerning their appearance, leisure activities and other interests. But the evidence seems to indicate that they still tend to turn to their parents for guidance on major questions of values. In a large British study, the vast majority of 14- and 15-year-olds believed their parents approved of their friends. Do you?

Parents sometimes resent other adults who appear to assume importance in their kids' lives, despite realising that alternative authority figures can be valuable resources at this time. They can be objective and helpful mentors and are important to a teenager's sense of broader community. Teenagers are fortunate to have access to caring adults other than their parents, particularly authoritative adults, who can also share the role of advocacy of young people (as we discuss in Chapter 17).

What about problem kids?

Let's not lay the whole responsibility for letting go at parents' feet. It's more complicated than that. Teenagers have to cooperate with this gradual lessening of parental control and be willing to gradually assume greater responsibility for themselves. Some teenagers, by virtue of being immature, depressed or unwell, for example, are too dependent and want to stay attached to the apron strings. They are not progressing normally. Beware, too, of the perfect kid, the one who is amenable to everything you ask, for the road to healthy adolescent development is never completely smooth and kids really do believe that what parents don't know won't hurt them. Remember to seek advice if things don't seem right.

On the other hand, some young people are too independent and take off too soon or too far. If this is a personality trait, you will have seen it coming for a long time. It's a bit awkward, however, if you've let children have a free reign throughout childhood. By adolescence, they will have become used to calling the shots, and trying to tighten up on discipline now will be fraught with difficulty. Hopefully, too, you will have encouraged a sense of wider community connectedness in your kids on the off chance they simply take off – or you get hit by a bus!

Taking a stand

Leadership takes courage. As parents, you can survive being unpopular. There are times when you have to grin and bear it, because, while trust is vital, it does not mean that anything goes. In fact, children feel distinctly insecure, and will come to interpret it as a lack of caring if limits are not clearly set.

Not having limits is like riding a bicycle across a narrow bridge with no railings. More importantly, during adolescence kids need limits to test themselves against and feel secure within. They need to know, at least, what a parent thinks about particular issues. As one teenager put it, 'If I don't know what my parents think, how can I do the opposite?'

Important matters

On some matters, certainly the important ones, parents have to take a stand. You can always compromise on less world-shattering issues, such as where the soap is supposed to be put in the bathroom. But when it comes to things like moderate behaviour in public or contributing something to family life, the expectations should be clear.

Rules and responsibilities define a household. They prescribe a family's particular way of living together. In fact, a cohesive family in which the child is expected to play a positive, clearly defined role is said to be the strongest thing a kid has going for it. Limits are not idle threats, harsh and unreasonable demands, nor 'here today and gone tomorrow' suggestions. Effective limits are firm, fair, explicit and consistent, and this is what we should aim for. However, limits do need to change over time. There's no special way to do this and personal views vary greatly. What most parents find is that they need to renegotiate around particular events. As teenagers grow up, there's always something new to contend with and a way (your way) to deal with it.

Mandatory retirement

There's a qualitative difference between turning in and coming in. A desire to have our kids safely under wraps at a reasonable hour is based on several factors: a need to know they are safe; a need to get a decent night's sleep ourselves; a concern about behaviour that may put them at risk (sex, drugs, overtiredness); a conviction that there are greater dangers after the witching hour (though even if we remind them of Cinderella, teenagers will never understand parental thinking on this one).

Whatever the reasons, it is a parent's prerogative to achieve an understanding about this and it can be approached in one of two ways:

- You will be home by midnight or else! This is a no-nonsense, authoritarian approach that usually buys trouble in the form of resentment or rebellion. It also does little to encourage your teenager's sense of personal responsibility (which is, after all, the goal of discipline).
- What time will you be getting home? Or what time do you think would be reasonable? These questions provide a basis for negotiation. A mutually acceptable arrangement can usually be arrived at, a better outcome for all concerned and more likely to be adhered to.

Some aspects of parenting never change. There is nothing outdated about needing to establish where kids are spending their time and with whom, and how and when they will get home. The mother of a 16-year-old girl states her case in this straightforward way: 'I want to know where you are. While we're together, we're accountable to each other. Would you like it if I were to go off for three days and you didn't know where I was?'

Logical consequences

Allied to the skill of setting firm, clear limits, is knowing what to do when they are breached. This is tricky, and the older the teenager, the harder it gets. There is much written about the importance of logical consequences. The idea is that transgressions are transformed into learning experiences. This means that consequences occur and have relevance to the 'crime'. Ideally, this will have been happening throughout childhood so that kids can progressively gain a sense of internal control, or at least know what to expect in a given set of circumstances.

A 14-year-old daughter took one of her father's favourite shirts to a school camp, and returned, nine days later, without it. 'It's missing!' Dad was infuriated, more by her laissez-faire attitude than by the loss itself. The girl had shared a dormitory with a dozen or so other girls. 'Maybe one of them took it by mistake,' she shrugged (in a world with starvation and strife, for goodness' sake, it's only a shirt). The incensed father insisted that she contact each and every girl and get it back (after all, it's his shirt and there's a principle at stake).

This is an example of logical consequences. An alternative punishment, such as having to wash up for a week, would not have carried the message: if you lose something belonging to someone else, at least make an effort to find it. But what if there's not an obvious flow on from the teenager's misdemeanour? This calls for creativity, and possibly some help from the culprit. One might ask, 'Which of the following activities or privileges would you care to forego?' Upfront, you're seeking to be reasonable – though all the while your thoughts might be running to grounding the kid for the next 25 years.

Harmony and conflict

Are you polite to your children? This is an important question and one, like responsible listening, that is frequently taken up in parenting guides. Who would dare suggest that this is anything but highly desirable? As a major pillar of parenting, however, there are one or two flaws. The following examples are representative of good advice one might read or hear about this issue:

- 'Treat your kids as you would treat guests in the house.' This would be fine if they behaved like guests and left after an appropriate period; it also sounds like a good way to turn them into strangers.
- 'Don't yell at the kids, it's not nice to be screamed at.' Of course it's not, and there are certainly more effective ways to express anger; but parents usually don't 'talk loudly' for nothing.

▶ 'Practise using firm but friendly facial expressions and gestures in front of the mirror.' But don't let anybody see you, they'll send for a straitjacket.

In reality, there cannot be amicable and positive interaction between parents and teenagers at all times. If there is, an awful lot is being suppressed. Nevertheless, as mentioned in Chapter 10, some parents become distraught in the face of ordinary adolescent backchat, occasional bad language, or the many other subtle (and not so subtle) signs that show teenagers want emotional separation. They try to gain distance in this way in order to see themselves more clearly. Not that it doesn't hurt. Adolescents have an uncanny, sixth sense about how to put the boot in, and being on the receiving end is not at all pleasant. Better that our self-esteem is not totally tied up in what our kids think of us or say to us, for if it is, we're in for hell. What we must tell ourselves, often, is that such behaviour is developmentally normal (clearly, easier said than done).

What if you're really angry?

A father had become very angry with his two teenage sons, and would let them know about it, often in no uncertain terms. Mostly, they were just being adolescent (giving a bit of cheek, taking their time over chores and so on). This dad was a screamer, and the fact that mum generally sided with the kids added to his frustration, sadness and disappointment. He felt that he had tried to do his best by them and considered them grossly unappreciative.

This is not an uncommon scene. Parents frequently argue about how to discipline and generally deal with teenagers. In the above instance, the mother believed that the father's behaviour was causing the boys' behaviour. While it probably was a factor, it is more likely that the boys were acting out the marital difficulties. If these parents were able to stop blaming each other long enough to find some middle ground (or get help if necessary), their mutual support might go a long way to easing the inter-generational conflict as well.

Some conflict is normal. When there is a lot of anger involving parents and teenagers, however, it may be serving as an alternative to experiencing pain – the emotional kind. As teenagers and their parents separate, these feelings inevitably surface. On both sides there will be sadness. So it makes sense that some people will fight to stay together, rather than face the feelings of loss associated with moving apart.

Of course, when the fighting becomes inexorable or is tinged with cruelty, or when it starts to affect the health of a family member or extends outside the family (to school failure, for example), it is time to take stock. Someone (perhaps mum and dad together) needs time out, or the family needs professional help.

A gift for life

A 50-year-old man confided in a friend that he wasn't doing too well in business: 'I'm not surprised really, Dad always said I'd never make a go of it.' The concept of self-fulfilling prophecy should be constantly on our minds where our children are concerned. In a very real sense, we are helping to mould their future lives.

The value of positive reinforcement is too often underestimated. It is as necessary a fuel for self-esteem as air is for life. The beliefs and attitudes we have about ourselves as individuals are acquired early, but the need for personal validation remains with us as we grow up and forever more. Our feelings of self-worth require care and maintenance, so being encouraging is a vital part of letting go – you might have a tear in your eye but you must have hope in your heart.

For parents, there are some basic dos and don'ts that have stood the test of time. Teenagers' self-esteem is not likely to be enhanced by the following:

- Being compared to other kids they know, their siblings or, worst of all, you as a teenager.
- Being deluged with 'righteous goodness' in the form of nagging, lecturing or moralising. Parents who do this all the time belong to the 'excessive virtue' group and are most likely to dominate teenagers through over-control and over-expectation.
- Being verbally put down: 'You're a clumsy idiot just like your father.'
- Being flippantly dismissed: 'Don't be so bloody ludicrous.'

More than anything else, young people want to be listened to, trusted, and given respect as individuals. Despite the ambivalent messages they sometimes give, they do want their comments and ideas to be taken seriously, and the people who are important to them to take an interest in their lives and activities. You can study a hundred self-help books or take a thousand courses, but in the final analysis, liking your son or daughter and letting it show will ultimately carry the day.

In fact, fostering healthy self-esteem in our children is probably our single most important task as parents. This is not a time-consuming exercise. As Dr Spencer Johnson suggests in *The One Minute Mother*, 'catch them doing something right'. A well-timed word, a well-placed touch may be all that is required to convey the message: You are a capable and competent person; your assets and strengths show. It's worth it. To grow up being able to feel good about yourself is, after all, a gift for life.

Leaving home – maybe later

According to the statistics, about 85 per cent of young people in Australia live with their families. Millions of parents will experience the confronting reality, at some point, of someone leaving home. Whether this is greeted with apprehension, fear and resentment or embraced with relief, gratitude and satisfaction, depends a lot on the timing and the circumstances involved. The American system in which teenagers 'go away to college' has a lot going for it. There, leaving home for the purpose of furthering one's education is simply expected as a normal part of family life, aiding and abetting the achievement of autonomy and self-sufficiency. In Australia, where we have no such routine, it's generally a more problematic and painful process on both sides.

Whatever the case, the ideal outcome of this most real of separations is for the young person to remain connected with the family through communication and visits. As we've discussed, adolescent resilience (the capacity to cope with life's trials and tribulations) is strengthened greatly by a supportive and nurturing relationship with one's family. The notion of 'independence' as a task of adolescence has given way to one of 'inter-dependence' as a goal of maturity. This is just as well because the past few decades have seen changing motivations for older teenagers to leave home:

- In the 1970s, they left home for vocational reasons or to marry.
- In the 1980s, they left home for reasons of conflict or to seek independence.
- In the 1990s, by and large, they thought twice before leaving home at all.

The conventional wisdom is that young people show little inclination to leave home and set up their own households. They're too comfortable, too broke, they can have sex at home and, if they're lucky, have mum (or dad) do the washing and ironing. The truth of the situation is a bit more complex. According to research by Judy Schneider of the Social Policy Research Centre at the University of New South Wales, since 1982 the proportion of 15- to 17-year-olds remaining dependent on their parents has risen from 79 per cent to 96 per cent. For 18- to 20-year-olds it's gone from 38 per cent to 62 per cent.

But a survey of 13,000 Australians reveals that the 20-something generation leaves home about the same age their parents and grandparents did – the change over 50 years has been remarkably small. Young people leave home all right, but return to it in hard times. If you take 25- to 29-year-olds, about 80 to 90 per cent will have left home, and of those still living at home, almost 75 per cent are returnees. They're called the 'Boomerang Kids' – they come and go according to their circumstances, using the family home as a bulwark against the pressures of life. An increasing number of young Australians are choosing to mix independence with the security of the family home as a haven. The factors influencing this trend include: more causal and insecure jobs, less affordable housing, the financial burdens post-graduation of university fee repayment, and the high rate of divorce, particularly among young parents.

Goodbye empty nest. So much for those attractive mid-life fantasies such as early retirement, future travel and downsizing from the spacious family home to something with a smaller garden. This rise in multi-generational families might actually help revive the institution of the extended family. As attractive as that might sound, extended families only work, of course, where a cooperative and communicative atmosphere prevails, together with a good sense of humour and respect for each other's space.

For parents who are less than thrilled about this prospect, there's literature out there now on how to get your teenager to leave home, suggesting for example, that you might 'suddenly make a habit of walking around in the nude'. If that doesn't work, nothing will. And then there's the following message which you could stick onto the kitchen fridge:

> *Children: tired of being harassed by your stupid parents? ACT NOW! Move out, get a job, pay your own bills, while you still know everything.*

Memories

A father of three children was asked what he enjoyed most about being a parent. He replied, 'Reliving each and every stage of childhood with them.' He's lucky to be enjoying it, because this process of reliving and remembering is not always pleasant or easy. We may not even be consciously aware that it's happening, but it is impossible to avoid. From time to time something will trigger an image or feeling from our own past. Occasionally parents have to relive and perhaps understand more clearly something important that happened to them many years ago.

Feelings from the past

Since every single experience we ever have is retained in the recesses of our mind, the tendency as a parent to relive your childhood experiences is not all that surprising. Perhaps you're playing with your four-year-old child and suddenly you remember how your grandmother would bake your favourite things when you were sick.

Becoming a parent can also reactivate many old conflicts, many of them to do with our parents. 'The trouble with parents,' someone once kidded, 'is that it's hard to think of them as people.' Just because they've lived longer than you, they always know best (even when you're fully grown). They may say and do the most outrageous things, and get hurt if you don't seem to understand that they're only thinking of what's best for you. And they can never quite believe, many of them, that you are actually capable of making a go of it, doing things your way.

As mentioned before, you become a parent, but you remain a son or daughter. Emotionally, there are always unresolved bits and pieces from your earlier life, and it's understandable that these can re-emerge. Parenting, it seems, has a powerful hold on your life. Sometimes memories of past experiences and the emotions associated with them may feel overwhelming (in which case it's important to seek help). Remember also to always try to reflect on the things your parents got right – happy and special times – and build on those.

Not enough to go on

Meanwhile, lots of things have changed. The social climate in which our children are growing up today is profoundly different to that of 40 years ago. Nostalgia may blur our recollections somewhat, but it does seem that there was a greater sense of continuity and coherence, a feeling that life was generally more settled.

While you may have fond recollections of relaxed Saturday afternoon matinees, meccano sets and careering down a hill on a homemade billycart, kids today are entertained by computer games with synthesised sound effects, walkman radios and expensive skate boards. More importantly, you may have managed to remain a virgin till 25 – many teenagers now become sexually active at 15! They are also taller, stronger, better developed and have many different ideas and aspirations.

The point is simply this: 'when I was young' has lost its clout. Your personal experience of adolescence (20 or 30 years ago or whatever) is not enough to go on, things have changed too much. Of course, this has always been the case. In the past century, there hasn't been a single decade in which parents were not confused about how to behave, about how best to raise their children.

Prevailing attitudes to discipline, for example, have changed dramatically: the popularity of spanking has come and gone (and is definitely 'out' at present); theories promoting reasoning with kids or just loving them and hoping for the best, have also seen their day. And by about 1970, a new feeling was emerging – to hell with them! The 'me generation' had arrived on the scene, coinciding, it seems, with parents' confidence in their ability to succeed as parents reaching an all-time low. Parents who felt they had nothing to offer would express feelings towards their teenagers like, 'It's your life, you live it the way you want to.'

These days the feeling has changed yet again. Our memories may not be enough to go on, but we're more aware of what's going on and more optimistic. Here we are, knowing so much about how kids grow and learn, realising that our words and actions affect their feelings and behaviour, accepting the creed of warmth, firmness and fairness, and understanding that our own personal needs are important too.

It's good to be a parent now. Freed from the tyranny of perfection, parents can now be good enough and take the good with the bad. Our view of our kids and ourselves can, at last, be more balanced and reasonable.

Some final thoughts

Let me test, let me try, let me reach,
Let me fly!
Push me out of the nest (but not too fast).
There is much I don't know.
There are things that I want – don't
Hide me from the sight of the world.
Give me room, give me time. There
Are things I'm not frightened
To try.
Let me tumble and spring, let me go,
Let me be. Wait and see –
I am growing, world.
Water me with the wisdom of
Your tears.

Cherie A. Millard, aged 17

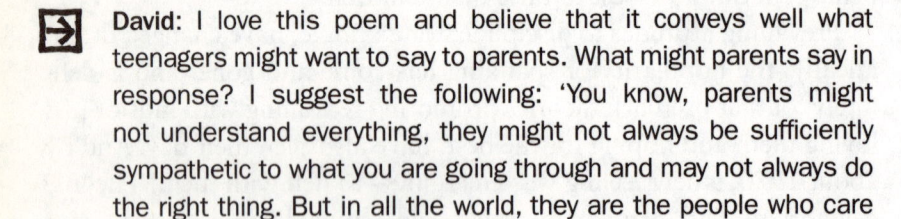

David: I love this poem and believe that it conveys well what teenagers might want to say to parents. What might parents say in response? I suggest the following: 'You know, parents might not understand everything, they might not always be sufficiently sympathetic to what you are going through and may not always do the right thing. But in all the world, they are the people who care about you the most.' After all:

- Parents are the people who want you to be safe and well, to do your best and to turn into competent and caring individuals whom everyone would be proud to know.
- Parents are there to provide you with guidance, to be a sounding board for your ideas and plans, not to do everything for you or carry you around on a stretcher.
- Parents are there to provide a place where you belong and give you unconditional love – that is, love for who you are, not for what you might achieve or become.
- Parents are also there to be role models for you to look up to – without a doubt, their values are the ones you will absorb, simply by living in their home.

Leanne: The suggestion that there is a right way to raise children of any age is clearly ridiculous. This notion has been aptly called the 'myth of parenthood' and is responsible for a great deal of unnecessary self-flagellation and guilt. I am not the first to note that children, parents, and the issues they face, separately and together, cannot be forced into a formula. For each teenager and each parent, there is a need to learn together, to work things out over and over again.

Since nobody finds the parenting of teenagers easy, you may derive some comfort from knowing that 'experience is a wonderful thing – it enables you to recognise a mistake when you make it again'. We can only do our best. Several decades ago, Benjamin Spock MD said to parents: 'Trust yourself, you know more than you think you do.' So, in letting go when you want to hold on, try not to be too hard on yourself, maintain a sense of humour and, above all, don't despair!

Section 3

It won't happen in our family

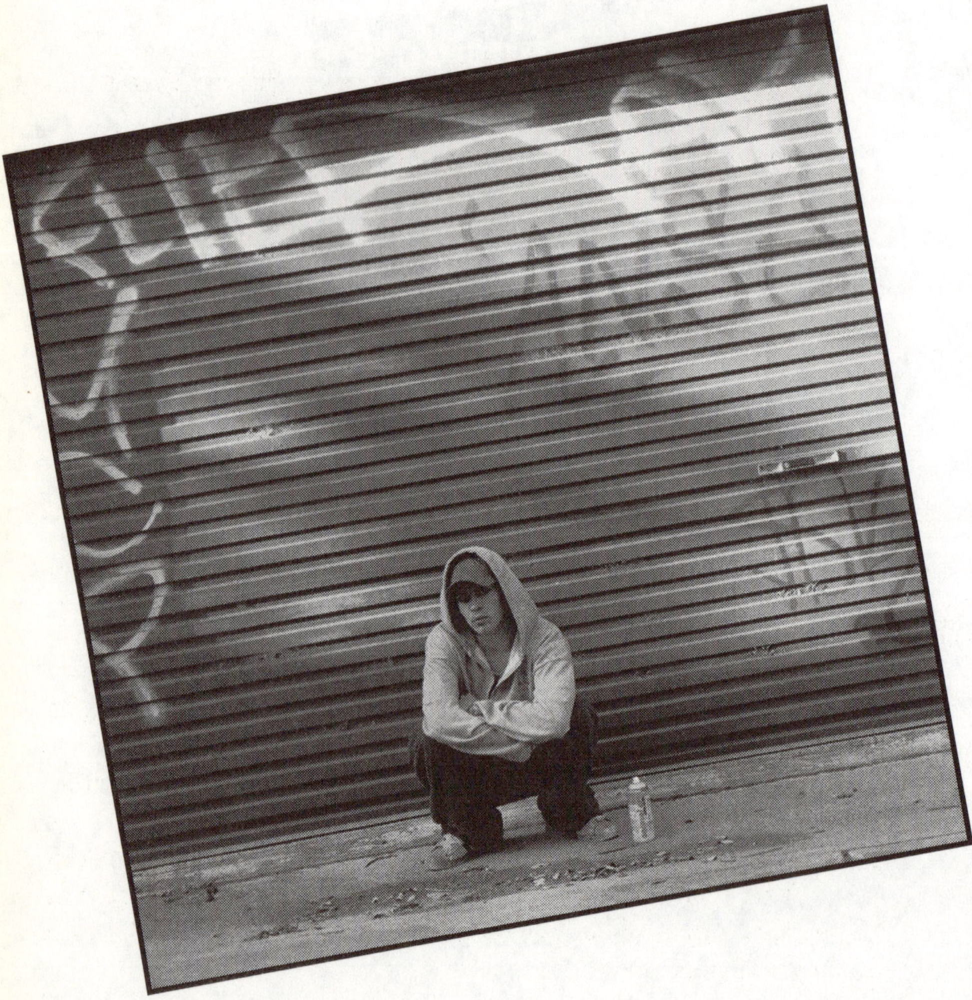

Chapter 14

Reducing the risk and minimising the harm

> *Alcohol is a release. I drink to fit in.*
> Sam, aged 15

Life is a risky business. We all take chances, and there are risks involved in practically everything we do. Taking risks is certainly a natural part of growing up. Teenagers have a special thirst for new experiences. They are eager to try out new skills, to test the limits of their abilities, to compete, to challenge, to rebel.

In the course of their exuberant experimentation, however, young people put themselves at risk of physical damage, or worse. It is normal for parents to worry about this, but preferable for them not to panic. This chapter looks at what risk-taking is about and discusses those 'health hazardous behaviours' that cause parents so much anxiety and anguish.

Why do teenagers take risks?

Young people are by nature experimental. How else can they work out what is not safe, and what is sensible and right for them? Only the most timid and fearful of parents would want a teenager to be a motionless blob who never take chances – and the outcome would be that they would never grow up. Obviously, however, there's more to risk-taking than mere experimentation. Multiple factors influence adolescent risk-taking, involving the individual, relationships with others, and the outside world.

At an individual level

The biology of the brain in adolescence is becoming better understood. While some areas of the human brain are mature by the end of childhood, the frontal and parietal lobes, responsible for such things as planning and self-control, continue maturing through the teenage years. In other words, the adolescent brain is still developing and the highest-level areas responsible for social judgement and self-control may not be completely mature until we hit our twenties. Teenage brains may be constructed in a way that makes their owners more open to ideas, more amenable to change, and also *more likely to experiment*.

At an individual level, therefore, it's no wonder that adolescents are curious about what life has to offer. Some experimentation is undertaken 'just to see what it's like' and there is often an exhilarating sense of freedom that comes with it. Remember, too, that those in the frenzied grip of hormones, bursting at the seams with testosterone-driven energy (particularly boys), are more or less programmed to be impulsive and thrill-seeking. This is why teenagers often do things on the spur of the moment, with little thought for the consequences. At the cognitive level, too, immature or changing thought processes may interfere with the actual perception of risk, leading to a sense of omnipotence and an apparently laissez-faire attitude. Inadequate information about risks and lack of prior experience are also relevant factors.

For a minority of teenagers, however, dangerous behaviour is motivated by psychological factors. Stressed kids are more likely to have accidents. Taking risks may offer them a means of escape from feelings and conflicts that are too painful to face (otherwise called 'acting out'), or they may have feelings of inadequacy, poor self-worth and even underlying suicidal wishes. Sometimes, risk-taking is associated with a lack of satisfaction in external things; if you're in rotten circumstances (homeless and unemployed, for example), perhaps getting high is the best thing going. As Los Angeles-based adolescent physician Richard MacKenzie notes: 'What adults see as problems, adolescents often see as solutions.'

An American survey of 600 high school students found that those who had been victims of child abuse (13 per cent) were more likely than their peers to engage in high-risk behaviour: three times more likely to drink alcohol or smoke cigarettes; almost twice as likely to use illicit drugs; six times as likely to induce vomiting while dieting; and five times more likely to attempt suicide.

At a relationship level

Most teenagers are pretty involved with other people, so what they do is not purely and simply a matter of individual choice. It is happening within the context of families and friends who have a strong influence on a young person's beliefs, behaviour and approaches to life. These influences contribute to a teenager's lifestyle which has both immediate and longer term effects on his or her health and wellbeing.

Much adolescent behaviour appears designed to impress one's friends, or at least to win their approval. This is largely why, for example, kids aged between 11 and 16 are the least likely to take precautions in the sun, even though research shows they are aware of the risks (that most sun damage is done before the end of the teen years and likely to emerge as cancers after age 50). More than 50 per cent reject the promotion of sun protection clothes as cool, dismissing them as 'daggy'. At a more dramatic level, flirting with illegal behaviour such as shoplifting (more common than any parent could possibly imagine) is unlikely to go undiscussed with peers.

In these and many other situations, the need to be 'one of the group' is a powerful motivation to behave in certain ways, to the extent that peer pressure sometimes achieves pride of place as a parent's number-one concern (not entirely unreasonable). But before over-reacting to this, remember that in seeking adult status (what growing up is all about), young people are drawn to what they perceive as 'adult activities'. They want to do what adults are doing, so who are they watching the closest?

Yes. Parents may inadvertently contribute to the risk-taking behaviour of teenagers in at least four ways:

- By the behaviour they 'model'. For example, a teenager is twice as likely to smoke if both parents smoke.

I tried to break away from my smoking friends but it was hard.
Steve, aged 17

- By the behaviour they disapprove of, especially when it comes in a stern 'it's bad for you and you must not do it' tone of voice. This gives kids something to rebel against.
- By the behaviour they 'set up' through subtle messages and vicarious enjoyment. Calling your child 'my big, strong son, the tough athlete' might lead him to believe he is bigger, stronger and tougher than he actually is.
- By behaviour they avoid. For example, not setting appropriate limits. If you say, 'It's your life, do what you want!' your child might take you at your word.

At the broader social level

There are influences in the outside world that are beyond personal and family control. Naturally, life would be a lot safer for young people if gigantic motorcycles, hotted-up cars, firearms and dangerous substances did not exist at all. But they do and they are very accessible to young people.

On the one hand, there are the depressing realities of troubled and confused families, unemployment and uncertainty about the future (giving rise to an understandable 'what the hell' attitude). On the other hand, the mass media delivers a constant bombardment of sexual innuendoes, a general glorification of violence and life in the fast lane, and the commercial exploitation of the young through alcohol and tobacco advertising (a package thoroughly deserving of the label 'ill-health promotion'!). Add to all these factors the absence of a recognised social status for the young, and we have a recipe for pushing a growing proportion of young people to the margins of society, with devastating consequences.

Statistical evidence indicates that risky behaviours are interrelated and that the factors that put a young person or peer group at risk are cumulative. There are definite correlations, for example, between the use of alcohol and the use of other drugs such as tobacco and marijuana. The greater the use of drugs, the more likely the involvement in other risk behaviours such as unsafe sexual activity, aggression and delinquency. Another reason for concern is that there is considerable continuity of health risk behaviour from adolescence into adulthood.

All my friends drink every weekend. I feel pressured to do it as well.
Sophie, aged 17

What risks do teenagers take?

Risk-taking can take a variety of forms, ranging from not getting enough sleep and eating the wrong food, to behaviour that constitutes a more serious threat to health, safety and life. In Chapter 7 we looked at sexual risk-taking (unprotected intercourse which can lead to unwanted pregnancy and/or exposure to sexually transmitted infections). The following section discusses accidents, tobacco, alcohol and other substance abuse.

Teenagers and 'accidents'

Where adolescents are concerned, accidents take on a somewhat different meaning. The usual implications of 'random and inevitable happenings' don't quite fit, especially when there is a multitude of contributing factors. 'Traumatic events' or 'non-intentional injuries' would be more appropriate terms in most instances.

Road crashes take more young lives than any other single cause.

Consider the following facts:

- Young males are involved in more road accidents than young females, mostly when driving at night and especially at the weekend, often after a party where they have had a few drinks.
- Nearly one-third of road accident deaths are in the 16- to 20 year age group and a quarter of injuries are sustained as a result of motorcycle crashes.
- More than half the alcohol-related accidents resulting in injury or death on the road involve young people between the ages of 16 and 24. A substantial proportion of the 16- to 20-year-old riders or drivers involved in serious accidents have a recordable blood alcohol level; 70 per cent of young men and 55 per cent of young women aged 16 to 25 who have accidents drive under the influence of alcohol or marijuana, or are passengers in cars driven by people under these influences.

Sitting behind the wheel of a car and travelling at breakneck speed is an exhilarating experience for a teenager. The question is, who's in control – the kid or the car? As a breed, young drivers tend to be impulsive, careless, easily distracted and think they are immortal. Not infrequently, it seems, they are also intoxicated! Even a blood alcohol level of 0.05 doubles the crash risk; at 0.15, a crash is 25 times more likely. (The legal blood alcohol level for drivers under 25 who have had a licence for less than three years is 0.02 in New South Wales.)

In our highly motorised society, getting a driver's licence is a rite of passage equal to none. Practically all teenagers want this desperately. One teenager recently said to his father: 'Dad, I would like to learn to drive in a different car, one with more power.' The dilemma seems to be that teenagers are learning to drive at the same time as they're learning to drink! We are yet to discover a satisfactory answer to this. Legislation relating to minimum drinking and driving ages, seat belts and helmets takes us only part of the way, although the decrease in road deaths in young people can be reasonably attributed to these mandatory interventions. Perhaps we need to combine two youth training campaigns: 'Learn to drive' and 'Learn to drink'.

While fatal accidents mainly occur on the road, non-fatal accidents are more common during sport (as discussed in Chapter 6) or in the workplace. Young people are particularly at risk in industry, where their lack of preparation, experience and care often make a dangerous combination. Workers between the ages of 15 and 24 have the highest rate of work accidents and it appears, from trends in compensation figures, that these rates are increasing.

Teenagers and violence

Violence has always existed in society, in common with communicable diseases, as a source of suffering, trauma, disablement and death. Violence certainly appears to be more widespread and more frequent in our modern societies than in the past, and aggression and violence intrude more and more into our daily lives (instantaneous and worldwide coverage by the media ensures that).

Another certainty is that adolescents, more than any other age group, are simultaneously the instigators of violent behaviour and its victims. Of particular concern is the violence that young people can turn against themselves. Self-aggression can join forces with delinquent behaviour in a curious sequence: crime, guilt, reaction of self-punishment. This may often explain truly suicidal behaviour at the wheel of a stolen car. Indeed, there is a fine line, sometimes, between accident and suicide.

Teenagers and smoking

Everyone knows that tobacco kills people. Legal drugs account for nearly 95 per cent of all drug-related deaths, a statistic that surprises most people. Of the 22,000 people who die annually in Australia from the direct or indirect use of drugs, tobacco is the biggest single killer, responsible for more than 80 per cent of all drug-related deaths and costing our community about $21 billion annually (about 60 per cent of the total social cost of drug-related damage). Over 19,000 Australians are killed each year by smoking-related illnesses. Despite our knowledge that 8 per cent of all burden of disease is related to smoking, teenagers are increasingly taking up this bad habit. Early exposure to smoking increases the risk of further drug use.

Have you noticed how many movie stars are smoking on screen lately? Julia Roberts, Gwyneth Paltrow, Wynona Rider, Brad Pitt, Arnold Schwarzenegger and Jim Carrey are, to name a few. In fact, 85 per cent of the top 25 box-office hits for each year from 1988 to 1997 included prominent smoking. Tobacco brands are shown in most films rated suitable for teenagers, as well as in 20 per cent of films for children. A new US study has found the more smoking that school children see in movies, the more likely they are to experiment with tobacco. Worldwide, the rates of smoking among 18- to 24-year-olds are rising. This is the age group most targeted by the tobacco industry, both in films and in other marketing, such as employing classy young men and women to promote cigarettes (free samples, of course) to their peers at cooperating clubs and bars.

In the latest *National Drug Strategy Household Survey* (2001), Australia's definitive document on drug use, the highest proportion of people smoking regularly was the 20–29 years age bracket for both males (29 per cent) and females (24 per cent). The statistics for teenagers are not too healthy either. In the 14–19 years age group, 14 per cent of boys were regular smokers (that is, smoke daily) and 6 per cent occasional smokers (smoke weekly or less often). The rates for girls were 16 per cent and 41 per cent respectively. To state the obvious, one in five teenagers is a smoker. During the high school years, the prevalence of daily smoking increases with age and there is no significant sex difference.

On the other hand, smoking among adults has decreased over recent years, and community attitudes are changing. 'Passive smoking', for example, is of far greater concern than it used to be, leading to smoking being banned in many public places. But adult smoking still has a major influence on children and young people. Children are getting hefty doses of nicotine, not to mention a heap of other pollutants, simply by living in a household with a smoker – the equivalent of 80 cigarettes a year, in fact, if both parents smoke. We also know that a teenager is twice as likely to smoke if both parents smoke, and four times as likely to smoke if parents and older siblings smoke.

Despite blustering denials by cigarette advertisers, a link has been made between smoking and sexual attractiveness for young women. It seems to be working. A lot of girls smoke in the belief that it will prevent them from getting fat (part of the same message). Some special concerns for young women need emphasising:

- An international study has shown that it takes teenage girls an average of three weeks from when they start smoking occasionally to when they become addicted (while it takes boys about six months).
- Women who begin smoking within five years of their first period have been shown to be at 70 per cent higher risk of being diagnosed with breast cancer before menopause. The research involved (a Canadian study of 2000 women) adds further weight to the theory that the breast is most susceptible to environmental carcinogens during and just after puberty.
- Teenagers who become pregnant and continue to smoke are not only endangering the health of their unborn babies (through the increased risk of stillbirth, prematurity and abnormally low birth weight), but they are more likely to suffer nausea, vomiting, diarrhoea, urinary tract infections, yeast infections, headache and backache themselves.
- Even the non-smoking daughters of women who smoked during their pregnancies are around 30 per cent more likely to miscarry their baby than the non-smoking daughters of non-smoking mothers; and if the daughter as well as the mother has smoked during pregnancy, the possibility of miscarriage is 60 per cent more likely (based on a study of 15,000 women in England, followed through pregnancy until their children reached the age of seven).
- Breastfed babies of smoking mothers may have nausea, vomiting, diarrhoea and a rapid heart rate and, compared to the children

of non-smokers, children of mothers who smoke have twice as many colds, are sick more often and take longer to recover from illnesses.

Fortunately, children and young adolescents are very open to positive health messages. Following a one-off discussion with Year 6 students on the evils of smoking, a bright-eyed youngster later penned this thought-provoking poem (printed here with kind permission):

> **Smoking, No Way**
> *Is smoking good or is it bad?*
> *Should you light up and take a fag?*
> *The answer to this, my friend, you see*
> *Is if you smoke you will be*
> *Absolutely manipulated*
> *By junk that should not be tolerated.*
> *In cigarettes, that you puff,*
> *They put all nasty kinds of stuff*
> *Like rocket fuel and tar,*
> *Also exhaust, like from a car,*
> *They put in floor polish,*
> *That will demolish*
> *Organs, like lungs, and the rest.*
> *So come on, mate, decide what's best,*
> *Don't go and smoke with all the rest.*
> *I really think that you should be*
> *A non-smoker, just like me!!*
> Mark Franklin (11 years old)

Mark would probably also be interested to know that cigarette smoke is radioactive. A person who smokes one or two packs a day will absorb the equivalent radiation dosages of 250 to 300 chest X-rays each year.

Nobody, apart from kids themselves perhaps, should need any convincing that teenage smoking is a major health problem. The longer term consequences in particular (a 15 times greater chance of developing lung disease and lung cancer and an eight times greater chance of heart disease) are bad. Thirty per cent of all fatal cancers could be prevented by people not smoking. Not everybody knows that

George Harrison's fatal brain tumour was caused by the spread of lung cancer resulting from his smoking. His early death reinforces an important message: smoking kills the people we love, and their music.

Teenagers who smoke soon develop a cough, produce phlegm and become short of breath on exertion, lose stamina, get a bad taste in the mouth, stains on their teeth and an unpleasant odour on their breath, fingers, hair and clothes. Smoke also irritates eyes, causes skin to wrinkle faster and hair to discolour, soon making smokers look older than their years. Not much going for it. Sometimes, it helps to say these sorts of things to young people, who may be more impressed by the implications of here-and-now unattractiveness than by some future, unseen threat.

There's another worry – nicotine is an extremely addictive drug. Recent research shows that kids can get hooked pretty quickly (perhaps after less than one pack) and actually need to continue smoking. Scientists had earlier assumed that addiction did not begin until teenagers were smoking 10 or more cigarettes a day – we now know it cuts in far earlier. According to an international study, young people smoking an average of only *two cigarettes a week* showed signs of addiction, and in two-thirds of the study sample, addiction appeared before daily smoking.

The reason that children and adults develop addictions to nicotine at different rates is that the adolescent brain is still developing and is therefore more vulnerable to the effects of drugs. As a result, juvenile onset nicotine dependence may represent a more serious disruption of neurological functioning than it does in adults. This also begs the question – how much passive smoke does a child have to be exposed to before they are more likely to become smokers themselves?

The more encouraging news is that if a young person under 25 is able to stop smoking, the health risks revert to normal. It takes seven to 10 days to be free from nicotine, and the cough, wheezing and mucus start to improve in two to three weeks. For teenagers who want to stop, 'Quit' kits and other help are readily available. A cute mobile advertisement for these kits was on the back of a cab: 'This taxi has given up smoking – you can too.' By the way, even for adult long-term smokers, the benefits of quitting are significant.

Teenagers and alcohol

Various youth-oriented media campaigns over the years (for example, those related to the Australian Government's National

Drug Offensive) have used television, radio and magazines to send anti-drug messages to young people. Girls have been told: 'You can lose a lot more than your memory if you get drunk.' Boys have been told, 'If you don't want to look a jerk, don't get drunk.' Another slogan asked, 'How will you feel tomorrow?' and a campaign looking at alcohol and violence was called 'Tears you apart'. The most recent Federal Government campaign, also seeking to combat irresponsible drinking, is aimed at 15- to 20-year-olds and links with the Australian pop music industry. The slogan is 'Drinking: Where are your choices taking you?' and funds are being invested in posters, music videos, print, online adverstising and band tours.

Unfortunately, worthy efforts such as these haven't helped much in the past. For one thing, they're competing with TV programs featuring characters who consume huge amounts of alcohol, such as certain high-profile Australian-made television shows targeting the young adult (16 to 35) demographic, that make alcohol look like a must-have accessory and a cool adventure (as mentioned in Chapter 4).

Overall, the 20–29 years age group has the highest proportion of hazardous and harmful drinking. But teenage drinking is also a serious problem, despite the law on underage drinking which states that alcohol may not be sold to people less than 18 years of age, even at private parties as part of a food package. Teenagers under 18 who are found drinking on licensed premises may be prosecuted.

The *National Drug Strategy Household Survey* of 2001 showed that, in the 14–19 years age group, 32 per cent of boys and 26 per cent of girls were regular drinkers (who consume alcohol on at least one day per week), while the rates for occasional drinkers (who consume alcohol less often than one day per week) were 41 per cent of boys and 49 per cent of girls. And according to a recent study undertaken by the Roy Morgan Organisation for the Salvation Army, this generation of drinkers starts younger, drinks more (twice as much as 10 years ago!) and indulges in binge drinking (defined as three times the 0.05 blood alcohol rate) to a greater extent than any previous generation. One-third of males aged 14–19 and more than half aged 20–24 admitted drinking between 11 and 30 alcoholic drinks in one session, mostly in sessions lasting no more than four hours!

Boys and girls have very similar rates of alcohol consumption, even in their mid-teens. The girls have caught up over the years, proof that the stigma once attached to female drinking has all but disappeared in

Australia. The teenagers of 20 years ago who furtively drank a limited range of beers and spirits would not recognise the abundance of new brands now on liquor store shelves. These include ready-made cocktails and fruit-based alcohols that appeal to the under-30s (let's hear it for advertising), particularly young women who dislike the taste of beer and prefer sweet drinks that don't taste like booze. Many drinks now have individual websites featuring computer games, competitions, jokes and marketing strategies that include the distribution of free beer samples for over-18 parties.

Why do teenagers drink alcohol? They say:

Some people act like they are drunk to get attention but this is really sad. Girls use alcohol to be more relaxed and confident. When you go to a new school, you want new friends and so you do things to fit in.

It's become the thing to do on a weekend to drink alcohol. Some people become really aggressive when they are drunk and they use it as an excuse for bad behaviour. Some people drink just to spite their parents, especially when they've been told not to.

The main reasons that young people drink are to 'fit in' or to relax. For many, partying with alcohol (and marijuana) often feels like an adolescent rite of passage. Wherever did they get the idea that you have to drink to relax? Notwithstanding our concerns about alcohol advertising, research shows that Australian teenagers who drink are much more likely to report that both parents drink, and are more likely to have been offered their first drink by parents or relatives. Surveys have found that when young people are asked what influences their decision to drink or not drink, more than 60 per cent say their parents are the main influence (with 28 per cent saying it's their peers).

We shouldn't be too surprised. Australia is in the top 20 countries in terms of alcohol consumption. In beer consumption, we are in the top 10 and our liking for table wines has increased, albeit marginally, in the past decade. Drinking is part of the Australian culture and, sadly, we tend to treat excessive drinking with a nod and a wink and give little thought to the health or social consequences. In fact, fewer than one in 10 Australians aged over 14 associates alcohol with a 'drug problem'.

What's depressing about all this is that alcohol-related illness is the fourth major health problem in Australia after heart disease, cancer and mental illness. Currently 3700 Australians die each year from complications related to alcohol abuse, with more than 62,000 people being admitted to hospital annually. It has recently been estimated that the net social costs of alcohol use in Australia amounts to over $7.5 billion a year.

The National Health and Medical Research Council defines low-risk drinking as no more than four standard drinks per day for men and no more than two standard drinks for women and at least two alcohol-free days per week. Can teenagers drink safely? Possibly, but even mild to moderate drinking may adversely affect the development of a young brain and body. Also, a drinking problem is not measured only by how much a person drinks, but also by how the drinking affects the individual's life and the lives of people around them. There are two main sets of consequences:

- The acute problems are bad enough: drunkenness, accidents, violence, arrests and unprotected sex. Alcohol is a depressant (not a stimulant as many people think) and is dangerously intoxicating, especially to young people. With binge drinking, it's possible to die from alcohol poisoning (blood levels in excess of 0.3 milligrams per 100 mls can be fatal) or from choking on your own vomit. Teenage deaths from toxic overdose have usually involved a dare to down a bottle of spirits. For most young drinkers, however, dangerous behaviour and drink-driving pose the greatest threat to life.
- Longer term problems are less obvious. While no one can say for sure whether or not teenage drinking patterns persist into adulthood, the earlier you start, and the heavier you drink, the earlier you get damaged. Also, people who drink regularly may become dependent on alcohol or develop a tolerance to alcohol, so they need more to get the same effect. The health consequences include: cirrhosis of the liver, some cancers, chronic malnutrition and the risk of infection and, of course, brain damage. Yes, heavy drinking does shrink your brain – it causes an irreversible loss of cortical tissue.

Parents won't have too much trouble noticing when a teenager staggers home reeking of alcohol or wakes up with a hangover. But there are some other early warning signs that might suggest that drinking is getting out of hand. For example: increased moodiness and aggressiveness; shaky hands; sleeplessness and anxiety; and deteriorating school or work performance (none of which, of course, are exclusive to alcohol abuse). Parents who are worried about their teenager's drinking can get advice from their local Community Health Centre (many of which employ specialist drug and alcohol workers), or call a 24-hour drug and alcohol information service (which is usually located at a hospital). For a very sick or unconscious teenager who's been drinking, the best thing to do is call a doctor or an ambulance.

Teenagers and other drugs

Young people take drugs for a variety of reasons: to get high (usually in a social setting), to be part of the group, to relieve boredom or gain relief from emotional pain (anxiety, depression, family problems), to go beyond the boundaries of ordinary experience, or simply to relax, reduce the pressure and slow down – the main reasons adults take drugs. Young people generally start off by experimenting with a drug (often to find out about the sensations it produces) as part of general risk-taking or rebellion, but it may become a habit when they think it solves their problems.

Before looking in more detail at drugs other than tobacco and alcohol, here are some general facts:

- Teenagers know more about drug use; drug use is glorified in popular culture; the use of needles has been demystified, has less of a 'junkie' association than in the past and young people are less afraid of it.
- Young people today are more commonly poly-drug users. For example, a relatively new fad is mixing caffeine-loaded energy drinks such as Red Bull with alcoholic drinks such as Vodka.
- Teenagers abuse easy-to-access over-the-counter drugs such as cough medicine (containing codeine), analgesics like paracetamol, antihistamines and decongestants, which may be dangerous if taken incorrectly.
- Young people sometimes steal drugs from the family medicine cabinet and sell them as party drugs.
- Common household products are being inhaled by teenagers and can be deadly.

- Many high school students take tranquillisers such as Serepax and Valium for stress-related symptoms (these are frequently abused by kids whose parents use them).
- Prescription drugs such as Dexamphetamine and Ritalin (used in the treatment of ADHD) are more available in schools these days, and are being abused as stimulants by teenagers who don't have the disorder.
- Cannabis and LSD now exist in forms that are more potent than in the 1960s, and have serious side effects such as mental illness.
- Dance parties called 'raves' are characterised by the use of drugs such as ecstasy which can cause severe psychological problems and occasionally death.
- Home laboratories for manufacturing methamphetamine (speed) have made this drug much more available for illegal use.

Despite all the statistics and known dangers concerning alcohol and tobacco, other drugs really worry parents the most. The biggest killer of people aged 14–34 is alcohol, accounting for about 60 per cent of drug-related deaths. Illicit drugs cause about 34 per cent of drug-related deaths in this age range. Of all the illegal drugs, cannabis is the most popular overall and the most used by young people. About 50 per cent of all high school students have tried cannabis, 10 per cent have tried amphetamines and LSD, five per cent have tried cocaine and ecstasy, and three per cent have tried heroin. The numbers of young people who are regular users or who are addicted to drugs are growing.

What are the signs of drug use? There is no precise profile of a drug-taking adolescent (or any other type of drug taker, in fact). A lot depends on what they're taking, how much, and in what circumstances. Mood swings and changes in behaviour patterns may be symptoms of drug abuse but, as we've seen, these may also be entirely normal. What we do know is that young people who misuse drugs go to great lengths to conceal their use. The smarter their parents, the harder they try to cover it up.

It's important to emphasise that, while many adolescents will experiment and take risks with alcohol and other drugs, only a small minority will go on to suffer serious substance abuse. The group with a serious risk of dependence are young people with psychiatric disorders who self-medicate with illicit drugs or alcohol to relieve their mental suffering. Predictors of continuing drug use are: engaging in antisocial behaviour, starting drug use at an early age, being seriously intoxicated repeatedly despite dangers, hanging out with older, more experienced, drug-using peers and being labelled as a substance abuser. Other factors predisposing a young person to drug use are the loss of a loved parent at a crucial time of development, as well as poor-quality family relationships and parenting skills.

If you suspect your kids are taking drugs, don't panic. Raise it with them as you would any other concern you had (this obviously goes for alcohol and tobacco too). Hopefully there will have been opportunities in the past to discuss the issue of drugs and the risks in a non-accusatory way.

> **The following, though not conclusive, are the signs of drug-taking to look for:**
>
> - A change in school attendance (frequently absent or late) or achievement (sloppy homework, apathy and lack of effort).
> - A change in peer group and a reluctance to introduce friends to the family.
> - Poor physical appearance and an extreme lack of regard for personal hygiene; red eyes, dilated or constricted pupils; drowsiness and confusion.
> - A marked change in emotional state, with unusual aggressiveness, temper flare-ups, or excessive tiredness or withdrawal.
> - Furtive behaviour, including lying, stealing or borrowing money (because drugs cost money); an unexplained need for more money.
> - Concerns expressed by friends, their parents or other adults.

If a teenager admits to using drugs, however, there are some sensible steps to follow: do some homework and become better informed about the subject; clarify the facts; clarify your own concerns in order to approach your teenager as a concerned and rational adult; try not to moralise about drugs. Not only is detailed drug information only a phone call away, but also there are counsellors who can advise and help you (see Appendix for help lines in your state, books and websites).

I know a guy who uses speed. He says drugs are cheaper than alcohol.
Matt, aged 18

> **Signs of addiction in the individual concerned include:**
>
> ▶ Spending a great deal of time using the substance.
> ▶ Using it more often than one intends.
> ▶ Thinking about reducing use.
> ▶ Making repeated unsuccessful efforts to reduce use.
> ▶ Giving up important social, family or occupational activities to use it.
> ▶ Reporting withdrawal symptoms after stopping using it.

Here is some brief information about other drugs commonly used by young people:

Cannabis

What does it look like? There are three main forms of cannabis: marijuana (dried leaves and flowers of the plant), hashish (dried resin in blocks) and hash oil (thick oily liquid rarely found in Australia).
How is it taken? Smoked, cooked.
Street names: Grass, pot, hash, weed, reefer, dope, herb, mull, buddha, ganja, joint, stick, buckets, cones, smoko, head.
Facts: Every year, more people become regular cannabis users, largely as a result of teenagers taking it up while baby boomers (this may come as a surprise) continue with their own use. Parents worry that smoking dope puts teenagers on a downhill run to heroin. While this is by no means an inevitable progression because most use it as a recreational drug only, it does mean that they're likely to be in contact with people who peddle a variety of drugs, and this is a worry.

Heated debates about the ill-effects of dope and whether or not laws should be changed rage on. Some young people believe that cannabis is in some way safer than cigarettes and is safer than the abuse of alcohol. But it's not safe, not by any stretch of the imagination.

Cannabis is a depressant drug that slows down the central nervous system, delaying messages between the brain and the body and causing the effects listed on the next page (which last for two to four hours).

- Increased awareness of sensation and colour, laughter and a sense of wellbeing, an altered perception of time (the illusion of time slowing down) and space.
- Stimulation of appetite.
- Less pleasant effects such as a dry mouth, dizziness, bloodshot eyes and in some users panic attacks as well as feelings of paranoia.
- Impaired coordination; problems with memory and the ability to think logically; confusion and hallucinations.

The long-term effects of cannabis are extremely worrying:

- Cannabis dependence is now recognised and there is a characteristic withdrawal syndrome. Chronic marijuana users also become very psychologically dependent and cannot or will not believe that it is causing them harm.
- Major drawbacks include a loss of energy and drive and impairment of short-term memory and concentration, effects that have been shown to persist long after people stop using the drug (and may not be reversible, suggesting physiological changes in the brain).
- Heavy long-term cannabis use can also lead to symptoms of airways obstruction and, because roll your own cigarettes (with loose tobacco) have far more tar than commercial cigarettes, there's an increased risk of lung cancer and chronic bronchitis as well as cancer of the mouth, tongue and jaw.
- The active chemical in cannabis (THC-9 tetrahydrocannabinol) can precipitate a wide variety of acute, disabling psychiatric syndromes, the most notable of which are an acute anxiety/panic state, and a brief psychosis; paranoia is particularly troubling to heavy cannabis users and symptoms can persist for up to a year after cessation of use.

The relationship between cannabis use and mental health problems is becoming of increasing concern to health professionals. Cannabis is associated with higher rates of depression and anxiety problems. Some psychiatrists recognise a probable link between the high rates of youth suicide and adolescent depression and the big increase in dope-smoking.

Inhalants

Street names: Glue, gas, sniff, huff, chroming (as in the use of chrome paint), poppers.

Facts: Solvent and aerosol sniffing is a popular form of drug experimentation for young adolescents. The substances used include glue, petrol, lighter fluid, cleaning fluid and paint thinner. About 30 per cent of students throughout the high school system have admitted to trying it, with equal involvement of girls and boys. Sniffing peaks at about 13 to 14 years and is rapidly given up by most.

The effects of sniffing include feelings of happiness, relaxation and drowsiness which last from one to three hours. The high from sniffing is similar to extreme drunkenness and there can be euphoria. Adverse effects include: drowsiness, agitation, flu-like symptoms (such as sneezing, coughing, runny nose), disorientation, problems with co-ordination, nausea and vomiting, diarrhoea, unpleasant breath, nose bleeds, sores and reckless behaviour.

Adolescents are largely unaware of the dangers in this practice, but sudden death by cardiac arrest can occur, even on the first occasion. In chronic abusers, depending on the solvent used, it may damage the nervous system, kidneys, liver or heart. (Such chronic abuse is rare, usually only occurring in deeply troubled young people.) It's dangerous stuff.

Heroin

What does it look like? Heroin comes as white to off-white granules or pieces of 'rock' packaged in 'foils' (aluminium foil) or coloured small balloons.

How is it taken? Most commonly injected into a vein but can be smoked ('chasing the dragon') or snorted.

Street names: Smack, skag, dope, H, junk, hammer, slow, gear, harry, horse, rock.

Facts: This highly addictive drug causes a sensation of euphoria and contentment. The adverse effects are related to a slowing down of bodily functions including breathing, blood pressure and pulse, causing drowsiness and nausea. The pupils of the eyes become smaller. In an overdose, breathing becomes very slow, body temperature drops and heartbeat becomes irregular. This can quickly lead to death. Combining heroin with other depressant drugs greatly increases the effects, and a relatively light dose of heroin can then become a heavy dose.

Street heroin is usually a mixture of pure heroin and other substances such as talcum powder, baking powder, starch, glucose or quinine. Sometimes other drugs, such as amphetamines and barbiturates, are also added. Sharing needles and syringes increases the risk of contracting hepatitis or HIV.

Dependence can be psychological or physical. Withdrawal symptoms from heroin may include diarrhoea, stomach cramps, vomiting and symptoms resembling a very severe bout of the flu.

Although only 2.2 per cent of Australians 14 and older have used heroin, deaths from heroin are increasing and the social cost in terms of crime and drain on the health system is significant.

LSD (lysergic acid diethylamine)

What does it look like? In its pure state, LSD is a white odourless powder. It usually comes in the form of liquid, tablets or capsules, squares of gelatine or blotting paper and is often diluted with another substance, such as sugar, or soaked onto sheets of blotting paper.
How is it taken? Can be swallowed, sniffed, injected or smoked.
Street names: Acid, trips, tabs, T.
Facts: This hallucinogenic drug heightens perception and causes hallucinations. Adverse effects include: enlargement of the pupils, rapid heart rate, changes in perception, nausea and loss of appetite, chills and flushing, shaking, paranoia, confusion and acute panic. Long-term effects can include flashbacks (intense nightmares) which occur days, weeks or even years after using the drug and people can also become psychologically or physically dependent. LSD is linked to mental illness.

Amphetamines

What does it look like? Amphetamines can be in the form of powder, tablets, capsules, crystals or red liquid. Amphetamine tablets vary in colour, and can be a cocktail of drugs, binding agents, caffeine and sugar.
How is it taken? Most commonly swallowed, injected (methamphetamine) or smoked. They are also 'snorted' or 'sniffed' through the nose.

Street names: Speed, up, fast, louee, goey, whiz, pep pills, uppers.
Facts: Amphetamines stimulate the central nervous system, providing a rush of energy and confidence and reducing fatigue. But in speeding up bodily functions, they increase the heart rate, respiratory rate and blood pressure. A dry mouth, increased sweating and enlargement of the pupils can occur. Amphetamines also cause reduced appetite and irritability, and high doses can cause headaches, dizziness, blurred vision, tremors, irregular heartbeat, stomach cramps and loss of coordination. Due to the unknown strength and mix of street amphetamines, some users have collapsed after overdosing and others have experienced strokes, heart failure and seizures. High amounts can also lead to 'amphetamine psychosis' including paranoid delusions, hallucinations and aggressive behaviour.

In contrast, amphetamines are safely prescribed for attention deficit hyperactivity disorder as the contents and dose of the drug are correct.

Ecstasy

What does it look like? Ecstasy usually comes in the form of small white or yellow- to brown-coloured tablets of various sizes, shapes and designs.
How is it taken? Swallowed or crushed and snorted. They can be inserted into the anus from where the drug is absorbed – referred to as 'shafting' or 'shelving'. Injecting ecstasy has recently become more popular.
Street names: Ecstasy is a street term for a range of drugs that are similar in structure to MDMA (Methylenedioxymethamphetamine). Ecstasy is also known as E, Vitamin E, XTC, eccy and the love drug.
Facts: This drug causes a sense of closeness and intimacy, feelings of love and affection. Ecstasy is like both amphetamines and hallucinogens in chemical structure and effect. It is a popular party drug and causes hallucinations, stimulates thirst and overheating. Death may occur after excessive drinking as in the well-known case of Anna Wood. New research suggests it causes permanent brain damage – it can impair memory, even when taken infrequently, and puts people at risk of developing a Parkinson's-like condition and other disorders.

After everything, the thing that really made me give up the drug was the look of hurt in my parents' eyes.
sean, aged 19

Fantasy

What does it look like? Fantasy, or Gamma-hydroxybutyrate (GHB), comes as a colourless, odourless, bitter or salty-tasting liquid usually sold in small bottles or vials. It also comes as a crystal powder.

How is it taken? Mostly taken orally; however, there have been reports of people injecting the drug.

Street names: Fantasy, grievous bodily harm (GBH), liquid ecstasy and liquid E.

Facts: Fantasy is another party drug that has depressant effects.

Cocaine

What does it look like? Most commonly a white, odourless powder called 'cocaine hydrochloride'. Cocaine may be mixed, or 'cut', with other substances such as sugar, baking soda and talcum powder. 'Crack' is a very pure form of freebase cocaine sold in the form of small crystals or rocks.

How is it taken? Inhaled (snorted) through the nose, or injected. Crack is smoked in pipes or in cigarettes, mixed with tobacco or marijuana.

Street names: C, vitamin C, coke, flake, nose candy, snow, dust, white, white lady, toot, crack, rock, freebase.

Facts: Cocaine causes exhilaration, a heightened sense of awareness, and reduces fatigue. The adverse effects include anxiety, paranoia and possible addiction. The other physical effects are increasing body temperature, heart rate, indifference to pain, enlarged pupils and sexual arousal. In greater quantities it can cause extreme aggression and hallucinations. Like other stimulant drugs, overdose causes death due to seizures, heart attacks, brain haemorrhage, kidney failure and stroke.

A supportive, harm reduction approach is best when we are talking to young people about drugs. Scare tactics and zero tolerance seem like good ideas but these approaches are not effective. Many young people will experiment with drugs regardless of their knowledge about adverse effects but parents can try to inform them of the risks and discuss the issue to lift the taboo around talking about drugs. Education needs to be targeted at the needs of the young person and to address the underlying issues associated with drug use. Why are they taking drugs? What will it take to minimise the harm, cut down their use or stop?

What do young people think about drug use?

I know a few people who are caught up in the drug scene but I don't know what to say to them. I have a few friends who smoke mull. They say: 'We're more relaxed – life's easier.' A guy I know uses speed. He says he can get up and dance all night and drugs are cheaper than alcohol. But these kids usually end up hurting their friends with their lies.

People say drugs are okay – I am just having fun. They are denying that they're really hurting themselves. You can't tell people to stop using drugs unless you offer them something else to do. Sometimes you can't do anything until the person wants to stop themselves. It's easier to forget about your problems than to deal with them.

Some people who try to stop smoking dope can't, because their friends all smoke and it's too hard. It's easier to say yes than no. Quick fixes seem more tolerable than long-term solutions.

Young people are drawn to drugs so strongly because, unfortunately, it seems to us that there is no other way to enjoy life. There is simply no hope in today's society. Take the government for instance. They are constantly pushing the statistics onto us. 'Half the youth are drug addicts, half of them are unemployed, and the rest of the world is lost in murder, rape, war and money.' Hearing that every day is going to give us hope for our future? I doubt it.

The problem is that drug use is a cool thing to do. They should activate a non-phoney campaign on young people's level that makes smoking and drugs seem daggy.

What drugs and alcohol do is give us a false sense of hope, confidence and peace, and we use them because we find it hard to believe that things can be achieved without them. But once you have built up a true sense of hope and confidence there is absolutely no need for drugs. I think that society realises that drugs are a major problem. At most schools, drugs are a taboo subject.

You get told that drugs are bad in a million different ways, but no one has the guts to give us the real hard facts. It is no wonder that young people use drugs when they are all around us but we are only given titbits of information. We are young, we are learning, we are trying to find out the facts of life and it is really sad that we are given the impression the only way to find out about them is to use them. There needs to be a compulsory program at every school that clearly shows the devastating effects of drug use. Guest speakers – (real young people, not just celebrities like Angry Anderson!) who use, have overcome their use, or who have ended up with hepatitis C or AIDS and are very likely to die, need to be brought right in close to us, to scare the shit out of us.

Homelessness in young people

This section on homeless youth has been included here because of the high incidence of risk-taking behaviour in this group. But the issue itself should be of concern to all caring adults. It is a problem of overwhelming proportions, with an estimated 80 million homeless children or more throughout the world. The situation in Australia can only be guessed at, but according to research undertaken by Brian Burdekin for the Human Rights and Equal Opportunity Commission back in 1989, 'There are at least 20,000 to 25,000 homeless children and young people across the country... likely figure is actually 50,000 to 70,000 children or young people who are homeless or at serious risk.' A review of the *Burdekin Report* is well overdue. Homelessness involving children, young people and even families is increasing.

There must be very few parents who don't love their children, although some, for a variety of reasons, have difficulty expressing it in a positive way. People can be so caught up in their own troubles that there is little left over for the kids. Some parents physically or sexually abuse their children, which is the reason why up to 60 per cent of homeless children leave home. In some households, the level of tension and conflict is so great that living there becomes intolerable. When a teenager runs away from home it is frequently an act of desperation. Parents may be left bewildered, frightened, angry or worried. However, they are still at home, while the young person has generally walked out of the frying pan and into the fire.

What must it be like to have nowhere to go, to think of home but feel unable to return there? Words like 'loneliness' and 'isolation' come to mind, but feelings go deeper than that. Young runaways (or throwaways as the case may be) typically have rock bottom self-esteem. Many feel they have no history and have no sense of future, only a core of emptiness. Homeless teenagers grieve the loss of their families, who may be out of sight, but are never for long out of mind. This is not something they discuss readily. Studies show that a majority of homeless kids have poor literacy and lack the skill to say how they feel. Not only does it seem to them that 'nobody gives a damn' but they feel, and usually are, powerless to change their circumstances.

Homelessness is not conducive to good health. 'Street youth' have little concern for self-care and have poor knowledge of their bodies and diseases. They tend to eat badly, sleep little and experience much stress, all of which interfere with normal growth and development. They often have exceptionally poor dental health, a high incidence of skin complaints such as scabies and eczema, chronic ear infections and hearing problems, asthma and other respiratory health complaints, including chronic bronchitis, and poor immunisation histories. And that's just on the physical side – mental health problems are also rife among this unfortunate population of young people.

In their grim and often desperate struggle for survival, drugs, prostitution, violence and brutality become part of their world. In the longer term, many street youth don't make it. High-risk lifestyles make them vulnerable to serious infectious diseases such as hepatitis B and C, gonorrhoea and other STIs and HIV/AIDS. Deaths resulting from suicide and motor vehicle accident (often one and the same) come as a surprise to no one.

To keep things in perspective, death holds less fear for many homeless young people than the family from which they ran. They adapt to the vicissitudes and abuses of the streets because, for the majority, they are no strangers to abusive situations. In her book, *Those Tracks on My Face*, former Children's Court Magistrate Barbara Holborow OAM writes:

> *Unfortunately, the public has very little insight into the plight of these children who are forced to live away from home. Children don't have a choice. Circumstances are such that it is often unsafe for them to live at home, unsafe emotionally, physically and for*

> *their wellbeing. For some reason, the general public has little patience for such children...*

And as hard as life on the streets is, there is some illusion of control over their circumstances. On the one hand they try to make the best of their forced independence among others who understand their feelings, but on the other, they have limited ability to overcome their poverty, poor living conditions and health problems.

Teenage boys and girls in this situation need access to strong and caring adults, which is easier said than done. They tend to avoid hospitals, doctors and social workers and have little trust in 'the establishment' and the veritable army of 'do gooders' and authority figures. Other reasons why street kids fall through the cracks in the health care system include: concerns about confidentiality; fear of receiving 'bad' health news; lack of money or even a Medicare or Health Care Card; a sense that services are inaccessible and non-'youth friendly'; a perception that health professionals are judgemental and cynical. In youth refuges, they find exhausted, relatively young and sometimes poorly informed workers, but rarely the stability and high-quality support they crave. Homelessness is often 'out of sight, out of mind' and society at large just doesn't see the risk – both to the kids themselves and to all of us. It is a monumental social problem.

Young people in trouble with the law

Studies of repeat young offenders in detention centres reveal major breakdowns in social bonding as the almost universal background to their difficulties, as well as their health-damaging legacies. Many homeless teenagers come before the courts, both in relation to their plight in unsafe and unsupported environments and because of anti-social and illegal behaviour. The picture that emerges is as follows:

A disrupted or dangerous home life: It is estimated that about 80 per cent of repeat young offenders come from families in which the marriage has broken down or is in the process of breaking down. Many of these young people become homeless, frequently (as mentioned) as a result of neglect, or emotional, physical or sexual abuse. A survey in one Sydney detention centre revealed that 87 per cent of inmates had previously been notified to authorities as being abused as children, 63 per cent on three or more occasions. According to staff of a young women's detention centre, over 90 per cent of residents claimed they'd been sexually abused, usually by someone known to them. A growing number of young male repeat offenders are now claiming they have been sexually abused.

A disrupted education and a sense of social inadequacy: Most repeat young offenders in detention have left school before completing Year 8! Their major deficits in literacy and numeracy skills not only minimise their chances of future meaningful employment, but also adversely affect their already depleted self-esteem. Most repeat offenders say that they feel like 'outsiders', alienated from their communities and greatly disadvantaged in terms of education, job opportunities and housing.

Risk-taking, depression and suicide: Many repeat young offenders claim they often become depressed, see little point in living and secretly wish they could die. More than 60 per cent of young people in detention centres claim they have seriously contemplated suicide, while as many as one in four report having attempted suicide.

Many repeat male offenders are reportedly involved in car stealing and reckless driving at high speeds for the 'thrills' involved, but, as noted, there may often be a correlation between this behaviour and suicidal tendency. For example, in the case of one teenage boy, he and his mother were often subjected to verbal and physical abuse by his alcoholic father and the boy would flee, often stealing motorbikes. He claimed that when he was riding he felt completely 'free' and 'totally in control' of the bike, and this helped him to escape from his home problems. He was killed at the age of 17 when the stolen bike he was riding inexplicably left a straight piece of road and hit a power pole. Accident or covert suicide?

Alcohol and other drug usage: A 1999 survey of 302 repeat young offenders in NSW (273 males and 29 females with average age of 16.5 years) revealed the following pattern of drug use: 92 per cent claimed they had used cannabis; alcohol use was predictably high at 87 per cent; 56 per cent admitted to having tried 'speed' or amphetamines, and 50 per cent admitted using heroin; the use of hallucinogens, such as LSD, was reported by 46 per cent of those surveyed; 34 per cent claimed to have tried cocaine; more than a quarter (27 per cent) had tried ecstasy or similar drugs; and, compared to similar previous surveys, there were significant increases in the reported use of injected illicit drugs. These young offenders attributed many of the problems in their lives to their drug use: legal and criminal problems; money problems; problems at work or school; problems with family and friends; physical and emotional health problems. Over half of those surveyed claimed they became aggressive and/or violent when using drugs or alcohol.

Contemporary approaches to juvenile crime

Not all the news about juvenile offenders is bad. A major study of almost 53,000 young offenders appearing before NSW Children's Courts over a nine-year period (January 1986 to December 1994) revealed that: 70 per cent did not appear before the Children's Court again; of the 30 per cent that did re-offend, around half returned to court only once; very few juveniles become persistent offenders but a small number of chronic or persistent offenders are responsible for a disproportionately large number of proven criminal offences. For example, nine per cent of juvenile offenders were responsible for 31 per cent of all the proven offences.

On the basis of this and other research about effective ways of dealing with young offenders the following strategies have been followed in NSW:

- Diversion of minor offenders from the formal criminal justice system through police warnings and cautions, and youth justice conferencing.
- Provision of more intensive, coordinated services to higher risk offenders.
- Emphasis on community-based rather than custodial services.
- Provision of programs to develop the educational, social and work skills of the most disadvantaged young offenders.

Positive youth development can and should be promoted within the juvenile justice system in the following ways:

Providing advocacy in the system: This concept is based upon the selection of a key worker, one who is able to develop a positive relationship with the young person, motivate and maintain their involvement in self-development. This key worker should be the person who introduces the young person to other staff, the various youth workers, nurses, teachers and specialist counsellors likely to be involved in the ongoing assessment process and casework.

Empowering the young person: Where there is truly client-centred casework, a young person is able to start making positive steps towards improving their life situation and accepting responsibility for their behaviour. Involving a detained teenager in their own case planning, for example, is more effective than an imposed process where they are merely onlookers or reluctant participants.

Tackling causes and effects: If a young person has left home to escape abuse and is on the streets, using drugs and thieving to support their habit, these problems need to be addressed. Individual counselling and groupwork will be needed to ameliorate the effects of the abuse, as well as focusing upon the offending behaviour itself (for example, the development of self-awareness and victim empathy). In due course, accommodation will need to be found so that the young person has some kind of 'home' to go to upon release.

Providing skills for dealing with stress: Many of the repeat offenders in the juvenile justice system act impulsively in response to the stresses they face on an almost daily basis. Some young people attempt to 'flee', while others try to fight aggressively through their problems. Because of their past negative experiences, most lack the trust needed to confide in adults so that they can unload their anxieties and gain much-needed advice or assistance. These challenges need to be faced.

Working with the family: Supporting positive youth development involves, whenever possible, working with the young person's family on issues likely to reduce their offending behaviour. Many different traumatic events occur within families that adversely impact on all family members. For example, one young person's offending behaviour commenced soon after the unexpected death of his father. The family members had become angry with him, believing that he had got into trouble when no longer subject to his father's discipline. In becoming alienated from his family, his antisocial activities increased. Eventually, in family sessions, he was able to reveal how shattered he was over his father's untimely death. All family members recalled that he had been close to his father and how he had withdrawn at the time, refusing to attend the funeral and remaining at home, shut away in his room, with his music. The family sessions enabled all family members, including the son, to talk about their loss and grief and, with greater understanding, the family bonded more closely and the young person's antisocial behaviour decreased.

Addressing educational and social deficits: Although most young offenders are of average or better intellectual potential, the majority have underachieved at school, generally due to environmental and emotional pressures, and dropped out early. Their ability to read, write and carry out simple mathematical calculations is thus severely limited, adversely affecting their self-esteem and social competence. Getting help to catch up a bit educationally, and receiving official recognition for their achievements (sometimes for the first time in their entire lives), are important ways to rebuild self-confidence in repeat young offenders.

Developing work skills: The vast majority of repeat young offenders entering the justice system are unemployed prior to their arrest and subsequent detention. Since most will live independently on return to the community, they need to acquire some basic employment skills if they are to gain work. Many accredited courses are now available to detained juveniles, through TAFE and other approved training bodies, to assist in the development of basic skills required for commonly advertised jobs.

Establishing supportive relationships: Meaningful relationships are the cornerstone of effective work with troubled young people. Since successful community integration should be the ultimate goal for repeat young offenders, every effort should be made from the outset to identify people who have been, or could become, significant others or mentors, willing to offer support and encouragement to each young person upon their return to the community. Leaving a supportive environment can be frightening and full of uncertainty (with some actually misbehaving in an attempt to be kept in detention). The weaning process needs to be carefully planned and will be helped if mentors are involved in the discharge planning process and available as soon as the young person is released from custody.

Informing about resources available in local communities: Because of the complexities of their problems, there is little doubt these young people will need various forms of assistance on their return to the community. While the process of adjustment will no doubt be assisted by mentoring, young people also need to know where they can seek help with health problems, accommodation, employment, emergency financial assistance, clothing and so on.

Not all young offenders are 'bad' kids, but kids who need our help. This deserves full community attention (like homelessness) and we must receive these kids with compassion and understanding when they return to 'our world'.

What can be done to prevent dangerous risk-taking?

No one would suggest that all risk-taking is problematic or even undesirable. If this were the message we were giving our kids, they might never climb a tree, ride a bike or bounce on a trampoline. Our concern here is about young people getting out of their depth, about the potentially dire consequences of the sorts of health hazardous behaviour we've been discussing. We want to find ways to protect our kids from these.

You have to start early, encouraging children to understand and care for their bodies (which has a lot to do with how you look after yours). If parents are heavily into the medicine cabinet for the slightest ache or pain, or heavily into tobacco or alcohol, kids will copy the behaviour. Nothing surer.

It is important to set limits for your kids. Negotiate with them about the time they should be home, discuss with them how to be safe on the road, to avoid the temptation to drink too much (and never drink and drive or get into a car with a driver who's been drinking). But remember, some limits need to be constantly revised; what might be appropriate for a 15-year-old is oppressive for a 17-year-old. Likewise, when you discuss non-negotiable limits, take the time to listen to your kid's views – lecturing, as tempting as it is, rarely has the desired effect.

Beyond this, everything we discussed in terms of stress management in Chapter 12 is also relevant here – encouraging your child's optimism, assertiveness and their abilities to solve their own problems will help your child to calculate risk. There is no special formula for preventing drug use among teenagers, or any other form of risk-taking for that matter. Kids get together and do what they're going to do no matter what. Whatever it is, some will, some won't. Most of the happenings involving young people cannot be controlled by any heroic acts of parental will. In fact, having had your quiet and sensible say, established trust and maintained open communication, set the best example you can and prayed hard, the rest is really up to them.

Some final thoughts

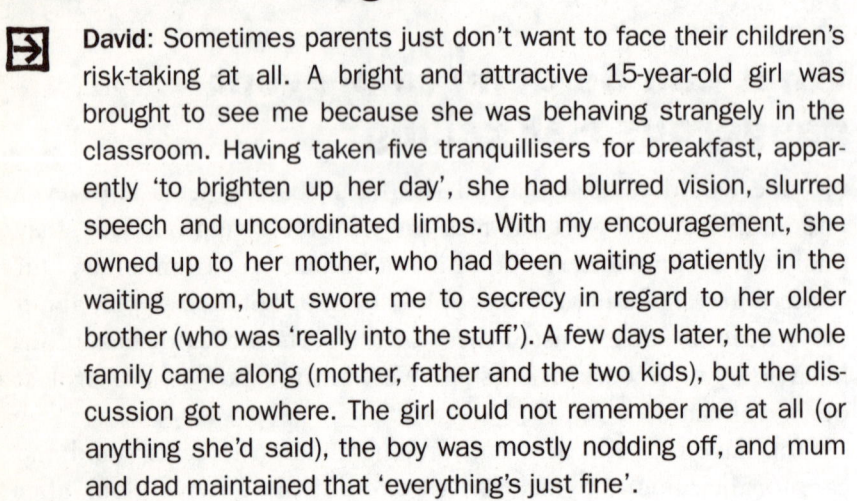

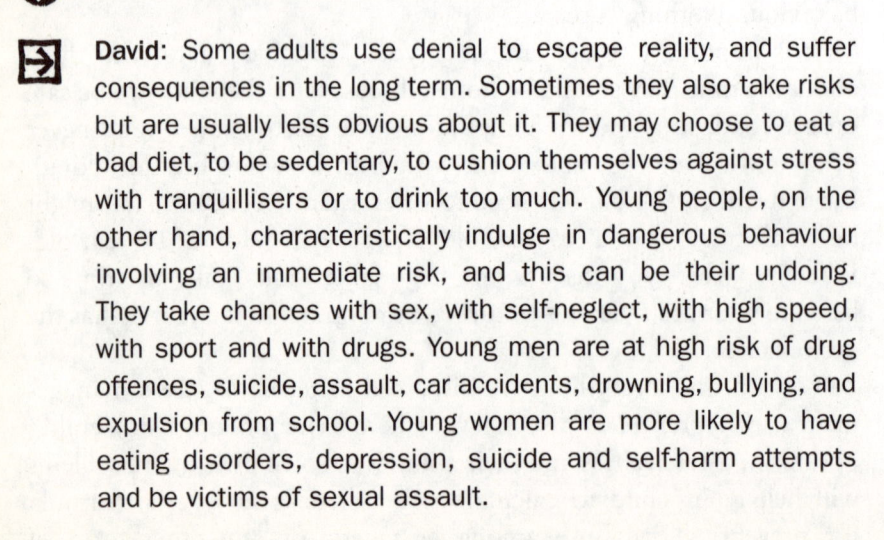

David: Sometimes parents just don't want to face their children's risk-taking at all. A bright and attractive 15-year-old girl was brought to see me because she was behaving strangely in the classroom. Having taken five tranquillisers for breakfast, apparently 'to brighten up her day', she had blurred vision, slurred speech and uncoordinated limbs. With my encouragement, she owned up to her mother, who had been waiting patiently in the waiting room, but swore me to secrecy in regard to her older brother (who was 'really into the stuff'). A few days later, the whole family came along (mother, father and the two kids), but the discussion got nowhere. The girl could not remember me at all (or anything she'd said), the boy was mostly nodding off, and mum and dad maintained that 'everything's just fine'.

Leanne: Unfortunately denial doesn't work, does it?

David: Some adults use denial to escape reality, and suffer consequences in the long term. Sometimes they also take risks but are usually less obvious about it. They may choose to eat a bad diet, to be sedentary, to cushion themselves against stress with tranquillisers or to drink too much. Young people, on the other hand, characteristically indulge in dangerous behaviour involving an immediate risk, and this can be their undoing. They take chances with sex, with self-neglect, with high speed, with sport and with drugs. Young men are at high risk of drug offences, suicide, assault, car accidents, drowning, bullying, and expulsion from school. Young women are more likely to have eating disorders, depression, suicide and self-harm attempts and be victims of sexual assault.

Leanne: No wonder parents look forward to teenagers growing up and slowing down. Then perhaps, at last, they can let out that long, lingering breath. Our good friend, the late Bronwyn Donaghy (author of *Leaving Early* and *Anna's Story*), gave us five pointers for keeping communication lines with our children open:

- Persevere – don't give up.
- Talk to them in proper conversations, ask about the music they like, films, their friends . . . Would you say to a friend, 'Have you done your homework? Don't leave your wet towels on the doona?'
- Listen to what they say – show them the respect they deserve.
- Watch how they behave – know what is normal and when to worry.
- Hug them. Just get in there and hold on.

Communication is our best weapon in the fight to minimise harm. Chapter 3 discussed more ways to show love.

The next chapter on mental health issues looks at what is behind the problems and what can be done to prevent and deal with them. These problems can range from the serious risk-taking just explained to simply not feeling that the child fits comfortably into the world. It is about promoting resilience.

David: This is a nice quote from Andrew Fuller (from his book: *From Surviving to Thriving*) about resilience:

Resilience is the happy knack of being able to bungy jump through the pitfalls of life. Even when the hardships and adversity arise, it is as if the person has an elasticised rope around them that helps them to rebound when things get low, and to maintain their sense of who they are as a person.

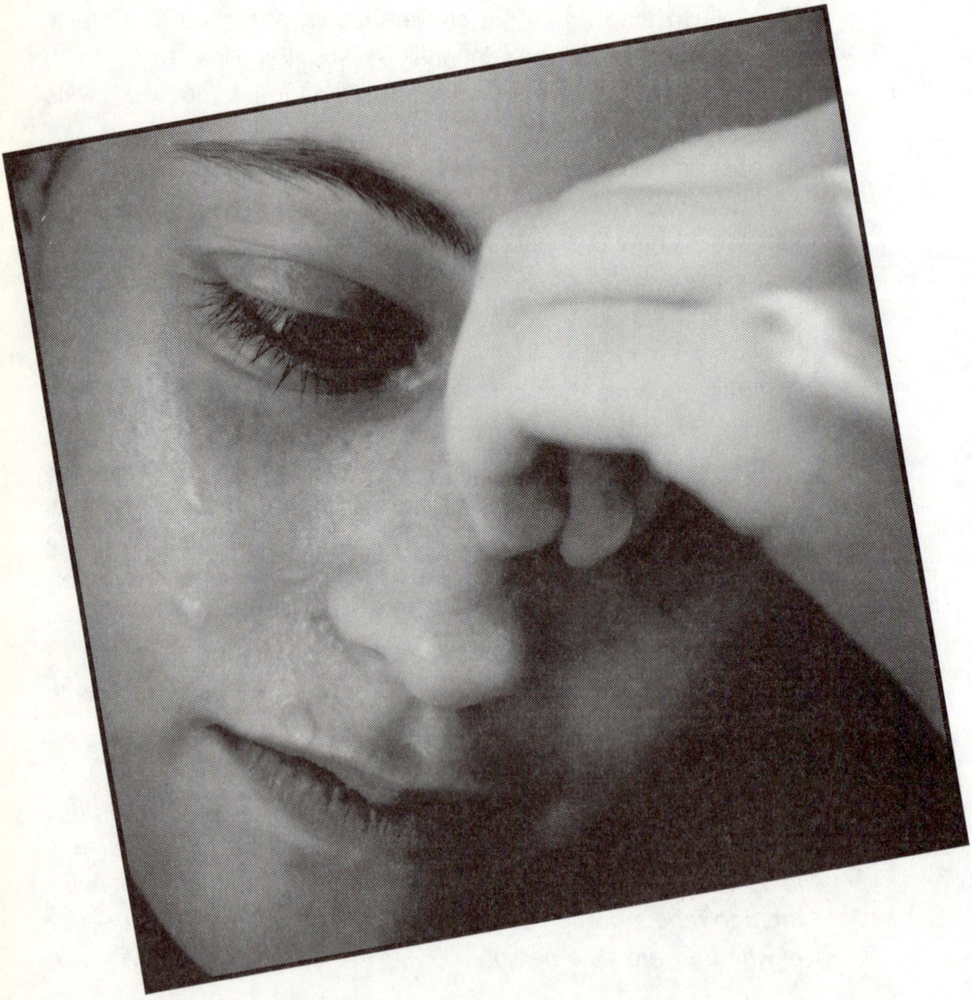

Chapter 15

It's in the mind

On a lot of days I feel empty and don't even know what I feel.
Jo, aged 14

During the ups and downs of adolescence, many parents will ask the question: Is this behaviour something to worry about? At a time when 24 per cent of young people develop mental health problems and suicide claims the lives of about 340 15- to 24-year-olds in Australia each year, parents have cause to worry. Mental health problems can happen to anyone and about 75 per cent of mental disorders begin in adolescence. This chapter discusses what we can do to prevent and deal with stress and common mental health issues such as depression, anxiety, panic attacks, eating disorders, psychosis and suicide.

Emotional pressures

I felt really empty and I told my mum. I said: 'I don't even know how I feel, but I feel nothing today.' She just sat me down and said: 'Don't worry, it's normal to feel that way sometimes. Be kind to yourself. Have a little rest and a drink and come and talk to me.' It was just a small thing, but now when I feel that way I just repeat my mum's words inside my head and things feel normal again.

Jack, aged 14

I still feel the crushing sense of failure in my stomach.
Lydia, aged 18

Adolescence is stressful. With pressures coming from all directions, inside and out, growing up can feel like negotiating your way through a maze. Unfortunately, many of the signposts and clues that could make this process easier are kept hidden from view. Teenagers do not always get the help and guidance they need.

The only people who are not stressed at all are dead. The rest of us have to cope with it as an unavoidable part of everyday life. Likewise, parents cannot create a stress-free environment for their kids. On the contrary, simply by being parents, parents are contributing to it. But there is much we can do to lessen the blows, particularly by taking the time to listen to our children's point of view and problems. As discussed in Chapter 10, home needs to be a sanctuary, a safe place where you can be yourself.

Stress – the good and the bad

Pressure in itself is not the problem. Without it we would get nowhere. If it motivates us and can be controlled, it is clearly a positive force. Particularly when there is an end in sight, pressure can lead to the pride of accomplishment and a boost in morale. In this sense, pressure is a desirable and healthy form of stress.

What is not so good is when pressure is prolonged or cannot be handled. Such pressure feels terrible, like you're being throttled or drowning in worries, and gives rise to the symptoms we recognise as stress. This is basically anxiety, and is like being revved up with nowhere to go, a feeling that is familiar to all of us.

A dry mouth, pounding heart, butterflies in the stomach and a sense of impending doom are due to the release of adrenalin. Other discomforts such as headache, backache and abdominal pain result from associated muscle tension. However, feeling dreadful is only part of the problem.

Why is adolescence stressful?

If stress is experienced by everyone from time to time, why should we be particularly concerned about adolescents? The writings of early theorists such as Anna Freud (Sigmund Freud's daughter) characterised adolescence as a time of 'storm and stress'. It was abnormal to be normal, as it were, and the turmoil of adolescence was seen as being essential for growth and development. This is no longer considered the case. Large-scale empirical research does not support the position that young people are in 'storm and stress' and, in general, they do not report themselves to be particularly unhappy, troubled or in turmoil. Nevertheless, for all sorts of reasons, adolescence can be tough.

> **Prolonged stress is damaging to the body, either directly or indirectly, in these ways:**
>
> - Blood pressure is increased and fats are released into the bloodstream.
> - The immune system is suppressed.
> - There is a greater likelihood of physical illness.
> - Highly stressed people are also more likely to have 'accidents'.

A confusing and competitive world

Everybody is affected by what is happening in the world. There is so much change and uncertainty, and so much competitiveness, those of us in Western society are living and struggling together in a truly tough culture. The media brings us a constant flow of bad news, of strife and destruction and man's relentless inhumanity to man. These 'windows on the world', particularly television and, more recently, the Internet, do little to create feelings of inner peace and security.

As young minds come alive to what is going on around them, no wonder they are touched with dismay. Having less to look back upon than adults, young people are greatly concerned with the future. And things are moving too fast. How can teenagers figure out where they fit into the scheme of things, if nothing around them keeps still?

The context in which young people are growing up is a society which focuses predominantly on productivity and competitiveness. Child and adolescent psychiatrist Professor Ken Nunn encourages a sense of perspective on this, where young people are concerned:

> *Every kid needs to know they have a niche. In the big swim of life, most of us are happy with a puddle. Not all of us want to be a salmon going up the waterfall, knowing there's a bear waiting to catch you on the way up. And when you get up there, you reproduce and then you die. In the dominant model of competitiveness*

in our society, either you're a salmon or a little, meaningless squiggle at the bottom.

He's right. Most of us are somewhere in the middle. Despite all this, teenagers have to adapt, somehow, to the world we live in – a task that can be made much easier by a sense of connectedness to caring adults (at home and at school) and being part of a community that gives you a sense of belonging.

A time of internal conflict

Of course, there's not a lot that parents can do about change; such things as the information explosion, increasing urbanisation and how the government handles the economy are beyond their control. Of more immediate concern are the individual conflicts that combine to cause stress in young people, right before our very eyes.

A basic formula for adolescent stress is the need to reconcile inner drives with outside expectations. This is a balancing act requiring great skill and finesse, for which no young person is fully prepared. In the course of everyday life, for example, a teenager must find a path between personal opinions, peer pressure and parental expectations. The difficulties they face include:

- The need to express oneself as an individual, which is in conflict with peer pressure to conform.
- The need to compete with one's friends, which is at odds with the need to win social approval.
- The need to achieve independence, which is complicated by the need for parental support and validation.

Little surprise then that teenagers behave erratically at times. It is impossible to please all the people (including themselves) all the time! Unbeknown to others, they are constantly practising the subtle art of compromise, perhaps without even being aware of it at a conscious level themselves. What will be noticeable to them, of course, is the stress involved.

> *I clear my mind of everything when I write it down.*
> *Mel, aged 15*

Remember, too, that adolescence is a time of new experiences and new feelings, of strong attachments and bitter losses. It is a time of demands and frustrations. Under normal circumstances, teenagers are stressed by everything, from their rapidly changing bodies and what is and isn't normal, to feeling that nobody understands or listens; from the pressure of exams or other performances, to the usual hassles with mum and dad.

What do teenagers say about stress?

Smoking was a thing to cope with stress. It used to be a new thing but now it is just normal. Most people wish they could quit. It's not cool any more.

It's important to find a balance with friends, study and personal space. I think to myself 'This is only a small hurdle in life – I will feel good about myself once I have done it and I will have achieved something.' My family will accept me and will be proud of me even if I don't do well. I worry that everyone else will be judging the outcome.

I think before I begin something stressful – I can only try my best. I only get stressed out if I compare myself to others. Small things can tip the stress scales – like not having enough hours in the day, the pressure to conform to rules and expectations. I have learnt not to jump to conclusions when things go wrong.

When I am doing something stressful, I think: 'It will be over soon and if something goes wrong, it's not the end of the world and my mother won't really kill me.' And no matter what, if I've tried my best I can never do better than that. It feels worse if I think: 'What if I mess this up?' I try to make myself feel better by thinking positively. There are two quotes I love: Only dead fish go with the flow. Have the courage to live, anyone can die.

In a stressful situation, I try to focus on the moment, but remind myself that what I am doing is going to help me in the future and I will be proud of myself afterwards. There is always the fear that things won't turn out how I hope, but because I have learnt to pace myself, I am confident I have at least tried my hardest. I think as long as you work hard to gain something, you can expect it to work out. It is when we sit back and wait for things to come to us and do not try, that we lose out. It's about taking a step forwards and facing the fear of the unknown. Not knowing what will happen once you take that step is scary but each step gets us closer to where we really want to be. If you set your own goals, you will achieve them. No one will talk you out of them.

Who is at risk?

Transient upsets and problems are simply part of being an adolescent. As discussed in Chapter 2, emotional ups and downs are to be expected, and it doesn't take much to provoke an attack of either one. Of course, it's not entirely trivial when the cat dies or an exam is failed. Parents are usually able to recognise an acute, discernible stressful experience when they see one, and most would not be so foolish as to underestimate the suffering involved. At such times, comfort and support are needed.

On the other hand, some young people are more vulnerable to the adverse effects of stress than their peers. Through having low self-esteem and feeling different and powerless, their experience of internal conflict may become unbearable. Certainly, some resilient individuals cope reasonably well despite the most difficult and trying circumstances, but many don't. It's those young people who have difficulty coping who are more likely to get into physical, emotional or social difficulty. The following types of teenagers should receive special consideration:

Young people who are different: Being 'different' can be a particular burden for adolescents. Those suffering from physical or intellectual impairment due to chronic illness or disability, those with an alternative sexuality, and teenagers from racial, religious or ethnic minorities (who often find themselves caught between two cultures) can be more vulnerable to stress.

Young people who experience serious losses or other traumas: Those who experience the loss of a parent through death or separation; parental rejection; physical, emotional or sexual abuse; having parents who are alcoholic or suffer from chronic or mental illness.

Young people in difficult external circumstances: Kids who are homeless, unemployed, very poor; those in institutional care or living in remote areas.

It is worth noting here that young immigrants and refugees can fit into all of these categories simultaneously. In the first place, being forced to flee from one's country is a process fraught with danger. The contexts include war, violence, invasions, dictatorship systems and political repression. Many families are split up before and during the period of flight, a time that can be highly traumatic and perilous. Research shows that young immigrants and refugees are at particular risk of mental health disorders, compared with the general population. For example, post-traumatic stress disorders are common, ranging from vague symptoms of depression, school failure, eating and sleeping problems, to high-risk behaviours such as drug abuse and sexual promiscuity. Psychotic breakdowns also occur in young people who have been exposed to uncontrollable violence.

Is this teenager really sick?

In one Australian health survey in the late 1990s, over half of the young people in the 12–18 age group reported that they had felt significantly unwell in the previous fortnight. And this is supposed to be the healthiest time of life? As a group, teenagers experience a lot of physical symptoms, some of which, no doubt, are merely growing pains. Others are more serious and debilitating, and interfere with their (and their family's) enjoyment of life.

Psychological stress has been implicated as a contributory factor in virtually all diseases, but that is another problem. Many sick young people, perhaps the majority, do not have a physical illness. Their malady is stress-related, what health professionals have variously referred to as 'functional illness', hypochondriasis or psychosomatic disorder. More recently the term 'somatisation' has come into vogue to describe patients with somatic (bodily) complaints that do not have an organic basis.

When a teenager presents with aches and pains (headache and abdominal pain are the most common), tiredness and lethargy or vague feelings of ill-health, and the doctor has ruled out such things as glandular fever, infectious hepatitis or withdrawal from too much coffee, the likelihood of a 'non-organic' condition will be suspected when the symptoms have the following characteristics:

- They are overvalued – that is, there is a preoccupation with their importance beyond what one would expect (for example, a teenager with headaches but who is otherwise well, who finds it hard to think about anything else).

▶ They are out of proportion to the physical findings – that is, a doctor can find no adequate evidence to account for the degree of discomfort or disability.
▶ They are enduring and distressing – that is, not merely minor or occasional complaints (like a momentary twinge).

In such cases, a frustrating medical merry-go-round in search of a 'respectable disease' will not provide the answer. The challenge is to understand what the illness might be telling us. Why is this young person behaving in an unwell manner, and why now? Are the symptoms 'inherited' from another family member (or from their own medical background)? What was happening at around the time the symptoms commenced?

Often the symptoms will be related to past or present distress within the family (such as bereavement, parental illness or an unhappy marriage). It is now more commonly understood that no medical illness (such as a prolonged viral illness) occurs without psychosocial repercussions (such as school absenteeism or depression), just as no psychosocial event (like a death in the family) occurs without some biological features (for example experiencing headaches or insomnia). In other words, there's been a helpful move in thinking from 'either/or' (biomedical or psychosocial) to 'both/and'. This is the basis for a collaborative approach called the 'medical family therapy model', which acknowledges that there is always a link between somatic and psychological factors.

For the patient, of course, none of this is happening at a conscious level, so it takes a bit of sorting out. When a young person continues to be unwell, therefore, and no obvious organic cause can be found, the help of the whole family may be enlisted.

An interview involving whoever lives at home (mum, dad, brothers and sisters, perhaps even grandma) can often lead to a better understanding of the situation. It is never a matter of seeking to blame someone. The goal of treatment is to find a more healthy and positive way for the family to cope so that the young person can get back to normal and get on with the job of growing up.

> *When you become depressed you get lost in it.*
> Charlie, aged 16

A boy called Jason
The family of a boy called Jason illustrates how things can work out when this approach is taken. Jason was a 13-year-old boy who had been sick for many weeks with a sore throat, abdominal pain, headaches and vomiting. Both his parents were very keen to find a physical cause for his symptoms (which had also occurred a number of times before), but many medical tests and consultations had failed to reveal one. During the course of several family interviews with a doctor and a social worker, the following information emerged:

- The father, a business executive, had recently changed his job (having lost his previous one) and this had led to significant marital tension.
- The mother, who also worked, suffered from frequent migraines and excessive tiredness (another instance in the family of medical symptoms reflecting stress).
- The children – Jason, his older sister and two younger sisters – griped a lot initially about household chores (particularly when things got tense between mum and dad). Eventually, they were able to express their fears that their parents might separate. Although Jason was the one presenting with an illness, they all had strong fears of being deserted by either their mother or their father.

The main outcomes of these preliminary family meetings were that Jason's symptoms rapidly became less overvalued and then settled, and the parents sought further help for themselves.

Fatigue and lack of energy
Young people do not uncommonly complain of tiredness. For example, when teenagers are going through their 'growth spurt' (as discussed in Chapter 1), they seem to need more sleep. We're not sure if this is to enable their growing to occur (under the influence of nocturnally activated hormonal bursts) or because of increasing energy expenditure or simply a more tiring lifestyle. Whatever the cause, young people need to be taught how to nurture themselves and to rejuvenate their bodies. Often a good meal and a good night's sleep will be all that's required to bring back energy levels. If fatigue persists (say for more than a week), however, a medical check-up is advisable.

The doctor will carefully consider which of the following four categories of causes is most likely:

Physiological fatigue: This occurs in everybody at times, and is usually the result of overexertion, overwork and/or lack of sleep. It is transient, improves with rest and, by definition, is not debilitating. Many young people do not understand how to settle themselves for sleep. Parents should recommend the following steps:

- Reduce alcohol and caffeine (including coffee, chocolate, high-caffeine soft drinks) and avoid exercise near bedtime, as this usually raises the heart rate and interferes with sleep. On the other hand, exercise during the day should be encouraged because it helps release tension and promote general relaxation.
- In the hour before settling down for sleep, try to dim the lights, listen to music, read a comforting book, drink a glass of milk, or practise some relaxation exercises. Finish with TV and homework or anything else that stimulates the mind (including arguments and emotional discussions) at least one hour before bedtime. Sleeping tablets are to be discouraged.

Psychological fatigue: This involves a feeling of weariness associated with a loss of motivation and interest, and a loss of a normal sense of pleasure. This type of fatigue characteristically fluctuates with mood and improves with activity. It is a common symptom of depression and anxiety in young people and a major aspect of chronic fatigue syndrome (both discussed in greater detail below).

Pathological fatigue: This is generally experienced as a debilitating physical sensation out of proportion to the person's level of activity and independent of mood. Although pathological fatigue may improve with rest, it is usually worsened by physical exertion. There are a number of common medical conditions that cause pathological fatigue in teenagers, including viral infections (with particular reference to glandular fever, otherwise called infectious mononucleosis), iron-deficiency anaemia (discussed in Chapter 5) and poorly controlled asthma.

Chronic fatigue syndrome (CFS): Sometimes called 'post viral fatigue syndrome', this is a serious health problem among adolescents, partly because the symptoms are so disabling for sufferers and partly because of the controversy that surrounds the diagnosis. The main feature of the syndrome is extreme fatigue in a person with no previous history of similar symptoms, which does not resolve with bed rest, is severe enough to significantly impair normal daily activities by at least 50 per cent and lasts for several months or more. Other recurring symptoms such as mild fever, sore throat, painful lymph nodes, sore muscles or joints, difficulty with concentration and generalised headaches, add to the miseries of the condition. CFS is more common in girls than in boys and is often associated with depression.

Opinion is divided on whether CFS is primarily an organic or primarily a psychological condition, each being as likely as the other, or, more likely still, a combination of both. It makes some sense to view it as a complex and intractable form of illness behaviour. One possible explanation is that a viral infection or other illness provides a starting point for the syndrome while other factors somehow keep it going. Certainly, physical and emotional factors soon become entwined and the situation tends to become self-perpetuating. Teenagers in certain sorts of families – for example, those families in which anxiety is readily experienced as physical symptoms – seem more vulnerable. While researchers continue to seek answers to these complex questions, teenagers who are extremely tired and unwell are missing out on lots of school and having a generally awful time.

As with any chronic health problem, outcomes probably depend more on the attitude of the person involved and the nature of the supports available, than on the specific condition itself. A teenager with chronic fatigue needs to be encouraged to view the situation not as a dreadful life-long sentence (which is why labels such as 'chronic fatigue syndrome' can sometimes be unhelpful), but as a challenge and learning experience. The team approach to treatment includes the following aspects:

- A doctor will monitor and review progress as well as prescribe suitable treatment for the physical symptoms – medications (such as analgesics for pain) and non-pharmacological methods (such as relaxation techniques).
- A well-balanced diet, adequate rest and some supervised exercise (optimally by a physiotherapist) tend to be helpful.
- A realistic modification of short-term goals for living and working is called for, together with liaison with the school to enable

a return to more normal activity levels. An occupational therapist is best equipped to help in these areas.
- A program of individual and family counselling. Again, those families willing to accept help to explore the relevant issues, including ways of relating and of dealing with stress, offer the best chances of recovery.

Acting out: another cry for help

Most adults are intolerant of adolescent behaviour that is irrational, aggressive or antisocial, and who can blame them? This is pretty threatening behaviour and we do hear a lot about it, particularly the 'crisis mentality' that would have us believe that adolescents (or youths) are basically rotten.

As a rule of thumb, it is often helpful to remember that most (probably all) behaviour has meaning. The challenge is to understand it. A lot of 'difficult' adolescent behaviour can be understood in terms of certain needs. For example, young people need:

- To be 'on the go'. Action and activity help kids to get rid of pent-up energy, as well as deal with anxiety, or even escape from trouble by riding off into the wild blue yonder. (Did it ever occur to you that the humble bicycle or skateboard served such a therapeutic role?)
- To test the limits of control. This goes on throughout childhood and adolescence, and requires a structure within which kids are free to experiment. Without clear limits, the testing may go outside the family and become of interest to the law! For example, a teenager from a very permissive home might get involved in acts of vandalism as a means of inviting some sort of restrictions (such behaviour is far more common than you would imagine, particularly in boys).

'Acting out' is different. This means that a person does something in order to avoid experiencing painful feelings. In a sense, thought is replaced by action, and the internal conflict is brought out into the open. It is acted upon, even though the action may not obviously relate to the feeling inside. For example, a teenager may be feeling very sad because his parents have separated, but instead of being able to articulate this feeling to others (let alone to himself), he may go out drinking or stay out all night.

One of the consequences of acting out is that the individual feels better (for example, less sad), without understanding what the behaviour means. But in so doing, the underlying feelings that cannot be directly faced and dealt with remain hidden. For this reason acting out must be viewed as a cry for help.

Acting out can take four distinguishable forms:

Occasional acting out: This is where behaviour seems unusual or out of character and is occurring in response to a specific circumstance or situation. The acting out may be an alternative to, say, feeling sad (as above) or guilty. Teenagers can feel guilty struggling against parents who are resisting their efforts to grow up – they may want to do what is expected of them but can't. For example, a teenager might not be allowed out at night or to spend time with his or her friends. Sneaking out through the window after one's parents are asleep (to go to a special party, perhaps) could qualify as acting out. Interestingly, guilt-laden adolescents sometimes commit a blatant delinquent act, such as stealing something, in order to be punished, after which they often feel greatly relieved without knowing why.

Habitual acting out: This is the so-called 'impulse-ridden adolescent' who acts out virtually all the time. They are thrill-seekers, who drive like maniacs and revel in danger and violence. Unaware of the underlying reasons for their behaviour, they are constantly in strife. Such teenagers have usually had a really rough time in infancy and childhood. Deprived of adequate care and affection in early life, they have difficulty getting close to people, and view the world and its inhabitants with suspicion and anger.

Acting out in search of the past: Some young people sense that something is missing from their lives. Crucial past events are either unknown or have been kept hidden, and the acting out represents a strange attempt at remembering. Foster children and children adopted late often fall into this category. Sometimes parents have kept the past a secret, ostensibly to protect the child, but more often to protect themselves. One troubled boy in all sorts of strife with stealing was actually the illegitimate son of the young woman he thought was his older sister.

Acting out on behalf of parents: The verbal instruction from the parent might be 'don't do it' (don't get pregnant, don't drive recklessly), but the 'twinkle in the eye' or the excessive interest in a detailed account of what subsequently happens provides a different message. In other words, the expected outcome appears different from the spoken statement, and teenagers readily pick up a covert nod to go ahead. In effect, a self-fulfilling prophecy derived from the needs of the parent is set in train. Of course, the 'forbidden' behaviour provokes much fuss and punishment, while the vicarious thrills and excitement are covered up. As with the other types of acting out, the underlying reasons are not experienced at a conscious level.

In practice, things would probably not be quite this clear cut. Maybe the kid really is just plain rotten, but generally it is more helpful to try to see 'bad' behaviour in context. Sometimes, as with severe emotional damage in early childhood, little can be done. In other circumstances, a troubled teenager can be helped by individual or family counselling. Sometimes, residential treatment would be ideal, but suitable facilities (that is, those offering a structured environment for adolescents who are acting out) are few and far between. Overall, the outlook will usually be better if parents do not distance themselves too far from what is happening. After all, whether or not parents are part of the problem, they need to be part of the solution.

What if a kid won't come out of their room and it's obvious something is up?

Child and adolescent psychiatrist Professor Ken Nunn gives a possible scenario:

> 'You know, I'm getting distressed. I'm actually losing it out here. I'm coming in.'
> 'Leave me alone.'
> 'Sorry, sweetheart, we have to talk. Otherwise, I'll have to call your friends and ask them what to do.'
> 'Don't do that.' (Because calling their friends is the last thing they want you to do.)
> 'Well, I'll just have to involve your father and you know how incompetent he is.'

He goes on to say:

> *One of the things parents are most frightened of is appearing unreasonable to their kids. But constructive nagging is important. Parents need to have a capacity to be unpopular with their kids ('You know, I love you so much, I'm gonna give you a bad time until you tell me what's going on'). And then they give a little bit out, just to get you off their back.*

Emotional problems

Adolescent depression

If the causes of stress are overwhelming or not dealt with in a healthy way, they can lead to emotional and physical disorders with potentially serious consequences. When is the situation more serious? It is time to seek help if depressed mood or irritability lasts longer then two weeks, there is a sudden change in behaviour or school performance in a previously well-adjusted teenager, and physical symptoms such as excessive weight changes or sleep disturbance appear. Suicidal thoughts and behaviours should always be taken seriously.

About three to five per cent of teenagers are clinically depressed at any given time. About 20 per cent of teenagers experience a period of significant depression at some time during their adolescence. Depression is now recognised as one of the most serious global public health problems and is predicted to become the second leading cause of disease burden worldwide by the year 2020. Unfortunately, only about 50 per cent of people with depression are diagnosed and of those recognised, only 50 per cent receive any treatment, largely because of the stigma attached to the condition.

> **Leanne:** I was struck by this fear of labelling and stigma when an eminent professor of psychiatry once stayed at our home and my children suddenly vanished. Later, when I asked my children why they had been so hard to find, they replied: 'We thought we had better disappear – we were scared he would diagnose us!'

Of course, with suicide (see pages 331–34 for detailed discussion), the focus is on the end point, but there is a process involved. Reaching a point of desperation does not occur overnight. What underlies increasing suicidal behaviour is an awful lot of adolescent depression and only recently has this been widely acknowledged. The late Bronwyn Donaghy, author of *Leaving Early*, believed there is a link between a stereotypical view of adolescents and rates of depression: 'An insidious danger is emerging from the popular conception of normal adolescence as a period of trauma and trouble. The danger is that genuine depression in young people is going unnoticed until it is too late.' She also made the important points that 'Parents are the best people to know what's normal in their own kids . . .' and 'No family is immune!'

What are the signs of depression?
Although there are similarities between the depressive illness suffered by young people and adults, there are also major differences. Teenagers are more likely to present with irritability and problems with behaviour and school performance. It's not always easy to tell, but teenagers generally reveal their depression in three ways:

- Depressed young people are usually sad and down-hearted and don't bounce back as you would normally expect. That is, the young person's emotions are no longer for them to command – they want to pick themselves up but can't. The mood doesn't lift and they often experience a sense of hopelessness. There is nothing unusual about sporadic tearful, sullen and 'out of sorts' behaviour, but when this goes on and on (for two weeks or more), it suggests something is amiss. There are also some indirect signs: they're not interested in anything and take little pleasure in activities they used to enjoy; they withdraw to their rooms, become apathetic and have trouble thinking and concentrating – deteriorating school work is a dead give-away. There's often a distancing from family and friends too. When parents start to feel 'I don't know you any more' and sad vibes are coming through most of the time, there's likely to be more to it than an ordinary bout of the 'downs'. Self-medication with alcohol, cannabis (one of the most potent factors that can actually lead to depression) and ecstasy is very common in depressed young people.
- Depressed young people are often physically unwell and may complain of frequent headaches, other aches and pains or the

general 'blahs'. Excessive tiredness and lack of energy are also very common, and research has shown that depressed young people tend to sleep longer than healthy individuals (and awake less fatigued, suggesting that the extra sleep may actually be helping them in some way). Sometimes they wake in the early hours and experience difficulty returning to sleep. Remember, too, that viral infections such as glandular fever can leave you feeling fatigued and depressed, sometimes for months. In depressed teenagers, there may also be significant loss or gain in weight.

Depressed young people may also show behaviour that is unusual for them, which can mislead people into thinking anything but the truth. One of the clearest signs of teenage depression is irritability – fierce, strong and uncharacteristic. In this situation, the depression is said to be 'masked', although the sadness will be evident if you look for it. Meanwhile, depressed kids who are hyperactive, disruptive, aggressive or frankly antisocial (for example, stealing), frequently become young offenders. Punishment at the hands of the authorities (school, welfare or the law) becomes their treatment, which is hardly appropriate!

Very depressed teenagers have morbid thoughts, feelings of anguish, loss and hopelessness and a mounting sense of frustration and alarm. This is an unbearably painful state and the idea of escape through suicide becomes very appealing. They think of death. Hopefully, before this advanced stage is reached, someone will have tuned into what is going on, a professional opinion sought and the appropriate counselling provided. It is literally a matter of life and death.

Depressed teenagers are likely to say:

I feel lonely.
I cry a lot.
No one loves me.
I feel that other people are against me.
I feel worthless and like a nobody.
I am nervous and tense.
I feel guilty.
I get easily embarrassed.
I am unhappy, sad, depressed, empty.
I worry a lot about everything.

I deliberately try to hurt myself.
I think about death.

As one young person described it:

When you're really depressed, you think, What is the point? You live, accomplish nothing and then die. Everywhere I go, I look into people's eyes and search for something that is not there.

Why do teenagers get depressed?

Depression: tends to run in families; is in part due to chemical imbalance in the brain; may be associated with personal tragedies or significant life changes; is more likely in people who are sensitive, emotional, perfectionists and dependent; may be a learned response for people who experience repeated losses, stress or who 'think depressed' (as discussed in Chapter 12).

The overriding themes in adolescent depression are loss and bereavement. Let's face it, if parents die, leave, become seriously ill, or if they are abusing, always drunk or constantly fighting, it would be abnormal not to be depressed. All of us become unhappy as a result of distressing situations in our lives and this is appropriate and human.

Less obvious, but equally important, is parental behaviour that destroys a young person's self-esteem. This can involve excessively high and inappropriate expectations or behaviour that is constantly critical or disparaging. Rejection can take many subtle forms and its effects are serious.

No age group is immune to depression, but it is important to know that older teenagers are at somewhat greater risk. This is because they generally have more emotional investment in people and things. For example, a relationship that breaks down can be quite devastating at 18 or 19 and would often lead to depression, whereas a 14- or 15-year-old kid, buffered by the peer group, would be more likely to just roll with it. Also, in the late teens and early twenties, a young person is less inclined to reach out to the family for support – the need to be grown up and independent gets in the way.

A girl called Lucy

It is her fourth cold in three months. She is chronically tired and has stomach pains, which are preventing her from going to school. Lucy is a small, shy, sensitive 15-year-old. Her parents have taken her to naturopaths, chiropractors and numerous other doctors. The consultation went like this:

I sense that something else is wrong.
No.
Are you worried about anything?
No.
How is school?
Good.
Who do you hang around with at school?
Nobody.

As tears welled in her eyes, she said:

My friends have dumped me, they swear at me. Older kids stole my bag. No one cares and everything is my fault. I'm bored and I've got nothing to do.

Is Lucy being bullied or is she depressed? Or both? How can you determine if someone is depressed?

In essence it is likely to be depression if the sadness lasts longer than two weeks, is associated with physical symptoms such as weight loss or gain, appetite and sleep changes and a sudden change in school performance or relationships.

The kinds of questions to ask Lucy are therefore:

How long have you been feeling sad?
How has your school work been going?
What are you interested in?
How do you find your friendships with other people?
How is your appetite? Have you lost or gained weight recently?
How are you sleeping?
If the bullying stopped, would you feel completely better? Would that fix everything?

What is the treatment for depression?

Depression is very different to normal unhappiness. It is prolonged intense sadness that interferes with our ability to function. On the positive side, depression, of all things in modern medicine and psychiatry, is one of the most responsive of any condition to treatment. But the characteristic of depression is to make you believe that nothing will work. (People living with someone with depression can get caught up in this feeling too – there's the capacity for it to be infectious.)

Even though depression is an illness that can be treated, many young people find it difficult to ask for help or to assist their friends to seek help because of the stigma attached to having a 'mental disorder'. One of the most important and helpful things that adults can say is: 'I don't always cope.' We must tackle the problem of stigma and prejudice related to mental illness, because the vast majority of people are touched by mental illness and suicide.

Above all, for the sufferer, we must not underestimate the value of a parent, a close friend, a trusted teacher or student welfare coordinator, someone who listens. Our lives are shaped by the inner stories we tell ourselves about our experiences. We move away from 'thinking depressed' by retelling the stories to trusted people, and thereby learning to understand them as challenging life experiences.

There are a number of strategies that can be used to overcome depression. Cognitive behavioural therapy (CBT) is the most effective, proven treatment for adolescent depression. The idea behind CBT is that thoughts, feelings and actions are connected. By challenging thinking we can change feelings and actions. Here are a few of the principles of cognitive behavioural therapy:

Challenging negative thinking: There are a number of patterns of negative thinking, including automatic, black and white, overgeneralising, mind-reading, making mountains out of molehills, and wasting time worrying.

You may be surprised how many times you automatically use negative self-talk. For example, you might have an underlying negative belief that: 'I must be good at everything to feel worthwhile.' CBT asks you to question the evidence behind such thoughts and ask yourself if the thought is helpful or unhelpful. However, you need to be gentle with yourself. Practise saying: 'I will try', 'I would prefer', rather than 'I should', and 'I must'. Through this process you can arrive at the more helpful thought that 'It's okay to make mistakes'.

Black and white thinking supposes things are either awful or perfect. For example, students may focus on one career, discounting all other options and predisposing themselves to feeling like a failure if their 'only' choice does not eventuate. The common belief that 'good things happen to good people' and 'bad things happen to bad people' (perpetuated in many cartoon shows and fairy tales) sets young people up to think that there must be something wrong with them when things go badly. CBT asks you to think about shades of grey and try to become aware of feelings and thoughts in between.

Common negative overgeneralisations include thoughts such as: 'I can't do anything', 'I'm so lazy', 'Nobody likes me'. The evidence for these generalisations needs to be challenged with questions such as 'What are my strengths?' 'What are the things I am proud of?' 'What are the ways I have contributed to this?'

Mind-reading involves the assumption of what someone else thinks or believes. Question the evidence for what you are assuming. How do you know? How can you be sure? Does your friend have something else on their mind?

Making mountains out of molehills includes beliefs such as, 'It will be awful, terrible, horrible. I can't stand it any more.' CBT asks you to consider how these statements make you feel, and to find a more helpful approach, such as: 'It will be difficult but I have got through before and I will try.'

Wasting time worrying speaks for itself. The challenge here is to focus on things we can do something about, rather than things we have no control over.

More specifically it can help to practise 'coping' thoughts before, during and after a stressful situation. For example, before an exam a student could practise thoughts such as: 'This is going to be hard but I know how to deal with it.' After the exam, positive thoughts may be reinforced with statements like: 'I'm doing better at this all the time.' 'I handled that well.'

It may also help to write down in a diary all the unhelpful and helpful thoughts that arise in specific situations. What do you really think and feel in certain uncomfortable or stressful situations? Teenagers can also monitor their progress and become more focused if they identify short-term and long-term goals.

Social skills: CBT also looks at social skills: eye contact, tone of voice, facial expression, body language, being interested in others, gaining attention in a positive way, dealing with arguments, negotiating compromise, listening, taking turns, expressing feelings, saying no, standing up for yourself, accepting criticism, asking for help. These social skills need experience and take practice, and they need to be taught by example, rather than by pointing out deficiencies and creating self-consciousness.

Understanding how to make friends is an important skill. Here is what teenagers say about the characteristics of a good friend:

- understanding, caring, trustworthy and honest
- loyal even with peer pressure
- listens to your problems
- accepts you for who you are
- lets you be yourself and have fun
- is not judgemental
- may have a different opinion but respects yours
- will still like you even if they disagree with you
- you can talk to them about anything
- is there in good and bad times.

It may be worth bringing this to the attention of your teenager.

Pleasant things: Depressed people often forget to seek pleasant things and often complain of boredom. Another aspect of CBT is for the young person to plan simple pleasurable things to do every day. It can be anything from breathing clean air to punching a bag; from bongo drumming to just lying on the ground and looking at the clouds. Anything.

Relaxation: Many of us try too hard to relax, and it usually helps to simply stop trying. The comment 'just relax' is counterproductive. Music, walking, exercise, yoga, thinking of a special place can be useful. Exercises in breathing, muscular relaxation and visualisation can be helpful too.

Breathing exercise
Sit comfortably in a quiet room. Count your normal breathing rate for 60 seconds. Then breathe in on the slow count of three (one . . . two . . . three . . .) and out for the slow count of three, for a full minute. Try counting your normal breathing rate over 60 seconds again and compare it to what it was before the exercise. The breathing rate often slows down, which in turn helps the heart slow down and this helps relaxation. It is an easy exercise to do at school or before a stressful task.

Muscular exercise
Lie on your bed and start with the breathing exercise. Next, become aware of the muscle groups in your body: face, neck, arms, hands, chest, tummy, back, legs, feet. Tense your facial muscles for a few seconds and let them go, take time to feel them lose the tension and relax. Next, move to your neck and repeat the same tension and relaxation. Continue this for all the muscle groups. Then repeat the breathing exercise.

Visualisation
Think of a pleasant, relaxing place and imagine you are there, smelling, tasting, feeling and breathing the sensations.

Communication: Communicating problems and concerns in a positive way can have a major impact on depression. It helps teenagers to express themselves, become less isolated and seek help. Active listening is a good skill to have. It involves 'listening with your eyes' by using eye contact and other body language to demonstrate that you are fully attentive. It can help to restate the problem by saying things like: 'It sounds as though . . .' 'Let's see if I understand what you are saying . . .'

Solving conflict has already been covered in Chapter 12. If discussing tense situations, try to focus on the present issue rather than raising multiple issues. Beginning statements with 'I feel . . .' rather than 'you make me . . .' are more positive than blaming and accusations. Also avoid interrupting, overgeneralisations ('you always', 'you never'), lecturing, sarcastic tone and bringing up the past. Keep statements brief, use a neutral tone and practise relaxation. Gradually, major issues causing common conflicts can be identified and dealt with.

Antidepressants

Antidepressant medication tends to be used for teenagers who are 'lost in their depression' and find the techniques of CBT and challenging thinking difficult. Levels of serotonin, a chemical in the brain, have been linked with depression. The antidepressants of choice are SSRIs – selective serotonin re-uptake inhibitors – to help restore normal levels of serotonin in the brain and relieve feelings of depression. The most frequently experienced side effects, particularly at the beginning of treatment, are nausea, headaches and diarrhoea.

These symptoms usually disappear within a week to 10 days of commencement and may be relieved by taking the medication with food, with paracetamol, or changing the time when the tablets are taken. Antidepressants are only prescribed by doctors and work best in combination with regular reviews and sympathetic counselling.

Other treatments have limited research evidence. However, the use of the herb St John's wort, folate, acupuncture, high-density air ionisation, light therapy, massage therapy, yoga and increasing fish in the diet show some promise and there is a need for further study into these areas. Avoiding alcohol and illicit drugs is also important in the treatment of depression.

Anxiety – more than a racing heart

The signs of anxiety include restlessness, irritability, muscle tension, poor concentration, disturbed sleep and fatigue. There are a number of psychiatric conditions that fall into the general category of anxiety, all of which require medical treatment and expert counselling.

Anxiety disorder: This is an illness where people worry constantly and irrationally about being harmed or about loved ones. Anxiety disorder also includes panic, phobia, post-traumatic stress disorder and obsessive compulsive disorder. Medical conditions such as thyroid disorders may also cause anxiety, as do prescription and illicit drugs and caffeine.

Panic attacks: These are unpleasant physical symptoms accompanied by a sense of panic, often occurring in situations where most people would not be afraid. There is often a sudden onset of intense fear with symptoms such as shortness of breath, trembling, shaking, nausea, abdominal pain, dizziness, racing heart, sweating, choking, flushes, chest pain, fear of dying and fear of losing control. The attacks are usually unexpected and agoraphobia sometimes results (a fear of going to places or situations that might provoke a panic attack).

Phobias: These are persistent fears about objects or situations or a fear that others will judge everything they do in a negative way. The fear is excessive and unreasonable and leads to isolation.

Post-traumatic stress disorder: This sometimes occurs after a major traumatic experience, such as an accident, violence, or war. In this situation people experience intense anxiety and recurrent flashbacks or nightmares.

Obsessive compulsive disorder: This involves unwanted thoughts that result in time-consuming rituals. People may constantly wash their hands or check doors are shut and this often causes embarrassment. These tasks seriously interfere with everyday life.

Eating disorders

Eating disorders are most common in adolescent girls and their onset is a distress call. With their increased recognition has come a greater understanding of what makes certain young people vulnerable to eating disorders. The broader societal influences are clearly relevant (as mentioned in Chapter 5), but the essential ingredient for the individual sufferer is a struggle for personal control. Psychologically, anorexics seemingly do not want to grow up, while bulimics (who are usually older) do not handle being grown up too well. However, both are characterised by a fear of weight gain, feelings of ineffectiveness and low self-esteem.

To reiterate the main factors:

- Australia has a strong culture that thinner is better and this is reinforced every day through the media, undoubtedly having a significant impact on the self-image of young women.
- Young people most at risk of developing an eating disorder are perfectionists, anxious, high achieving or competitive; they fear loss of control and have low self-esteem.
- Families may be very close and protective, providing little privacy for the young person, as well as having high expectations of their children. However, parent blaming is very counterproductive and the parent–teenager alliance against the eating disorder is one of the main keys to successful treatment.

Treatment can range from acknowledging normal hunger and promoting a healthy diet and exercise pattern, to improving underlying problems related to self-esteem, family and other relationships. In finding solutions, it is important to discourage self-surveillance, which is very characteristic behaviour of people with eating disorders because it perpetuates the underlying cause of the problem. If left untreated, both anorexia and bulimia can cause serious illness or even be fatal. When severe, both illnesses cause kidney problems, dehydration, constipation, depletion of important minerals, and damage to vital organs including the heart, which may cause sudden death. If you suspect your child may have an eating disorder, contact your doctor for more information and advice on early treatment.

In the meantime, here are some facts about anorexia nervosa and bulimia nervosa.

Anorexia nervosa: Anorexia, the third most common chronic illness in adolescents (after obesity and asthma), is a condition where someone refuses to maintain a minimal, normal weight for their age and height. There is an intense fear of gaining weight or becoming fat, even though the person is underweight. Sufferers often resist admitting anything is wrong and girls may stop having periods. The ratio of females to males with this illness is approximately 10:1, with an increasing incidence in younger boys.

Anorexia nervosa typically occurs in a high achieving and previously well-adjusted child. It may start insidiously, often after a chance remark about weight or fatness, but the end result is that dieting gets out of control.

For parents, it's possible to tell that something's not right. Apart from noticing that your teenager looks underweight for their age and height, other behavioural clues include: they're telling you that they're fat no matter how thin they become; they're saying they have a sense of control when they say 'no' to food; they're avoiding eating with the family or going straight to the bathroom after eating (to throw up); they're wearing loose clothing to hide their body.

Admission to hospital becomes necessary when weight loss leads to medical complications such as low body temperature (under 35.5°C), slow pulse rate, low blood pressure and changes in blood chemistry. Management of anorexia nervosa is complex and requires an integrated team approach. In hospital, the usual program requires re-feeding (either orally or by a nasogastric tube), a psychiatric assessment, individual, family and nutritional counselling, physical rehabilitation, schooling and (where available) involvement in group programs (the best of

> *We need to look at who people are not what they look like. Some girls and boys think people only appreciate them for the way they look, not love them for who they are.*
>
> Joanne, aged 15

which include creative arts activities). The young person's family needs to become allies with the professional team if satisfactory progress is to occur.

> **The main characteristics of anorexia nervosa:**
>
> ▶ A loss of weight – 15 per cent or more of ideal body weight or failure to gain the equivalent amount of weight – in the absence of any physical illness (this usually happens over six to 12 months).
> ▶ A preoccupation with foods and fat avoidance.
> ▶ A distortion of body image, continued complaints about a protruding tummy or fat thighs, and a relentless pursuit of thinness, more or less to the exclusion of all normal concerns of adolescence.
> ▶ A loss of menstrual periods (for more than three months) due to the reduction in body weight and fat, and a curtailment of normal adolescent development; there may be hair loss and the development of fine, downy hair called lanugo on the face and body.
> ▶ A tendency to frenetic physical activity ('hooked on exercise') or other behaviours aimed at losing weight, such as self-induced vomiting or excessive use of laxatives.
> ▶ A risk of death from prolonged fasting or purging, usually over many years, or from a direct suicide attempt (related to severe depression); overall, suicide is the most common cause of death in cases of anorexia nervosa.

Bulimia nervosa: Bulimia is about binge eating. A person with bulimia nervosa is generally of average weight or slightly overweight and experiences a repeated compulsion to eat large amounts of usually high-kilojoule food. A binge involves eating much more than most people would eat in a similar period of time.

The condition is rare before the age of 15 and becomes more prevalent among women in their late teens and early twenties (it is rare among men and boys), often in association with mood disorders such as depression. Abdominal pain, falling asleep or self-induced vomiting usually end the binge. Typically, a bulimic attempts to resist doing this and has fears about not being able to stop voluntarily. She tends to be secretive and often feels guilty and depressed after a binge. Bulimia nervosa is characterised by repeated cycles of bingeing and guilt feelings relieved by purging, which occur three or more times a week for three or more months. Menstrual irregularities are common.

Dramatic fluctuations in weight are very common in cases of bulimia nervosa. Those suffering from bulimia may initially lose weight, but most often gain all of it back and sometimes more because of the ineffectiveness of purging and the body's natural resistance to changes in weight. Extreme methods of weight control are also potentially dangerous:

- Recurrent vomiting causes loss of fluids and salts and can also lead to erosion of tooth enamel and tooth decay from retention of stomach acid in the mouth.
- Excessive laxative use causes diarrhoea with the loss of water and salts from the large bowel.

In both these instances, food is digested and absorbed in the small bowel and little is achieved in terms of weight loss. With bulimia nervosa, weight loss, body image and menstrual disturbance tend to be far less severe than with anorexia nervosa. Treatment is usually successful on an outpatient basis with medical monitoring, counselling and the use of SSRI (selective serotonin re-uptake inhibitor) medications, if these are considered appropriate by the doctor.

> **Some things parents and friends can do to help someone suffering anorexia or bulimia:**
>
> - Let the person suffering from an eating disorder know you are concerned and there to help.
> - Try to find out where she can go for support and encourage her to seek it (this may turn out to be for the whole family).
> - Read as much as possible about eating disorders and the dangers of dieting — the more you know, the more you can help.
> - Provide her with information to help her understand the effects of anorexia, bulimia and dieting.
> - Don't force her to eat and don't make comments about food and weight.

Family relationships are relevant in both these conditions, particularly in anorexia nervosa. People who are too close and caring, and who tend to avoid conflict, unwittingly create an environment in which a young person may react in this way. What then follows is a self-destructive struggle for independence, accompanied often by personal despair, low self-esteem and a fear of proceeding with personal development. Expert, professional help is urgently needed.

We see many young people, their families and healthcare teams struggling painstakingly together over long periods of time. But recovery is achievable. A beautiful young woman who was seriously malnourished and suicidal was hospitalised with anorexia nervosa when she was 16. Two years later she wrote her own encouraging story which concluded:

> *Today I am no longer worried about my weight. I control my life through other means by making sure I eat, sleep and study at specific times ... All that matters today is that I am a normal, happy and healthy girl with a different outlook on my life, my education and my future. At last I have learnt to understand that nothing one does is going to change circumstances out of their control, not even through anorexia.*

Of course, some people are naturally thin and this will carry no health risk as long as they have an adequate, balanced diet.

Just a little crazy

The feeling that everybody's just a little crazy (apart from you and me) is pretty normal. Of course, truly strange people generally don't know that they're strange, and would a friend tell them? Actually, that's a serious concern – odd characters tend not to have many friends.

The loner, for example, is easy to pick. The young person who shuns friends and remains aloof, isolated and seemingly self-contained is said to have a withdrawn (or schizoid) personality. Chances are that such kids are basically okay and will simply grow up to become fairly withdrawn and isolated adults. But in later adolescence, when stresses tend to build up, there is a possibility of becoming more seriously disturbed (for all the reasons discussed earlier in relation to depression).

On the other hand, some teenagers are unable to develop a mature identity and become lost in endless self-questioning and soul-searching (so-called 'identity disorder'). Despite intellectual or other abilities, such individuals fail to fulfil their potential, feel like misfits, despair of ever forming worthwhile relationships and frequently drop out of the mainstream.

Psychosis

This is a group of serious mental illnesses which cause a loss of contact with reality. The signs of this may be confused thinking, delusions, hallucinations, changed feelings, mood swings and changed behaviour. The teenager has a lack of insight that there is anything wrong. There are different types of psychosis and it is sometimes related to illegal drugs including cannabis. The causes of the psychosis are not clear, but the age of onset of psychosis is usually in the teenage years. It is important to seek help and treatment early as research shows early medication leads to a better future outcome. The following conditions require life-long management.

Schizophrenia: This is characterised by deteriorating school performance, withdrawal and loss of drive, inappropriate responses to people (such as laughing inanely when nothing funny has happened), an inability to think normally, disjointed speech, imagined happenings or voices (hallucinations), feelings of persecution, delusions and, at times, markedly childish behaviour. Schizophrenia often starts as depression, anxiety and extreme fears.

Contrary to the popular stereotype, schizophrenia has nothing to do with split personality but definitely is a serious and mostly life-long psychiatric disorder involving a breakdown in the machinery of the mind. It affects one in 100 Australians at some time in their lives.

Schizophrenia may come on acutely or insidiously and can occur any time after the age of seven, but the incidence tends to increase between the years of 15 and 20. Before adulthood, for reasons that are not understood, the condition is three times as common in males but, thereafter, the sexes are equal. The cause of schizophrenia is unknown, although there are probably many factors involved (genetic, biochemical, family).

Bipolar mood disorder: This is another rare but very serious mental illness that requires early management. It is characterised by extreme mood swings from intense sadness to elation, prolonged elevated mood, increased energy, irritability, rapid thinking and speech and reduced need to sleep. The manic phase may be associated with lack of inhibitions and grandiose plans and beliefs.

Needless to say, if a young person becomes totally manic and wants to buy the Harbour Bridge or takes to washing his or her feet a hundred times a day, you will know who to call. Obviously, whenever serious emotional or psychiatric problems are suspected, seek professional advice. They do not go away of their own accord.

These conditions require urgent, early medical treatment and life-long management.

A boy called Tim

Tim is 14, attends Year 8 at high school and is the middle of three boys. His father is an engineer and his mother is a management consultant. Tim has always been a sociable, pleasant and happy kid with plenty of friends. Neither his parents nor his teachers were worried about him except that they felt he could do better academically. However, over recent months, they have noticed that Tim has changed. He has become 'obnoxious', rude, argumentative, both at home and at school and, of course, his room is a mess. He is a good basketball player and now wants to drop out of the team and he no longer wants to continue with his clarinet lessons.

What could be happening here? Is this behaviour part of normal adolescence or something to worry about?

Unfortunately, when this case is presented in forums, many parents respond with comments such as:

- This is normal 14-year-old behaviour.
- The other children in the family turned out fine, so it can't be the parents' fault.
- It is his mother's fault because she is working.
- His behaviour is common and it's completely inexplicable.

Any sudden change in behaviour is a cause for concern. There is always a reason – absent parents, permissive parenting, parental marital problems, bullying at school, early onset of mental illness . . .

The first questions to ask are: Does Tim think there is a problem? What does he think it is due to? Why?

If the behaviour continues or deteriorates, Tim's parents can focus on:

- Creating a loving environment at home.
- Looking at ways of overcoming family conflict in more constructive ways.
- Enlisting the help of a caring adult friend or relative to talk to Tim (another reason parents need to encourage their teenagers to have other caring adult mentors).
- Visiting the class teacher to discuss school performance.
- Consulting the school welfare coordinator with Tim, to ensure the school understands there is a problem and to encourage Tim to talk to trusted teachers at school.
- Asking the school welfare coordinator about other youth agencies and workers who might be able to help.
- Going back to the school to inform them, if nothing is working.
- Encouraging Tim to invite his friends home, to gain an understanding of his peer relationships.
- Visiting their GP to gain support and appropriate referral if necessary.
- Creating a safety net of family, friends, school and community.

What happens when these approaches do not work?

Parents often complain that nothing seems to work. If this is the case, Tim's parents need to follow the steps above and try again. While weathering the problems, parents must remember to focus on what they can do, rather than creating more problems by trying to control what they cannot control. Parents have the power to show love and respect, the power to connect, the power to teach by example, the power to listen, to understand, to do their best to prevent further problems, reduce the risk and minimise the harm. They have the power to seek the right help and to persevere. Young people respond well in the long term to consistency, quiet confidence and perseverance through difficult times.

Well, as it happens, Tim's behaviour has deteriorated. He has started going out every Saturday night with his friends and coming home with cigarette smoke on his clothes and alcohol on his breath. He is getting home later and later. He doesn't see that there is a problem. Now his behaviour has become quieter. He is moody and refuses to go to school. His circle of friends has shrunk and he no longer goes out much. He fluctuates between being agitated and withdrawn.

What can his parents do?

Loss of friends and withdrawal are key signs of major problems. Tim's parents must recognise the behaviour is more serious and deteriorating. It is likely that he has a mental illness such as depression. Tim must have professional help and the first step is often a GP.

Suicide: a one-way ticket

I know how to kill myself. I heard Mum and Dad talking about a guy who had his car fixed, changed the spark plugs and everything, then drove to a quiet place and put a hose from the exhaust pipe into the back window. All you have to do is keep the car running and the windows shut.

James, aged 13

There is justified community alarm at the high suicide rate and suicidal behaviour among young people. Australia and New Zealand have among the highest suicide rates for young people and young adults in the developed world. It is closely related to the increase in depression in this age group. It is also related to unemployment, parental divorce, alcohol and other drugs, secularisation (young people who are religious are at less risk), and access to means (such as guns). Suicide is an issue commonly discussed by young people. In the *National Survey of Mental Health and Wellbeing* in 2002, 12 per cent of 13- to 17-year-olds reported considering suicide in the previous year.

Of course, many more young people make an attempt on their lives than actually succeed. The ratio is about 100:1. Although more girls than boys try to kill themselves, boys are more likely to use an effective method (such as hanging or shooting themselves), which is why they succeed more often. A girl might take an overdose of pills (tranquillisers, for example) or cut her wrists, and make sure someone knows about it pretty soon afterwards. Tragically, some teenagers who make half-hearted attempts end up losing their lives anyway.

> Risk factors for suicide increase if you: are male, have previously attempted or threatened suicide, have a history of depression or suicide in the family, have suffered depression, have psychotic illness, abuse alcohol and drugs, have conduct disorder, eating disorder, significant losses, family problems; are a young person with poor social supports, a loss of hope and a suicide plan.

Young people may be getting brainwashed into believing that there is no future worth living for, an insidious and sinister process that should be of great concern to us all. While suicide is defined as voluntary, intentional, self-inflicted death, there are three ways in which adolescent suicides can occur:

- A young person takes his or (less commonly) her life through a deliberate and obvious suicidal act.
- In some cases, an accidental death (say, in a car or motorcycle accident) is actually a 'disguised suicide' in a depressed teenager.
- Suicide can occur indirectly when young people choose to take drugs or live a lifestyle that slowly kills them.

It's important to distinguish 'self-harm' from suicidality. In self-harming behaviour, there is no intent to kill themselves but to get relief. They have overwhelming emotions and cut themselves, for example, to get relief. This is mostly a problem with young women, and parents often don't know that it's happening. There are three main groups of young people who self-harm: those with post-traumatic stress; those experiencing chronic trauma and abuse; those with emotional instability.

The truly suicidal young person, on the other hand, wants to go to sleep and never wake up. They want to be gone. These young people are seeking an out to an intolerable problem and are not always aware of the finality of death.

This subject is complex and distressing and, not surprisingly, many people view it as something that is happening 'out there'. But a lot of lives are touched by it. The difficulties faced by parents after adolescent suicide have not been well documented, but bereavement is surely complicated by the additional problems of guilt and hostility, the pain of police investigation and coronial inquest and the social stigma. In a poignant press article, a mother whose daughter had committed suicide made this plea:

> *If you are a teenager reading this, don't give up on life. Death is a one-way ticket, marked 'not negotiable'. That body in the morgue is no longer yours to make choices with. Suicide is a game where everybody loses – your parents, your friends and, most of all, you.*

Mentioning suicide will not put the idea into someone's head. Any troubled young person should be asked if they have ever thought of harming themselves. At an appropriate time, a less intrusive question may be easier: Many young people who have these problems feel like hurting themselves. Have you ever felt like that?

Mostly (more than 90 per cent), depressed and suicidal young people confide in a friend before they take their life. It's extremely important therefore to give friends a way to help. Once a friend is worried, everyone should pull out all the stops. Sometimes it's too difficult for one friend to deal with the situation. Schools need to encourage students to talk with friends and tell someone in authority together. This is a time for dobbing. It is the one situation where it's okay not to keep a secret. The one thing that trumps confidentiality is safety!

> *A friend was self-harming and I told my mum and she told my friend's mum. My friend didn't talk to me for ages but I didn't want to feel the guilt if she had really hurt herself.*
>
> Jane, aged 17

A common precipitant for a suicide attempt is a relationship break-up, particularly against a background of not feeling supported, not being sure of backup. There are usually multiple factors that have been lingering for months or years. Suicide is rarely inexplicable as the media would have us believe.

If a young person admits to being suicidal, don't: brush it off or play it down; be judgemental; be sworn to secrecy; get into a panic; leave the young person alone. Take it seriously, take action and get help. If health professionals do not respond to your distress call, be assertive, make a formal complaint to a senior person (for example, the manager of the local mental health service) and try again. The following list is great advice by Margaret Appleby.

> **What parents can do when a teenager threatens suicide**
>
> - Talk about it openly. Ask them if they feel so bad that they are thinking of hurting themselves.
> - Listen to them. Watch their non-verbal behaviour.
> - Tell them that if they need help, you are there for them.
> - Offer to go with them to get help.
> - Ask them why they want to die.
> - Tell them you don't want them to get hurt or die because you will miss them.
> - Take time to listen and be with them — time is a precious gift to give.
> - Consult a professional if you are concerned about a young person's behaviour.

Some final thoughts

David: This chapter has discussed what we can all do to prevent and deal with common and serious mental health problems and when to worry and act. When the major danger signals go on for more than two weeks, the emotional problem may be a mental illness, and outside help should be sought immediately.

Leanne: I remember a very disturbing experience when I was working in an Accident and Emergency Department. A 17-year-old unconscious boy had been rushed in by ambulance. As I quickly positioned his neck to insert a tube into his throat to help him breathe, I found a small bloodstained wound under his chin. It is difficult to describe how it feels to have to tell a loving and unsuspecting family their son has died by suicide by putting a bullet into his brain.

What haunts me now is that the boy's parents described their son as a normal teenager, who had many friends and did well at school. However, in the three months before his death, he had become withdrawn and spent a lot of time lying on his bed holding a crucifix. Did he, like so many who die by suicide, have unrecognised depression? Contrary to the myth that suicide is inexplicable, there are usually many clues in retrospect.

After listening to so many sad stories over many years of my career, I have learnt to believe in the courage and resilience of young people and to never give up. One of the most significant days of my work at Clockwork Young People's Health Service, Geelong, started very badly. I had been delayed by a number of people in crisis; a 14-year-old girl with an eating disorder was kicked out of home; a homeless 16-year-old admitted that her uncle had been sexually abusing her over many years; and a distraught mother rang me after the suicide of her son. At the time, I was fighting with the government bureaucracy to keep the Clockwork service open and had a frustrating meeting about another cut in funding.

I arrived late to pick up my son from school and he had already gone to after-school care. I sat on the bench outside his classroom, to breathe in the normal world and to listen to the children laughing in the school grounds, when my son's teacher called me into the classroom. That day, the 4th Grade had been doing a project on people who had changed the world. The children had nominated people such as Gandhi, JFK, the Queen and Mother Teresa and my son had nominated me. Later, I told my 10-year-old son that I was having a lot of difficulties at Clockwork and was feeling overwhelmed by my work. His words have remained with me since:

You've had hundreds of problems at Clockwork and you've always fixed them. You will fix this one too. Your work with teenagers is more important than any other job. You've taught me that you never give up.

I am convinced now that the way we as adults persevere through difficulties teaches young people about resilience. In the words of Winston Churchill, never, never, never give up.

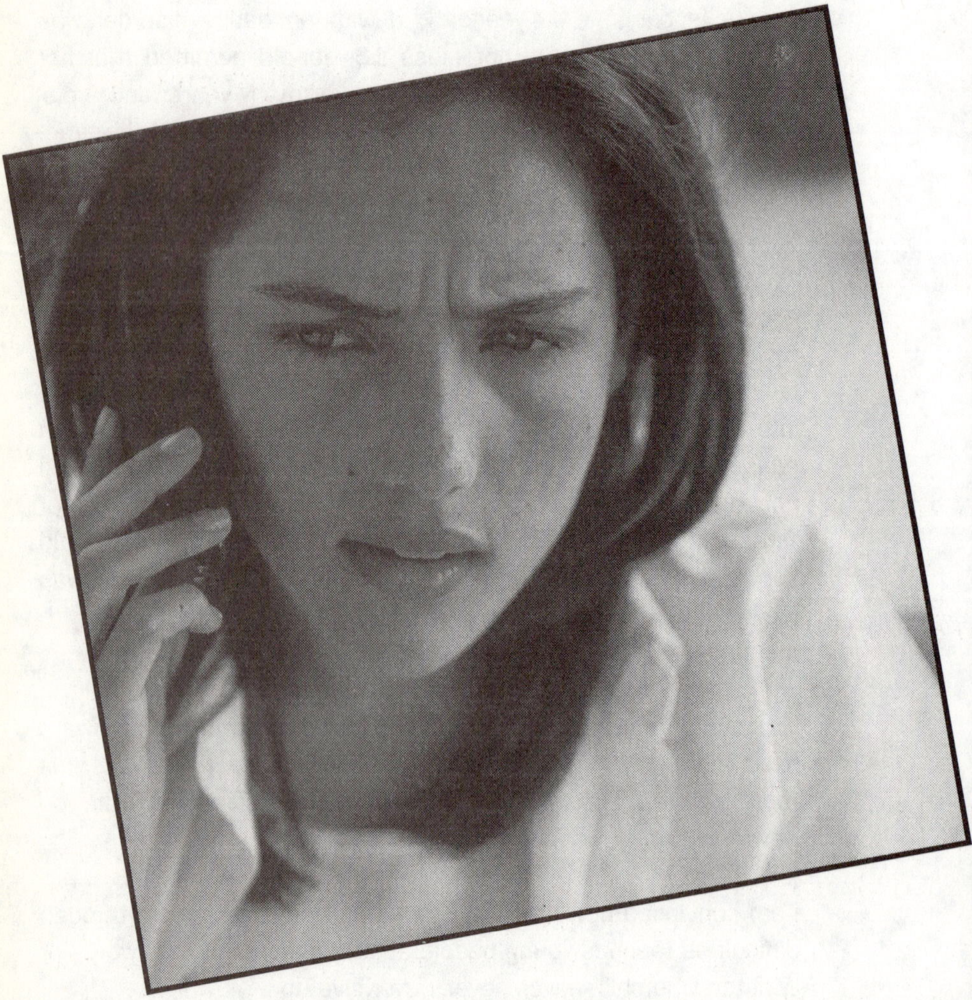

Chapter 16

When, how and where to ask for help

*I seek help when my life reaches a tangled snag.
I turn to people who are great knot untiers.
Abby, aged 16*

It is important to note that 80 per cent of teenagers sail through adolescence. However, as we've seen, significant numbers of teenagers don't. Many factors put young people at risk. Some overcome terrible adversity and bounce back, while others may be very sensitive to the pain of the world around them and quietly or not so quietly self-destruct.

Helping young and vulnerable people comes down to understanding what is normal and what is abnormal and to being more proactive in preventing problems, intervening early and persevering if minor to serious problems arise. As a general rule, if a teenager's behaviour suddenly changes, parents need to seek advice.

But seeking outside help can be confronting, for both parents and teenagers. It's always a sensitive issue, as these comments from young people show:

When I feel down, it helps if people make small gestures to show they understand. Things like: 'Get over it' or 'You need help' are not helpful.

Some people are really good at hiding things and you don't really know they are in pain. A lot of people don't want to admit they've got a problem or that they're a head case. I wouldn't go to the school counsellor. I know he's there but I don't want anyone to know I'm seeing him. Sometimes it is easier to go to a total stranger.

Going to a psychiatrist was daunting and scary. I felt as though I was under the spotlight. You feel as though you have to say the right thing – feel as though you are getting graded. It's not a human atmosphere.

A girl called Kim

Sixteen-year-old Kim is in trouble. There have been behavioural problems for years – foul language, isolation, the wrong friends, crying, mood swings, damage to property or self-harm. The situation has quickly deteriorated into crisis – Kim is now highly at risk of taking drugs, overdose, leaving school and home, violence, accidents, pregnancy, a criminal record or suicide.

Her parents reach for help. The school doesn't understand. There is no appointment with a counsellor for two weeks. Kim doesn't want help anyway. She expects her parents to trust her. Kim tells her parents that she hates them. She wants to be left alone.

What do we do?

Parents often say: 'We are changing schools because we spoke to the teachers and they didn't help.' Teachers often say: 'The child saw a psychologist or went to that service and it didn't work.' Sometimes the school fit is wrong but there is no quick fix. The situation has been brewing for years. The expectation that the school or counsellor will fix this is unrealistic. Changing schools, workers, doctors or psychologists can give a message that we give up if we don't get a quick fix. By persevering, enduring difficulties and uncomfortable times and being there for the long haul, we teach teenagers not to give up; we are, in effect, teaching them about resilience. The priority is to get the right help early and to persevere.

Teenagers will often react against parents and teachers. Despite this, a parent's and a teacher's role and support in a crisis are crucial. Somehow, parents have to find a way to endure the storm. In a crisis, the first concern is immediate safety. When home has become a battleground, it may help to arrange for the angry teenager to stay with an adult relative or friend while things cool off.

Kim began to steal from her parents and in one heated argument, she slapped her mother and bit and kicked her father, when he tried to restrain her. She was dragged to the local mental health service, but was diagnosed as having behavioural problems and referred back to the local GP. The next day, Kim used a razor blade to cut the word 'fuck' into her wrist. She admitted to smoking cannabis. Fortunately, Kim had an aunt who was willing to look after her for a few days until the situation defused.

A parent's role is to reassure love, but to set firm limits around unsafe behaviours. Parents are not counsellors. An adult friend may take a caring (not interfering), listening, non-judgemental, supportive role. But they are not counsellors either.

Things that don't work in situations like Kim's are:

- allowing the teenager to do whatever they like
- physical restraint
- physical punishment
- zero tolerance
- ultimatums
- telling them to get out (this most commonly results in homelessness).

Kim obviously needs professional counselling. But it is important to remember that professionals do not have quick fixes for complex problems.

Seeking the right help

People who have the courage to seek help will quickly discover a very cruel fact: Australia has a lack of services for young people. The services that do exist are sometimes uncoordinated, focused on single issues (for example only mental health or drug problems but not both) and stigmatising to young people. How can parents and their teenagers navigate the maze, without getting lost on the way? The first step is to turn to a professional who can provide counselling and/or advice.

> **Professionals who can help include:**
> - A teacher whom the teenager connects with and trusts.
> - The student welfare coordinator at the school.
> - A youth worker (often employed by the local council) who may help with linking the teenager into alternate school programs, activities or other relevant help.
> - A GP is in a good position to help parents because the cost is mainly or completely covered by Medicare and GPs understand the broad range of issues such as family relationships, mental health, drug abuse, sexual health and how to access other help. However, the family doctor may not be the right person to look after the teenager because of concerns about confidentiality. Another GP with a special interest in adolescent health may be better placed to care for the young person while the parents attend the family GP for support.
> - A psychologist or psychiatrist.

Providing the right support

The right counsellor (be it a teacher, student welfare coordinator, youth worker, GP, psychologist or psychiatrist) is someone with qualifications and experience, who offers a low-cost (the teenager must be able to afford this help without parents' permission), confidential, and non-judgemental service. They must be open to positive and negative feedback and prepared to be there for the long haul. And: *it helps if the teenager likes the counsellor*.

Young people are sometimes hard nuts to crack, but if we appeal to the little part of a young person that wants help, trust will develop over time. Teenagers cannot be forced to attend counsellors and they do not like repeating their story to different professionals. It is important to avoid having too many people involved in a teenager's care and to ensure that someone takes overall responsibility so the teenager does not fall through the gaps between services.

In Kim's case, she decided to live with her aunt for a time while attending regular counselling. Over this time she began to share her story, and eventually professional family mediation was organised to try to settle the family conflict. At one point Kim admitted that in the past she had not cared about anyone or anything, but that she was now starting to care. She wanted to go home but she did not think her parents would forgive her. At this point her parents were invited into the counselling sessions and, to everyone's relief, they were open to allowing Kim back into their home, despite the past trauma.

When there is a lot of conflict it helps if a young person attends their own counsellor. Parents must seek their own sources of support and respect the confidentiality between teenager and counsellor. They may only contact the counsellor with the young person's permission, unless there is a safety issue. While many parents feel they must contact the counsellor to give the full picture, teenagers will refuse to attend if they think there is a conspiracy. Parents must not ask counsellors to keep their contact or letters secret – this threatens trust and risks progress. It is often very difficult for parents to refrain from interfering, but if young people sense this is happening they tend to drop out of counselling. This experience tends to deter them from seeking help again. Parental interference can sometimes make the teenager more at risk.

However, it is important at an appropriate time to come together as a family and, under the guidance of the counsellor, try to identify needs, mediate problems and make plans for possible future crises. This may involve writing down scenarios, based on past experiences, including the proposed action to take if each scenario occurs and developing a list of after-hours telephone numbers for emergency advice and assistance. For instance, if a teenager regularly leaves home in anger and does not come home overnight, the consequences of this need to be clearly stated.

A crisis plan may be negotiated with the teenager, parents and counsellors, by documenting the answers to these questions:

- What is the behaviour of concern?
- What triggers it?
- What are the dos and don'ts?
- What works and what doesn't?
- Who has what role and what responsibility?
- Do the adults know what to do in an after-hours situation?
- Do the teenager and parents each have a copy of the plan, in case of crisis?

A young person's message to parents

My family and I have been through enough anger and sadness to last a lifetime. There have been times when we have hated each other, times when I felt they would rather disown me than put up with me and times when we have cried and cried in each other's arms. I cannot remember half of the things I have done in the past that have caused heartache in my family, but they have always forgiven me and done what they could to help me.

I have left home countless times without explanation, but my parents have always accepted me back when I needed to come home. They have helped repair and clean the many dingy houses and tiny flats that I lived in and carried my boxes of possessions in and out from house to house.

Although, since I have left home, I have always tried to be independent and take care of myself, there were many times I needed food or money. At this time we were hardly even speaking. I had left on very bad terms with them and they did not agree or understand why I left. But despite all this my mum would make me casseroles and lend me money when I needed it and my father would repair parts of the house that I had broken.

While all this was going on they were having their own counselling to help them understand the problems between us and come to terms with the fact that their daughter had left, probably forever. But after living with friends and trying to take care of myself, I am home again and things have never been better.

It must be hard for parents to stop themselves rushing in to help. But they need to remember that we are young and must go through hard times and good times to grow into real adults.

They must remind themselves that we are all different people and we may want and need different things in our lives. I guess every parent wants to see their child follow in their footsteps, but if that doesn't happen, they need to be able to accept this and love their children for their own individuality.

One day I hope to establish a program that counsels kids, teaches physical skills like mechanics, organic planting, designing and sewing of clothes, painting and music – and help them to come to know and love themselves. I want to show children every beautiful aspect of Nature. This is how I hope to contribute to the world. It is my dream.

I would just like to say to anyone who feels angry, hopeless, lost or alone that no matter what the situation, there is always a way out of it. There is always someone who cares, who you care about or someone to help you. Life does not have to be painful, it can be beautiful and fun. You do not have to hate yourself or the world, everyone deserves better. There really is help out there, you just have to find it. There really are people who have lived horrible lives who have felt just as much pain as you have and now dedicate their lives to helping others.

I have lived through hell. And when people told me they knew what I was going through and that they had changed their lives and now felt happiness, I thought, 'Yeah, but for how long?' I never believed this happiness could last, I always thought the pain would come back. But as you take each step towards a better life, the pain begins to die. Your energy and will to live will kill it. I would never have learnt what I know now if I had not gone through all that pain. But there is only so much hell that one person can take and it is up to that person to decide enough is enough. So it is up to you to decide when you tell yourself, 'No more crying. I want to live.'

Jo Sherwell, aged 17

Choosing a doctor

Not surprisingly, it's taken a long time for teenagers, as a group, to come to the attention of doctors. After all, aren't young people supposed to be the healthiest group in the community? Haven't they survived the chickenpox and made it to the teens with reasonable immunity? And aren't they too young to have the sorts of health problems that beset people of their parents' vintage?

All true. Despite many developments in adolescent health care in Australia in the past 25 years, in many ways teenagers remain seriously underserved by the health system. They often fall through the cracks: too old for paediatricians, too young for adult physicians,

It must be hard for parents to stand back and watch their kids stumble.
Marieke, aged 18

and too mistrustful, at times, of the family GP. Consequently, many of their concerns and problems tend to go unnoticed. Also, if adults find it difficult to cope with the medical maze, how much more difficult is it for teenagers? Less naïve than small children, but less aware and experienced than adults, they often get the worst deal of all.

For parents, it is not always easy to see the situation through their children's eyes. While kids are young enough to take along to see the doctor, at least you're in a position to advocate. But as they get older, this is certainly not what they want. Even teenagers with a chronic illness, who require ongoing medical care and attention, will want to cope with their own relationships.

Doctors have something special to offer young people. They do this by being accessible to them, by understanding what's happening to their bodies and minds, by recognising the intimate relationship between their health and behaviour (which, of course, is true at any age), and by making every effort to encourage their sense of personal responsibility in relation to their health and wellbeing. Someone expressed it like this: 'The goal is to assist teenagers to achieve good health, reasonable fitness, emotional stability, and the capacity to cope with challenges and opportunities.'

When a teenager visits a new doctor, it probably takes about three seconds to 'suss' out what sort of encounter it's going to be. Young people have a sixth sense about it and can read the clues: how the doctor greets you, whether or not you're given an opportunity to talk for yourself, the way questions are put and (later) how the physical examination is conducted.

After all, what's the point of consulting a doctor about something if you don't feel comfortable enough to mention the real reason you came? What's the point of getting an ordinary old check-up, if the whole experience leaves you feeling embarrassed and even more worried? Obviously, being treated decently, as an intelligent and reasonable person, is important in any medical encounter at any age. With teenagers, however, there are a number of special considerations.

In a medical journal article entitled 'What a Doctor Should Be', a 16-year-old girl offers some important advice to medical practitioners. These are useful insights for parents to have:

To put it plainly, a doctor should simply be himself or herself. Any put on or false front could destroy a teenager's hope for understanding and help.

Teenagers don't want a doctor to talk, dress or act like a teenager – they already know lots of kids who do that. They want a doctor to be comfortable, friendly and professionally competent.

Because the teenager is a patient, just like any other, the doctor must always bear in mind his or her right to confidentiality and should encourage discussion of things that might not fall on such a sympathetic ear at home. The doctor must always assume that the patient is an individual. Over-reliance on contact with parents tends to destroy much confidence between the doctor and his teenage patient.

Parents can find this change of focus a difficult transition, but it is important to accept it graciously. A doctor who hears the teenager out, whether in your presence or in private, is going to be a valuable resource to your son or daughter. For young people, this is part of growing up and assuming responsibility, and the ultimate goal is protecting and promoting their health.

Some points about confidentiality:

- Confidentiality is cited by young people as the most important quality of their relationship with a health professional (surveys have shown that many teenagers will actually avoid seeking help if they believe confidentiality might not be respected).
- Confidentiality shows respect for the individual privacy of the adolescent and recognises that they are increasingly capable of exercising rational choice and giving informed consent (even with teenagers under the age of consent, 16 years, common law recognises the concept of the 'mature minor').
- Confidentiality does not preclude encouraging a young person to confide in and seek support from their family and others who care about their wellbeing.
- Confidentiality is necessary to enable young people to trust their doctor with sensitive information, but their safety would sometimes take priority.

Dr Melissa Kang, a colleague in adolescent health, puts it like this:

> *Anything we discuss will be kept confidential. That means that I will not repeat anything you tell me to anyone else, unless I think it would help you and you give me permission to do so. There are a few situations, however, where I will not be able to keep confidentiality; for example, if I am concerned that you could harm yourself or someone else, or if I am concerned that you are being harmed or at risk of being harmed because of somebody else (and you are under 16). In these situations it would be my duty to ensure that you are safe. I would tell you if I need to notify somebody about something that you've told me and I would make sure that you have as much support as possible.*

There is no fixed age at which a young person is deemed legally competent and therefore entitled to confidentiality. The degree of understanding and judgement will differ from teenager to teenager and the doctor is permitted to assess whether they are in a position to make their own decisions. Therefore many teenagers are entitled to visit a doctor before the age of consent without their parents' consent.

Teenagers can be wary of adults anyway, so someone who appears busy and distracted is not going to get very far in an interview. It's more the feeling that someone is 'with you', taking an interest in you as a person, than the actual time spent that counts. A doctor who can listen quietly for the hidden, tangential ways in which young people convey their concerns has something very special to offer.

The problem itself may not be a threat to life, or even to health, but only an insensitive practitioner would treat an adolescent's bodily (or any other) concerns as trivial. A teenager's 'presenting complaint' represents something important: it gains them entry to the doctor's surgery, and often there's more to it than meets the eye. A 14-year-old boy who turns up with a cough or a pain in the chest, for example, could well be inviting the doctor to discover the lump he's noticed under his right breast. How nice to be reassured that it's normal and harmless (the condition called gynaecomastia), and not cancer or the first sign of some abnormal sexual transformation.

The manner in which a physical examination is performed can leave a lasting impression on a young person too. A doctor who respects an adolescent's privacy and modesty, keeps up a running dialogue of reassurance (in comprehensible language) and takes the opportunity to teach kids something about how to care for their bodies, has done more than justice to the whole procedure. A doctor who is perfunctory, rough or ominously silent (a frown of intense concentration without explanation means you're dying, right?), does not.

Possibly the most sensitive procedure that a teenage girl can experience is an internal examination. Some girls may want their mothers present the first couple of times, others won't. There's generally a good reason for having an examination, such as severe menstrual problems or undiagnosed abdominal pain – which could mean an infection such as chlamydia – or because she has become sexually active and needs an annual pap smear. It can be extremely unpleasant, even painful, if it's not approached with gentleness and tact. This means a quiet explanation of what's to be done, the use of a warmed speculum (there's a special small one for girls whose hymen is intact), and a kindly appreciation that embarrassment is normal.

A psychosocial biopsy

When a teenager consults a doctor (or any other health professional for that matter), this is a golden opportunity to tune into what's happening in their life, whatever the presenting complaint or concern. Health is a dynamic state, constantly changing, and there is nothing to gain by taking a narrow view of it. The World Health Organisation has defined health broadly as 'the presence of physical, emotional and social wellbeing, not merely the absence of disease or infirmity'. Perhaps we should concern ourselves with spiritual, creative, imaginative and soulful wellness too.

An important contribution to adolescent health care comes from the Division of Adolescent Medicine at the Children's Hospital of Los Angeles, the so-called HEADSS (Home; Education; Activities; Drugs; Sexuality; Suicide) guide. This simple guide to 'getting into a teenager's head' has been around for a long time, encouraging doctors in particular to move beyond physical issues and enrich a professional encounter with a teenager by sensitively exploring these psychosocial dimensions. As well as indicating an interest in the whole person, not just the illness or problem, and establishing a professional rapport, this approach enables a doctor to obtain a sense of the young person's circumstances, lifestyle, interests and health risk behaviours.

Many doctors seem wary of doing this, possibly for fear of opening up a Pandora's box of problems and not knowing how to proceed.

Some think it is just beyond their medical brief. But it's catching on nevertheless and HEADSS is becoming a routine way to assess a young person.

For example, a gentle enquiry such as: 'Have you ever felt really unhappy, like life just isn't worth living?' is not an easy thing to ask, but in certain circumstances to leave it out is unwise.

Using the health care system

About 90 per cent of the Australian population sees a GP each year. A GP will often be the first contact for distressed families. It is important for young people to be taught how to choose and visit a GP because they often keep their distress to themselves. The following basic information needs to be provided to young people to encourage them to seek confidential advice and treatment through the health system.

Making an appointment: To ensure an appointment with a doctor meets your needs, ask the doctor's receptionist:

- For an appointment with the doctor of your choice.
- For a long visit if the problem will take longer than 15 minutes.
- For an urgent appointment if the problem is urgent (though it's better to try to make the appointment before the problem becomes a crisis).

You can also ask the receptionist:

- What the consultation will cost and if the doctor will bulk bill (bulk billing means that you sign a form and you do not have to pay).
- To ring the Medicare hotline for your Medicare number if you do not have a Medicare card.
- To help you obtain your own Medicare card.
- To cancel your appointment if you can't make it.

How to get a Medicare card: If you need to visit a doctor and you don't have a Medicare card, the doctor's receptionist will take your name and call the Medicare hotline to get your parent's or guardian's

Medicare number (your visit to the doctor will be strictly confidential). If you are unable to pay, you can ask the doctor or the receptionist if it is possible to sign a bulk billing form. This means that Medicare pays for the full cost of your visit to the doctor and a bill will not be sent to your parents. If you are 16 or over, you can have your own Medicare card. All you need to do is visit your local Medicare office with identification such as a birth certificate and fill in a Medicare enrolment form. If you don't have any identification, you can give your parent's or guardian's name. Your name will then be taken off your parent's card and you will get your own Medicare card. This card will be sent to you in the mail. When visiting your doctor, remember to take your Medicare card. For more information, contact the Medicare hotline on 132011. If you have any problems with this, ask your doctor or the receptionist.

How to get a Health Care Card: If you are receiving or about to receive benefits from Centrelink, you will instantly get a Health Care Card. If you are under 16 and your parents have a Health Care Card, then you can use their card. If you don't live at home, you may be entitled to the youth homeless allowance from Centrelink. It is helpful to see a social worker to determine if you are eligible to seek this allowance. If you are over 16 and earn less than a certain amount, you may qualify for a Health Care Card. Visit your Centrelink office with some identification and staff will help you fill in an application form. A Health Care Card has many benefits such as cheaper health care, cheaper medicines and travel concessions.

Rights of young people when seeking health care: You have the right to:

- Be encouraged and supported to make your own informed decisions about your life.
- Privacy. Everything you say will be treated in a confidential manner.
- Not be pressured into making any decisions you are unhappy with.
- Non-judgemental responses and treatments.
- Be respected.
- A second opinion.
- Have a complaint heard and dealt with fairly.

What if a teenager at risk will not seek help?

> The most helpful and mature decision I have ever made was to seek counselling. This was at a time when I felt completely hopeless.
> Kim, aged 16

It can be very difficult for parents when a teenager refuses their help, and then refuses to seek help themselves. Sometimes it helps just to keep in touch, send a supportive card or letter, or provide written information and educational brochures about relevant conditions including sexuality, drugs and mental illness. It may also help to obtain some leaflets about local youth services or lists of GP names and clinics, to make your teenager aware of services, and reassure them about confidentiality. It is unfortunate that some young people have to reach crisis point before they will seek help, but if they have some useful telephone numbers or websites, they are likely to seek the right help at this time (an extensive list is provided in the Appendix of this book). If a teenager is self-harming, professional help must be enlisted. If young people are violent, they must be warned that the police may be called.

It can be difficult to keep communication lines open in times of crisis. Sometimes it helps to ask some gentle questions.

Here are some questions to ask teenagers who will not seek help:

Can you tell me what is happening?
What has happened to upset you?
What is playing on your mind?
What needs to change?
What can I do to help?
What effect is this problem having on your life?
Is it positive or negative?
How can you express your anger?
What is the argument in your head?
What would you be doing if the depression was not there?
What are the steps we can take to mend it?
Do my concerns concern you? Why or why not?
Who are the people you trust, feel close to or have things in common with?
Can you contact them now and talk to them?
How do you know that people care?
What can I do to support you?

> *Many people who experience this distress feel like hurting themselves. Have you ever had these thoughts?*
> *What are the questions you would like me to ask?*
> *When you are happier what do you find yourself doing?*
> *Imagine your problems had been solved. How would you know this had happened? What changes would you notice? What steps could you take to make those changes?*

Leanne: One evening, I was telephoned by a senior bank manager, who had just found out that her 19-year-old son, Max, had been taking a mixture of illicit drugs, including heroin, for the past two years. I saw Max the following day and he could not sleep, was highly anxious and requested help with his drug problem. He was also very depressed and Max's parents were insistent that he be referred to a private psychiatrist urgently. Unfortunately, Max did not attend the psychiatrist after the first few sessions and left home, much to the despair of his parents. About six months later, Max came to me on his own after his relationship with his girlfriend broke up, again asking for help with his drug problem. Over 12 months he attended regularly and his depression and drug addiction responded to treatment. This case illustrates that sometimes young people have to hit a crisis before they will seek help. When they ask for help, they need to know where to turn for the right help; help that is affordable, confidential and accessible to them.

Through my work, I have learnt to be patient, to just listen, to hang in there and to try to keep young people safe until they find their own resources to come through. We can't judge young people – we have to accept them for who they are and not try to make them something they are not or force them in a direction that they don't want to go. When I think about some of the tortured young people I have seen and how at risk they were, it is remarkable now that they are even alive. It is inspiring to see them come through and to now be living as responsible young adults.

Teenagers in hospital

Teenagers have accidents, take overdoses, get pregnant and suffer from a variety of serious diseases (such as diabetes, cystic fibrosis, juvenile rheumatoid arthritis and spina bifida), all of which can require a hospital bed. In fact, according to some research, as many as one in 10 Australian adolescents may have an admission to hospital in any given year. So we cannot pretend it's not important.

For a teenager (or anyone, for that matter), being in hospital is rarely a terrific experience. It's not too difficult to figure out why, but it shouldn't be as awful as it frequently is. On the first occasion it's just plain scary, as Claire Williams wrote in the *Canteen Newsletter* (published by the Australian Teenage Cancer Patients Society):

> *When I first went into hospital I was 13, upset, frightened. Unsure what was going to happen to me. It was as if the impossible had come true. My whole world was shaken up. Upside down.*
>
> *There were many children playing, laughing, crying. Nurses, rushing about their duties.*
>
> *Worried faces. Parents. Talking, walking, whispering, hoping, praying. Mother. Thin, flustered, grey hair, weak smile. Comfort. On a bed, a bony, pale child. His dark eyes, innocent, weary. As if this was a normal world. Everyone lived like this.*
>
> *My bed was standing at attention. In line with all the others – identical, starched, regimental. Faces watching, wondering. Whitewashed walls. The smell of disinfectant.*
>
> *Greetings. People smiling, warmly, exhaustedly, understandingly. Questions answered, barriers broken. No longer an outsider. I was one of them.*

Settling in can be easier said than done. If, on top of illness, pain and anxiety, a young person is confronted with 'inhospitable circumstances', coping becomes even more difficult. Even after many years of developments in adolescent health care, only a mere handful of Australian hospitals (mostly children's hospitals) arrange for teenagers to be grouped together. Generally they are not, which is most unfortunate. At no other time in life is the urge to be with mates of one's own age more intense. When given the opportunity, teenagers support, teach, reassure and entertain each other. Why not in hospital?

For one thing, hospital staff do not always find teenage patients easy going. They are different, unpredictable. A sick adolescent may be reasonable, cheerful, calm and cooperative at one moment, and the next moment depressed, disruptive, demanding, manipulative, obstructive and defiant. Some nurses actively favour a divide and conquer approach, preferring that they be scattered around. Put them all together and – heaven knows! Noise and mayhem? Graffiti and loud music? Sex and depravity?

The opposite view, as it happens, appears more humane and more valid. There is much research to show that teenagers do not thrive in hospital wards that deprive them of contact with peers, understanding staff, a reasonable timetable, and appropriate activities with which to occupy their time. As young people see it, there are different concerns and problems depending on where they are:

- In a children's ward, where they are disturbed by younger children and crying babies, teenagers often feel infantilised, resented or ignored, irritated by the small furniture and lack of facilities for teenagers, embarrassed by a lack of privacy, infuriated by having to turn the television off at a 'ridiculously early hour' (8.30 pm, for example), and dissatisfied with the food (who isn't?).
- In an adult ward, which is usually more austere and ominous, there are even greater chances for the whole experience to be emotionally unsettling. Adolescent patients are psychologically more vulnerable than adults and are more likely to be very troubled by being in close proximity to the elderly and the dying. In comparison with adult in-patients, they have been shown to be more self-conscious about their bodies, have a greater fear of death and mutilation, greater levels of separation and general anxiety, and to feel much more dissatisfaction with their physical surroundings.

The Association for the Welfare of Child Health works tirelessly to lobby hospitals and governments to ensure that children and young people are appropriately and safely accommodated as in-patients. In some hospitals there are assigned children's wards, but retaining them for children only is a well-recognised problem. Particularly after hours, if a bed in a 'children's section' is empty, an adult may be popped into it, which not only changes the atmosphere and morale of staff, but also brings with it potential risks to the children or teenagers. And where young people are housed with adults in adult wards, there are dangers associated with that as well (especially in adult mental wards, for obvious reasons).

A 14-year-old girl with leukaemia experienced these 'adult ward' problems first-hand. Her mother, in anguish, wrote about it, concluding the letter with these sentiments:

Regardless of the prognosis, an adolescent's stay in hospital should be conducive to as happy a mental disposition as possible, and not such that the actual mental recovery could be hindered by circumstances such as I have described. I hope that hospital care more suited to the needs of our youth will not be too long forthcoming.

On being chronically ill

Adolescence is a rotten time to have something seriously wrong with your body, but it's not all that uncommon – about one in 15 young people (possibly more) have a significant, medical condition or physical abnormality requiring ongoing care and support (that is, a chronic disease). For such kids, things can come to a head during the teenage years, growing up can become a much more painful journey. And, of course, the whole family is affected.

Let me be a teenager

The parents of ill or disabled teenagers have an awful lot to cope with: they usually feel stressed, guilty, and anxious about the future; marital relationships can suffer; or siblings can feel, and actually be, neglected.

The temptation to overprotect sick kids, to somehow make amends or take on their pain as your own, is almost overwhelming. Unfortunately, this is the absolute opposite of what they need and desire. The obstacles to a healthy adolescence are many and varied, but ironically, the most insurmountable ones are often those created by people who mean well and care the most.

What does a chronically ill teenager want more than anything else in the world? To be a teenager, to do 'normal' things and to make up his or her mind what to do.

Obstacles to growing up

Many aspects of normal adolescence become a greater challenge:

- Not being able to do certain things for yourself, as well as the overprotectiveness mentioned above, may interfere with efforts to grow up and become an individual, reasonably separate from but still connected to the family. This enforced dependence makes kids very angry, and periodically they may become uncooperative about their treatment (for example, a diabetic teenager bingeing on cake, or an asthmatic teenager smoking cigarettes between puffs of Ventolin). Doctors call this behaviour 'non-compliance' or 'non-adherence' and it worries everybody concerned, but there's clearly an element of healthy adolescent rebellion in it.

- How you look, and how you think you look (body image), are extremely sensitive matters during adolescence. Any deformity or imperfection, obvious or hidden, real or imagined, can be very troubling to an ill or handicapped young person. For example, having to wear a body brace if you need treatment for curvature of the spine (scoliosis). Sometimes and with certain disabilities, adolescents experience feelings of disgust, loathing and shame. This has implications in regard to personal hygiene and to an acceptance of one's sexuality (not that the opportunities to express it are likely to be all that great).

- Missing a lot of school or having a condition that rules out certain vocational goals, raises questions about getting a job and eventually becoming economically independent. Of course, a kid with epilepsy can do a lot of things other than becoming an airline pilot. A greater problem is dealing with community prejudices and a shrinking labour market for young people in general. Having something wrong with you does not tip the scales in your favour.

- Finally, how are you supposed to end up feeling good about yourself if the rough and tumble of mixing with friends has been denied you? In some ways, the greatest handicap of all for the disabled young person is loneliness. Problems relating to mobility, transport and access on the one hand, and shyness, embarrassment and poor self-esteem on the other, keep kids out of the mainstream of adolescent life, or render their involvement in it awkward and traumatic.

A question of attitude

There is a poster that features a teenager saying 'What's a girl like me doing with cystic fibrosis? Fighting it!' Some chronically ill teenagers are among the most inspiring people one could ever meet. Under the most trying and adverse personal conditions, with little or no hope for improvement or recovery, they have soldiered on (while healthy people around them continue whingeing about life's small imperfections). They are (or were) special individuals, carrying their burden with dignity and courage.

A particular young woman in this category was, as a result of her disease, physically wasted and partially paralysed, but she loved life and made the most of it. Her wry sense of humour and indomitable spirit seemed out of place with her tiny body and difficult circumstances. But she lived each day at a time and managed to work until the day she died.

In her book *Hannah's Gift: Lessons from a life fully lived*, Maria Housden writes about her daughter who lost her battle against cancer in 1994 when she was just four. Hannah taught those around her 'that the truest measure of life is not its length, but the fullness in which it is lived.'

Why have adolescent services?

We are fortunate in Australia to have a comprehensive and relatively accessible health system. We say relatively, because most services are designed for adults or young children and are often less than ideal for teenagers. Some of our major paediatric hospitals have done something over the years to address the imbalance by setting up special adolescent units, as well as academic centres of excellence on adolescent health, but these are usually based in major capital cities. In comparison with need, there are very few established adolescent health services in country areas.

Research indicates that there are many obstacles to young people accessing, for example, the publicly funded community health centres that exist across the country. They either do not know they're available (especially for mental health problems) or find them non-youth friendly. A study about access to health services for adolescents undertaken by the NSW Centre for the Advancement of Adolescent Health shows that other barriers include concerns about confidentiality, and discomfort about disclosing health concerns.

Despite the overall paucity of adolescent services, however, many effective and enduring models of care have been created over the past quarter century. Some are medically oriented but incorporate the skills of psychosocial and other allied health personnel. The Royal

Alexandra Hospital for Children (now The Children's Hospital at Westmead, Sydney) was the first hospital in Australia to establish an Adolescent Medical Unit along these lines. Other services cater more to the social, recreational and mental health needs of young people, like The Second Storey in Adelaide or Youth Link in Perth. Clockwork Young People's Health Service is an innovative service for at-risk young people in Geelong, Victoria, staffed by altruistic GPs who bulk bill the clients. In some instances (albeit rarely) there are linkages between hospital- and community-based services enabling a seamless system of care. The Centre for Adolescent Health in Melbourne, for example, is responsible for health care in the entire Victorian juvenile justice system.

Much is now known about what works well. The essential feature is a friendly and supportive service, provided by interested and experienced health professionals from a variety of disciplines, where young people can start to relax, build relationships with caring and competent adults and deal with their health concerns.

Historically, the first hospital-based adolescent unit in the world was established in 1951 at the Boston Children's Medical Centre by Dr J. Roswell Gallagher. Since the establishment of the International Association for Adolescent Health in 1987, a network of concerned health professionals has shared information about developments throughout the world. The international field is growing rapidly, with over 20 national associations for adolescent health worldwide, which means that much is happening in far off places, often with limited resources, that can inspire and encourage our own efforts.

The case for special services for teenagers is based on the following points:

- Teenagers are neither children nor adults and generally do not fit well into existing systems of health care.
- Teenagers have special physical and emotional needs and require different types of treatment and care.
- Teenagers need and deserve health care providers who are able to relate comfortably to young people.
- Teenagers are advantaged, directly and indirectly, by being grouped together (for example, they support each other, provide a resource for teaching, stimulate clinical research into their needs, and receive better and more comprehensive care).

The wheels, however, continue to move slowly; there is resistance to change. As English author Wilfred Trotter put it: 'The mind likes a strange idea as little as the body likes a strange protein and resists it with similar energy.' But there's more to it than that. The subject of adolescent health care invariably takes us into the sticky waters of medical politics in hard economic times. While some governments are starting to look more seriously at the need for prevention and early intervention with young people (especially in the area of child and adolescent mental health), none seem prepared to properly fund the clinical services that are needed. The adolescent health field, together with other adults who care and young people themselves, needs to come together to address this problem in creative ways and advocate strongly for what should be happening.

Engaging creativity in care

Within each of us there is the capacity to be innovative and creative. In adolescent health care, there is a need to call upon the talents, creativity and active involvement of young people in their own care, to introduce new and exciting experiences and to facilitate growth and change. These ideas are not new, but they represent an important challenge for health professionals and can be taken up in a variety of ways.

Creative expression has been given a special recognition at the Royal Alexandra Hospital for Children, in two very different settings: an adolescent ward and a community-based centre for homeless and at-risk youth. When artists and musicians enter into stimulating relationships with ill or troubled young people, working comfortably alongside their more traditional (but often equally creative) health care givers, magic is in the making. After almost two decades of pioneering work by the hospital's Youth Arts Program, activities such as the creation of games, drawings, murals, masks, sculptures, film, slides, stories, songs, plays, magazines, totems and mosaics have become commonplace. Their impact, however, is often profoundly positive.

Why youth arts in hospitals? In the gentle words of author and therapist Thomas Moore in *Soul Mates: Honouring the Mysteries of Love and Relationships*: 'Art, broadly speaking, is that which invites us into contemplation... In that moment of contemplation, art intensifies the presence of the world. We see it more vividly and more deeply.'

The inclusion of an artist in a hospital setting creates a special feeling and special opportunities, particularly for chronically ill young people with repeated or lengthy admissions. For them, hospitalisation may represent a major crisis point in their adolescence, imposing considerable restrictions on lifestyle, self-concept, skills development and peer and family relationships. Given an unexpectedly stimulating milieu and program, however, it can be an exciting, transformative and healing experience.

In a project called Art Injection, art students helped adolescents to make sculptures from old hospital equipment. The results were startling. A wheelchair encased in plaster of Paris houses a twisted figure made of rubber hose and plaster feet. Another wheelchair is covered with babies' bottle teats. 'Nil by Mouth', the work of a young man who required frequent surgical treatment to release pressure within his brain, is a robotic angular sculpture with an intravenous giving set (the apparatus which times the drip) for a head, a drip stand body, metal rod limbs, all wreathed in red and blue plastic tubing. A giant doctor towers over it all, a white coat suspended on stilts made from crutches; inside the coat the doctor's body is a tangled mass of wires and his dangling hands are inflated rubber gloves.

Understandably, many of the hospital staff found the raw emotions expressed in these sculptures disturbing. The teenagers themselves, however, evidently enjoyed breaking the taboos of hospital life by dismantling and adopting medical equipment into art forms. They were able to poke fun at their perceived torturers (the medical staff), the instruments of torture (the equipment), and to express the frustration of being chronically ill. A seriously ill boy named Kane expertly created his first major artwork (within a two-hour time limit) on a hospital sheet. In one corner of the sheet he painted a faint, ghost-like face fading away into clouds, while another haunted and tearful face sinks quietly into water. He called this powerful painting 'Tear of Thought' and explained it as follows:

This painting represents the helplessness of life slowly fading away. The loss of identity, becoming something you once would not have recognised. There is need for expression that comes from being trapped inside a world of inescapable sickness and continued hospitalisation.

In an environment of openness, trust and respect, young people (and human beings generally) are able to accommodate and survive the most difficult experiences. What is needed are settings that allow a reconnection with human warmth, caring and love. In such circumstances, a young person's inner strength and resilience are engaged and supported, enabling him or her to move forward to a better destiny. Our society depends on this capacity in people.

One of the most challenging problems in adolescent health is dealing with angry, despairing, disaffected young people, particularly those who are homeless. Cellblock Youth Health Centre (which derives its name from its original site in an old police station) is an innovative youth health centre in Sydney. Established in 1990, it epitomises the successful integration of creative arts activities with health promotion programs and health services. On one of its doors, a staff member had placed the statement: 'Practise random acts of kindness and senseless beauty.' Creativity in its various forms played a major role in formulating the centre's comprehensive and humane approach to health care for marginalised teenagers. For example, an imaginative anti-smoking billboard was designed and painted by young people; a drama group created and performed original plays about issues such as juvenile justice, family breakdown and school stress; poetry reflecting pain and suffering was set to music and performed by bands made up of young musicians with something to say – often loudly!

Artistic expression provides a poignant voice to those who cannot express their often tortured experiences in other ways. An art show entitled 'The Body of Work', a unique and innovative blend of art, medicine and technology, showcased the creative contributions of homeless and troubled young people. Shannon, a young woman with a long history of abuse, despair and suicide attempts, stood proudly beside a series of small, colourful drawings. 'They are based on a poem about me,' she said, and proceeded to recite an excerpt from it amid the milling crowd. The first drawing showed a young woman with a jaggedly 'broken heart'; the last was a scene in which a pale yellow sun rises above a distant horizon, tentative rays reach upward from the sun on which is written, ever so faintly, 'hope'! It seems that her connection, in particular to the artist at Cellblock at the time, played a part in saving her life.

Some final thoughts

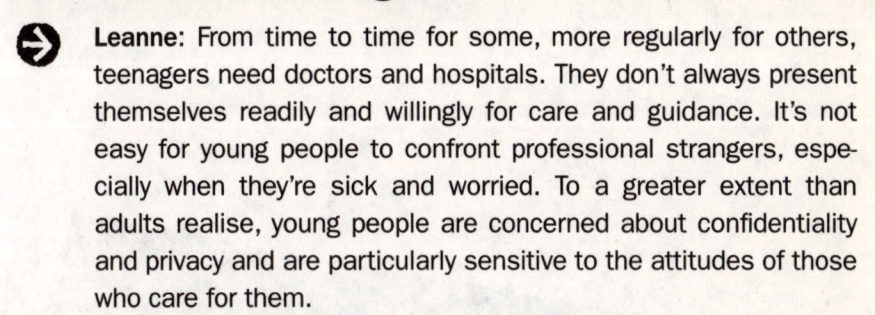

Leanne: From time to time for some, more regularly for others, teenagers need doctors and hospitals. They don't always present themselves readily and willingly for care and guidance. It's not easy for young people to confront professional strangers, especially when they're sick and worried. To a greater extent than adults realise, young people are concerned about confidentiality and privacy and are particularly sensitive to the attitudes of those who care for them.

David: Parents are not outside this issue. Even though you are gradually and appropriately giving up the reins of control and increasingly allowing your teenaged children to negotiate the health system on their own behalf, your interest in their getting the best possible deal is not going to diminish. You'll be on the lookout for doctors having a reputation for being 'good with teenagers'. You'll be happy for them to attend 'youth friendly' GPs, special adolescent units and youth-oriented facilities and programs. And last but not least, you'll be encouraging governments to put resources into adolescent health – our society cannot really afford to do otherwise. Cure is costing us much more than prevention.

YOU CAN BOMB THE
ORLD TO PIECES...BUT
OU CAN'T BOMB THE
WORLD TO
PEACE!

Chapter 17

What about the future?

> *I often overhear adults talking about teenage drug use and depression as if it is all hopeless. Have they ever stopped to ask us why we are so unhappy?*
> Daniel, aged 17

What's wrong with young people these days? It is a problem in itself that many people who ask this complex question want a simple answer. There is no quick fix for the deepening despair and declining health of about 20 per cent of our young people.

These problems ruin the lives of families from all socio-economic groups, so the answers are not as simple as living conditions, financial security, education and employment. Many people have theories: lack of spirituality, an ineffective education system, family breakdown, working mothers, increasing mental illness, drugs, childhood abuse, media and peer influence.

Here is a simple message about three things you can do today: minister, media and mentor.

Minister

Despite enormous advances in health technology, preventable and self-inflicted disorders in young people are increasing significantly. In Australia, despite open acknowledgement of the importance of

> *I was desperate when I went to the mental health service. They told me I wasn't suicidal and referred me to the drug and alcohol service. Then they referred me back to the mental health service for my 'mental health problem'. How suicidal do you have to be to get help?*
> *Emma, aged 17*

young people, we have a major national issue of relatively uncoordinated, short-term and inadequate funding for youth health by many different Government departments. Taskforces on suicide and 'wars' on drugs tend to produce glossy reports and short-term pilot projects, but few long-term well-evaluated strategies have resulted.

Many youth health strategies still fail to consider the social determinants of health, including education, welfare and employment. This failure is leading to increased discrepancies in health status between higher and lower socio-economic groups and a younger generation with more health problems than their parents' generation. History will judge our generation harshly. How much wider will the gap become before we act?

In our professional work, we have been confronted by many despairing young people who now have positive lives. Their stories demand that we ensure there are safety nets to protect these young people and our community: a suicidal 17-year-old who steals cars, drives dangerously and doesn't care whom he takes with him; a young person with untreated psychosis, who is planning a mass shooting; a 16-year-old girl who has been injected with heroin by her parents for two years. They are all now living and working constructively after receiving the right support and professional help.

As noted in the previous chapter, there are few youth-specific or youth-friendly services on offer to help teenagers, particularly those who live in rural areas or who are marginalised.

Australia needs:

- A political commitment to improve deteriorating youth health statistics and caring concern about the distress behind them.
- Coordinated strategies to promote youth health, education, justice, social welfare, housing and employment.
- Improved quality of and access to youth-specific and mainstream services.
- Ongoing meaningful youth and community consultation.

The Ministry for Children and Youth Affairs is currently focused on small children and the issues and needs of the earliest years. Australians should be aware of and support the Government's current positive initiatives for teenagers. However, we also need to express our concerns over deteriorating youth health statistics and the largely unmet need for focused and evaluated youth programs, services and funding.

Write to the Office of the Prime Minister to ask for a copy of the Government's vision for young people and plans to support their transition to adulthood.

Media

Eighty per cent of young people travel well through their adolescence, but their creativity and achievements are rarely reported by the media. About 80 per cent of the images of young people in our media are negative. The dominant images are of teenage crime, vandalism, pregnancy, truancy, dole bludgers and young people dying on the end of needles. The pervading stories are about violence, death, sex, environmental disasters, human rights abuses and social injustice.

Fashion, music and the media are integral components of youth culture. However, it is hypocritical for society to allow the media to sexualise young people while failing to accept the need for sexual health education in schools; to promote a perfect body image and then fail to fund adequate programs for young people with eating disorders; and to expose young people to violent, depressing images but simultaneously stigmatise depression and mental illness.

Blaming the hypocrisy and negativity of the media will not of course change its influence on our young people. Commercial media provides us with images that sell. Television could be a vehicle for promoting positive images of young people, positive role models, parenting and relationship education, public health education campaigns, particularly mental health promotion, and information about youth services. There is an enormous need and public demand for a TV program on relationships, parenting and adolescent issues.

> *The world is changing so quickly and I am constantly changing to keep up. But my parents aren't changing in the way they respond to me. I feel like I am leaving them behind.*
> *Paul, aged 18*

Write to television stations and newspapers to support the need for programs about parenting, relationships and positive images of young people.

Mentor

In the normal process of striving for independence, most young people go through a time when they find it difficult to discuss personal issues with their parents and at this time it is important they feel connected with at least one other caring adult. Young people choose their own mentors but relatives, teachers and adult friends need to make themselves available. A trusted mentor has the opportunity to encourage communication, values, participation, contribution, a belief in the future and a healthy lifestyle. All young people are affected by our society's spiritual desert, by emotionally distant relationships and by increasing family breakdown. A caring mentor can offer support, listen, provide small kindnesses and live an example.

When peer influence takes over family influence, a safety net is needed for the 20 per cent of young people who struggle with depression, suicidal thoughts and substance abuse. Families must create this safety net from early childhood, before problems manifest in adolescence. Schools must provide compulsory advocacy and mentoring programs to keep young people connected. Communities must help schools care for children who do not have family support. Significant numbers of carefully selected adult mentors are needed to connect with the growing number of young people who have little family support, or come from broken or depressed families, to protect them from exploitation.

This can be seen in a number of schools where volunteer parents on a roster system cook sausages and eggs before school for young teenagers. These young people would otherwise have no morning meal and care. This simple gesture provides nourishment and nurturing. There are great rewards in winning the respect of a difficult adolescent.

My father was dying and of all people I turned to my anatomy professor because he left the door to his office open to students and asked me 'How are you really?' It was a gift.
Elana, aged 19

Consider making yourself available as a mentor to young people and ensuring your own children from a young age have trusted mentors outside your immediate family.

There is no quick fix. However, if we believe the issues are too difficult and that society will not change, we unknowingly give our own children a message of hopelessness for their future. So if you do not agree with these strategies, develop three of your own. Confront the uncomfortable fact that youth problems are at least in part a measure of our generation's apathy. After all, the extent to which we nurture the idealism of our young people and protect their vulnerable transition to adulthood is a critical measure of a caring society.

The solution is not something you can buy or something governments can impose. The statistics will only change with something much bigger and need to be community driven. Communities, parents and individuals have to believe in the future. By this example, children will learn to take responsibility for something bigger than themselves, to have a lifetime commitment to involvement in community, to be sensitive to the suffering of others and to persevere through difficulties. This is what we and many other parents want to teach our children. It is not a government's role to initiate this, but it is government's role to support it.

We need only a groundswell of public concern to demonstrate that we care. By doing nothing, we are contributing to the problems. What is wrong with young people? If we insist on a simple answer, we need look no further than ourselves. The simple answer to what is wrong with young people is that we do not believe we can change things. We need to believe in the power of our voices.

Appendix

Sources

Chapter 1
p. 5   Early puberty in girls in step-families comes from Hetherington M., Kelly J., *For better or For Worse: Divorce Reconsidered*, WW Norton, 2002.

Chapter 3
p. 43 Information on authoritative parenting comes from 'We know some things: Parent–Adolescent Relationships in Retrospect and Prospect', Steinberg, Lawrence, Temple University, *Journal of Research on Adolescence,* 2001, Vol. 11, No.1, pp. 1–19.
p. 43 Australian Temperament Project, 1983–2000 Australian Institute for Family Studies, *Pathways from Infancy to Adolescence.*

Chapter 4
p. 57 Some of the material in this chapter was drawn from 'Children, Adolescents and the Media in the 21st Century': Strasburger, Victor C. and Donnerstein, Ed, *Adolescent Medicine: State of the Art Reviews*, Vol. 11, No.1, February 2000, pp. 51–68.
p. 57 'It's not surprising . . . that many of the newest generation can click a mouse before they can tie a shoe, and that they've become just as comfortable with e-mail and with PCs as with pen and paper': David Britt, CEO, Children's Television Workshop, 1977 (quoted in Strassburger and Donnerstein's 'Children, Adolescents and the Media in the 21st Century').
p. 58 Statistic on percentage of children who recognise Arnold Schwarzenegger's *Terminator* character comes from Groebel, J., 'The UNESCO Global Study on Media Violence', *Children and Media Violence*, Carlsson, U. and von Feilitzen, C. (eds), Goteborg, Sweden, UNESCO International Clearing House on Children and Violence on the Screen, 1998, pp. 181–199.
p. 58 This quote is from Barbara Holborow OAM: *Those Tracks on My Face*, Random House, 1997.
p. 59 'Dolly Doctor' column written by Dr Melissa Kang, a primary care adolescent health physician in Sydney, and courtesy of *Dolly* magazine.
p. 64 From an article on the Internet by Jon Casimir, *Sydney Morning Herald*, August 2002.
p. 66 Andrew, Fuller, *Raising Real People: A guide for parents of teenagers*, the Australian Council for Educational Research Ltd., Melbourne, 2000.
p. 67 Albert Einstein quote comes from *The Big Little Book of Jewish Wit and Wisdom*, Berk, Sally Ann (ed.), Black Dog & Leventhal Publishers Inc, New York, 2000.
p. 69 Eckersley, R., *Media, Culture and the Twenty-first Century*, Australian Press Council News, August 1996.

Chapter 5

p. 74   Booth, M.L. et al, 'The Epidemiology of Overweight and Obesity Among Australian Children and Adolescents, 1995–1997', *Australian and New Zealand Journal of Public Health*, 2001, Vol. 25, pp. 162–169.

p. 76   Field, A.E., Cheung, L., Wolf, A.M. et al, 'Exposure to the Mass Media and Weight Concerns Among Girls', *Pediatrics*, 1999, p. 103, endnote 36.

p. 76   Shandler, Sara, *Ophelia Speaks: Adolescent Girls Write About Their Search for Self*, Doubleday, 2000.

Chapter 6

p. 91   Metzl, Jordan and Shookhoff, Carol, *The Young Athlete: A Sport Doctor's Complete Guide for Parents*, Little, Brown and Company, Boston, New York, London, 2002, p. 80.

Chapter 7

p. 100   Comment on pornography comes from Steve Biddulph: *Raising Boys*, Finch Publishing Pty Ltd, Sydney 1997/8.

p. 102   Information on female masturbation comes from *The Hite Report*: Hite, Shere, 1976.
Comment on masturbation also from *Raising Boys*, Steve Biddulph, as above.

p. 104   Figures on teenagers and intercourse: Rosenthal, Doreen A. et al, 'Personal and Social Factors Influencing Age of First Intercourse', *Archives of Sexual Behaviour*, 1999, Vol. 28, No. 4, pp. 319–333.

p. 105   Woody Allen quote comes from *The Big Little Book of Jewish Wit and Wisdom*, Berk, Sally Ann (ed.), Black Dog & Leventhal Publishers Inc, New York, 2000.

p. 105   Statistics on 'first intercourse' and 'contraception the first time' come from 'The Australian Study of Health and Relationships' 2001/2, University of New South Wales, University of Sydney and La Trobe University, Melbourne.

p. 109   Comment on seeking contraception: by Jeffrey Cubis in *Breaking Out: Challenges of Adolescent Mental Health in Australia*, Kosky, Robert; Eshkevari, Hadi Salimi; Kneebone, Gary (eds), Canberra: Australian Government Publishing Service, 1992.

p. 110   Comment on heterosexual expectations for girls comes from *Ophelia Speaks: Adolescent Girls Write About Their Search for Self*, Shandler, Sara, Doubleday, 2000.

p. 113   Statistics come from 'The Australian Study of Health and Relationships' 2001/2, University of New South Wales, University of Sydney and La Trobe University, Melbourne.

p. 114   Reference to teen pregnancy and personality types: Blum, R.W. & Resnick, M.D. 'Adolescent Sexual Decision-making: Contraception, pregnancy, abortion, motherhood', *Pediatric Annals* 1982 Oct; Vol. 11, No. 10, pp. 797–805.

p. 119   Reference to risky sex and mental disorders: 'Adolescent Mental Health and Risky Sexual Behaviour', invited editorial by Bennett, David and Bauman, Adrian, *British Medical Journal*, 2000, Vol. 321, pp. 251–252.

Chapter 8

p. 130   Checklist on symptoms of mid life adapted from an article by psychiatrist John Ellard entitled 'Middle Age', *Modern Medicine of Australia*, August 1983.

p. 137   Bloomfield, Harold and Felder, L., *Making Peace with Your Parents: The Key to Enriching Your Life and All Your Relationships*, Ballantine Books, New York, 1983.

p. 140   These reflections are from a list about self-esteem developed by Ron Luyet, an international human relations consultant. © Ron Luyet, BConWSA, 2000.

Chapter 9

p. 145   Comments on the impact of culture come from Eckersley, Richard, *Casualties of change: The predicament of youth in Australia*, Commission for the Future, 1988.

p. 151 Quotes by Henry Kissinger and Erica Jong come from *The Big Little Book of Jewish Wit and Wisdom*, Berk, Sally Ann (ed.), Black Dog & Leventhal Publishers Inc, New York, 2000.

p. 155 Hetherington, Mavis E. and Kelly, John, *For Better or For worse: Divorce Reconsidered*, W.W. Norton, 2002. An article entitled 'On Their Best Behaviour' by Adele Horin on this research appeared in *The Sydney Morning Herald*, March 9–10, 2002.

p. 156 Eleanor Berman's comment comes from her book *The New Fashioned Parent: How to make your family style work*, Prentice Hall Inc, Englewood Cliffs, New Jersey, 1980.

Chapter 10

p. 160 Moore, T., *Care of the Soul: A guide for cultivating depth and sacredness in everyday life*, HarperCollins Publishers, New York, 1992.

p. 169 Haim Ginott's comment is from Ginott, H.G., *Between Parent and Teenager*, Avon Books, New York, 1969.

p. 169 Quote by Rev Bill Crews AM, Chairman of the Exodus Foundation: *Love This Life: A forum on depression, despair and resilience* chaired by Dr Brendan Nelson, Federal Member for Bradfield, co-sponsored by Lindfield Rotary Club, Sydney, 2001.

p. 171 Information on authoritative parenting comes from 'We Know Some Things: Parent–Adolescent Relationships in Retrospect and Prospect', Steinberg, Lawrence, Temple University, *Journal of Research on Adolescence, 2001* Vol. 11, No. 1, pp. 1–19.

Chapter 11

p. 188 *Report on Government Services 2003* (www.pc.gov.au).

p. 189 *Realising Australia's Commitment to Young People: Scope, benefits, costs, evaluation & implementation*. A report for the Dusseldorp Skills Forum, Applied Economics, November 2002 (www.dsf.org.au).

p. 189 The Smith Family's *Learning for Life* program, which was established in 1988, supports education as the key to ensuring children's future health and wellbeing.

p. 194 *Boys: Getting it Right*, Commonwealth Government Standing Committee on Education and Training, October 2002.

p. 202 Bullying findings come from a survey by psychologist Robert Parada of 4500 high school students from Western Sydney (quoted in the *Sydney Morning Herald*, 2000).

p. 204 Newington College's Anti-Bullying Policy.

p. 205 Harvey Fierstein quote comes from *The Big Little Book of Jewish Wit and Wisdom*, Berk, Sally Ann (ed.), Black Dog & Leventhal Publishers, Inc, New York, 2000.

p. 207 Green, C. & Chee, K., *Understanding ADD: Attention Deficit Disorder*, Doubleday, Sydney, 1994; Serfontein, G., *The Hidden Handicap: How to Help Children Who Suffer Dyslexia, Hyperactivity and Learning Difficulties*, Simon & Schuster, Sydney, 1990.

p. 215 Costs of raising teenagers from 'The People the Pollies Forgot – Teenagers', Ross Gittins, the *Sydney Morning Herald*, 2 April, 2003. Research by the Social Policy Research Centre at the University of NSW.

p. 221 Wilson, Jan, *The Teenager and You*, Hedges & Bell, Melbourne, 1982.

Chapter 12

p. 228 Brown, P. & Hooper, J., *Accessible Interventions for Depression in Rural and Remote Areas*. Royal Queensland Children's Bush Health Scheme 1998.

p. 229 Alexander, C.N., Rainforth, M.V. & Gelderloos, P., 'Transcendental meditation, self-actualization, and psychological health: A conceptual overview and statistical meta-analysis', *Journal of Social Behaviour and Personality* 1991; Vol. 6, No. 5, pp. 189–247.

p. 228 Seligman, Martin E.P., Reivich, Karen, Jaycox, Lisa, Gillham, Jane, *The Optimistic Child: A proven program to safeguard children against depression and build lifelong resilience*, HarperCollins Perrenial, New York, 1996.

p. 241 The dialogue provided by child and adolescent psychiatrist Professor Ken Nunn is from *Love This Life: A forum on depression, despair and resilience* (as before).

Chapter 13

p. 246 Ginott, Haim, *Between Parent and Teenager*, Avon Books, New York, 1969.

p. 256 Johnson, Spencer, *The One Minute Mother*, Columbus Books, London, 1984.

p. 256 Information about kids leaving home from 'Surprise, Surprise – Just When You Thought They Would Never Leave Home', Adele Horin and Brigid Delaney, the *Sydney Morning Herald*, 14 March, 2003.

p. 260 Poem by Cherie A. Millard quoted in *Young Girls: A Portrait of Adolescence*, Konopka, G., The Haworth Press, New York, 1976, p. 14.

p. 261 Benjamin Spock quote comes from *The Big Little Book of Jewish Wit and Wisdom*, Berk, Sally Ann (ed.), Black Dog & Leventhal Publishers Inc, New York, 2000.

Chapter 14

p. 266 Richard MacKenzie quote from a talk on the history of the high risk youth program at the Division of Adolescent Medicine, Children's Hospital of Los Angeles, 1976.

p. 271 Movie stars smoking on screen: 'Smoking: Dying to See the Stars, Lifematters', Life Education Australia, 21 December, 2001.
National Drug Strategy Household Survey 2001.

p. 273 The poem 'Smoking, No Way' by Mark Franklin (aged 11) was inspired by a talk to Mark's Year 6 Class by David Bennett. Mark is now 23 years old.

p. 274 Addictiveness of smoking: from a study undertaken at the University of Massachusetts by Joseph DiFranza, published in the Journal *Tobacco Control*, September, 2002.

p. 275 Study of alcohol use in 614 Australians aged 14 and over by Roy Morgan Organisation, commissioned by The Salvation Army in 2002.

p. 280 Comments on when to worry about adolescent drug use from Dr Raymond Seidler, a Sydney-based GP.

p. 280 Palin, Martin, *Drugs and your Teenager: A 'don't panic' guide for Australian parents*, Maxibooks, Springwood, 1993.

p. 288 Human rights and Equal Opportunity Commission, Brian Burdekin, 1989.

p. 289 Comments on homeless children and young people from Barbara Holborow OAM, *Those Tracks on My Face: A mind-opening journey into the world of children in trouble*, Random House Australia, 1997.

p. 291 Case example provided by Ken Buttrum AM, previous Director General of the NSW Department of Juvenile Justice.

p. 292 Cain, Michael, *Recidivism of Juvenile Offenders in NSW*, Department of Juvenile Justice, 1996.

p. 292 Strategies for dealing with young offenders come from: McGuire, James (ed.), *What Works. Reducing Re-Offending: Evidence-based practice*. This was part of the Crime Prevention Strategy launched by the Home Secretary, July 1998.

p. 292 Suggestions for promoting positive youth development in the juvenile justice system come from Ken Buttrum AM.

p. 293 Anecdote on family influences on a young person's offending behaviour provided by Ken Buttrum AM.

p. 297 The late Bronwyn Donaghy presented her 'Five pointers for keeping communication lines open with our children' at *Love This Life: A forum on depression, despair and resilience* (as before). Bronwyn Donaghy also wrote *Anna's Story* (1996), *Leaving Early* (1997) and *Unzipped* (1999).

p. 297 Quote about resilience is from *From Surviving to Thriving: Promoting mental health in young people*, Fuller, Andrew, ACER Press, 1998.

Chapter 15

p. 300 Many studies have challenged the beliefs of early theorists including Anna Freud, Peter Blos and Erik Erickson that adolescence is 'a time of storm and stress'.

p. 301 The statement by child and adolescent psychiatrist Professor Ken Nunn was made at *Love This Life: A forum on depression, despair and resilience* (as before).

p. 305 Pilowski, I., 'Abnormal illness behaviour', *British Journal of Medical Psychology*, 1969, Vol. 42, pp. 347–351 quoted in Rickarby, G., Blyth, D., Bennett, D.L., 'Abnormal Illness Behaviour as a Required Family Role', *Psychiatric Medicine*, 1987, Vol. 5, pp. 115–122.

p. 312 The statement by child and adolescent psychiatrist Professor Ken Nunn was made at *Love This Life: A forum on depression, despair and resilience* (as before).

p. 314 Comments by the late Bronwyn Donaghy at *Love This Life: A forum on depression, despair and resilience* (as before).

p. 315 Compas, B.E., 'Psychosocial Stress and Child and Adolescent Depression', *Handbook of Depression in Children and Adolescents*. Reynolds, W. M. and Johnson, H. (eds). Plenum Press, 1994.

p. 321 Beck, J.S., *Cognitive Therapy: Basics and beyond*, Guilford Press, New York, 1995.

p. 321 Clarke, G.N., Lewinsohn P.M., et al., *The Adolescent Coping with Depression Course: A psychoeducational intervention for unipolar depression in high school students*, Castalia Press, 1990.

Hawton, K., Salkovikis, P.M., et al, *Cognitive Behaviour Therapy for Psychiatric Problems: A practical guide*, New York, Oxford University Press, 1996.

Reynolds, W.M., 'Depression in Adolescents: Contemporary issues and perspectives', *Advances in Clinical Psychology*, 1994, Vol. 16, pp. 261–316.

Stark, K. and Kendall, P.C., *Treating Depressed Children: Therapist manual for taking action*, Ardmore PA, Workbook Publishing, 1996.

p. 327 *The Secret Language of Eating Disorders* by Peggy Claude-Pierre challenges traditional treatment.

Cooke, Kaz, *Real Gorgeous*, WW Norton and Company, 1996.

McCoy, Kathy & Wibbelsman, Charles, *The Teenage Body Book: Nutrition, health, fitness, emotions, sexuality*, Perigee, 1999.

p. 327 The quote from a recovered anorexic comes from 'Surviving Anorexia – one Woman's Tale', written by Catherine Morena in 1998 when she was 18.

p. 329 The case of Tim was provided by Professor Doris Young, Head, Department of General Practice, University of Melbourne.

p. 331 *National Survey of Mental Health and Wellbeing, 2002*.

p. 334 'Hearing the Cry' by Margaret Appelby and Margaret Condonis, quoted in *Leaving Early* by Bronwyn Donaghy.

Chapter 16

p. 344 Quotes come from 'What a Doctor Should be', Quale, Jackie, in *Pediatric Annals*, June 1973, Vol. 2, No. 6, pp. 79–83. Jackie was a Year 11 student at the time.

p. 345 The statement about confidentiality is from 'Adolescence', Bennett D.L., Kang M., in *Child Health: A Practical Manual for General Practice*, Editors RK Oates, Kathryn Currow, Wendy Hu, 2001.

p. 347 The HEADSS guide comes from Goldenring, J.M. and Cohen, E., 'Getting into Adolescents' Heads', *Contemporary Paediatrics*, 1988, pp. 75–90.

p. 352 Claire Williams, Canteen Newsletter, Australian Teenage Cancer Patients Society.

p. 353 The Association for the Welfare of Child Health (AWCH) advocates for a holistic, family-oriented approach to child and adolescent health care.

p. 356 Housden, Maria, *Hannah's Gift: Lessons from a life fully lived*, Bantam, 2002.
p. 356 *Access to Health Care Among NSW Adolescents*, Booth, M.; Bernard, D.; Quine, S.; Kang, M.; Usherwood, T.; Alperstein, G.; Beasley, L.; Bennett, D.L., NSW Centre for the Advancement of Adolescent Health, The Children's Hospital at Westmead, 2003.
p. 357 Peppard, J., 'An outbreak of adolescent health and the side effects', *AAAH Newsletter* (Australian Association of Adolescent Health), 1999; Vol. 1, pp. 4–6.
p. 357 For more information about the history of adolescent health care see Bennett, D.L., Tonkin. R. 'Adolescent Health Care and International Developments in the Past 30 Years', *International Journal of Adolescent Medicine and Health*, 2001 Vol. 13, No. 4, pp. 265–285.
p. 358 Trotter, Wilfred, 'Has the Intellect a Function?' *Lancet*, Vol. 1, 1939, pp. 14–19.
p. 358 Important papers concerning pevention and early intervention: Patton, George, 'The Scope for Youth Health Development', a briefing paper for The National Public Health Partnership, Centre for Adolescent Health, Royal Children's Hospital, Melbourne; Wise, M. Bennett, D.L., Alperstein, G., Chown, P., *Better Futures for Young People*, 2002, NSW Centre for the Advancement of Adolescent Health, The Children's Hospital at Westmead, Sydney.
p. 358 Quote about art: Moore, T., *Soul Mates: Honouring the Mysteries of Love and Relationship*, HarperCollins Publishers, New York, 1994.
p. 359 *Art Injection: Youth Arts in Hospital*, Adolescent Medical Unit, The Children's Hospital at Westmead. For additional information about the Youth Arts Program, see Thwaite, P.; Bennett, D.L.; Pynor, H.; Zigmond, H, 'Art and "the language of wellbeing" in adolescent health care', *Annals, Academy of Medicine, Singapore*, 2003, Vol. 32, No. 1, pp. 171-77.

Chapter 17
p. 365 *Footprints to the Future*, report from the Prime Minister's Youth Pathways Action Plan Taskforce, 2001.

Bibliography and further reading
Books about growing up, health and nutrition
Cooke, Kaz, *Real Gorgeous*, WW Norton and Company, 1996.
Covey, Sean, *The 7 Habits of Highly Effective Teens*, Simon & Schuster, October 1998.
Darvill, Wendy, and Powell, Helsey, *The Puberty Book: A guide for children and teenagers*, Hodder, Revised 2nd edition, 2002.
Donaghy, Bronwyn, *Unzipped: Everything teenagers want to know about love, sex and each other*. Harper Collins, February 1999.
Friel, John L., Friel, Linda D., *The 7 Best Things (Smart) Teenagers Do*, Health Commission Inc., Florida 2000.
Lewellyn-Jones, Derek and Abraham, Suzanne *Everygirl*, Oxford University Press, 1996
Martino, Wayne, and Pallota Chiarolli, Maria, *Boys Stuff: Boys Talking About What Matters*, Allen & Unwin, 2001.
Martino, Wayne, and Pallota Chiarolli, Maria, *Girls Talk: Young Women Speak Their Hearts and Minds*, Finch Publishing, 1998.
Mayle, Peter, *What's Happening to Me? A Guide to Puberty*, Sun Books, Melbourne, 1975.
McCoy, Kathy, *The Teenage Body Book: Nutrition, health, fitness, emotions, sexuality*. Perigee Trade Paperback, September, 1999.
McVeagh, Patricia and Reed, Eve, *Kids, Food and Health 3*, Finch Publishing Pty Limited, Sydney, 2001.
Metzl, Jordan M.D. with Shookhoff, Carol, *The Young Athlete: A Sport Doctor's Complete Guide for Parents*, Little, Brown and Company, New York, 2002.
Rowe, Leanne, *girl X_ Recreated, Hopes and Dreams of Young People*, Random House, 2002.
Shandler, Sara, *Ophelia Speaks: Adolescent Girls Write About Their Search for Self*, Harper Collins, Young adult, 2001.

Walker, Ross, *If I Eat Another Carrot I'll go Crazy*, Kingsclear Books, 1999.
Walker, Ross, *The Cell Factor*, Pan MacMillan Australia, 2002.

Books about life, partnership and family life
Amato, Paul and Booth, Alan, *A Generation at Risk: Growing Up in an Era of Family Upheaval*, Harvard University Press, 1997.
Currie, Paul, Carnegie, Jon, & Stynes, Jim, *A Hero's Journey*, TGS Press, 1997.
Edgar, Don, *The Patchwork Nation*, HarperCollins, 2000.
Gladwell, Malcolm, *The Tipping Point: How Little Things Can Make a Difference*, Little Brown, 2000.
Gottman, John and Silver, Nan, *The Seven Principles for Making Marriage Work*, Three Rivers Press, May 2001.
Hetherington, Mavis E., and Kelly, John, *For Better or For worse: Divorce Reconsidered*, W.W. Norton, 2002.
Housden, Maria, *Hannah's Gift: Lessons from a life fully lived*, Bantam, 2002.
Mackay, Hugh, *Turning Point: Australians choosing their future*, Macmillan, 1999.
Marsden, John, *Secret Men's Business*, Pan MacMillan Australia, 1998.
Moore, Thomas, *Soul Mates: Honouring the Mysteries of Love and Relationship*, HarperCollins Publishers, New York, 1994.
Pryor, Jan, and Rodgers, Bryan, *Children in Changing families: Life After Parental Separation*, Blackwell, 2001.
Schnarch, David, *Passionate Marriage: Love, sex and intimacy in emotionally committed relationships*, Henry Holt and Company, May 1998.
Stynes, Jim, *Whatever It Takes*, Celebrity Publishing, 1995.

Books about risky behaviours and kids at risk
Claude-Pierre, Peggy, *The Secret Language of Eating Disorders*, Random House, 2000.
Donaghy, Bronwyn, *Anna's Story*, HarperCollins, 1996.
Donaghy, Bronwyn, *Leaving Early: Youth Suicide: the horror, the heartache, the hope*. HarperCollins, 1997.
Fuller, Andrew, *From Surviving to Thriving: Promoting mental health in young people*, The Australian Council for Educational Research Ltd., Melbourne, 1998.
Holborow, Barbara, *Those Tracks on My Face: A mind-opening journey into the world of children in trouble*, Random House Australia, 1997.
Pipher, Mary, *Reviving Ophelia: Saving the selves of adolescent girls*, Doubleday. 1999.
Rey, Joseph, *More Than Just the Blues*, 2nd edition of *Is My Teenager in Trouble?* Simon and Schuster Books, 2002.
Seligman, Martin E.P., Reivich, Karen, Jaycox, Lisa, and Gillham, Jane, *The Optimistic Child: A proven program to safeguard children against depression and build lifelong resilience*, Perrenial, September 1996.
Tanner, Susan, and Ball, Gillian, *Beating the Blues: A self-help approach to overcoming depression*, Doubleday, Sydney, 1991.

Books about parenting
Biddulph, Steve, *Raising Boys: Why boys are different – and how to help them become happy and well-balanced men*, Finch Publishing Pty Limited, Sydney 1997.
Carr Gregg, Michael and Shale, Erin, *Adolescence: A guide for parents*, Finch Publishing Pty Limited, July 2002.
Chopra, Deepak, *The Seven Spiritual Laws for Parents: Guiding your children to success and fulfillment*, WW Norton and Company, 1996.
Fuller, Andrew, *Raising Real People: A guide for parents of teenagers*, The Australian Council for Educational Research Ltd. (ACER), Melbourne, Vic 2000.
Grose, Michael, *Raising Happy Kids: A guide to happy parenting*, HarperCollins 1999.
Panzarine, Sue, *Teenagers and the Internet: What every parent should know*, Town Book Press, 2002.

Strasburger, Victor C. and Wilson, Barbara J., *Children, Adolescents, & the Media*, Sage Publications, 2002.

Web addresses and contacts
www.health.gov.au/hsdd/mentalhe/ (Mental Health and Wellbeing)
www.mbsr-nyc.com (Mindfulness Based Stress Reduction)
www.parentingideas.com.au (Parenting ideas by Michael Grosse)
www.relationships.com.au (Relationships Australia)
www.rch.unimelb.edu.au/cah/index.cfm (Centre for Adolescent Health)
www.aifs.org.au (Australian Institute for Family Studies)
www.caah.chw.edu.au (NSW Centre for the Advancement of Adolescent Health)
www.naah.org.au (NSW Association for Adolescent Health)
www.adolescenthealth.org (The Society for Adolescent Medicine)
http://www.dest.gov.au/schools/Publications/2000/bullying.htm (Commonwealth Dept of Education, Science and Training)
www.thesource.gov.au (Australian Government Youth Site)
www.youngaustralians.org (The Foundation for Young Australians)
http://makeanoise.ysp.org.au (Make a Noise)
www.oxygen.org.au (OxyGen organisation for quitting smoking)
www.quitnow.info.au (Quit)
www.adca.org.au (Alcohol & other Drugs Council of Australia)
www.nationalalcoholcampaign.health.gov.au (Teenage alcohol campaign)
www.adf.org.au (Australian Drug Foundation)
www.somazone.com.au (Somazone Youth Advisory Group)
www.reachout.com.au (Reachout)
www.kidshelp.com.au (Kids Helpline)
www.lifeline.iinet.net.au (Lifeline)
www.getontop.org (Get on top, a guide to mental health)
www.beyondblue.org.au (Beyond Blue, National Depression Initiative)
www.centrelink.gov.au (Centrelink)
www.fpahealth.org.au (Family Planning Australia)
www.betterhealth.vic.gov.au (Better Health Channel)
www.cybersmartkids.com.au (Cybersmart Kids online)
www.healthinsite.gov.au (Health information)
www.also.org.au/outreach (Outreach, gay and lesbian information)
www.lawstuff.org.au (Know your rights)
www.smithfamily.com.au (The Smith Family)

National telephone contacts

Kids Help Line	1800 551 800
Lifeline	131 114
SANE Helpline	1800 688 382
Centre for Adolescent Health	(03) 9345 5890
NSW Centre for the Advancement of Adolescent Health	(02) 9845 3338
Australian Institute of Family Studies	(03) 9214 7888
Alcohol and other Drugs Council of Australia	(02) 6281 0686
Australian Drug Foundation	(03) 9278 8100
Medicare Card Information	132 011

Index

A
abortion 114, 115
accidents
    road 269
    workplace 270
achievement, academic 187–88
'achievement imperative' 220–21
acne 17–19
acting out 266, 310–12
addiction
    cannabis 282
    nicotine 274
    signs of 281
adipose tissue 5–6
adolescence, transition to 170
adolescent medical units 356–57
adoption 165–66
Adoption Information Act, 1990 165
adoptive families 165–66
adult wards 353–54
advertising
    alcohol 62, 275
    food choices 83
    hygiene and grooming 89
advice, perception of 169
aerobic exercise 94
ageing, double standards about 134
aggressive habits 58
AIDS 116, 118–19
alcohol
    abuse 84, 275, 277–78
    advertising 62, 275
    depression 314
    harmful practices 275, 276, 277
    health effects 277
    low-risk levels 277
    media campaigns 274–76
    music videos 64
    reasons for use 276
    related accidents 269–70
    risk-taking behaviour 267, 268
    young offenders 291
Allen, Woody 105, 169
alone, need to be 25, 331
alternative families 166–67
amphetamines 279, 284–85, 291
anaemia, iron-deficiency 77, 308
anal sex 111, 116
andropause 131–32
anger
    expression of 203
    parent–teenager 254–55
anogenital warts 118
anorexia nervosa 76, 323–27
anti-bullying programs 204
antidepressants
    depression 321–22
    menopause 134
anti-drug messages 275
anxiety 322–23
anxiety disorders 322
appearance, reaction to 30–31
appetite suppressant drugs 75
application, letters of 221
arguments
    chores 231, 233
    general 170
Art Injection 359
artistic expression 358–60
assertiveness 141, 230
Association for the Welfare of Child Health 353
'athletes foot' 89
attention, undivided 171–73
attention deficit disorder (ADD) 207, 209
attention deficit hyperactivity disorder (ADHD) 207–9
'auditory processing problems' 195
authoritarian parenting 50, 171
authoritative parenting

benefits of 171
reasons for 43–44
showing love 44–46
authority
alternative figures 250
questioning of 187

B
'baby boomers' 148–49
Bagshaw, Dr Sue 242
bedrooms
messy 28–29, 36–37
refusal to leave 312–13
bedtime, preparation for 308
behaviour
criminal 178
emotional roller coaster 24–25
'forbidden' 312
'non-compliant' 355
oppositional 169–70, 187
at school 212–13
sudden change in 329–31, 337–39
belonging, sense of 224
bereavement
coping with 193
disintegrating family 155
juvenile crime 293–94
bickering 170
Biddulph, Steve 14, 100, 102–3
binge drinking 275, 277–78
binge eating 325–26
bipolar mood disorder 329
birth control *see* contraception
birth families, contact with 165–66
black and white thinking 318–19
blame, giving up 141
blended families 163–64
body
odours 89–90
understanding 87
body hair 10
body image
chronically ill 355
feminine shape 76–77
media influence 76
middle age 135, 142–43
positive 94
'Body of Work, The' (art show) 360
body piercing 119, 231
bones, brittle 77–78, 81
'Boomerang Kids' 257
boys
access to sexual images 100–101
alcohol use 275–76
breast enlargement 9–10, 21
constant movement 27

difficulty at school 194–96
early maturity 13
gender roles 98
growth spurt 12–13
increase in muscle 5
masturbation 102–3
personal hygiene 88–89
physical changes 9–12
risk-taking behaviour 296
shortness 13–14
suicide 331–32
breakfast 79
breast cancer
effect of smoking 272
HRT 134
breasts
development of 6
enlargement in boys 9–10, 21
lumps 6, 346
breathing exercise 320
Buddhists 240
bulimia nervosa 76, 323, 325–26
bulk billing 348–49
bullying 202–5

C
cancer
beneficial diet 77
smoking 272, 273–74
see also breast cancer
candida 116, 117
cannabis 279, 281–82, 291, 314
Canteen Newsletter 352
canteens, school 82–83
Casimir, John 64–65
casual sex 99–100, 104
catastrophising 319
CBT (cognitive behavioural therapy) 318–21
Cellblock Youth Health Centre 360
Centre for Adolescent Health, The (Melbourne) 357
CFS (chronic fatigue syndrome) 308–10
changes
effect on teenagers 301–2
job market 217
limiting beliefs 141
in marriage 151
mid-life 131–36
social climate 259
'chasing the dragon' 283
chastity, premarital 99, 121
child abuse
detecting 179
facts on 177–79
high-risk behaviour 267

mental health 120–21
young offenders 290–91
childhood, reliving 258
Children's Hospital, Westmead 357
children's wards 353–54
chlamydia 116, 117
chocolate 80
chores
arguments over 231, 233
flexibility 182
chronic fatigue syndrome (CFS) 308–10
chronically ill 354–56
cleanliness 88–90, 95
Clockwork Young People's Health
Service (Geelong) 357
Clonidine 134
clothes, reaction 30–31
coaching 198
cocaine 279, 286, 291
coercive parenting 52
cognitive behavioural therapy (CBT)
318–21
Comfort, Alex 124
comments of teenagers
ADD 209
adversities in life 146, 147
drug use 287–88
friends 193
limits 51
parents 44–45, 47, 48–49, 260,
342–43
racism 205–6
school 211
seeking help 337–38
sexuality 121–22
stress 303–4
teachers 191–92
working fathers 180
working mothers 181
commitment, in marriage 151
communes 166
communication
as a family 172–73
in marriage 151
open lines of 139–41, 297
parent–teenager 168–69
positive 321
community, connection to 213–14
competitiveness
at school 187–88
Western society 301–2
complementary therapies, menopause
133
compromise 251–52
computer use, health consequences of
66

concern
parental 48–49
teenagers' perception of 169
condoms, use of 108, 109
confidentiality, medical 345–46
conflict
family crisis 338–39, 340–41
internal 302–3
within marriage 151
parent–teenager 169–70
resolution process 230–35
between siblings 175–76
conformity
of family type 167
with parents 28, 51
with peer group 31–32, 267
pressure for 187
connectedness
to community 213–14
health benefit of 228
to parents 145–47, 156
sense of 302
Connolly, Billy 102
consequences, logical 252–53
contraception
failed 112–13
not used 107–9
use of 105
control, parental 49–51
coping mechanisms
for parents 32–33, 37
school pressures 187–88
teenagers 319
counsellors 340–41
creative arts activities 358–60
creeps 31–32
Crews, Reverend Bill, AM 68, 169
crisis, family 338–39, 340–41
crisis plan, negotiated 341
crushes, same-sex 110
Crystal, Billy 98
Cubis, Dr Jeffrey 109
cults, religious 31
curfews 53, 252
curvature of the spine 19, 355

D
dance parties 279
daydreaming 33–34
debate, school 237–38
dependence
disabled youth 354–55
drugs 279–80, 281, 282
on parents 219–20, 223, 250, 257
depression
occurrence of 313–14

reasons for 239, 316–17
signs of 314–16, 331
thinking patterns 227–28
treatment for 317–22
young offenders 291
diabetes, type 2 73
diet *see* eating
dieting 76
diets, fad 75, 78–79
disabled teenagers 354–55
discipline
consistency in home 171
disagreement about 254
school options 212–13
trends 259
divorce 154–56, 162
doctors, choosing 343–48
Donaghy, Bronwyn 297, 314
drinking see alcohol
Drucker, Paul 168
drugs
abuse victims 267
amphetamines 279, 284–85, 291
anti-drug messages 275
cannabis 279, 281–82, 291, 314
cocaine 279, 286, 291
early school leavers 193
ecstasy 279, 285, 291, 314
fantasy 286
general facts 278–81
hallucinogens 291
harm reduction approach 286–87
heroin 279, 283–84, 291, 364
inhalants 278, 283
LSD 279, 284, 291
in the media 62
over-the-counter 278
prescription 279
risk-taking behaviour 268
seeking help 351
signs of addiction 281
signs of use 280
sniffing 278, 283
speed 279
teenagers' thoughts on 287–88
tranquillisers 279, 296
young offenders 291–92
'dry runs' 102
dysfunctional families 177, 290–91

E
early childhood development 146–47
eating
advertising influence 83
binge eating 325–26
changing habits 82
excess intake 74
healthy 72
larger portions 82
nutritional requirements 77–79, 92–93
parental influence on 84–85
teenage habits 71, 72, 79, 84
unhealthy 77–78
eating disorders 76, 77, 323–27
Eckersley, Richard 69
ecstasy 279, 285, 291, 314
education
need for 185–86
private 196–97
public 196
sex 112–13, 122–25
vocational relevance 189
ejaculation
competitions 102
first 11
spontaneous 21
employment *see* work
empty nest fantasy 257
energy
getting rid of 310
lack of 307–10
exams 199–200
exercise 90–94
expectations 25–26
experimentation 266
extended families 164–65

F
face
changes to 17
hair on 10
fad diets 75, 78–79
fair play, sense of 176
families
basic needs 168
dysfunctional 177, 290–91
getting along 167–73
need for 159
organised communication 172–73
as sanctuary 182–83
transition to adolescence 170
types of 160–67, 257
unemployment problems 219–20
unhappy 153–54, 157, 177
fantasy (drug) 286
fast food 80–82, 84
fasting 79
fat, dietary 80, 82
fat stores 5–6, 77
father–daughter relationship 175

fathers
    incest 177
    non-custodial 162
    teenage 115
father–son relationship 174–75
fatigue 77, 307–10, 316–17
fears
    about parents' marriages 156–57
    private 146
feelings, having 141
ferals 30
fiddles 26
fidgets 26
fitness 90–95
fluid intake 92
food
    additives 78
    wide choice 85
    see also eating
foster families 166
'free love' movement 148
friends
    characteristics of 320
    comments on 193
    influence of 31–33
    loss of 331
    parents' concern 32
    see also peer pressure
Fuller, Andrew 35, 66
future
    hope for 220–21
    keys to 222
    prospects for 363–67
    world's 238–40

G
Gamma-hydroxcybutyrate (GHB) 286
gangs, street 32
gender roles 98
'generation gap,' notion of 170
genital herpes 116, 117
genital human papillomavirus (HPV) 118
genital warts 116
genitalia, negative view of 7
Ginott, Haim 169, 246
girls
    alcohol use 275–76
    benefits from sport 91
    bullying tactics 202
    early maturity 5, 13
    effects of smoking 272–73
    fat stores 5–6
    gender roles 98
    growth spurt 12–13
    masturbation 102
    personal hygiene 88–89
    physical changes 6–9
    reasons for sex 106–7
    risk-taking behaviour 296
    school achievement 195
    single-sex schools 197
    suicide 331
gonorrhoea 116, 117
'Good Wife's Guide, The' (article) 149
goths 30
'grandparents, premature' 115
'grazing' 72
grown up, meaning of 129–30
growth, adolescent 12–17, 307
gynaecomastia 10, 346

H
habitual acting out 311
hair
    body 10
    facial 10
    pubic 6–7, 10
    styles 38
    underarm 7, 10
hallucinogens 291
Harrison, George 274
hash oil 281
hashish 281
HEADSS (Home; Education; Activities; Drugs; Sexuality; Suicide) guide 347–48
health
    maintaining 84–85
    unemployment lifestyle 219
    WHO definition 347
Health Care Cards 349
health care system
    adolescent services 356–58, 361
    adolescents' rights 349
    national needs 364
    using 348
health foods 81–82
health strategies, youth 364
hearing damage 29–30
heavy metal music 63
height
    growth spurt 12–13
    short 13–15
    tall 15–16
help
    list of options 340
    professional 339–43
    refusing 350–51
    seeking 337–39
    teenagers' perception of 169
hepatitis B 116, 118
Herman-Giddens, Marcia 5

heroin 279, 283–84, 291, 364
high school
    boys' difficulty with 194–96
    canteens 82–83
    changing direction 186
    choice of 196–97
    early leavers 188–89, 291
    a family affair 196–201
    good 190–94
    poor attendance 210–12
    poor behaviour 212–13
    poor performance at 201
    pressure of 186–88
    racism 205–6
    refusal to go 210–11
    reports 200–201
    single-sex 197
    system basis 185–86
    transition to 197
HIV/AIDS 116, 118–19
Holborow, Barbara, OAM 58–59, 289–90
home, leaving 183, 256–58
homelessness 178, 288–90
homework 198–99
homosexual families 167
homosexuality 109–12, 121–22
hormones
    effect of 24–28
    growth 14–15
    menopause 132–33
    in middle age 136
hospitals
    adolescent units 356–58
    adolescents' experience 351–54
    creative arts in 358–60
Housden, Maria 356
housework
    arguments over 231, 233
    shared 181–82
    thankless task 180
HPV (genital human papillomavirus) 118
HRT (hormone replacement therapy) 133–34
hygiene 88–90, 95
hymen 7

I
'identity disorder' 328
illness see sickness
immigrants, young 304–5
incest 177–79
independence 137–38, 260
individuality 38, 187
infatuations, first 102

information overload 67–68
inhalants 278, 283
inspiration, sources of 240
intellectual abilities, new 33
intercourse see sex
inter-dependence 256–58
International Association for Adolescent Health 357
Internet
    explicit sex sites 65–66
    material available 64–66
    pornography 100–101
    usage control 66–68
interviews 221–22
introspective withdrawal 25
iron intake 77, 92

J
jobs see work
'jock itch' 89
judgement, postponing 141
juvenile crime 290–95, 315

K
Kang, Dr Melissa 346
King, Martin Luther 206
kissing games 60
kyphosis, adolescent 19

L
language, disrespectful 47–48
'late-onset' diabetes 73
laxative use 326
learning difficulties 207–10
leaving home 183, 256–58
letting go
    challenge of 245–46
    health care 361
    learning trust 246–51
    leaving home 183, 256–58
    memories 258–59
    sense of loss 254
    by teenagers 250–51
life
    learning about 237–41
    recipe for 140–41
    search for meaning 138
    speed of change 301–2
lifestyle
    healthy 75
    stress-reducing habits 228
    unemployment 219
limits
    need for 51–53, 251
    need to test 310
    negotiated 295

listening
    active 321
    responsible 253
literacy, poor 194–95
    loneliness
    depression 317
    disabled youth 355
loners 327
love, showing 44–46, 241–42
LSD (lysergic acid diethylamine) 279, 284, 291
lumps
    beneath the knee 19–20
    breast 6, 346
Luyet, Ron 140–41

M
magazines
    letters to 59–61
    sexual images 100–101
make-up, use of 59–61
male menopause 131–32
marijuana 268, 281
marriage
    effect of teenagers 152
    as framework for life 156
    impact on children 152–56
    making it last 148–52
    mid-life crisis 152
    rating 153
    teenagers' view of 148
    tips from 1955 149
masturbation 102–3
maturity, gaining 130
McDonald's fries 82
'me generation' 259
meal replacement diets 75
mealtimes
    arguments 232–33
    breakfast 79
    evening 85
    family 172–73
media
    depiction of youth 23, 365–66
    eroding self-worth 69
    risk-taking behaviour 268
    sexual images 59, 68
    sexual violence 61–62
    violence 58–59
'medical family therapy model' 306–7
Medicare see health care system
Medicare cards 348–49
meditation, transcendental 229
'Memo to my parent' 42
memories 258–59

menopause
    female 132–34
    male 131–32
menstrual blood 8–9
menstruation 7–9, 20–21
mental health
    benefits of marriage 150
    cannabis use 282
    immigrants and refugees 305
    non-custodial fathers 162
    risky sexual behaviour 119–21
    sexual abuse 120–21, 178
mentors, need for 367–68
messiness 28–29, 36–37
methamphetamine 279
Metzl, Dr Jordan 91
middle age
    acknowledging 130
    body image 142–43
    changing bodies 135
    fantasies of 257
    realisation of 138–39, 142
    sexuality 135–36
    symptoms checklist 130–31
    taking stock 137
    urge for changes 131–36
mind-reading 319
minister to youth 363–65
Ministry for Children and Youth Affairs 365
Mistral, Gabriela 147
mobile phones 35
modesty, upsurge of 88
mollycoddling 49–50
mooching around 36
mood swings 24–25
Moore, Thomas 160, 358–59
morals as life guidelines 240
morbid thoughts 315
mother–daughter relationship 173–74
mothers, working 232–33
mother–son relationship 174
movement, constant 27
movies, smoking in 62, 271
multiculturalism 205–6
multi-generational families 257
muscles
    food for 92–93
    increasing bulk 5
muscular exercise 321
music, volume levels 29–30
Music Television (MTV) 63–64
music videos 63–64
'myth of parenthood' 261

N

National Drug Strategy Household Survey (2001) 271, 275
negative thinking 227–28, 237–38, 318–19
negotiation
    crisis plan 341
    level of messiness 29
    limits 52
    loud music 29–30
    phone usage 35
Nelson, Dr Brendan 195–96
Newington College 204
nicotine 274
'Nil by Mouth' (sculpture) 359
NSW Childhood Obesity Summit (2002) 83
nuclear families 161
Nunn, Professor Ken 241, 301–2, 312–13
Nurcomb, Professor Barry 120
nutrition
    for sporting activities 92–93
    teenage requirements 77–79
    see also eating

O

obesity
    contributory factors 72
    dealing with 75–76
    genetic component 73, 74
    health problems 73
    hormonal changes 74
obsessive compulsive disorder 323
occasional acting out 311
oestrogen 4, 5, 16, 24
'option shock' 67–68
oral contraceptives 108–9
oral sex 118
Osgood-Schlatter disease 19–20
overcontrol 49–51
overexpectation 50
overgeneralisation 319
overindulgence 52
overprotection 50

P

paedophilia 111
panic attacks 322
parenting
    consistency in home 171
    good characteristics 53
    harmonious 253–54
    less successful styles 43, 50, 52
    motivated by guilt 52
    'myth of parenthood' 261
    suggestions list 41–42
parents
    commonality with teenagers 135–38, 142
    connectedness 145–47
    coping mechanisms 32–33
    eating habits 84–85
    exam time 199–200
    helping with homework 198–99
    hope of 220–21
    leadership of 251
    memories of own youth 141–42
    non-custodial 162
    response to homosexuality 111–12
    response to pregnancy 115
    as role models 295
    role of 260
    strange behaviour 139
    teenagers' comments 42–43, 44–45, 48–49, 342–43
    unhelpful comments 45–46, 47–48
    unresolved issues with 137–38
    working 179–82
    youth suicide 332–33, 334–35
parties, teenage 248–50
partnership *see* marriage
passive smoking 271–72
past
    acting out in search of 311
    feelings from 258
pathological fatigue 308
peer pressure
    adult version 38
    eating habits 84
    risk-taking behaviour 267
    at school 193–94
pelvic inflammatory disease (PID) 117
penises, size of 10–11, 21
perimenopause 132
periods *see* menstruation
permissive parenting 52
phobias 322
phone calls 34–35
physical examinations 346–47
physical fitness 90–95
physiological fatigue 308
PID (pelvic inflammatory disease) 117
piercing, body 231
Pill, The 108–9
pitching in 181–82
pituitary gland 4
pocket money 215
poor performance, academic 201
pornography 100–101
positive reinforcement 256–58
'post viral fatigue syndrome' 308–10

post-traumatic stress disorder 305, 322–23
pregnancy
  smoking effects 272
  teenage 113–15
premenstrual syndrome 9
pressures
  academic achievement 187–88
  emotional 241, 299–300
  high school 186–88
  internal 187
  see also stress
privacy 25
problem-solving process 235–36
Propranolol 134
'protected sex' 107, 116
psychological fatigue 308
psychosis 328
puberty
  increase in fat 77
  new intellectual abilities 33
  normal changes 4–6
  parental encouragement 20
  physical growth 12–16
  signs of 4
  see also boys; girls
pubic hair 6–7, 10
punishments 233
puppy fat 6, 74

R
racism 205–6
radiation, cigarette smoke 273
rappers 30
'raves' 279
reassurance 20
rebellion 28, 169–70
refugees, young 304–5
rehearsal 229
relationships
  maturing 103–4
  parents' new 164
  parent–teenager 169–70, 173–75
  types of 160–67
  see also families
relaxation 229, 320–21
religious cults 31
remarriage, impact on children 163–64
reports, school 200–201
resilience 297
respect
  for changing needs 46–50
  demanded 51
responsibility
  to family 251–52
  for self 140

risk-taking behaviour
  broader social level 268
  early school leavers 189
  forms of 269–81
  individual level 266–67
  need for 265–66
  parents' influence 267–68
  prevention of 295–96
  relationship level 267–68
  sexual activity 120
  street youth 289
  young offenders 291
risk-taking groups 32
rituals, family 172–73
Roaccutane 18
road accidents 269–70
rock music 62–64
romance
  growing interest in 101–4
  short-lived 103
rosters, housework 182
routines, family 172–73
Roy Morgan Organisation for the Salvation Army study 275
Royal Alexandra Hospital for Children 356–57, 358
rules 251–52

S
safe sex practices 107, 116
salt 80
sanitary napkins 9
schizophrenia 328
school *see* high school
scoliosis 19, 355
sculptures in hospitals 359
Second Storey, The (Adelaide) 357
self talk 229–30
self-awareness 140
self-esteem
  common problem 240
  damaging comments 255
  developing 145–46, 256
  improving 140–41
  parental behaviour 316
self-harming behaviour 332
self-sufficiency 256
semen 11
separation
  emotional 254
  leaving home 183, 256–58
  from marriage 154–56
sex
  anal 111, 116
  casual 99–100, 104
  devaluation of 121

double standards 98–99
education 112–13, 122–25
experimental play 102
first experience 104, 105–6
forced 106
growing curiosity 101–4
a health hazard 112–21
house rules 124
ignorance about 122–23, 125
Internet adult sites 65–66, 68–69
media influence 59–62
moral hypocrisy 99–100
oral 118
pressure to have 121
questions to magazines 60–61
readiness for 106
reasons for 106–7
within relationships 104
risky behaviour 111, 119–21
survey of practices 104, 106, 113
sex toys 118
sexual abuse, child *see* child abuse
sexual activity, music videos 64
sexual development 12, 13
sexual images, in media 59, 68
sexual orientation, spectrum of 110
sexuality
confusing messages 97–100
cultural influences 104–5
developing 122–23
father–daughter relationship 175
homosexuality 109–12, 121–22
increasing interaction 103–4
maturing 123–24
middle age 135–36
mother–daughter relationship 173–74
parents' reaction to 135–36
sexually transmitted infections (STIs) 116–19
'shafting' 285
Shandler, Sara 76, 110
share household families 166
'shelving' 285
shoplifting 267
shortness 13–15
siblings, strife between 175–76
sickness
caused by depression 314–15
chronic 354–56
stress-related 305–7
single mothers
difficulties of 114
parental help 115
single-parent families 161–62
skaters 30
skeleton, developing 19–20

sleep, preparation for 308
sleeping over 247–48
slipped capital femoral epiphysis 20
'smart cards' 82–83
smoking
health effects of 84, 273, 274
in movies 62, 271
risk-taking behaviour 267
teenage 271–74
'Smoking, No Way' (poem) 273
SMS (short message service) 35
sniffing 278, 283
social change 259
social skills
desirable 319–20
young offenders 291
soft drinks 81
Sole Parents Benefit 114
speed 279
sperm, adolescent 11
spine, developing 19
Spock, Benjamin, MD 261
sports
benefits of 91–93
non-participation 93–94
squabbling 170
SSRIs (selective serotonin re-uptake inhibitors) 321–22
statistics
adoption 165
alcohol use 269–70, 275, 277–78
child sexual abuse 178
drug use 279
drug-related deaths 271
HIV/AIDS 119
homelessness 288
juvenile crime 292
sexual orientation 111
soft drink consumption 81
teenage pregnancy 113, 114
young offenders' drug use 291–92
youth suicide 331
youth unemployment 216–17
Steinberg, Professor Lawrence 43, 171
step-families, girls' maturity 5
stepfathers, incest 177, 178
stereotypes
sex roles 98
sexual 109–10
steroids 92–93
STIs (sexually transmitted infections) 116–19
Strasburger, Dr Victor C. 58, 59, 65
street gangs 32
street youth 288–90
stress

adolescence 300–305
   good and bad 300
   health damage 301
   management 228–30
   psychological 305
   those at risk 304–5
'stretched' families 167
substance abuse 279–80
success
   in life 240–41
   in marriage 151–52
suicide
   accidents and 270
   depression 313–16
   gay adolescents 111
   risk-taking behaviour 267
   taskforces 364
   threat of 334
   young offenders 291
   youth 331–35
sun protection 267

T
TAFE (Technical and Further Education) 222
tallness 15–16
tampons 9
tattoos 118–19, 231
teachers
   good 190–94
   lack of males 195
   teenagers comments on 191–92
teaching techniques, modern 186
team sports 91–93
'Tear of Thought' (painting) 359
technokids 30
technology, unprepared for 57
teenagers
   cost of 215
   impact of divorce 154–56, 162
   impact of marriage 152–56
   'parentified' 162
   parent's remarriage 163–64
telephone use 34–35
television
   alcohol use on 275
   violence on 58
termination of pregnancy 114, 115
testicles, self-examination of 11
testosterone 4, 5, 16, 17, 24, 27
thinking
   black and white 318–19
   depressed 227–28
thinness 76–77
three Ps 242
thrill-seekers 311

thrush 116, 117
Tibolone 134
time
   gift of 171–73
   wasting 33–36
'time out' 25
tobacco *see* smoking
tooth decay 77, 81
toxic shock syndrome 9
traditional families 161
tranquillisers 279, 296
transcendental meditation 229
trichomonal infection 116, 117
Trotter, Wilfred 358
truancy 211
trust, learning 246–51
type 2 diabetes 73

U
underachievement, academic 201
underage drinking 275
underarm hair 7, 10
unemployment 216–24
university 222

V
vagina 7
vegetarianism 77, 78–79, 85
Venlafaxine 134
violence
   media depiction of 58–59
   MTV videos 63–64
   part of life 270
   sexual 61–62
virginity 99, 121
virgins 104, 105
visualisation 321
vitamin B6 81
vitamin C 81, 92
vitamin supplements 92
vitamin therapy 81
voice
   changes to 9
   tone of 51
vomiting, recurrent 326

W
weight
   increasing fat stores 5–6
   losing 75–76
   too fat 73–76
   too thin 76–77
   see also obesity
wet dreams 11
Williams, Claire 352
withdrawal 25, 331
Women's Health Initiative Study, 2002 134

work
    attitude towards 180
    developing skills 294
    disadvantaged children 189
    motivation for 217–18
    next step in life 214–22
    realistic expectations 215–16
working fathers 179–80

working mothers 180–81, 232–33
workplace, changes in 217
worrying 238

Y
Youth Arts Program 358
Youth Link (Perth) 357